# A Practical Guide To Planning, Highways And Development

## Tom Graham

BATH PUBLISHING

Published May 2019

ISBN 978-0-9935836-9-8

Text © Tom Graham

Typography © Bath Publishing

Bath Publishing Limited

27 Charmouth Road

Bath

BA1 3LJ

Tel: 01225 577810

email: info@bathpublishing.co.uk

www.bathpublishing.com

Bath Publishing is a company registered in England: 5209173

Registered Office: As above

**TO**

Thomas, my favourite grandson

and

Linda, my favourite wife!

# About the author

Tom Graham is a solicitor and a non practising barrister with over 35 years experience in town & country planning and highway law and practice. He has advised in both the private and public sectors and taken the lead in a number of major highway schemes.

# Introduction

Rumour has it that the late Christopher Hitchins once said that *"Everybody does have a book in them, but in most cases that's where it should stay."* It follows that there must be a plausible excuse for taking up the metaphorical pen. Mine is that I hope this will be a useful book.

The overall objective of the book is to examine the ways in which highway considerations are taken into account in the development process, starting from the grant of planning permission and following through to the construction or improvement of roads associated with these projects. I have lectured on what I describe as this "interface" for many years and, since my talks are normally well received, I thought there might be a book in it - which, hopefully, would be equally well received.

The general idea, last June, was that I would render some of my many monographs into book form whilst reciting: *"How hard can it be?"* to myself. Alas, the book decided to write itself, with the said idea of usefulness uppermost in its mind and with scant regard to my previous utterances on the topic.

The structure is, therefore, predicated from this basis.

The book is in three parts. First, there is, what I hope to be, a relatively readable commentary on law and practice. Secondly, I have set out some annotated statutes which go into more depth for those who wish to do so. Finally, I have provided a number of example documents. The latter are derived from my practical experience of negotiating and settling many of them over 35 years. Thus, I hope this will be a compact desk-top book rather than an academic tome which gathers dust on a shelf.

Those who have attended my seminars will recall that I press my audience to read the actual sources of legal rules rather than relying on the often capricious hearsay of others, no matter how distinguished those others might be. This approach is followed in this book and, I hope, I have followed the tenet of scholarship laid down by Edward Gibbon:

> *"I have always endeavoured to draw from the fountain-head; that my curiosity, as well as a sense of duty, has always urged me to study the originals; and that, if they have sometimes eluded my search, I have carefully marked the secondary evidence, on whose faith a passage or a fact were reduced to depend."*

Tom Graham

May 2019

# Acknowledgments

I have derived much assistance from many fine works of scholarship, but I would like to give three special mentions. First, the seminal Pratt & Mackenzie's *"Law of Highways"*. I was first referred to it in 1982 when I was given the, then, bewildering task of deciding whether a public park was subject to a public right of way. I was told to speak to the former town clerk who advised me to find a volume of this work and look it up. I now own three editions. I am not sure what this says about me, but I have delved into the 21$^{st}$ Edition on many occasions during the past months. Next, I have had recourse to Stephen Sauvain QC's excellent *"Highway Law"* and I am duly indebted. Finally, whilst it might seem to be a compact guide on the surface, I have found Michael Orlick's *"An Introduction to Highway Law"* to be very helpful throughout.

I thank David Chaplin and Helen Lacey at Bath Publishing. Taking on the challenge of launching a new book is no small risk and I hope that the outcome is what they expected. I suspect that Helen is now one of the few people on the planet who can make sense of the cryptic manuscript comments which I visit upon unsuspecting draft documents.

Finally, thanks to Linda Jackson and Umi Filby for choosing the cover.

# Bibliography

- Pratt & Mackenzie, *"Law of Highways"* (21$^{st}$ Edn. - 1967) Butterworths

- Michael Orlick, *"An Introduction to Highway Law"* (4th Edn. - 2018) Sweet & Maxwell

- Hancox & Wald, *"Highways Law & Practice"* (2002) Butterworths

- Stephen Sauvain QC, *"Highway Law"* (5$^{th}$ Edn. - 2013) Sweet & Maxwell

- Martin Goodall, *"A Practical Guide To Permitted Changes of Use"* (2$^{nd}$ Edn. - 2016) Bath Publishing

- Alistair Mills, *"Interpreting the NPPF: The New National Planning Policy Framework"* (2018) Bath Publishing

# CONTENTS

## PART 1: COMMENTARY

### Chapter 1: Foundations Of Highway Law

### Chapter 2: The Highway Authorities

### Chapter 3: How Highways Come Into Being

# Chapter 8: Planning Applications And Highways

# Chapter 9: Transport Assessments, Transport Statements And Travel Plans

# Chapter 10: Road Safety Audits

# Chapter 11: Planning Conditions

# Chapter 12: Planning Obligations

# Chapter 13: Agreements Under Section 38 Of The Highways Act 1980

# Chapter 14: Forced Adoption

# Chapter 15: Highway ("Section 278") Agreements

## Chapter 16: Land Compensation Act 1973

## Chapter 17: Structures Over And Under The Highway

## Chapter 18: Cranage Licences

## Chapter 19: Cognate Highway Agreements & Licences

# PART 2: ANNOTATED STATUTES

# PART 3: DRAFTING EXAMPLES

# Table Of Cases

# Table Of Statutes

# Table Of Statutory Instruments

# Table Of Conventions

# Table Of Frameworks

# PART 1

# COMMENTARY

# Chapter 1

# Foundations Of Highway Law

## 1.1    What is a highway?

The word "*highway*" does not have a single fixed content in law and so its meaning must be established according to the situation one is examining.

The point has to be laboured before proceeding down this path because it is a source of much confusion both to many who are new to highway law and to some who appear to be schooled in the topic.

It is sometimes misleading to try to define something without first trying to understand the context within which it is being used. There is the tale of the philosopher who observed that no man ever steps in the same river twice.[1] As with many things philosophical, this is more Penn & Teller than useful analysis. To the farmer, the "*stream*" is the flowing water which he hopes to trap for the purposes of irrigation. To the cartographer, a "*stream*" is a physical characteristic of the landscape which he seeks to map. That is to say, the description of the properties of a thing can vary according to the predisposition of the person who is forming the description.

Thus, moving from the fluvial metaphor, a lawyer might be keen to understand those metaphysical properties of a "*highway*" which matter to a lawyer as a lawyer, whilst an engineer might be more interested in the physical components of a visible mode of transportation. An engineer might look at a made-up road and say that it is "*for*" vehicular traffic, but his real meaning might be that it is physically "*suitable for*" vehicular traffic. The legal rights of passage and repassage over it are matters for the lawyer.

Many express surprise that the Highways Act 1980 (which is the principal source of statute law on the point) does not provide a self-contained definition of "*highway*",[2] but, it would be more surprising if the Parliamentary draftsman had sought to pin down something which varies according to the observer.[3] This introductory chapter seeks to describe the most salient properties of this difficult concept.

In *London Borough of Southwark & Anor v Transport for London* [2018] UKSC 63, Lord Briggs helpfully referred to two elements:[4]

---

[1]    Commonly attributed to Heraclitus of Ephesus (c. 535 – c. 475 BC). He also is said to have said that "*the path up and down are one and the same*" when, according to his metaphorical river, they should not have been!

[2]    See Hancox & Wald, "*Highways Law & Practice*", Butterworths, (2002) @ p.6 and Orlick, "*Highway Law*" Shaws, (4th Edn @ p.2).

[3]    Any similarities to a description of the role of the "*observer*" in quantum mechanics is unashamedly mischievous. Aside from my aside, both Sauvain (ibid @ p.2) and Orlick (ibid @ p.2) exemplify the point. They begin by focusing on legal rights, which is, perhaps, consistent with their assessments of their target audiences.

[4]    @ para. 32

- "... the incorporeal rights of the public in relation to the locus in quo ...", which appears to mean, in non-technical language, public rights of passage, whether on foot, on horseback or in (or on) vehicles over the way.[5]

- "... a reference to its physical elements", which appears to mean the physical fabric of the way, including its surface, structures, bridges etc.

This separation turns on the observer and those matters which touch and concern him and, it is suggested, it forms a good starting point.[6]

The reference to the *"incorporeal rights of the public"* takes up the fact that, at one time, a *"highway"* was conceived as being no more than right of passage, the classic exposition being that adopted by Lord Mansfield:

> *"The King has nothing but the passage for himself and his people, but the freehold and all profits belong to the owner of the soil."* [7]

However, the advent of heavy traffic meant that, over the years, the law had to evolve to encompass the creation of surfaced ways (as an alternative to the pre-existing swamps of mud) and to provide a status for, and rights in respect of, those engineered artefacts; that is to say, the *"physical elements"*.[8]

Furthermore, to the lawyer, the expression *"highway"* is a generic one because there are different classes of highway which are distinguished by the *"incorporeal rights of the public"* over them. These are as follows:

- *"Footpath"* – means a highway over which the public have a right of way on foot only, not being a footway.

- *"Bridleway"* – means a highway over which the public have the following, but no other rights of way, that is to say, a right of way on foot and a right of way on horseback or leading a horse, with or without a right to drive animals of any description along the way (NB: Section 30 of the Countryside Act 1968 permits cycling on bridleways).

---

[5]  NB: the word *"way"* is used in this book as a neutral word which does not seek to ascribe any particular legal or physical characteristics to the *"way"* which is thus mentioned, albeit (predictably) there is an idiosyncratic use of the word in the London Building Act 1930!

[6]  Indeed, this is seems to be the very starting point used by Sauvain in the first sentences of the 3rd edition of his work: Sauvain, *"Highway Law"* (3rd Edn. 2004), @ p.1. Per: *"A highway is essentially a public right to pass over a defined route. The term highway may be used to refer to the nature of the right but more usually relates to the physical feature over which the right is exercised."*

[7]  In *Goodtitle d. Chester v Alker & Elmes* (1757) 1 Burr. 133.

[8]  Well described by Hancox & Wald, ibid @ pp.7 – 19. For scholars, the locus classicus is *"The Story of the Kings Highway"* by Sidney & Beatrice Webb (1913). See *www.ForgottenBooks.org* for a re-print.

- *"Footway"* – means a way comprised in a highway which will also comprise a separated[9] carriageway being a way over which the public have a right of way on foot only.

- *"Carriageway"* – means a way constituting or comprised of a highway being a way (other than a cycle track) over which the public have a right of way for the passage of vehicles. Unless constrained by a site specific statutory instrument or process, a carriageway is an *"all purpose"* highway; meaning that it is also open to all other forms of traffic.

The phrase *"special road"* appears from time to time. Whilst the word *"motorway"* does not appear in primary legislation, a *"special road"* is, for all practical purposes, a motorway.[10] That is to say, it is a trunk road which is open to vehicular traffic only and provided pursuant to a scheme made under section 16 of the Highways Act 1980.

## 1.2 The public right of passage

Members of the public have a right to pass and repass along a highway according to the particular class of highway in question. If, however, a member of the public is doing something other than passing or repassing, that person may be committing a trespass which is actionable by the owner of the highway. The right of the public to pass and repass on a highway is *"subject to all reasonable extensions which may from time to time be recognised as necessary to its existence in accordance with the enlarged notions of people in a country becoming more populous and highly civilised, but they must be such as are not inconsistent with the maintenance of a paramount idea that the right of the public is that of passage"* (*Hickman v Maisey* (1900) 1 Q.B. 752).[11] For example, therefore, parking a car for a reasonable length of time will not constitute a trespass: see *Carey v Chief Constable of Avon & Somerset* [1995] R.T.R. 405.

---

9    The Highways Act 1980 does not use the word *"separated"*, but it is an essential characteristic of a footway. Otherwise, one could be describing a *"shared surface"*. The American phrase *"sidewalk"* is a better one.

10   It is defined in secondary legislation: i.e. The Motorways Traffic (England and Wales) Regulations 1982 (S.I. 1982, No. 1163).

11   See now *DPP v Jones* [1999] 2 A.C. 240 and *UK Oil & Gas Investments Plc v Persons Unknown* [2018] EWHC 2252 (Ch).

The actions must be reasonable when set against the exercise of the right of passage. Where the highway surface vests in the highway authority, the highway authority may be able to take action based on trespass.

## 1.3      The legal elements of a highway

To qualify as a highway, a way must be:

- open to the public at large;

- the public use must be as a right;

- the public right must be for passage; and

- the public right of passage must follow a defined route.

If the way is only open to a select class of the public, then it will not be open to the public at large for the purposes of establishing a highway, for example an access way to a golf course only. Thus one can say, with proper conviction, that the phrase "*public highway*" is a meaningless tautology; because the one characteristic which all classes of highway share is that they are "*public*".[12]

If the landowner allows the public to use a way by way of permission or licence, then that public use will not be as of right. Such a way is commonly called a "*permissive way*". This means that the landowner reserves the right to bar the public from the use of such a way at his absolute discretion. Thus, for example, if a landowner allows the public to use the way but, in doing so he erects signs which state that the use of the way is by way of permission or licence, then this will be a "*permissive way*" only.

The essential characteristic of highway rights is that they are available to the public for passage and repassage. If members of the public are using a particular area for sport and recreation or something similar, then this is not used as a highway. It might, perhaps, be use that is appropriate to a town or village green, but the fact that members of the public are not using the land for passage and repassage militates against the establishment of a public right of way.

There is no common law right to wander across somebody else's land and, therefore, it is an essential characteristic of a highway that it follows a defined route.

All four of these elements have to be established by those who claim that a particular way is a public right of way.

---

[12]     A point made with justifiable force by Orlick in his 2nd Edn. @ p.2. Unfortunately, no less than *Pratt & Mackenzie* fell into this distracting solecism in their leading work.

## 1.4     "Once a highway, always a highway"

Highway rights cannot be lost by disuse only, notwithstanding that the physical fabric of the way may have changed with the passage of time.[13] This is enshrined in the axiom *"once a highway, always a highway"*.

This concept is important to would be developers because it bears not only on the status of land within a proposed development site, but also relates to rights of access to frontage highways: see Chapter 5.

In *Dawes v Hawkins* (1860) 141 E.R. 1399, Byles J said: *"It is also an established maxim, once a highway always a highway: for, the public cannot release their rights, and there is no extinctive presumption or prescription"*.

Adverse possession (aka *"squatter's rights"*) cannot be asserted if the effect would be to exclude the public from part of a highway, and that is so even if the part concerned had not been used, as such, for a number of years.

In *Harvey v Truro District Council* [1903] 2 Ch 638 a dispute turned on a strip of land that it was conceded formed part of the highway. In 1886, or 1887, a wooden building was constructed, partly on the strip and partly on what was formally part of the metal surface of the highway. Joyce J concluded that this was an encroachment and said in relation to it:

> *"The possession of a squatter on the highway since 1886 cannot bar the public right."*

The Court of Appeal endorsed this principle in *R (Smith) v Land Registry (Peterborough)* [2011] Q.B. 413.[14]

---

[13]     Unless the whole of the land upon which the highway formerly subsisted has been destroyed: e.g. by coastal erosion.

[14]     But note Sauvain's criticism of some of the obiter dicta in that case: ibid @ pp.5 & 6.

# Chapter 2

# The Highway Authorities

## 2.1 Introduction

Section 1 of the Highways Act 1980 identifies the various highway authorities.

The Secretary of State for Transport is the highway authority for trunk roads in England. In keeping with section 10 of the Highways Act 1980, the "*trunk roads*" are normally taken to be the national system of routes for through traffic in England and Wales.

In practice, the Minister's functions have, since 2015, been discharged by Highways England (formerly the Highways Agency).

Highways England describe themselves as being the government company "*charged with operating, maintaining and improving England's motorways and major A roads*": viz,

> *We are responsible for motorways and major (trunk) roads in England. Our road network totals around 4,300 miles. While this represents only 2 per cent of all roads in England by length, these roads carry a third of all traffic by mileage and two thirds of all heavy goods traffic.*[15]

The Minister for public paths is the Secretary of State for the Environment, Food and Rural Affairs (still known by the acronym "*DEFRA*").

Outside Greater London the council of a county or metropolitan district are the highway authority for all highways in the county or the district which are not highways for which the Minister is the highway authority.

The council of a London borough or the Common Council is the highway authority for all highways in, respectively, the borough or in the City which are not highways for which the Minister is the highway authority.

In Wales, the Welsh Government is the highway authority for trunk roads; i.e. 75 miles of motorway and over 1,000 miles of trunk road.[16] The council of a county or county borough are the highway authority for all highways in the county or the county borough which are not highways for which the Welsh Government is the highway authority.

## 2.2 The interface between the Minister and local highway authorities

There are some cases where development schemes have effects on both trunk roads and local highway networks. Those acting for developers should be aware that both the Town

---

[15] See https://highwaysengland.co.uk/highways-england-about-us/.
[16] See https://gov.wales/topics/transport/roads/?lang=en and https://gov.wales/docs/det/publications/151021-wales-trunk-roads-map-en.pdf.

and Country Planning Act 1990 and the Highways Act 1980 contain provisions which can be used to manage this overlap between the responsible highway authorities.

For example, the traffic generated by the *"Meadowhall"* shopping complex near Sheffield impacts, as locals will know, not only on the nearby roads managed by Sheffield City Council but also on junction 34 of the M1. In 2017, Sheffield City Council gave planning permission for an extension which would have made Meadowhall the fourth largest shopping centre in the United Kingdom. The traffic impacts were complicated by the fact that a new IKEA store had been built on nearby land and, thus, both the City Council and Highways England were involved in assessing the cumulative traffic impacts of the existing and proposed schemes.[17]

Measures for managing the (very complex[18]) junction interfaces between the M1 and the local highway network were provided by the Section 106 Agreement which preceded the grant of the permission. However, it was contemplated[19] that long term measures could include the use of an agreement pursuant to section 5 or section 6 of the Highways Act 1980 to deal with the management of slip roads and nearby local roads around the junction points.

## 2.3    Section 4, Section 5 and Section 6 agreements

Section 4 of the 1980 Act provides for the making of agreements for exercise by Minister or strategic highways company (aka *"trunk road authority"*) of certain functions of local highway authority as respects highway affected by construction or improvement of a trunk road.

The agreement would relate to a highway that crosses or enters the route of a trunk road or is or will be otherwise affected by the construction or improvement of that trunk road and provide that any functions specified in the agreement, being functions of improvement exercisable as respects that highway by the local highway authority, shall be exercisable by the trunk road authority. The trunk road authority shall have the same powers (including highway land acquisition powers) as the local highway authority have for that purpose.

Section 5 of the 1980 Act provides that the local highway authority may, by agreement with the Minister, undertake the maintenance and improvement of a highway in the local highway authority's area, being a highway (other than a trunk road) which the Minister proposes to construct or has constructed.

Section 6 provides that the trunk road authority may, by agreement with a county council, a metropolitan district council, or a London borough council, delegate to that council all or any of his or its functions with respect to the maintenance and improvement of, and other dealing with, any trunk road or any land which does not form part of a trunk road but which has been acquired by him or it in connection with a trunk road. This delegation arrangement will normally take the form of a "Section 6 Agreement".

---

[17]   Albeit, this scheme has been held over. A revised scheme was submitted to the council in 2018.
[18]   Junction 34 is, in fact, a *"dumbell"* junction. The end bells are known, respectively, as *"34 North"* and *"34 South"* with an underpass joining them.
[19]   The author was one of those who drafted the Section 106 Agreement.

# Chapter 3

# How Highways Come Into Being

## 3.1 Introduction

This chapter is very selective and concentrates on those modes of creation which are of direct relevance to the matters discussed in this book.

## 3.2 Construction by Minister or Highway Authority

Section 24 of the Highways Act 1980 provides that "*The Minister may ... construct new highways ...*" and that "*A local highway authority may construct new highways ...*". These very short statements form the basis for the very substantial powers of construction given to the highway authorities.

A highway constructed under these provisions will be maintainable at the public expense without further ado: see section 36 of the Highways Act 1980. It is not necessary that some form of document or instrument is produced by the authority. It should be sufficient that the completed way is thrown open to public passage and repassage.

## 3.3 Creation under section 228 of the Highways Act 1980

The section 228 procedure is normally used where street works have been carried out in a private street in accordance with the Private Street Works Code or the Advance Payments Code and the Street Works Authority has resolved to adopt the way as a highway maintainable at the public expense.[20]

## 3.4 Creation of public rights of way by dedication and acceptance

If a landowner dedicates a right of passage across his land for use by the general public, then this may create a highway. Such dedication may be by way of a written document or it may be implied from the fact that the landowner has allowed public passage across the route for a considerable period of years.

A highway can be created by public user over a period of time. This is known as "*dedication and acceptance*".

The respective modes of creation by dedication and acceptance can be summarised under the following headings:

- creation by express dedication;

- dedication and acceptance at common law; and

- deemed dedication under the Highways Act 1980.

---

[20] See para. 13.20 below. The phrases "*street works*", "*private street*", "*Private Street Works Code*" and "*Advance Payments Code*" are defined terms: see Chapter 7.

## 3.5    Creation by express dedication

The owner of land is entitled, should he so wish, to create a highway over it. He can do so simply by opening the way and then allowing the public to use it as a highway. The owner's act in opening the way to the public is known as *"dedication"* and the user of it by the public is known as *"acceptance"*. A highway will not be created unless both elements are present. Whilst the owner does not need to execute a written document dedicating the land, this is a common method of doing so. Such a written document can be a unilateral declaration which is published in some way (e.g. by the posting of a public notice) or it can be a bilateral agreement between the landowner and the highway authority.

Express dedication is often achieved by way of agreements under sections 25 or 38 of the Highways Act 1980 and the *"acceptance"* in such cases occurs when the highway authority accepts the land as a highway on behalf of the public.[21]

## 3.6    Dedication and acceptance at Common Law

At common law a highway will be established over a route by use by the public *"as of right"* if the following elements are established:

- it is open to public at large;

- the landowner has not given permission;

- there was no force;

- no secrecy;[22]

- public right must be for passage; and

- must follow defined route.

Lord Blackburn said in *Mann v Brodie* (1885) 10 App. Cas. 378:

> *"... where there has been evidence of a user by the public so long and in such a manner that the owner of the fee, whoever he was, must have been aware that the public were acting under the belief that the way had been dedicated, and has taken no steps to disabuse them of that belief, it is not conclusive evidence, but evidence on which those*

---

[21]  See *Secretary of State for the Environment, Transport and the Regions v Baylis (Gloucester) Ltd* [2000] 4 W.L.U.K. 463.

[22]  Whilst repeated with due solemnity by many, the reference to *"no secrecy"* is something of a nonsense in the context of highway law. It is difficult to see how the public could traverse open land without being seen. The present author has never (in nearly 40 years of practice) come across a case where this has been in issue. In the *Sunningwell Case* [2000] 1 A.C. 335 (@ 357), Lord Hoffman alluded to the user which is *"so trivial and sporadic as not to carry the outward appearance of user as of right"*. But, with respect, this proposition appears to carry a self-evident contradiction within it.

> *who have to find that fact may find that there was a dedication by the owner whoever*
> *he was."*

In *Folkestone Corporation v Brockman* [1914] A.C. 338, Earl Loreburn said:

> *"... dedication may be and, indeed, ought to be presumed in the absence of anything*
> *to rebut the presumption from long-continued user of a way by the public. Two things*
> *have to be made good, that the user has been sufficient in its duration and character,*
> *and that the presumption then arising has not been rebutted."*

The public use should normally be for a period of years – but the period of user needed to establish the route will vary according to the facts of each case. In some cases, the highway can be established by a relatively short period of public user. *Pratt & Mackenzie* stated that there is no fixed minimum period of public user which must be proved to show acceptance by the public and where the facts show an intention to dedicate, a highway may be created almost at once by public user.[23]

This point is important in the context of this book because it can determine whether a newly constructed estate road has become a highway at common law and also goes to determining the extent of highways fronting development sites and, further, frontage rights of access to those highways.

In *North London Rail Co v St Mary Islington, Vestry* (1872) 27 L.T. 672, a period of public user of 18 months was held to be enough. In *Rowley v Tottenham Urban District Council* [1914] A.C. 95, a period of three years was enough. In *R v Petrie* (1855) 4 El. & Bl. 737, the period was about nine years or less.

It follows that a developer who has created a new estate road and then opened it as a passage to and from a highway might have done so at his peril. Not only might the way have become a highway at common law, but the developer will then be responsible for its maintenance and will be liable for any accidents caused by the condition of the ways. Accordingly, both the developer and the local highway authority should be alert to, and seek to manage, the ramifications of this situation, particularly in the context of highway agreements.[24]

The position is mitigated for certain post-2006 ways by section 66 of the Natural Environment and Rural Communities Act 2006: see para. 3.8 below.

### 3.7 Deemed dedication under the Highways Act 1980

Section 31 of the Highways Act 1980 has simplified the position in that, if a way has been actually enjoyed by the public as a right and without interruption for a full period of 20 years, then that way is deemed to have been dedicated as a highway unless there is sufficient evidence that there was no intention during that period to dedicate it. If the public

---

[23]   Ibid @ p.33.
[24]   For which see para. 13.13 below.

in general pass and repass over a defined route for a period in excess of 20 years, then this will normally be enough to establish that the route is a public right of way.

A landowner may demonstrate that he had no intention to dedicate the way as a highway by placing an appropriate notice in close proximity to the route in question. He may also supply to the highway authority a map of his land showing the ways that he admits to have been dedicated and declaring that no further ways have been dedicated. In the absence of evidence to the contrary, the filing of these documents will negative an intention to dedicate: Highways Act 1980, section 31(6).

**3.8      Section 66 of the Natural Environment and Rural Communities Act 2006**
Section 66(1) of the 2006 Act provides that no public right of way for mechanically propelled vehicles is created after 2 May 2006 unless it is:

(a)    created (by an enactment or instrument or otherwise) on terms that expressly provide for it to be a right of way for such vehicles, or

(b)    created by the construction, in exercise of powers conferred by virtue of any enactment, of a road intended to be used by such vehicles.

Section 66(2) provides that, for the purposes of the creation after 2 May 2006 of any other public right of way, use (whenever occurring) of a way by mechanically propelled vehicles is to be disregarded.[25]

The provision does not use the word *"carriageway"*, but uses the phrase *"public right of way for mechanically propelled vehicles"* and, arguably, they are not the same.

The 2006 Act imports its terminology from the Wildlife and Countryside Act 1981[26] and this does not appear to encompass carriageways which form estate roads.

By section 66 of the 1981 Act *"right of way"* means *"a right of way such that the land over which the right subsists is a public path or a byway open to all traffic"*. A *"byway open to all traffic"* means *"a highway over which the public have a right of way for vehicular and all other kinds of traffic, but which is used by the public mainly for the purpose for which footpaths and bridleways are so used"*.

The forgoing is an apt description of what is sometimes called a *"green lane"* or *"green road"*, and section 66 has to do with limiting the establishment of rural ways which will be used by four wheel drive vehicles, motorcycles etc. In particular, section 66 reverses the effect of *Bakewell Management Ltd v Brandwood* [2004] UKHL 14, which was a case involving the creation of a green lane. Accordingly, it is difficult to see its relevance to bespoke estate roads which are created, and surfaced, to accommodate vehicular traffic.

---

[25]    The leading case on these provisions is *Fortune v Wiltshire County Council* [2012] EWCA Civ 334.
[26]    Per section 71 of the 2006 Act.

## 3.9    Ancient highways – and why they are important

The highway can also arise in the form of what is known as an "*ancient highway*".

This might appear to be an aside in a book which is aimed at the practicalities of development; however, it is of considerable importance in some cases.

An "*ancient highway*" is a carriageway highway which has been in existence since before 1835 or a public path which has been existence since 1949. Its existence and status will normally be proved by reference to historical documents including OS maps, enclosure awards and tithe maps.

If a would be developer can show that his site has a connection to an ancient highway, then this might provide him with an access which he might otherwise not enjoy or the ability to widen an existing access.

Also, the discovery that a road is an ancient one might absolve him of the costs of future maintenance of it. If the way is an ancient highway, then it is maintained at the public expense: see section 36 of the Highways Act 1980.

On the other hand, the discovery, by another person, of an ancient highway across his site might pose difficulties for the development of the site. Given the axiom "*once a highway, always a highway*", it matters not that a highway has been unused for many years. The public retain their historical rights of passage and repassage over it and any interference with those rights is unlawful. Clearly, this can pose a great problem for the developer who has purchased a site in blissful ignorance of the fact that his site is crossed by such a highway.

There is some relief in that, as from 1 January 2026, all unrecorded rights of way will be extinguished if the only evidence to support their existence is historical evidence. Otherwise, the hapless developer will be forced to think in terms of a stopping up or diversion order or a scheme which accommodates the way.

All of which suggests that the prudent developer should, at the least, commission a map based desk-top study by a suitably qualified expert[27] before his purchase, so as to assess the possibility of the existence of such ancient highways.

---

[27]    Something of a rarity! In reality, the best bet is an expert in public rights of way with a track record in rights of way claims and inquiries.

# Chapter 4

# The Extent Of The Highway

## 4.1    Why this is important

There are two main aspects to this topic; namely, the width of the highway and its vertical extent, both in terms of the subsoil and the airspace above it. Either or both may be of considerable importance to some development schemes.

Given that many development sites abut highways, it should follow that it is important to understand where the boundary between the two lies. A developer should determine the boundaries of his own site, or the site he is about to purchase, as one of his first tasks. It would be unfortunate if he finds that land which he believed to be within his site is actually part of the highway, perhaps because boundary markers have been misplaced.[28] All experienced highway lawyers will have had to deal with cases where an innocent purchaser has found this to be the fact, and it can be unpleasant for all concerned.

On the other hand, the discovery that a highway is narrower than was previously believed might provide the adjacent landowners with a windfall in terms of the frontage land thus released.

The vertical extent of a nearby highway might be of considerable concern to the developer who wishes his scheme to overhang or oversail it, whether temporarily during the construction process or permanently by way of an overhanging building.

## 4.2    The width of the highway

It is helpful to consider the relationship between what might, today, be perceived as soft highway verge and the metalled part of the highway, because it is often the case that the verge is subject to the same public rights of passage and repassage as the running course. This stems from the fact that, in many cases, the metalled part of the way was not taken to the full width of highway which preceded the making up of that running course. It was not unknown for an ancient unsurfaced road to be many yards in width, due, of course, to the problems of navigating what would, sometimes, be a mud-bath in bad weather.[29]

Such a way would be a highway for its whole width and the highway status of each and every part of the way would not be lost or diminished when a part of that width only was metalled. This is due to the axiom "*once a highway, always a highway*"; meaning that highway rights cannot be lost by disuse: see para. 1.4 above. The fact that the unmetalled part of the way becomes, in effect, a soft verge will not reduce the highway rights which applied to it in earlier times.

---

[28]    Again, bear in mind the axiom "*once a highway, always a highway*".

[29]    See Abbott LCJ in *Steel v Prickett* (1819) 2 Stark 463 NP.

It follows that the broad starting point is often said to be that, when one finds a metalled carriageway bordered by unmetalled[30] margins and beyond the margins by hedges or fences, then it may, in the absence of evidence to the contrary, be presumed that all the width between the hedges or fences (including the verges) is highway. However, this is a starting point only and each case has to be assessed on its individual merits.

Unfortunately, the caselaw on this *"fence to fence"* presumption is not remarkable for its clarity.

In *Neeld v Hendon Urban District Council* (1889) 81 L.T. 405, Lord Russell of Killowen stated:

> *"It seems to me very difficult to give assent to such a general proposition as this, that under all conditions where you find a metalled road bordered by unmetalled margins and beyond the margins by hedges, there is an invariable presumption that all the space between the hedges is highway. The question whether such a space is all highway would depend, to a great extent, I think, on many other circumstances, such, for instance, as the nature of the district through which the road passes, the width of the margins, the regularity of the line of hedges, and the levels of the land adjoining the road. These are all circumstances which should be taken into account before any presumption of law can arise as to the width of the highway. It seems to me that it is not safe to say, as a general proposition, without knowing the conditions of each particular case, that in such a case as I have mentioned all the space between the hedges is part of the highway."*

Not all judgments are as clear as that of Lord Russell of Killowen.

In *Offin v Rochford Rural District Council* [1906] 1 Ch 342, Warrington J stated:

> *"... the mere existence of fences on either side of the highway is not enough to raise the presumption. You have to find whether those fences are prima facie to be taken to have been made in reference to the highway, and, therefore, to the boundaries of the highway, ...".*

Thus far this is uncontentious and consistent with the *Neeld* case, but then His Lordship added:

> *"... and, further, I think that, having regard to the judgment of Vaughan Williams LJ, if you find a fence by the side of the highway, then prima facie that fence is the boundary of the highway, unless you can find some reason for supposing that it was put up for a different purpose."*

Arguably, when taken together, these statements by Warrington J appear to contain a degree of circularity. Either one asks the question about whether the fence was erected by reference to the highway or one does not. This statement seems to say that a prima facie

---

[30] A way is said to be *"metalled"* when it is surfaced by some durable material. Despite more interesting explanations, the word probably has its prosaic etymological origins in the old Latin word for minerals *"metallum"*.

inference arises from the mere fact that the fence is "... *by the side of the highway* ...". However, Lord Russell of Killowen stated (in *Neeld*) that one has to take account of a number of local circumstances before drawing any inferences. Ergo, Warrington J's dictum seems to be something of a gloss by a Divisional Court on the Court of Appeal in the *Neeld* case, albeit not a particularly convincing one. For example, the "*by the side of the highway*" test might be scotched immediately in a case where, on an examination of local factors, there is a significant difference in levels between the fence-line and the metalled way. Arguably, it might be that this type of situation was intended to be covered by the phrase "*unless you can find some reason for supposing that it was put up for a different purpose*". But, if it is plain as a pikestaff that the fence cannot possibly relate to the highway, then it serves no useful purpose to try to then divine why it was erected in the first place.

In *Attorney General v Beynon* [1970] Ch 1, Mr Justice Goff stated that:

> "... the mere fact that a road runs between fences, which of course includes hedges, does not per se give rise to any presumption. It is necessary to decide the preliminary question whether those fences were put up by reference to the highway, that is, to separate the adjoining closes from the highway or for some other reason. When that has been decided then a rebuttable presumption of law arises, supplying any lack of evidence of dedication in fact, or inferred from user, that the public right of passage, and therefore the highway, extends to the whole space between the fences and is not confined to such part as may have been made up."

Unfortunately, he added:

> "... one is to decide that preliminary question in the sense that is to say that the fences may prima facie be taken to have been originally put up for the purpose of separating land dedicated as highway from land not so dedicated."

Again, this seems to involve the unhelpful gloss on the *Neeld* case mentioned above.

Hopefully, the historical anomaly has been put to rest by the Court of Appeal in *Hale v Norfolk County Council* [2001] Ch 717. There, Mrs Hale owned a residential property fronting onto a highway. There was a dispute between Mrs Hale and the local highway authority, the Council, regarding a part of her garden which was immediately next to the made-up carriageway. The Council asserted that part of the garden was part of the highway. The dispute came to a head when Mrs Hale erected several posts and a chain on the disputed land. The Council served a notice on Mrs Hale under section 143 of the Highways Act 1980 requiring her to remove them. She failed to do so and so the Council removed the posts and chain itself. Litigation ensued and the matter eventually came before the Court of Appeal. The Court of Appeal held in favour of Mrs Hale.

Chadwick LJ said:

> "... the first question to be decided is whether the fence was erected (or the hedge established) in order to separate land enjoyed by the landowner from land over which the public exercised rights of way ..."

He added:

> "... In other words, did the landowner intend to fence against the highway? If that question is answered in the affirmative, then there is a presumption, which prevails unless rebutted by evidence to the contrary, that the land between the fence and the made-up or metalled surface of the highway has been dedicated to public use as highway and accepted by the public as such".

Consistently with *Neeld*, Chadwick LJ further stated:

> "... Whether it is right to infer, as a matter of fact in any particular case, that the landowner has fenced against the highway must depend, ... on the nature of the district through which the road passes, the width of the margins, the regularity of the line of hedges, and the levels of the land adjoining the road; and (I would add) anything else known about the circumstances in which the fence was erected."

One can see the significance of this judgment to the developer, or would be developer, where his frontage land appears to, or is said to, encroach on an adjacent highway.

To summarise, it is necessary to have regard to:

- the nature of the district through which the road passes;

- the width of the margins;

- the regularity of the line of hedges/fences;

- the levels of the land adjoining the road; and

- anything else known about the circumstances in which the fence was erected or hedge planted.

If the way crosses open land and is not fenced, the presumption is that the width of the highway is the width of the made-up way or beaten track only: see *Easton v Richmond Highway Board* (1871-72) L.R. 7 Q.B. 69.

The principles in *Hale* were applied by Mr Richard Sheldon QC (Sitting as a Deputy Judge of the High Court) in *Goodmayes Estates Limited v First National Commercial Bank Limited & Essex County Council* [2004] EWHC 1859 (Ch). The Claimant asserted that proposed highway works, which were required in connection with a proposed development on nearby land by the Defendant developer, would be trespass to his land. The central issue was the location of a boundary between land owned by the developer and highways running adjacent to that land. The developer contended that the boundary line lay on the edge of the metalled footway and the kerb line on the relevant road. The owner of the disputed land contended that the boundary line fell outside the proposed highway works and relied on the (in this case) "*hedge to hedge*" presumption.

The Deputy Judge's very thorough examination of the facts included a site visit and he was assisted by considerable expert evidence and, again, it is important to stress that many of these cases turn on their facts.[31] It is common ground that the roads were of some antiquity and appeared on a map dated 1777. Consistent with *Hale* (and *Neeld*) the Deputy Judge noted that the district was characterised by roads with verges running between hedges. The lines of the hedges on the site and in the neighbourhood were regular and ran in lines broadly adjacent to the roads. Per para. 28:

> "*Applying the principles in Hale, the foregoing features would tend to suggest that the fence to fence presumption should apply and that the boundary line should be drawn along the centre of the hedge.*"

In *Easton v Richmond Highway Board* (1871-72) L.R. 7 Q.B. 69, an unfenced metalled way crossed a village green and there was no difference between the grass abutting the way and the rest of the green. Cockburn J stated:

> "*It cannot be meant that the whole green was a highway, and the statement is expressly that the public have not exercised any greater or other right of passage over the grass adjoining the metalled road than they have over the rest of the green. In the first place, a highway may exist which is not metalled road at all; but generally a part is metalled and a part left which is not hard road; and, in general, when the highway is between two fences all the ground that is between the fences is presumably dedicated as highway, unless the nature of the ground or other circumstances rebut that presumption. In the present case there are no fences, and there is nothing to raise the presumption that one part of the open green more than another beyond the actual road has been dedicated.*"

Finally, it is worth mentioning *Portsmouth Corporation v Hall* (1907) 71 J.P. 564, where it was held that, if a highway is of a varying and indeterminate width, then the highway authority and the frontagers may agree a width on a "*give and take*" basis. There is now a statutory procedure to give effect to such an agreement in section 256 of the 1980 Act.

---

[31] Per para. 13: "At the invitation of all the parties, I conducted a site visit on the afternoon of the first day of the trial, accompanied by, amongst others, counsel and the experts. I found this to be an invaluable exercise. I was able to acquaint myself with the features of the site and the neighbouring areas without which it would have been difficult, if not impossible, properly to decide the issues in the case. The site had been pegged to mark the boundary as proposed by Mr Wright, the Claimant's expert surveyor, and to mark a line showing the extent of the proposed highway works."

## 4.3      The vertical extent

It is necessary to consider the vertical extent of the highway in terms of both the subsoil beneath it and the airspace above it.

The usual extent of ownership of the freehold owner of land stems from the time honoured legal principle which is encapsulated in the somewhat picturesque (and overblown) maxim:

> *"Whoever has the land itself, his also is everything up to the vaults of Heaven and down to the floor of Hell."*

This principle (if indeed there is one) is heavily modified in connection with the rights of a local highway authority in a highway which is maintainable at its expense.

Section 263 of the Highways Act 1980 provides, so far as is relevant, as follows:

> *"Subject to the provisions of this section, every highway maintainable at the public expense together with the materials and scrapings of it, vests in the authority who are for the time being the highway authority for the highway..."*

Lord Briggs explained the nature of the rights given to the highway authority by this vesting provision in *London Borough of Southwark & Anor v Transport for London* [2018] UKSC 63:

> *"First, it was a determinable, rather than absolute, fee simple, which would end automatically if the body responsible for its repair ceased to be so responsible (eg if the road ceased to be a public highway): see Rolls v Vestry of St George the Martyr, Southwark (1880) 14 Ch D 785. Secondly it was inalienable, for so long as that responsibility lasted. Thirdly, and most importantly for present purposes, statutory vesting conferred ownership only of that slice of the land over which the highway ran, viewed in the vertical plane, as was necessary for its ordinary use, including its repair and maintenance."* (Emphasis added).

As to the subsoil beneath the made-up surface, Lord Briggs adopted the decision of the House of Lords in *Tunbridge Wells Corporation v Baird* [1896] A.C. 434, where (@ p.442) Lord Herschell said:

> *"My Lords, it seems to me that the vesting of the street vests in the urban authority such property and such property only as is necessary for the control, protection and maintenance of the street as a highway for public use."*

There it was held that the local highway authority was not entitled to construct public toilets under the *"Pantiles"* in Tunbridge Wells without the consent of the subsoil owners.

Turning to the airspace above the highway, Sauvain has observed:

> *"The same basic rule applies to the air above a highway as it does to the subsoil beneath the highway. The interest of the highway authority is limited to that area which is required by it for the exercise of its powers and the performance of its statutory duties."* [32]

In *Finchley Electric Light Company v Finchley Urban District Council* [1903] 1 Ch 437 the Council had acquired statutory rights in relation to Regents Park Road in London under a direct statutory predecessor of section 263 of the 1980 Act but could not restrain the running of a power cable by the plaintiff at a height of 34 feet above its surface.

In the *Southwark* case (ante), Lord Briggs characterised the vertical plane as including "*a modest slice of the airspace*" and no more; viz:

> [9] *"That slice of the vertical plane included, of course, the surface of the road over which the public had highway rights, the subsoil immediately beneath it, to a depth sufficient to provide for its support and drainage, and a modest slice of the airspace above it sufficient to enable the public to use and enjoy it, and the responsible authority to maintain and repair it, and to supervise its safe operation."*

Whilst the *Southwark* case has the outward appearance of providing clear guidance on this point, it is submitted that the analysis does not cover the situation where a structure or mechanism with potential to cause harm oversails a highway maintainable at the public expense above this "*modest slice of the airspace*". It would seem to be odd if the highway authority is devoid of any common law rights to restrain such an inchoate hazard rather than having to wait until a member of the public is injured. These matters were not canvassed in the *Southwark* case and so it should not be taken as being conclusive on points which was never discussed by the court. They are considered at Chapter 18 in connection with the cranes which oversail the highway.

---

[32] @ para. 3-16.

# Chapter 5

# The Landowner's Right Of Access To The Highway

## 5.1    The importance of this topic

A landowner has a common law right of access to the highway from any part of his property which abuts it. It is a private right which is distinct from public law rights in the highway. Clearly, the right of access has significant implications where a developer is seeking to bring forward a site which has a boundary which touches an adjacent highway but does not, as yet, have an existing access point. This is because, at common law, the landowner is entitled to create an access without permission from the local highway authority.

## 5.2    The right of access

This right is not dependent upon whether the adjacent landowner also owns the subsoil to the highway: *Ramuz v Southend Local Board* (1892) 67 L.T. 169. The landowner may require the removal of any obstruction which impedes his access to the highway and seek damages: *East Riding of Yorkshire County Council v Company of Proprietors of Selby Bridge* [1925] Ch 841; *Marshall v Blackpool Corporation* [1935] A.C. 16 and *Rowley v Tottenham Urban District Council* [1914] A.C. 95.

The right of access does not, however, give the landowner any rights which are greater than those of the public when it comes to loading and unloading from the adjacent highway. He is entitled to make a reasonable use of the highway for the purposes of loading and unloading of goods and materials, but the rights of the public are higher than the private rights of the owner. Therefore the owner must act reasonably, and is not entitled to cause a serious obstruction to the public whilst in the course of loading and unloading: *Vanderpant v Mayfield Hotel Co Ltd* [1930] 1 Ch 138.

In *Fritz v Hobson* (1880) 14 Ch D 542, the defendant's premises were approached by means of three passages, and the Defendant, in rebuilding his premises, carried on building operations for several months. Fry J held that it was not reasonable to use one passage only, though the most convenient, for the carriage of building materials and rubbish, but that the inconvenience created thereby should have been distributed over the three passages, and that the Defendant ought not to have carried such materials and rubbish during the busiest hours of the day, but should have diminished the inconvenience by carrying them early in the morning or late at night. The jury are not to consider solely what is convenient for the business of the Defendants.[33]

A landowner may gain access to his adjacent land by heavy machinery notwithstanding that consequential damage is caused to an intervening footway: *St Mary Vestry, Newington v Jacobs* (1871-72) L.R. 7 Q.B. 47.

---

[33]    Per *Pratt & Mackenzie* @ p.121.

Similarly, the owner has a right of access from the highway in order to repair or maintain the fabric of any building on his adjacent land: *Cobb v Saxby* [1914] 3 K.B. 822. Again, this right must be exercised reasonably, as against the public, both in terms of duration and extent: *Harper v Haden & Sons* [1933] Ch 298. Thus, in the case of repairing a house, the public must submit to the inconvenience occasioned necessarily in repairing the house; but if this inconvenience is prolonged for an unreasonable time the party may be indicted for a nuisance: *R v Jones* (1812) 3 Camp. 230.

### 5.3    Statutory limitations on right of access

As is often the case, this common law right of access is subject to limitations or constraints imposed by statute.

First, planning permission is required for the creation of a new access onto a classified road. Given that the local highway authority will normally be a consultee in respect of an application for planning permission, one can anticipate that a proposed access which fails to meet appropriate highway safety standards will be subject to an objection from that authority.

Secondly, statute provides a local highway authority with a number of powers in respect of private accesses. In *Ching Garage Ltd v Chingford Corporation* [1961] 1 W.L.R. 470, Lord Radcliffe said (@ 478):

> *"In my opinion, it is well-settled law that a highway authority exercising statutory powers to improve or maintain a street or highway, such as to raise or lower its level, to form a footpath, to pave or kerb or to erect omnibus shelters, is empowered to carry out its works even though by so doing it interferes with or obstructs frontagers' rights of access to the highway."*

Nowadays, the principal statute is the Highways Act 1980. Section 80 provides that a highway authority may erect and maintain fences or posts for the purpose of preventing access to a highway maintainable at the public expense by them, notwithstanding that to do so might impede access to adjacent private land: *Cusack v London Borough of Harrow* [2011] EWCA Civ 1514. Section 124 allows the highway authority to close an existing access if it considers the access likely to cause danger to, or to interfere unreasonably with, traffic on the highway. Section 184 allows the highway authority to require that a made-up vehicle crossing be installed over a footway or verge and then to charge the occupier of the relevant premises with the costs of doing so.

### 5.4    "Ransom strips"

The existence of a *"ransom strip"* between a frontage property and the adjacent highway can have very significant financial ramifications for the developer who must cross the strip in order to provide a site access. There are two typical, but very different situations. First, there is the classic *"ransom strip"* situation where the person with the benefit of the strip is seeking a share in the development value of the scheme.[34] Secondly, there is the situation where the person with the benefit of the strip is simply using it so as to frustrate the development. In many cases, the strip of land is part of a highway verge and is held by a highway authority.

The first point to make is that an unmetalled area which could be properly described as *"highway verge"* might, as a matter of law, be subject to the same public rights of passage and repassage as the metalled part. This point is discussed in Chapter 4 above in connection with, among other authorities, *Neeld v Hendon Urban District Council, Hale v Norfolk County Council* [2001] and *Goodmayes Estates Limited v First National Commercial Bank Limited & Essex County Council* [2004].

The greatest unresolved difficulty with this topic is where a highway authority has acquired land for the purposes of constructing a highway, but then has used all of this land in the project. That is, what might be perceived to be *"verge"* or *"amenity land"*, in fact, land which was left over from the project. Then, the question which might be asked is whether the authority can seek to impose financial charges on those who then seek to access the new highway from adjacent land over land which was left-over from the scheme. This is difficult because the authority put itself into the position of becoming the owner of land to discharge its public duties as a highway authority.

Some guidance can be gained from *R v Northamptonshire CC ex. p. Commission for New Towns* (1991).[35] There, the Commission agreed to sell an area of land to the County Council, subject to the grant of planning permission and completion of access agreements. The Commission was responsible for the costs of access over land, sold by the Commission to the Council for highway purposes some years before with reservation of full and free rights of way over the roads or intended roads. However, the Council was now demanding a £5m payment. This was the only available access land and as yet no road had been built and the land had never been used as a highway. Macpherson J held that the Commission had a right of access. The Commission had a legitimate expectation that access would be provided to its land without the payment of a ransom sum, because this was the intention when the land was acquired by the County Council for highway purposes and there was no evidence that the parties ever changed their intention to provide a link to the Commission's land. The Council had a duty to act fairly.

In *Bexley LBC v Maison Maurice Ltd* [2006] EWHC 3192 (Ch) the highway authority had built a road next to Maison Maurice's property following a compulsory purchase order, but had retained a strip of land along Maison Maurice's frontage boundary. With the agreement of the authority, Maison Maurice constructed a new access across the strip to the road in place of its old access and used the access for some years without complaint from the authority. The authority later demanded that Maison Maurice should enter into

---

[34] Often called a *"Stokes v Cambridge"* payment by those who have either never read *Stokes v Cambridge Corporation* (1962) 13 P. & C.R. 77 or have misunderstood it!

[35] [1991] 10 W.L.U.K. 255.

a temporary licence in return for a relatively modest fee, which Maison Maurice disputed. Lewison J gave judgment for Maison Maurice.

It was clear that the authority had not constructed a highway whose boundary was contiguous with the boundary of Maison Maurice's property; however, Maison Maurice had complied with all the planning conditions set by the local authority and both parties had behaved as if Maison Maurice had a right of way over the new crossover in place of its old right of way. Maison Maurice could therefore reasonably expect that it would receive a new permanent and safe access in substitution for the old without additional payment other than the local authority's costs, which it had paid. The local authority was therefore estopped from denying that Maison Maurice had a permanent means of access to the highway over the new crossover.

Having reviewed those authorities, Sauvain suggests[36] that it must be wrong in principle for a highway authority to seek to charge for the right to cross land which was acquired either by agreement or by compulsory acquisition for the purpose of constructing a highway, when the vendor had properly assumed that his remaining land would have access over the new or improved highway, and where the purchase price or compensation paid may have reflected that assumption.

The bigger problem, however, is that *R v Northamptonshire CC ex. p. Commission for New Towns* (1991) and *Bexley LBC v Maison Maurice Ltd* [2006] were exceptional cases. In reality, there are usually no grounds for claims turning on *"legitimate expectation"* or estoppel for the simple reason that many road schemes do not use up all of the land acquired for them. That is to say, surplus areas are not uncommon. It makes sense that the prudent highway authority will acquire sufficient land to allow for flexibility in the precise boundaries of the finished highway by, quite properly, drawing the *"red line"* widely.[37] In theory, land which is not used should be offered back to the original landowner under the *Crichel Down rules*; but this is not always the case in practice. However, it is suggested that it does not follow that the authority should, somehow, distance itself from the *Crichel Down rules* by the passage of time, so as to put itself into the position where it can demand a ransom payment either from the original landowner, his successors or, even, a third party. Unfortunately, an examination of these matters falls outside the scope of this book.

Furthermore, it is wrong to presume that all land which is used in connection with a road scheme is always part of the *via trita* and therefore subject to public rights of passage. The most obvious example is a steep retaining embankment which is necessary in order to support land adjacent to a highway or to support the highway against a slope. Notwithstanding that the embankment is maintained by the highway authority, it would be most odd if this rampart is deemed to be available for passage and repassage, even if a vehicle capable of driving along it could be devised. The more difficult case is where the authority purchases

---

[36]   Ibid @ p.110.
[37]   It might be apocryphal, but it is understood that this happened with land purchase for the Channel Tunnel Rail Link.

land to mitigate the environmental effects of a road scheme and incorporates that land as nominal "*amenity land*". It would be most unfortunate if this carefully landscaped and vegetated land is then used for the passage of public motor vehicles.

# Chapter 6

# Extinguishment And Diversion Of Highways

## 6.1 Introduction

It is often the case that a developer must seek to stop up (i.e. extinguish) or divert a highway in order to carry out a development. There are numerous statutory powers relating to the extinguishment and diversion of highways. This chapter discusses those which tend to be most common in this connection, namely:

- Section 116 of the Highways Act 1980

- Section 118 of the Highways Act 1980

- Section 119 of the Highways Act 1980

- Section 247 of the Town and Country Planning Act 1990

- Section 257 of the Town and Country Planning Act 1990

## 6.2 Section 116 of the Highways Act 1980

A magistrates' court can, on an application by a highway authority, authorise the stopping up of, or diversion of, a highway provided that the highway is "*unnecessary*" or can be diverted, to make it nearer or more commodious to the public.

Section 116(1) provides that if it appears to a magistrates' court that a highway (as respects which the highway authority have made an application under this section) is unnecessary, or can be diverted so as to make it nearer or more commodious to the public, the court may by order authorise it to be stopped up or, as the case may be, to be so diverted.

The highway authority is obliged to give notice to the following:

- in cases where the highway is in a non-metropolitan district, the Council of that district and if it is in Wales the Council for the area in which it is situated if they are not the highway authority; and

- in England the parish council and in Wales the Council (if any) of the community in which the highway is situated.

In the event that within two months of service of the notice the district council, parish council or community council refuse to consent to the making of the application then the application shall not be made.[38]

---

[38] The prudent developer would do well to canvass these councils before initiating the process.

Any person who uses the highway and any person aggrieved by the making of the order has a right to be heard in the magistrates' court.

An order made under these provisions shall not be made unless the written consent of every person having a legal interest in the land which is to be diverted is produced to and deposited with the court, and shall not authorise the stopping up until the new part to be substituted has been completed to the satisfaction of two justices of the peace.

In *Ramblers' Association v Kent CC* (1990) 154 J.P. 716 the Divisional Court, whilst emphasising that the question whether a highway is unnecessary is essentially a question of fact for the magistrates, attempted to lay down some guidance as to the principles which may assist in this determination. The way must be unnecessary for the public. It should be unnecessary for the sort of purposes for which the justices would reasonably expect the public to use that particular way, which may be to reach a specific destination or which may be recreational in character. Where there is evidence of use of a way, it will, prima facie, be difficult for the justices properly to come to the conclusion that a way is unnecessary unless the public are, or are going to be, provided with a reasonably suitable alternative way. In deciding whether an alternative way is reasonable, it must be a way which is protected, so far as duration is concerned, in the same way as the existing way is protected. It must also be suitable or reasonably suitable, for the purpose for which the public were using the existing way.

Section 117 of the Highways Act 1980 provides that a person who desires a highway to be stopped up or diverted, but is not authorised to make an application for that purpose under section 116, may request the highway authority to make such an application; and if the authority grants the request they may, as a condition of making the application, require him to make such provision for any costs to be incurred by them in connection with the matter as they deem reasonable.

### 6.3    Section 118 of the Highways Act 1980

Section 118 of the Highways Act 1980 makes provision for a council[39] to make an order to stop up a footpath on the grounds that it is not needed for public use.

Section 118(1) provides that:

> *"Where it appears to a council as respects a footpath or bridleway in their area ... that it is expedient that the path or way should be stopped up on the ground that it is not needed for public use, the council may by order ... extinguish the public right of way over the path or way."*
>
> *An order under this section is referred to in this Act as a 'public path extinguishment order'".*

Section 118(2) provides that the Secretary of State shall not confirm a public path extinguishment order, and a council shall not confirm such an order as an unopposed order, unless he, or they, are satisfied that it is expedient so to do:

---

[39]    NB: this power is not limited to local highway authorities.

- having regard to the extent (if any) to which it appears to him or them that the path or way would, apart from the order, be likely to be used by the public; and

- having regard to the effect which the extinguishment of the right of way would have as respects land served by the path or way.

If it is an opposed order, it is subject to confirmation by the Secretary of State. If unopposed, it can be confirmed by the authority.

## 6.4　Section 119 of the Highways Act 1980

Section 119 of the Highways Act 1980 allows an authority to make a public path diversion order in the interests of the owner, lessee or occupier of land crossed by a path or way or alternatively if it is in the public interest. The order is subject to confirmation of the Secretary of State and creates a new way and extinguishes the old.

Section 119(1) provides that:

> *"Where it appears to a council as respects a footpath or bridleway in their area ... that, in the interests of the owner, lessee or occupier of land crossed by the path or way or of the public, it is expedient that the line of the path or way ... should be diverted ... the council may ...*
>
> *(a) create ... any such new footpath or bridleway as appears to the council requisite for affecting the diversion, and*
>
> *(b) extinguish ... the public right of way over so much of the path or way as appears to the council requisite as aforesaid."*
>
> *An order under this section is referred to as a 'public path diversion order'".*

## 6.5　Sections 247 and 257 of the Town and Country Planning Act 1990

Sections 247 and 257 of the Town and Country Planning Act 1990 permit orders to be made for the stopping up or diversion of highways, footpaths and bridleways. In the case of a carriageway, the order must be made by the Secretary of State and in the case of the footpath or bridleway, by the local planning authority subject to the confirmation by the Secretary of State, or as an unopposed order by the Planning Authority.

The pre-condition for orders under the 1990 Act is that the Secretary of State, or the local planning authority, must be satisfied that the stopping up or diversion is necessary in order to enable development to be carried out in accordance with planning permission, or by a government department. This means that such an order cannot be obtained if the development has already taken place. An order can be made, however, when the relevant work has yet to be completed.

In *Ashby v Secretary of State for the Environment* [1980] 1 All E.R. 508 the Court of Appeal held that the stopping up of a highway under this section could not be authorised with retrospective effect. The words *"to be carried out"* meant that the power was not exercisable where all the permitted development on the line of the highway had already been completed. For an authority, or the Secretary of State, to be satisfied that an order "is" necessary to enable development to be carried out there must still be some development to be carried out.

In *Vasiliou v Secretary of State for Transport* [1991] 2 All E.R. 77, the Court of Appeal had to consider whether that meant that planning objections must be disregarded by the Secretary of State when confirming an order under this section. The Secretary of State had decided that the effect of the stopping up order on the Appellant's trade was not a material consideration under this section, but was instead a matter to be taken into account by the local planning authority when considering the application for planning permission for the proposed development. The Court of Appeal held that, in making the stopping up order, the Secretary of State ought to take into account the adverse effect his order would have on those entitled to the rights which would be extinguished by his order, especially as the statute made no provision for compensation to those whose rights were being extinguished.

See also *R v Commissioner for Local Administration for England ex. p. Odds* [1995] E.G. 168 (C.S.) and *R (Batchelor Enterprises Ltd) v Secretary of State for the Environment* [2004] J.P.L. 1222.

# Chapter 7

# The Advance Payments Code

## 7.1 Introduction

If a developer's scheme will involve the construction of ways to access buildings within it, then the "*Advance Payments Code*" might apply, with the result that the local highway authority must secure and supervise the construction of those ways and is given statutory powers to do so. In many cases, the authority's objective will be to ensure that the ways are built to standards which allow them to be adopted as highways maintainable at the public expense.

The Code is, therefore, of central importance to many developers.

This chapter forms an overview and a detailed discussion can be found at pages 201 to 227 below.

## 7.2 The Advance Payments Code

The "*Advance Payments Code*" means the statutory code provided by sections 219 to 225 of the Highways Act 1980: section 203(1). The Code has the effect of securing payment of the expenses of the execution of "*street works*" in "*private streets*"[40] adjacent to new buildings: section 204(2). In practical terms, this can be taken to mean works for the construction of estate roads in a scheme for built development.

The Code ensures that a sum equivalent to the likely costs of making up the private street is paid to the street authority or secured before a new building is erected, the objective of the exercise being to put the "*Street Works Authority*"[41] in the position of being able to step in and carry out the street works in the event that the developer fails to do so.

Importantly, a developer is not entitled to commence work on a building served by the private street, and for which building regulation approval is required, unless and until he has paid to the highway authority a sum equivalent to the likely costs of making up the street (aka the "*Advance Payment*") or provided an equivalent security (normally a bond or other financial guarantee).

The general principle is subject to a number of exemptions, the most notable being the entry by the owner into an agreement under section 38 of the Highways Act 1980.

The authority must (unless the works are exempted) within 6 weeks from the date when plans are passed under the Building Regulations in respect of construction of the new building serve a notice (usually called an "*APC Notice*") requiring payment or a security. This is a statutory duty which is imposed on the authority and, as such, it has no discretion in the matter. An authority which fails to discharge this statutory duty can be challenged

---

[40]  Both "*street works*" and "*private streets*" are defined terms: see section 203(2).
[41]  Another defined term, but normally the local highway authority: see section 203(2).

by judicial review or by a complaint to the local commissioner for administration: see *R (Hughes) v Local Government Ombudsman* [2001] EWHC Admin 349.

It is a criminal offence to carry out such works if an Advance Payment is not made or security given in the absence of an exemption: section 219(2).

If the developer makes up the street, then the Advance Payment is refunded or the security is released. If the developer does not make up the street then the Street Works Authority can make up the street under the Private Street Works Code and recover its costs from the Advance Payment or the security: section 222.

If street works are carried out, then the authority may, if it chooses to do so, make a declaration so that the street then becomes a highway maintainable at the public expense or a majority of the frontagers may (if at least one of them has made an advance payment) require that such a declaration is made: section 228.

### 7.3     Where does the Advance Payments Code apply?
Section 204(2) provides that the Advance Payments Code applies:

(a)     in all outer London boroughs;

(b)     in all areas in counties in which the advance payments code in the Highways Act 1959 (which is replaced by the advance payments code in the 1980 Act) was in force immediately before 1 April 1974; and

(c)     in any parish or community in which the advance payments code in the Highways Act 1959 was, after 1 April 1974, adopted in accordance with Schedule 14 to that Act, or in which the advance payments code is adopted in accordance with Schedule 15 to the 1980 Act.

The areas in which the Advance Payments Code applies include any area in Wales which is, or is in, a county borough and in which the code applied immediately before 1 April 1996: section 204(3).

### 7.4     Payments to be made by owners of new buildings
Section 219(1) provides that where:

(a)     it is proposed to erect a building for which plans are required to be deposited with the local authority in accordance with building regulations, and

(b)     the building will have a frontage on a private street in which the Street Works Authority have power under the Private Street Works Code[42] to require works to be executed

---

[42]   The *"Private Street Works Code"* is the statutory code set out in sections 205 to 218 of the Highways Act 1980; see section 203(1).

or to execute works,

no work shall be done in or for the purpose of erecting the building unless the owner of the land on which it is to be erected or a previous owner thereof has paid to the Street Works Authority, or secured to the satisfaction of that authority the payment to them of, such sum as may be required under section 220 in respect of the cost of street works in that street (i.e. broadly the sum which would be recoverable under the Private Street Works Code).

The *"Building Regulations"* are regulations currently made pursuant to the Building Act 1984. The authority must (unless the works are exempted) within 6 weeks from the date when plans are passed under the Building Regulations prior to the commencement of construction of the new building serve a notice requiring an Advance Payment or a security: section 220(1).

### 7.5 Some definitions

Section 203(2) provides that a *"private street"* means a *"street"* that is not a highway maintainable at the public expense. It is necessary to analyse this less than straightforward definition in some depth.

The word *"street"* is itself defined in section 329(1) as having the same meaning as in Part III of the New Roads and Street Works Act 1991. Section 48(1) of the 1991 Act states:

> *"In this Part a "street" means the whole or any part of any of the following, irrespective of whether it is a thoroughfare –*
>
> *(a) any highway, road, lane, footway, alley or passage,*
>
> *(b) any square or court, and*
>
> *(c) any land laid out as a way whether it is for the time being formed as a way or not.*
>
> *Where a street passes over a bridge or through a tunnel, references in this Part to the street include that bridge or tunnel".*

This definition makes it clear that the concept of a *"street"* is not confined to highways only. The use of the phrase *"road, lane, footway, alley or passage ..."* in addition to the preceding word *"highway"* can be construed to mean that this part of the definition is not limited to highways only – otherwise the words following *"highway"* would be redundant. The words *"... any land laid out as a way whether it is for the time being formed as a way or not ..."* clearly includes ways which have yet to be constructed.

Section 203(2) goes on to provide that a *"private street"*:

(a)     includes any land that is deemed to be a private street by virtue of a declaration under section 232; and

(b)   for the purposes of the Advance Payments Code, includes any land shown as a proposed street on plans deposited with respect to any building either under building regulations or on an application for planning permission under the Town and Country Planning Act 1990,

but the fact that a part of a street is a highway maintainable at the public expense does not prevent any other part of it from being a part of a private street.

As to (a), section 232(1) states that section 232 applies to land defined by a development plan as the site of a proposed road or as land required for the widening of an existing road which is of less than byelaw width and is designated by the plan as land to which section 232 applies.

Section 203(3) provides that *"Street Works Authority"* means:

(a)   as respects a street outside Greater London, the council of the county or metropolitan district in which the street is situated,

(b)   as respects a street in a London borough, the council of the borough, and

(c)   as respects a street in the City, the Common Council.

Section 203(3) provides that *"street works"* means any works for the sewering, levelling, paving, metalling, flagging, channelling and making good of a street, and includes the provision of proper means for lighting a street; and *"paving, metalling and flagging"* includes all methods of making a carriageway or footway.

### 7.6      Does the Advance Payments Code apply to ways which are proposed or in the course of construction?

This is an important question because new buildings are often constructed in advance of the completion of access roads and it should follow that the highway authority ought to be in the position to exert controls at an early stage, otherwise developers could easily evade the Advance Payments Code by failing to progress construction of their estate roads.

It is necessary to go back to the definition of *"private street"* to find the answer.

The definition of a *"street"* in section 48 of the New Roads and Street Works Act 1991 includes *"... any land laid out as a way whether it is for the time being formed as a way or not."* This clearly includes ways which have yet to be constructed.

The definition of *"private street"* in section 203(2) includes *"... any land that is deemed to be a private street by virtue of a declaration under section 232."* In turn, the section 232 definition relates to land which may or may not be laid out at the time that the declaration is made.

For the purposes of the Advance Payments Code, the definition of "*private street*" in section 203(2) also includes "*... any land shown as a proposed street on plans deposited with respect to any building either under building regulations or on an application for planning permission under the Town and Country Planning Act 1990.*" Again, there is reference to a way which may or may not be laid out at the time that the application is made.

The position seems to be relatively clear; however, the arguments advanced, but not resolved, in *R (Hughes) v Local Government Ombudsman* [2001] EWHC Admin 349 have not assisted matters: see discussion below.

## 7.7     The exemptions
The Advance Payments Code provides a number of exemptions in section 219. The exemptions are discussed at pages 205 to 214 below.

## 7.8     Is highway status inevitable?
The Advance Payments Code is not designed to ensure that all ways to which it applies will become highways regardless of the wishes of the landowners. The owners might have good reasons for keeping a way private. They might wish to maintain or surface the way in a particular manner, install their own traffic calming or to control any future development which may gain access from the way.

A way does not automatically become a highway simply because street works have been carried out on it. If the Street Works Authority wish to adopt the street, then they have the option of making a declaration to this effect under the procedure in section 228. If they do not make such a declaration, then the street need not become a highway maintainable at the public expense. Whether it becomes a highway at common law or by deemed dedication under section 31 of the Highways Act 1980 is another matter.[43] If the owners or developers erect signs at the start of construction which make it clear that the new way is private (e.g. "*Private – Construction Traffic Only*"), then any usage by the public will not give rise to highway rights. The owners can then erect and maintain the usual signs to preclude the creation of highways by public user at common law or lodge statements and plans with the Street Works Authority under section 31(6) of the Highways Act 1980.

If, however, the owners are content that the way will become a highway, then (if the Street Works Authority agrees) there is no compulsion on them to have it maintained at the public expense.

---

[43]   See discussion @ para. 3.6 above.

# Chapter 8

# Planning Applications And Highways

## 8.1    Introduction

The town and country planning process is one of the central themes in formulating and delivering development schemes. It is important to view the highway aspects of the development process as flowing from the town and country planning stages through to the provision of roads and road works when the scheme is being constructed.

This chapter provides an overview of the application process. The important matter of transport statements and assessments is discussed in Chapter 9 including the details and documents which accompany a planning application. It is, also, important that both the local planning authority and the developer pay attention to the conditions which may be attached to a permission and any planning obligation which may accompany it, and they are discussed at Chapter 11 and Chapter 12 respectively.

## 8.2    The Local Planning Authorities

The local planning authorities are district councils, London borough councils, metropolitan district councils, county councils in relation to any area in England for which there is no district council, the Broads Authority and the National Park authorities.[44]

## 8.3    The need for planning permission

Planning permission is required for the carrying out of the *"development"* of land: see section 57 of the Town and Country Planning Act 1990; and *"development"* can, for present purposes, be taken to comprise *"material change of use"* or *"operational development"*. Section 55 of the 1990 Act provides that *"development"* means the carrying out of building, engineering, mining or other operations in, on, over or under land, or the making of any material change in the use of any buildings or other land.

So far as day to day practice is concerned, engineering or building operations are normally referred to as *"operational development"*. Not surprisingly, *"mining"* is usually called *"mining"* or *"minerals"*.

*"Operational development"* is the carrying out of operations which effect permanent changes to physical fabric of the land itself, for example the erection of buildings. So far as building operations are concerned, they are further defined as including the demolition of buildings, rebuilding, structural alterations of or additions to buildings and other operations normally undertaken by a person carrying on business as a builder; see section 55(1A). By section 336(1) of the 1990 Act, *"engineering operations"* includes the formation or laying out of means of access to highways and *"means of access"* includes any means of access, whether private or public, for vehicles or for foot passengers, and includes a *"street"*.[45]

---

[44]    See sections 37(4) and (5), of the Planning and Compulsory Purchase Act 2004.
[45]    Not defined in the 1990 Act.

A "*material change of use*" will take place when the way in which land is used is changed but without changing the physical fabric of the land, for example the use of land for a market or for the parking of vehicles. There is no statutory definition of "*material change of use*" and the concept has, therefore, evolved over the years by way of judicial precedent.

Both material change of use and operational development can have effects on traffic flows and generation and so highway considerations may be material to the question of whether planning permission should be granted.

Some forms of activity are expressly excluded from the definition of "*development*" by the 1990 Act.

Section 55(2)(b) provides that the carrying out on land within the boundaries of a road by a local highway authority of any works required for the maintenance or improvement of the road shall not be taken for the purposes of the Act to involve development of the land and therefore does not need planning permission. However, it goes on to say that, in the case of any such works which are not exclusively for the maintenance of the road, this exemption does not include any works which may have significant adverse effects on the environment.

## 8.4 Permitted development

Planning permission may be granted by a local planning authority or a minister, but it is often the case that permission is granted by subordinate legislation without the need for an application. Such permission is called "*permitted development*" and is currently given by the Town and Country Planning (General Permitted Development) (England) Order 2015 (S.I. 2015, No. 596) (aka the "*GPDO*").

Part 9 of Schedule 2 to the GPDO provides for development relating to roads. The carrying out by a highway authority:

(a)     on land within the boundaries of a road, of any works required for the maintenance or improvement of the road, where such works involve development by virtue of section 55(2)(b) of the 1990 Act; or

(b)     on land outside but adjoining the boundary of an existing highway of works required for or incidental to the maintenance or improvement of the highway,

is permitted development and, therefore, does not need the grant of an express planning permission. The word "*road*" is not defined in the 1990 Act and there is no reason to believe that it is limited to highways only. In particular, in *Spackman v Wiltshire County Council* [1977] 1 All E.R. 257 it was held that a private drive, albeit serving one house only, was a "*road*" within what is now section 56(4)(d) of the 1990 Act. It is also important to note that the boundaries of a road or highway are not limited to the made-up carriageway or other metalled parts, but often encompass verged areas: see Chapter 4.

So far as it may be material, section 336(1) of the 1990 Act provides that *"improvement"*, in relation to a highway, has the same meaning as in the Highways Act 1980 and section 329(1) of the 1980 Act provides, in turn, that *"improvement"* includes works within the powers of improvement in Part 5 of that Act.

The formation, laying out and construction of a means of access to a highway which is not a trunk road or a classified road[46] is permitted development where that access is required in connection with development permitted by any Class in the Schedule to the GPDO: Part 2, Class B. However, this power does not apply where the access involves the erection, construction, maintenance, improvement or alteration of a gate, fence, wall or other means of enclosure. It is further limited by Article 3(6) which excludes the right where an access would obstruct a sight-line or cause a danger.

The carrying out on land within the boundaries of an unadopted street or private way of works required for the maintenance or improvement of the street or way is permitted development: Part 9, Class E. For these purposes *"unadopted street"* means a street not being a highway maintainable at the public expense within the meaning of the Highways Act 1980. In its circuitous way, the 1980 Act then provides that *"street"* is defined in the New Roads and Street Works Act 1991: see section 48(1) of the 1991 Act and para. 7.5 above. This power is available to private persons and is not limited to highway authorities or street managers.

Unfortunately, the application of the provision can be a source of difficulty where the status of the way is unclear. The limitation to unadopted streets and private ways contains a trap for the unwary because it is not always readily apparent that a way is not maintainable at the public expense. It might be the case that the way is not listed by the highway authority as a highway maintainable at the public expense, yet it might be so, as a matter of law, if it is an *"ancient highway"* or a pre-1949 public right of way (see para. 7.5 above). Determining whether this is the case or not is, often, problematic. This may be compounded by the fact that, in many cases, the exact boundaries of an ancient road can be difficult to determine. This would suggest that, in cases of doubt, the person who wishes to carry out such works should seek a certificate of proposed use or development from the local planning authority pursuant to section 192 of the 1990 Act. It is also worth bearing in mind that extensive works in environmentally sensitive areas might trigger the need for an environmental impact assessment in any event.

## 8.5    Permitted changes of use

Some types of change of use are allowed by the Town and Country Planning (Use Classes) Order 1987 (S.I. 1987, No. 764) (aka the *"UCO"*). The broad effect of the UCO is that where a building or other land is used for a purpose of any class specified in the Schedule to the UCO, the use of that building or that other land for any other purpose of the same class shall not be taken to involve development of the land: see Article 3. For example, Class A1 allows an operator to switch between any shop-based uses mentioned in Class A without

---

[46]    Defined at Article 2(1).

the need for planning permission. Class A includes (among others) use for the retail sale of goods other than hot food, as a post office, for the sale of tickets or as a travel agency, for the sale of sandwiches or other cold food for consumption off the premises and so on.

The UCO and the GPDO also operate in tandem to allow further changes of use without the need for planning permission. Thus, Part 3 of the GPDO allows development consisting of a change of use of a building from a use falling within Class A3 (restaurants and cafés), A4 (drinking establishments) or A5 (hot food takeaways) of the Schedule to the UCO, to a use falling within Class A1 (shops) or Class A2 (financial and professional services) of that Schedule.

An in-depth examination of the GPDO and the UCO can be found in two books by Martin Goodall; namely, *"The Essential Guide to the Use of Land and Buildings"* and *"A Practical Guide to Permitted Changes of Use"*.[47]

## 8.6 Types of planning permission

Planning permissions are usually characterised as being either *"full"* permissions or *"outline"* permissions.

There is no statutory definition of *"full planning permission"* but it is taken to mean a planning permission which sets out all the details of the development. In practice, many so-called *"full"* permissions are subject to conditions which require the settling of matters of detail before the development can be started.

Article 2(1) of the Town and Country Planning (Development Management Procedure) (England) Order 2015 (S.I. 2015, No. 595) (aka the *"DMPO"*) defines an *"outline planning permission"* as meaning a planning permission for the erection of a building, which is granted subject to a condition requiring the subsequent approval of the local planning authority with respect to one or more reserved matters. Article 2(1) of the DMPO goes on to add the following definitions:

> *"reserved matters"* in relation to an outline planning permission, or an application for such permission, means any of the following matters in respect of which details have not been given in the application:
>
> (a) access;
>
> (b) appearance;
>
> (c) landscaping;
>
> (d) layout; and

---

[47]   By a happy coincidence, also published by Bath Publishing.

(e) scale.

"*access*", in relation to reserved matters, means the accessibility to and within the site, for vehicles, cycles and pedestrians in terms of the positioning and treatment of access and circulation routes and how these fit into the surrounding access network.

The references to "*... accessibility ... within the site ...*" and "*circulation routes*" means that "*access*" is not confined to the particulars of the junction arrangements with the surrounding highway network and extends to on-site estate roads.

"*layout*" means the way in which buildings, routes and open spaces within the development are provided, situated and orientated in relation to each other and to buildings and spaces outside the development.

It is notable that the word "*routes*" encompasses on-site estate roads and that, in any event, it would be difficult to particularise the other aspects of layout without an understanding of the estate roads. There is, therefore, an overlap with reserved matters in respect of access.

Article 5(2) provides that where the authority who are to determine an application for outline planning permission are of the opinion that, in the circumstances of the case, the application ought not to be considered separately from all or any of the reserved matters, the authority must within the period of 1 month beginning with the date of receipt of the application notify the applicant that they are unable to determine it unless further details are submitted, specifying the further details they require.

Article 5(3) provides that an application for outline planning permission must also indicate the area or areas where access points to the development will be situated, even if access has been reserved.

An applicant can choose to submit details of any of the reserved matters as part of an outline application.

Notwithstanding that "*access*" and "*layout*" can be reserved for subsequent approval, applicants often provide details of the junction arrangements to the highway network when applying for outline permission. Rightly or wrongly, this is then usually described as being a "*non-reserved matter*". It is, however, wrong to say that, therefore, "*access*" is not a reserved matter for the purposes of that development because the definition of "*access*" includes circulation routes within the development site and these might not be thus detailed: ibid Article 2(1).

Outline applications are often accompanied by one or more illustrative master-plans which show how the application site could be developed. An applicant may supply supporting information "*for illustrative purposes only*" (or may otherwise indicate that they are not formally part of the application), and these materials will not be treated as part of the application.

Applications for approval of reserved matters must be made within a specified time-limit, normally 3 years from the date outline planning permission was granted: section 92 of the Town and Country Planning Act 1990. This period can be shortened by the local planning authority.

## 8.7        Design and Access Statements

Article 9(1) of the DMPO provides that a Design and Access Statement is required for an application for planning permission which is for:[48]

(a)      development which is *"major development"*; or

(b)      where any part of the development is in a *"designated area"*, development consisting of:

    (i)      the provision of one or more dwellinghouses; or

    (ii)      the provision of a building or buildings where the floor space created by the development is 100 square metres or more.

By Article 2(1) *"major development"* means development involving any one or more of the following:

(a)      the winning and working of minerals or the use of land for mineral-working deposits;

(b)      waste development;

(c)      the provision of dwellinghouses where -

    (i)      the number of dwellinghouses to be provided is 10 or more; or

    (ii)      the development is to be carried out on a site having an area of 0.5 hectares or more and it is not known whether the number of dwellinghouses to be provided is 10 or more;

(d)      the provision of a building or buildings where the floor space to be created by the development is 1,000 square metres or more; or

(e)      development carried out on a site having an area of 1 hectare or more.

The Design and Access Statement must be about:

(a)      the design principles and concepts that have been applied to the development; and

(b)      how issues relating to access to the development have been dealt with.

---

[48]      Note the limitations in Article 9(4).

The Design and Access Statement must:

(a)    explain the design principles and concepts that have been applied to the development;

(b)    demonstrate the steps taken to appraise the context of the development and how the design of the development takes that context into account;

(c)    explain the policy adopted as to access, and how policies relating to access in relevant local development documents have been taken into account;

(d)    state what, if any, consultation has been undertaken on issues relating to access to the development and what account has been taken of the outcome of any such consultation; and

(e)    explain how any specific issues which might affect access to the development have been addressed.

The National Planning Practice Guidance website states:

> *"A Design and Access Statement is a concise report accompanying certain applications for planning permission and applications for listed building consent. They provide a framework for applicants to explain how the proposed development is a suitable response to the site and its setting, and demonstrate that it can be adequately accessed by prospective users. Design and Access Statements can aid decision-making by enabling local planning authorities and third parties to better understand the analysis that has underpinned the design of a development proposal.*
>
> *The level of detail in a Design and Access Statement should be proportionate to the complexity of the application, but should not be long."* (Paragraph: 029; Reference ID: 14-029-20140306 - Revision date: 06 03 2014).

For additional information see:

http://www.designcouncil.org.uk/resources/guide/design-and-access-statements-how-write-read-and-use-them.

## 8.8    The development plan

Section 38(6) of the Planning and Compulsory Purchase Act 2004 provides that, if regard is to be had to the development plan for the purpose of any determination to be made under the planning Acts, the determination must be made in accordance with the plan unless material considerations indicate otherwise.

For the purposes of any area in Greater London the development plan is the spatial development strategy, the development plan documents (taken as a whole) which have been adopted or approved in relation to that area, and the neighbourhood development plans which have been made in relation to that area: section 38(2).

For the purposes of any other area in England the development plan is the regional strategy for the region in which the area is situated (if there is a regional strategy for that region), and the development plan documents (taken as a whole) which have been adopted or approved in relation to that area, and the neighbourhood development plans which have been made in relation to that area: section 38(3).

For the purposes of any area in Wales the development plan is the National Development Framework for Wales, the strategic development plan for any strategic planning area that includes all or part of that area, and the local development plan for that area: section 38(4).

The statutory definition of *"development plan documents"* is circuitous in the extreme. In practice, one would normally be looking to the *"Core Strategy"* produced by the relevant local planning authority together with any daughter documents such as, for example, site allocation development plan documents.

The Croydon Local Plan (2018) provides a recent example of a local plan policy:

> *Policy DM29: Promoting sustainable travel and reducing congestion*
>
> *To promote sustainable growth in Croydon and reduce the impact of traffic congestion development should:*
>
> *(a) Promote measures to increase the use of public transport, cycling and walking;*
>
> *(b) Have a positive impact and must not have a detrimental impact on highway safety for pedestrians, cyclists, public transport users and private vehicles; and*
>
> *(c) Not result in a severe impact on the transport networks local to the site which would detract from the economic and environmental regeneration of the borough by making Croydon a less accessible and less attractive location [sic] in which to develop.*

If there is an adopted Neighbourhood Development Plan for the locality, then this will be a part of the development plan. Given that section 38(5) of the 2004 Act gives priority to the last development plan document to be adopted, it follows that this will probably give priority to Neighbourhood Development Plans in most cases because they will often be the last to be adopted.

## 8.9 National policy

National policy is a material consideration in the determination of planning applications by local planning authorities, planning inspectors and the Secretary of State. It is provided by the National Planning Policy Framework (2019)[49] (the *"NPPF"*); albeit that, on occasion, expressions of policy are supplemented by ministerial statements.

---

[49] Note that the NPPF was re-issued in February 2019.

Additionally, a Government website usually called the "National Planning Practice Guidance" (aka the "*NPPG*") provides a rolling commentary. Unfortunately, it is often unclear as to whether the authors of the NPPG are providing policy statements or attempting technical advice. If the latter, then this is usually made difficult by the fact that the authors frequently fail to observe the customary tenets of technical writing, such as providing sources, citations or any technical justification for their assertions. Indeed, it is not clear whether the authors possess any technical expertise, because they are not identified.[50] Arguably, given these shortcomings, practitioners are well advised to place greater weight on bespoke expert advice and standards in soundly based publications, such as the "*Design Manual for Roads and Bridges*".

## 8.10    The National Planning Policy Framework
The NPPF (2019) contains a number of statements which relate to sustainable transport and they will be taken up below.[51]

Paragraph 108 states that, in assessing sites that may be allocated for development in plans, or specific applications for development, it should be ensured that:

(a)    appropriate opportunities to promote sustainable transport modes can be – or have been – taken up, given the type of development and its location;

(b)    safe and suitable access to the site can be achieved for all users; and

(c)    any significant impacts from the development on the transport network (in terms of capacity and congestion), or on highway safety, can be cost effectively mitigated to an acceptable degree.

Paragraph 109 of the NPPF provides that development should only be prevented or refused on highways grounds if:

•    there would be an unacceptable impact on highway safety, or

•    the residual cumulative impacts on the road network would be severe.[52]

It is important to note that the "*severity*" test relates to impacts on the road network and not to highway safety.

The question on safety is whether there would be an "*unacceptable impact*" on highway safety.

---

50    For example, see the author's criticism of the misleading NPPG "*advice*" on Section 106 Agreements at para. 12.13 below.
51    Alistair Mills has provided a useful analysis of the NPPF in his book on the 2018 version of the NPPF "*Interpreting the NPPF*" (2018) which, coincidentally, is published by Bath Publishing. This guidance is still relevant to the 2019 version for the purposes of this book.
52    And see Mills ibid @ p.104 – 105.

So far as impacts on the highway network are concerned, it is important to have regard to the Delphic phrase *"residual cumulative impacts"*. In *Redhill Aerodrome Ltd v Secretary of State* [2014] EWCA Civ 1386, Sullivan LJ described this phrase as meaning: *"... those traffic impacts which would remain after any highway improvement to limit the significant impacts of the development have been carried out"*.

This assessment would, it is suggested, encompass three elements.

First, that the impact of the proposed development should be assessed not only on the traffic generated by the scheme but also by reference to the aggregate impacts of the scheme and other developments in the area.

Secondly, the highway authority must assess traffic generation by reference to the *"fall-back position"* for the site. Any assessment of a possible *"fall-back"* position is comprised of two components:

- An assessment of such lawful development as may be carried out on the site in the event that a planning application is refused. The assessment will include the consideration of any rights available to the landowner by way of planning permissions, permitted development or the Use Classes Order.

- A determination that there is a likelihood or real prospect that the alleged fall-back use will be taken up.[53]

Thirdly, as per Sullivan LJ, the developer's proposed mitigation measures, and any other proposed improvements to the local highway network, should be taken into account.

Paragraph 110 states that, within this context, applications for development should:

(a) give priority first to pedestrian and cycle movements, both within the scheme and with neighbouring areas; and second – so far as possible – to facilitating access to high quality public transport, with layouts that maximise the catchment area for bus or other public transport services, and appropriate facilities that encourage public transport use;

(b) address the needs of people with disabilities and reduced mobility in relation to all modes of transport;

(c) create places that are safe, secure and attractive – which minimise the scope for conflicts between pedestrians, cyclists and vehicles, avoid unnecessary street clutter, and respond to local character and design standards;

---

[53] In *PF Ahern (London) Limited v The Secretary of State for the Environment* [1998] J.P.L. 351, it was held that the test is whether there is a real possibility that any theoretical fall-back use will be taken up.

(d)     allow for the efficient delivery of goods, and access by service and emergency vehicles; and

(e)     be designed to enable charging of plug-in and other ultra-low emission vehicles in safe, accessible and convenient locations.

Mills notes[54] an apparent tension between Paragraphs 109 and 108(c). The latter notes that it should be ensured that any significant impacts, in terms of capacity and congestion or on highway safety, can be cost effectively mitigated to an acceptable degree. It is difficult to understand what the draftsman had in mind, what parameters for this mooted examination of cost effectiveness might be and what this adds to Paragraph 109.

Mills also notes[55] another apparent tension, this time between Paragraphs 109 and 108(b); namely, that safe and suitable access to the site can be achieved for all users. Again, it is difficult to see how this adds to Paragraph 109. The short answer is that Paragraph 108(b) is an unnecessary statement of the obvious. It would be bizarre if a local planning authority decided to grant a permission for a development with a manifestly unsafe access.

The exhortation to give priority to pedestrian and cycle movements in Paragraph 110(a) goes directly to the way in which estate roads are designed and managed. That is, they should not be dominated by vehicular traffic. Paragraph 110(c) goes to the same objective. Paragraph 111 provides that all developments that will generate significant amounts of movement should be required to provide a travel plan, and the application should be supported by a transport statement or transport assessment so that the likely impacts of the proposal can be assessed. These points are discussed at some length in Chapter 9 below.

---

[54]   Ibid @ p.105.
[55]   Ibid @ p.105.

# Chapter 9

# Transport Assessments, Transport Statements And Travel Plans

## 9.1 Introduction

Almost all applications for developments which impact on the highway will have to be accompanied by some explanation of the likely highway impacts of those proposals.

If those impacts might be significant, then a *"transport statement"*, *"transport assessment"* or *"travel plan"* might be required. Paragraph 111 of the NPPF states:

> *All developments that will generate significant amounts of movement should be required to provide a travel plan, and the application should be supported by a transport statement or transport assessment so that the likely impacts of the proposal can be assessed.*

## 9.2 Transport assessments and statements

The glossary to the NPPF (2019) describes a *"transport assessment"* as:

> *"A comprehensive and systematic process that sets out transport issues relating to a proposed development. It identifies measures required to improve accessibility and safety for all modes of travel, particularly for alternatives to the car such as walking, cycling and public transport, and measures that will be needed deal with the anticipated transport impacts of the development."*

A *"transport statement"* is described as:

> *"A simplified version of a transport assessment where it is agreed the transport issues arising from development proposals are limited and a full transport assessment is not required."*

The National Planning Practice Guidance (*"NPPG"*) website states:

> *Travel Plans, Transport Assessments and Statements are all ways of assessing and mitigating the negative transport impacts of development in order to promote sustainable development. They are required for all developments which generate significant amounts of movements.* (Paragraph: 002; Reference ID: 42-002-20140306 - Revision date: 06 03.2014).

The website states:

> *Transport Assessments and Statements are ways of assessing the potential transport impacts of developments (and they may propose mitigation measures to promote sustainable development. Where that mitigation relates to matters that can be addressed by management measures, the mitigation may inform the preparation of Travel Plans).*
>
> *Transport Assessments are thorough assessments of the transport implications of development, and Transport Statements are a 'lighter-touch' evaluation to be used where this would be more*

*proportionate to the potential impact of the development (i.e. in the case of developments with anticipated limited transport impacts).*

*Where the transport impacts of development are not significant, it may be that no Transport Assessment or Statement or Travel Plan is required. Local planning authorities, developers, relevant transport authorities, and neighbourhood planning organisations should agree what evaluation is needed in each instance.* (Paragraph: 004; Reference ID: 42-004-20140306 - Revision date: 06 03 2014).

The website states:

*Paragraph 111 of the National Planning Policy Framework sets out that all developments that generate significant amounts of transport movement should be supported by a Transport Statement or Transport Assessment.*

*Local planning authorities must make a judgement as to whether a development proposal would generate significant amounts of movement on a case by case basis (i.e. significance may be a lower threshold where road capacity is already stretched or a higher threshold for a development in an area of high public transport accessibility).*

*In determining whether a Transport Assessment or Statement will be needed for a proposed development local planning authorities should take into account the following considerations:*

- *the Transport Assessment and Statement policies (if any) of the Local Plan;*

- *the scale of the proposed development and its potential for additional trip generation (smaller applications with limited impacts may not need a Transport Assessment or Statement);*

- *existing intensity of transport use and the availability of public transport;*

- *proximity to nearby environmental designations or sensitive areas;*

- *impact on other priorities/strategies (such as promoting walking and cycling);*

- *the cumulative impacts of multiple developments within a particular area; and*

- *whether there are particular types of impacts around which to focus the Transport Assessment or Statement (e.g. assessing traffic generated at peak times).* (Paragraph: 004; Reference ID: 42-004-20140306 - Revision date: 06 03 2014).

## 9.3 Travel plans
The glossary to the NPPF describes a *"travel plan"* as:

*"A long-term management strategy for an organisation or site that seeks to deliver sustainable transport objectives and is regularly reviewed."*

The National Planning Practice Guidance website states:

> *Travel Plans are long-term management strategies for integrating proposals for sustainable travel into the planning process. They are based on evidence of the anticipated transport impacts of development and set measures to promote and encourage sustainable travel (such as promoting walking and cycling). They should not, however, be used as an excuse for unfairly penalising drivers and cutting provision for cars in a way that is unsustainable and could have negative impacts on the surrounding streets.* (Paragraph: 003; Reference ID: 42-003-20140306 - Revision date: 06 03 2014).

Then, under the heading *"When is a Travel Plan required?"*, the website states:

> *Paragraph 111 of the National Planning Policy Framework sets out that all developments which generate significant amounts of transport movement should be required to provide a Travel Plan.*
>
> *Local planning authorities must make a judgement as to whether a proposed development would generate significant amounts of movement on a case by case basis (ie significance may be a lower threshold where road capacity is already stretched or a higher threshold for a development which proposes no car parking in an area of high public transport accessibility).*
>
> *In determining whether a Travel Plan will be needed for a proposed development the local planning authorities should take into account the following considerations:*
>
> - *the Travel Plan policies (if any) of the Local Plan;*
>
> - *the scale of the proposed development and its potential for additional trip generation (smaller applications with limited impacts may not need a Travel Plan);*
>
> - *existing intensity of transport use and the availability of public transport;*
>
> - *proximity to nearby environmental designations or sensitive areas;*
>
> - *impact on other priorities/ strategies (such as promoting walking and cycling);*
>
> - *the cumulative impacts of multiple developments within a particular area;*
>
> - *whether there are particular types of impacts around which to focus the Travel Plan (e.g. minimising traffic generated at peak times); and*
>
> - *relevant national policies, including the decision to abolish maximum parking standards for both residential and non-residential development.* (Paragraph: 009; Reference ID: 42-009-20140306 - Revision date: 06 03 2014).

The National Planning Practice Guidance website further advises, under *"How do Travel Plans, Transport Assessments and Statements relate to each other?"*:

> *The development of Travel Plans and Transport Assessments or Transport Statements should be an iterative process as each may influence the other.*

> *The primary purpose of a Travel Plan is to identify opportunities for the effective promotion and delivery of sustainable transport initiatives eg walking, cycling, public transport and tele-commuting, in connection with both proposed and existing developments and through this to thereby reduce the demand for travel by less sustainable modes. As noted above, though, they should not be used as way of unfairly penalising drivers.*

> *Transport Assessments and Transport Statements primarily focus on evaluating the potential transport impacts of a development proposal. (They may consider those impacts net of any reductions likely to arise from the implementation of a Travel Plan, though producing a Travel Plan is not always required.) The Transport Assessment or Transport Statement may propose mitigation measures where these are necessary to avoid unacceptable or "severe" impacts. Travel Plans can play an effective role in taking forward those mitigation measures which relate to on-going occupation and operation of the development.*

> *Transport Assessments and Statements can be used to establish whether the residual transport impacts of a proposed development are likely to be "severe", which may be a reason for refusal, in accordance with the National Planning Policy Framework.* (Paragraph: 005; Reference ID: 42-005-20140306 - Revision date: 06 03 2014).

And under *"What key principles should be taken into account in preparing a Travel Plan, Transport Assessment or Statement?"*:

> *Travel Plans, Transport Assessments and Statements should be:*

> * *proportionate to the size and scope of the proposed development to which they relate and build on existing information wherever possible;*

> * *established at the earliest practicable possible stage of a development proposal;*

> * *be tailored to particular local circumstances (other locally-determined factors and information beyond those which are set out in this guidance may need to be considered in these studies provided there is robust evidence for doing so locally);*

> * *be brought forward through collaborative ongoing working between the local planning authority/transport authority, transport operators, rail network operators, Highways Agency where there may be implications for the strategic road network and other relevant bodies. Engaging communities and local businesses in Travel Plans, Transport Assessments and Statements can be beneficial in positively supporting higher levels of walking and*

*cycling (which in turn can encourage greater social inclusion, community cohesion and healthier communities).*

*In order to make these documents as useful and accessible as possible any information or assumptions should be set out in a clear and publicly accessible form:*

- *the timeframes over which they are conducted or operate should be appropriate in relation to the nature of developments to which they relate (and planned changed to transport infrastructure and management in the area);*

- *local planning authorities should advise qualifying bodies for the purposes of neighbourhood planning on whether Travel Plans, Transport Assessments and Statements should be prepared, and the benefits of doing so, as part of the duty to support.*

*Local planning authorities may wish to consult the relevant bodies on planning applications likely to affect transport infrastructure, such as rail network operators where a development is likely to impact on the operation of level crossings.* (Paragraph: 007; Reference ID: 42-007-20140306 - Revision date: 06 03 2014).

Under: *"What information should be included in Travel Plans?"*:

*Travel Plans should identify the specific required outcomes, targets and measures, and set out clear future monitoring and management arrangements all of which should be proportionate. They should also consider what additional measures may be required to offset unacceptable impacts if the targets should not be met.*

*Travel Plans should set explicit outcomes rather than just identify processes to be followed (such as encouraging active travel or supporting the use of low emission vehicles). They should address all journeys resulting from a proposed development by anyone who may need to visit or stay and they should seek to fit in with wider strategies for transport in the area.*

*They should evaluate and consider:*

- *benchmark travel data including trip generation databases;*

- *information concerning the nature of the proposed development and the forecast level of trips by all modes of transport likely to be associated with the development;*

- *relevant information about existing travel habits in the surrounding area;*

- *proposals to reduce the need for travel to and from the site via all modes of transport; and*

- *provision of improved public transport services.*

*They may also include:*

- *parking strategy options (if appropriate – and having regard to national policy on parking standards and the need to avoid unfairly penalising motorists); and*

- *proposals to enhance the use of existing, new and improved public transport services and facilities for cycling and walking both by users of the development and by the wider community (including possible financial incentives).*

*These active measures may assist in creating new capacity within the local network that can be utilised to accommodate the residual trip demand of the site(s) under consideration.*

*It is often best to retain the ability to establish certain elements of the Travel Plan or review outcomes after the development has started operating so that it can be based upon the occupational and operational characteristics of the development.*

*Any sanctions (for example financial sanctions on breaching outcomes/processes) need to be reasonable and proportionate, with careful attention paid to the viability of the development. It may often be more appropriate to use non-financial sanctions where outcomes/processes are not adhered to (such as more active or different marketing of sustainable transport modes or additional traffic management measures). Relevant implications for planning permission must be set out clearly, including (for example) whether the Travel Plan is secured by a condition or planning obligation.*

*Travel Plans can only impose such requirements where these are consistent with government policy on planning obligations.* (Paragraph: 011; Reference ID: 42-011-20140306 - Revision date: 06 03 2014).

For further information see: http://www.highwayengineer.co.uk/transport_assessment.htm.

# Chapter 10

# Road Safety Audits

## 10.1    Introduction

The subject of Road Safety Audits is important because they are often referred to in both planning documents and highways agreements.

Road Safety Audits derive from the "Design Manual for Roads and Bridges" (the "*DMRB*"), daughter document "GG 119 - Road safety audit".[56] Whilst drafted for trunk roads, the DMRB is often used to set standards for local roads and is often incorporated into the arrangements for the creation of new highways or alterations to existing highways.

## 10.2    The four stages of Road Safety Audits

There are four different stages of Road Safety Audit:

- Stage 1 Road Safety Audits are undertaken at the completion of preliminary design. The preliminary design will normally be complete before a highway agreement is executed.

- Stage 2 Road Safety Audits are undertaken at completion of the detailed design stage of the works.

- The Stage 3 Road Safety Audit should be undertaken when the highway works are substantially complete and, preferably, before the works are open to road users. The Audit Team should consider whether the design has been properly translated into the scheme as constructed and that no inherent road safety defect has been incorporated into the works. Particular attention should be paid to design changes which have occurred during construction.

- Stage 4 involves post-opening monitoring the new road during the first year following it being made open to traffic. Monitoring will include recording and assessing any personal injury collisions that might occur during that period, so that any serious problems can be identified and remedial work arranged quickly. A Stage 4 RSA report is not needed where no road traffic collisions have been recorded in the vicinity of the highway scheme over the 12 month period following opening to traffic: para 5.34 of GG 119. This is one reason why a "maintenance period" should be not less than 12 months; also, why it is important that the way is open to traffic for this 12 month period.

---

[56]    GG 119 replaced HD 19/15 in January 2019.

# Chapter 11

# Planning Conditions

## 11.1 Introduction

Local planning authorities often seek to impose controls over, or requirements in respect of, highway matters by attaching appropriate conditions to the grant of planning permissions.

The now revoked guidance in *"Planning Policy Guidance 13: Transport"* gave some examples:

> *"81. Where clearly justified and in accordance with the usual statutory and policy tests, conditions may legitimately be used to require on-site transport measures and facilities as part of development or to prohibit development on the application site until an event occurs, including:*
>
> 1. *provision of secure cycle parking and changing facilities and safe pedestrian and cycle routes*
>
> 2. *provision of facilities for public transport, such as bus stops and lay-bys*
>
> 3. *specifying the number of parking spaces, and their size, including those for disabled people*
>
> 4. *the management and use of parking spaces, so that, for example, priority is given to certain categories of people, e.g. disabled people, people with children, visitors, or cars with more than one occupant*
>
> 5. *the removal of parking spaces (other than those for disabled people) after a specified period, or when access to the site is improved by public transport, walking and cycling (such as when a bus route is introduced to the site)*
>
> 6. *the provision of information to staff and visitors about public transport, walking and cycling access to the site, including information for disabled people*
>
> 7. *arrangements for deliveries to the site and removals from the site, covering specification of types of vehicles and hours of operation, design of delivery areas and specifications for lorry parking and turning spaces*
>
> 8. *new or improved junction and road layouts*
>
> *This list is not exhaustive, and particular care is needed in the drafting of conditions relating to some of these measures to ensure they are enforceable. ... Some of these or other measures may form part of a travel plan and a condition may therefore be used to require aspects of a travel plan to be implemented."*

## 11.2    Typical uses of conditions for highways purposes

Planning conditions can be used to secure highway objectives in many ways. Some typical examples are:

- To secure on-site highway works (e.g. perhaps in connection with traffic calming).

- To impose prohibitions on the use of certain access points to the site for certain types of traffic (e.g. perhaps in connection with lorry routing).[57]

- To require that works are carried out in accordance with a "Construction Method Statement".

- Provision of footways:

  *"No development shall take place unless and until details showing the provision of a footway across the whole of the site frontage have been submitted to and approved in writing by the local planning authority. No building forming part of the development shall be occupied unless and until the footway has been completed."* [58]

- Surface water run-off:

  *"No development shall take place until details of preventing surface water run-off from hard paved areas within the site onto the highway have been approved in writing by the local planning authority. These works or facilities shall be carried out in full before any access or parking facilities are brought into use."* [59]

- Driveways:

  *"No loose material shall be used to surface on any driveway or parking area within 10 metres of the highway."*

- Traffic signage:

  1.  *The [****] road shall not be opened to public traffic until a signage scheme advising motorists of the new road and junction layouts resulting from the development has been submitted to and approved in writing by the local planning authority [in consultation with the [****] [highway authority]] and the signage in the approved scheme has been installed.*

  2.  *The signage scheme must include details of any temporary signage and that signage must be provided and maintained for the duration of the construction period and for*

---

[57]    Query whether better served by a Section 106 Agreement.
[58]    The discharge of this condition will probably turn on a highways agreement with the local highway authority.
[59]    Query whether long term maintenance should be considered.

*a minimum period of three months following the date when the [\*\*\*\*] road is first opened to public traffic.*

3. *All temporary signs, road markings and other access measures are to be removed and the highway reinstated in accordance with the scheme approved pursuant to Condition [\*\*\*\*] by not later than the expiry of the fourth month following the date when [\*\*\*\*] road is first opened to public traffic.*

- Access to local services:

  1. *The development shall not commence until -*

     (a) *a report identifying where and when the road access or egress to or from any local services may be affected by temporary changes to any road during and arising from the construction of the authorised development has been submitted to and approved in writing by the local planning authority; and*

     (b) *a scheme providing details of temporary signage and access arrangements to any local services identified in the report approved pursuant to and works of reinstatement to the highway following removal of the signage and access arrangements has been submitted to and approved in writing by the local planning authority in consultation with the [\*\*\*\*] [highway authority].*

  2. *The temporary signage and access arrangements measures mentioned in the scheme approved pursuant to Condition [\*\*\*\*] must be provided and maintained for the duration of the construction period.*

  3. *For the purposes of this condition, the phrase "local services" shall include facilities such as and including the [\*\*\*\*] garage, the [\*\*\*\*] store and the [\*\*\*\*] veterinary practice and all other similar facilities.*

- Control of deposits on highways:

  1. *The development shall not commence until details of a scheme to minimise the deposit of mud, stone, gravel or other debris or materials onto any road by any vehicles leaving the land have been submitted to and approved in writing by the local planning authority [in consultation with the [\*\*\*\*] [highway authority] and [Highways England]].*

  2. *The approved scheme must include details of the provision, locations, maintenance and use of wheel wash and vehicle body washing equipment within the site throughout the construction period.*

  3. *The measures and equipment mentioned in the scheme approved pursuant to Condition [\*\*\*\*] must be provided and maintained for the duration of the construction period.*

4. *All vehicles leaving the site shall be cleaned or otherwise treated in accordance with the approved scheme.*

- Traffic management:

    1. *A Transport Management Plan must be submitted for approval by the Council [in consultation with the [****] [highway authority]] and no part of the development may commence until such a plan covering the full construction period has been approved by the Council in writing.*

    2. *The Traffic Management Plan must include details of routing, schedules and timings of movements, details of escorts for abnormal loads and temporary directional and warning signing for the duration of the construction period.*

    3. *The measures and equipment mentioned in the Transport Management Plan approved pursuant to Condition [****] must be provided and maintained for the duration of the construction period.*

- Highway approvals and site accesses:

    1. *No part of the development is to commence until details of the proposed [****] all movements grade separated junction together with linking slip roads to access and egress the A1 trunk road referred to in [****] have been submitted in writing to and approved in writing by the local planning authority [in consultation with Highways England on behalf of the Secretary of State for Transport.]*

    2. *No part of the new road is to be opened to vehicular traffic until the highway works approved in accordance with [****] have been constructed.*

    3. *All highway and associated works must be designed and constructed in accordance with the [****] [highway authority's] standard specifications. Any temporary site accesses must be designed and constructed generally in accordance with Type [****] of the [****] [highway authority's] standard specifications.*

    4. *Turning facilities for all vehicles, including abnormal loads, must be provided within the site to enable all vehicles to enter and leave the highway in a forward gear at all times. The development must not commence (other than the construction of turning, storage and parking areas) until such provision has been made.*

• Conditions regulating the use of cranes over or near the highway:

> *No crane or other equipment shall oversail the [\*\*\*\*] road from the site[60] (whether loaded or unloaded) unless and until a licence to do so has been granted to the developer by the [\*\*\*\*] [highway authority].*

Examples of acceptable conditions for use in appropriate circumstances from Appendix A of Circular 11/95[61] include:

• Accesses:

> *14.[62]    Means of vehicular access to the permitted building shall be from ... Road only.*
>
> *15.    The building shall not be occupied until a means of vehicular access has been constructed in accordance with the approved plans.*
>
> *16.    The building shall not be occupied until a means of access for [pedestrians and/ or cyclists] has been constructed in accordance with the approved plans.*
>
> *17.    Development shall not begin until details of the junction between the proposed service road and the highway have been approved in writing by the local planning authority; and the building shall not be occupied until that junction has been constructed in accordance with the approved details.*

• Sight-lines:

> *18.    No structure or erection exceeding metres in height shall be placed to the [east] of a line from ... to ... [as shown on the plan attached hereto].*

• Service roads:

> *19.    No [dwelling] shall be occupied until that part of the service road which provides access to it has been constructed in accordance with the approved plans.*

• Parking:

> *20.    No [dwelling] shall be occupied until space has been laid out within the site [in accordance with the plan attached for [number] cars to be parked [and for the loading and unloading of [number] vehicles [and for vehicles to turn so that they may enter and leave the site in forward gear].*

---

[60]   This may be extended to any adjacent land which is to be used in connection with the project, provided that the developer has control over it.

[61]   The current NPPG refers to Appendix A of Circular 11/95 in connection with the use of model conditions: see Paragraph: 021; Reference ID: 21b-021-20180615 - Revision date: 15 06 2018.

[62]   Para number as per Circular 11/95.

*21.     No [dwelling] shall be occupied until space has been laid out within the site [in accordance with the plan attached for [number] bicycles to be parked.*

*22.     The building shall not be occupied until the area shown on the plan attached hereto has been drained and surfaced [or other steps as may be specified] [in accordance with details submitted and approved by the local planning authority], and that area shall not thereafter be used for any purpose other than the parking of vehicles.*

- Transport:

  *23.     Development shall not commence until details of the proposed [bus/railway station(s) or stop(s) have been approved in writing by the local planning authority; and the building(s) shall not be occupied until [that/those station(s) or stop(s) have been constructed in accordance with the approved plans.*

- Access for disabled people:[63]

  *37.     Before the development hereby permitted is commenced a scheme indicating the provision to be made for disabled people to gain access to [****] shall have been submitted to and approved by the local planning authority. The agreed scheme shall be implemented[64] before the development hereby permitted is brought into use.*

- Hours of use: to apply time-limits on vehicular access to a site (e.g. perhaps where HGV movements or parking at unsocial hours would cause unacceptable noise/vibration disturbance to residential properties):

  *65.     No machinery shall be operated, no process shall be carried out and no deliveries taken at or despatched from the site outside the following times [****] nor at any time on Sundays, Bank or Public Holidays.*

  *66.     The use hereby permitted shall not be open to customers outside the following times [****].*

- Hours of deliveries:

  *68.     No deliveries shall be taken at or despatched from the site outside the hours of [****] nor at any time on Sundays, Bank or Public Holidays."*

---

[63]   Note the need to take section 149 of the Equality Act 2010 into account and also see para. 110(b) of the NPPF (2019).

[64]   The word "*implemented*" is unclear as to whether it relates to making a start or completing an action. Better phrases might be "*carried out*" or "*completed*".

## 11.3   Legal limits on conditions

Section 70(1) of the Town and Country Planning Act 1990 provides that a local planning authority may grant a planning permission unconditionally or *"subject to such conditions as they think fit"*.

The power to impose conditions is not as wide as the literal words of section 70(1) might appear to suggest. The courts have, on numerous occasions, held that local planning authorities must observe certain legal principles in imposing conditions.

In *Newbury DC v Secretary of State for the Environment* [1981] A.C. 578 the House of Lords identified these principles as follows:

- a condition must be imposed for a planning purpose only and not for any ulterior motive;

- the condition must fairly and reasonably relate to the development permitted by the planning permission; and

- the condition shall not be so unreasonable that no reasonable planning authority could have imposed it.

In the *Newbury* case, a condition of a temporary permission required the removal of two pre-existing aircraft hangers upon expiry of the permission. The condition was invalid because it did not address anything arising from the change of use.

These principles have been developed by the courts in a number of later cases.

## 11.4   The need for precision

Conditions which relate to highway matters are often burdened with the task of conveying technical requirements in a few words. This is not an easy task. The courts have held that a condition may be invalid if it fails to convey its message in terms which should be understood by the reader or fails to provide a formula that can be applied with accuracy in practice; however, the defects must be extreme.[65]

Whilst not a planning case, *R v Secretary of State for the Environment, ex. p. Watney Mann (Midlands) Ltd* (1976) J.P.L. 368 exemplifies the point. There a magistrates' court had made an order, under the Public Health Act 1936, requiring the abatement of nuisance caused by music played in a public house. The order required that the level of noise in the premises should not exceed 70 decibels. The Divisional Court held that the order was void for uncertainty because it did not specify the position where the noise reading was to be taken. The local authority had made the mistake of setting a testable standard in

---

[65]   See *Fawcett Properties Ltd v Buckinghamshire CC* [1961] A.C. 636; *Alderson v Secretary of State for the Environment* [1984] J.P.L. 429; Sullivan J in *Carter Commercial Developments Ltd v Secretary of State* [2002] EWHC 1200 (Admin) (affirmed @ [2002] EWCA Civ 1994); and *Green v Secretary of State for Communities and Local Government* [2009] EWHC 754 (Admin).

the order but failing to set out the parameters which were essential to the carrying out of the test. One can easily see why this case is important in the context of noise conditions relating to highway matters.

The position is not made better by the use of subjective language instead. A classic example comes from the world of planning enforcement.

In *Metallic Protectives Limited v Secretary of State for the Environment* [1976] J.P.L. 166, an enforcement notice required the occupier of premises to install *"satisfactory soundproofing"* of a compressor and to take all possible action to minimise the effects created by the use of acrylic paint. The Divisional Court held that the notice was a nullity. The mistake was, of course, that the recipient of the notice was not supplied with clear instructions about the nature of the soundproofing. What might or might not be *"satisfactory"* will vary according to the subjective opinions of those one may consult.

Circular 11/95 called such conditions *"discretionary or vetting"* conditions:

> *32 ... Conditions requiring that tidiness, for example, shall be "to the satisfaction of the local planning authority" make the applicant no more certain of just what is required ... .*

However, the same paragraph continued:

> *" ... Conditions which raise these difficulties, however, are not to be confused with conditions which require the submission of a scheme or details for approval which will, when granted, provide the precise guidelines to be followed by the developer ...".*

Thus, a condition requiring a *"satisfactory means of access"* would be defective for lack of precision; likewise, a condition requiring a road of *"proper"* width. A condition which is defective in this way cannot be rescued by the addition of *"tail-piece"* words such as *"unless otherwise agreed with the local planning authority"* for two reasons; first, because the defect goes to the heart of the condition - it is a fundamental misdirection and so, at law, there is nothing to thus *"vary"*; secondly, because the *"tail-piece"* might be defective itself: see para. 11.18 below.

If the case is marginal, then the courts might tip the balance in favour of the local planning authority: see *Crisp from the Fens Ltd v Rutland County Council* (1950) 48 L.G.R. 210.

## 11.5     Policy constraints on conditions

The National Planning Policy Framework (2019) advises:

> *55. Planning conditions should be kept to a minimum and only imposed where they are necessary, relevant to planning and to the development to be permitted, enforceable, precise and reasonable in all other respects. Agreeing conditions early is beneficial to all parties involved in the process and can speed up decision making. <u>Conditions that are required to be discharged before development commences should be avoided, unless there is a clear justification</u>[23].* (Emphasis added).

The underlined words allude to "*Grampian type*" conditions, also known as "*pre-commencement conditions*" or "*conditions precedent*": see para. 11.10 below. They indicate the Secretary of State's concerns that such indiscriminate use of such conditions may slow down the planning process. The footnote refers to sections 100ZA(4-6) of the Town and Country Planning Act 1990 which require the applicant's written agreement to the terms of a pre-commencement condition, unless prescribed circumstances apply.

The former version[66] referred to the so called "*six tests*"; namely, that planning conditions should only be imposed where they are:

- necessary;

- relevant to planning and;

- to the development to be permitted;

- enforceable;

- precise and;

- reasonable in all other respects.

The National Planning Practice Guidance states that any proposed condition that fails to meet any of the six tests should not be used. This applies even if the applicant suggests it or agrees on its terms or it is suggested by the members of a planning committee or a third party. Every condition must always be justified by the local planning authority on its own planning merits on a case by case basis. Also, conditions which place unjustifiable and disproportionate financial burdens on an applicant will fail the test of reasonableness.[67]

The Guidance states that planning permission should not be granted subject to a positively worded condition that requires the applicant to enter into a Section 106 Agreement, or an agreement under other powers, because such a condition is unlikely to pass the test of enforceability. It adds that a negatively worded condition limiting the development that can take place until a planning obligation or other agreement has been entered into is unlikely to be appropriate in the majority of cases.[68]

The Guidance includes the time honoured preference for the use of conditions over planning obligations; namely, that it may be possible to overcome a planning objection to a development proposal equally well by imposing a condition on the planning permission or by entering into a planning obligation. In such cases the local planning authority should use

---

[66]  At the time of writing, the NPPG has not caught up with the 2019 version of the NPPF and still refers to the 2012 version: see Paragraph: 003 Reference ID: 21a-003-20140306 - Revision date: 06 03 2014.

[67]  Paragraph: 005 Reference ID: 21a-005-20140306 - Revision date: 06 03 2014.

[68]  Paragraph: 010 Reference ID: 21a-010-20140306 - Revision date: 06 03 2014.

a condition rather than seeking to deal with the matter by means of a planning obligation.[69] The unstated rationale is that a developer has rights of appeal against any condition which he disputes. Whether this holds good in the 21st Century is debateable. Despite this policy statement, it is not unlawful to have a planning obligation which secures matters which could have been secured by planning conditions: *Good v Epping Forest DC* [1994] 1 W.L.R. 376.

## 11.6    Conditions referring to land controlled by the applicant

A condition may impose obligations in respect of any land within the application site, whether that land is owned or controlled by the applicant or not: see *Atkinson v Secretary of State for the Environment* [1983] J.P.L. 599. If a condition refers to land outside the application site, then this must be land which is within the control of the applicant: see *Peak Park Joint Planning Board v Secretary of State* [1980] J.P.L. 114.

Section 72(1)(a) of the 1990 Act provides that a condition may regulate the development or use of any land under the control of the applicant (whether or not it is land within the application site) or require the carrying out of works on any such land so far as it appears to the local planning authority to be expedient for the purposes of, or in connection with, the permitted development.

In practice, most local planning authorities invite the applicant to show the application site edged in red on the location plan which accompanies the planning application and to show land which is outside the application site but controlled by the applicant edged in blue. This gives the authority the ability to see whether it may impose conditions which include this "*blue land*"; for example, in connection with the provision of visibility splays. Otherwise, the inclusion of land outside the application site might have to be by way of a planning obligation with the relevant landowner.

In *R v Derbyshire County Council ex. p. North East Derbyshire DC* [1980] J.P.L. 398, it was held that such a condition can have the effect of granting planning permission for the use specified in the condition. Given that the condition in question related to aftercare on a mining site, it is highly questionable whether the principle would extend to off-site works (for example, the construction of visibility splays). Furthermore, one wonders whether this principle still holds good in the very different legal and administrative climate of the 21st Century. For example, it would, clearly, be wrongly applied where additional works require an environmental impact assessment.[70]

## 11.7    Conditions seeking financial contributions

It might seem to be that a local authority which seeks a financial contribution by way of a condition is acting laudably if that money is going to be used to benefit the public. However, executive bodies (which include local planning authorities) cannot obtain money from the public unless authorised to do so by Parliament. No pecuniary burden can be imposed upon the public, except under clear and distinct legal authority.

---

[69]    Paragraph: 011 Reference ID: 21a-011-20140306 - Revision date: 06 03 2014.
[70]    See also *R v Surrey County Council ex. p. Monk* (1987) 53 P. & C.R. 410.

In *R v Bowman* [1898] 1 Q.B. 663 it was held that justices who were charged with issuing liquor licences were acting unlawfully in requiring applicants to make payments for public purposes; namely, that the applicant should pay £1,000 in reduction of the rates.

These principles were affirmed by the House of Lords in *Total Network SL v Commissioners of Customs and Excise* [2008] UKHL 19.

If a local planning authority is seeking a financial contribution from a developer, then the best course is to consider whether the use of an agreement under section 106 of the Town and Country Planning Act 1990 might be possible: see Chapter 12 below.

## 11.8     Conditions interfering with land ownership
The courts have tended to lean against conditions which interfere with rights of land ownership, particularly when a condition has the effect of expropriating land without the compensation which would otherwise be payable.

In *Hall & Co Ltd v Shoreham by Sea Urban District Council* [1964] 1 W.L.R. 240, the plaintiffs obtained planning permission to develop land for industrial purposes. The main road was overloaded with traffic and, in the interests of highway safety, the local planning authority granted permission, subject to conditions, that provided, among other things, that the plaintiffs "*shall construct an ancillary road over the entire frontage of the site at their own expense and as and when required by the local planning authority, and shall give right of passage over it to and from such ancillary roads as may be constructed on adjoining land*" and that "*the new access shall be temporary for a period of five years initially but the local planning authority will not enforce its closure until the ancillary roads ... have been constructed and alternative access to the main road is available*". The conditions were struck down by the Court of Appeal.

In *Westminster Renslade Ltd v Secretary of State for the Environment and Another* (1984) 48 P. & C.R. 255, the High Court quashed a planning inspector's refusal of planning permission where he held, among other things, that the developer should have made a contribution to off-site public car parking.

These principles were confirmed in *Bradford City Council v Secretary of State for the Environment and McLean Homes Northern Ltd* [1986] 1 E.G.L.R. 199.

If a local planning authority is seeking this type of arrangement from a developer, then, again, the best course is to consider whether the use of an agreement under section 106 of the Town and Country Planning Act 1990 might be possible: see Chapter 12 below.

## 11.9     Positive conditions and actions outside the developer's control
A local planning authority is not entitled to impose a condition which the developer plainly will not be able to discharge. It can only relate to matters over which the developer has control.

A positive condition which requires the developer to carry out works on land outside his control is invalid because he does not have the immediate ability to comply with the condition. Thus a condition requiring the developer to carry out works on the highway outside his site is invalid, viz:

> *"The off-site highway works shown on drawing X shall be constructed within one year following the commencement of the development".*

In *Birnie v Banff CC* [1954] S.L.T. (Sh. Ct.) 90 planning permission had been granted for the erection of a house, subject to a condition requiring the construction of an access over land not belonging to the applicant. The access was not constructed and the local planning authority took enforcement action. It was held that the authority had no power to impose a condition requiring the carrying out of works on land other than land under an applicant's control and the enforcement notice was quashed.[71]

In *British Airports Authority v Secretary of State for Scotland* [1980] J.P.L. 260, a condition was imposed concerning the flight paths of aircraft taking off and landing at Aberdeen airport. The condition was void because it related to matters over which the applicants had no control. Only the Civil Aviation Authority could control the directions of aircraft.

In *Mouchell Superannuation Trust Fund Trustees v Oxfordshire CC* [1992] 1 W.L.U.K. 212, it was held that a condition requiring that *"Vehicles shall travel to and from the site via the A57 and the M1 only"* was invalid because it was unenforceable. Obviously, the landowner would have no control over the movements of vehicles owned or operated by others on the A57 or M1 and could not comply with the condition.

These cases should be contrasted with *Davenport v Hammersmith & Fulham LBC* [1999] J.P.L. 1122. There, planning permission had been granted for the use of land for motor vehicle repairs. A condition prohibited vehicles which had been left with, or in the control of, the applicant being parked on the highway adjacent to the premises; namely, *"no vehicles which have been left with or are in the control of the applicant shall be stored or parked in Tasso Road"*. Following non-compliance with the condition, the Council served a breach of condition notice and then prosecuted the owners for non-compliance with the notice. The owners challenged the validity of the condition; however, the Divisional Court upheld the condition. Whilst the highway was outside the control of the owners, the condition did not require them to have control of the land in question. They were able to comply with it because the vehicles were left with them and were within their control. That is to say, the vehicle owners handed in their car keys when leaving their cars at the garage.

In *Andrews and Andrews v Secretary of State for the Environment, Transport and the Regions and North Norfolk District Council* [2000] P.L.C.R. 366 a condition imposed by a planning inspector in respect of a taxi office was struck down by the High Court. The condition provided:

---

[71] Cited by Sullivan J in *R v Rochdale MBC ex. p. Tew* [2000] J.P.L 54 @ p.36.

> *"No taxis or mini-cabs belonging to the applicant, nor those belonging to freelance drivers operating through the radio control at the premises, shall call at the office hereby permitted for the purposes of waiting, taking orders and instructions, collecting clients or for taking refreshment."*

The court held that it was not convinced that the Inspector had properly considered whether such a condition would solve the planning objections about on-street parking. However, it is arguable that the condition was flawed by the fact that it sought to make the operator responsible for the actions of freelance drivers.

In *R v Rochdale MBC ex. p. Tew* [2000] J.P.L 54 Sullivan J held (@ p.38) that even if a condition was theoretically enforceable it would be invalid if it was not reasonably enforceable. The enforceability of any planning condition had to be considered in the light of the particular facts. A condition which is not reasonably enforceable is not a reasonable condition for the purpose of the *Newbury* tests. Enforceability should be considered in a pragmatic and not in a theoretical manner, and should be considered by reference to the terms of the particular conditions, the specific development and the particular site in question.

## 11.10    "Pre-commencement" conditions

Given that it is often important to secure the carrying out of off-site highway works to allow a development to go ahead, these limitations on the use of positive conditions are not helpful. However, it is possible to circumvent the problem by way of a negative *"Grampian"* condition.

A negative condition may provide that the permitted development shall not commence unless and until a particular event has occurred. Such conditions are named after *Grampian Regional Council v City of Aberdeen* [1984] J.P.L. 590, where the particular event in question was the closure of an off-site highway.

So called *"Grampian Conditions"* are now commonly called *"pre-commencement conditions"* or *"conditions precedent"*. Such a condition is said to be *"negative"* in the sense that it prohibits the carrying out of some action on the development site unless and until something else happens (usually off-site). For example:

> *"No part of the development shall be begun unless and until the highway works shown in drawing X have been constructed".*

The *Grampian Regional Council* case is important in the highway context and so it is appropriate to consider it at some length.

The Regional Council applied to two local planning authorities for planning permission for the change of use of land lying across the local planning authorities' boundaries. The local planning authorities failed to determine the application within the statutory time-limit and the Regional Council appealed to the Secretary of State for Scotland. The Minister's Reporter, after a public local inquiry, considered that traffic to and from the site would constitute such a hazard as to justify the refusal of planning permission. He felt that the hazard would be removed if an existing road could be closed, but concluded that it would not be competent to grant planning permission subject to a condition requiring the closure of the road, his reason being that it did not lie wholly within the power of the Regional Council to secure the closure; that is, any closure order that they might make required confirmation by the Secretary of State, which would not necessarily be granted. He accordingly dismissed the appeals.

The First Division of the Inner House of the Court of Session allowed an appeal by the Regional Council, holding that, while a condition requiring something to be done that was not within the control of the first respondents would be incompetent, a pre-commencement condition requiring that no development be commenced until the road had been closed would be competent. The House of Lords agreed and held that there was a crucial difference between a positive condition and a negative type of condition in that the latter was enforceable while the former was not; that the reasonableness of any condition had to be considered in the light of the circumstances of the case and that in the present case, where the proposals for development had been found by the Reporter to be generally desirable in the public interest, it would have been not only reasonable but highly appropriate to grant planning permission subject to the condition in question.

The distinction between positive and negative conditions may seem a narrow one; however, it is based on sound legal reasoning. As a matter of law, section 72(1)(a) of the 1990 Act confines the power to impose conditions in respect of land in the control of the developer only. The crucial characteristic of a pre-commencement condition is that it does, indeed, apply to land within the control of the developer; namely, the development site itself. A pre-commencement condition places an embargo on the carrying out of the development, or a specified part of the development, unless a defined event has occurred.

The use of pre-commencement conditions to secure off-site highway works now forms an important linkage to highway agreements (whether under section 278 of the Highways Act 1980 or otherwise) and should be used to provide such a linkage. If a condition requires that certain off-site highway works be completed before the development goes ahead, then the developer is placed in the position of having to enter into a highway agreement with the highway authority in order to carry out the works and then, in turn, to start his development.

### 11.11    Failure to discharge a pre-commencement condition

If the developer fails to discharge a pre-commencement condition and goes ahead with the development, then the breach of planning control can go beyond a mere breach of condition. The development itself may be unauthorised and is then deemed to be without the benefit of planning permission. Thus the failure to comply with such a condition can be fatal. This is because all planning permissions are granted on the basis that each permitted development must be begun within a period stipulated in the conditions to the permission – if the development is not started lawfully within the time-limit, then the permission will lapse. That is, an unlawful act of purported commencement will not count. In the case of operational development, a lawful act of commencement will be by carrying out a *"material operation"* within the meaning of section 56 of the 1990 Act and, in the case of material change of use, this will be the initiation of the permitted use. It is now trite law that such acts of commencement count to crystallise a permission if they are lawful and that the carrying out of such an act in breach of a pre-commencement condition will not normally be lawful for these purposes.

This is sometimes called the "*Whitley principle*" after the leading case on the point.

In *F. G. Whitley & Sons Co Ltd v Secretary of State for Wales* [1990] J.P.L. 678, planning permission had been granted for mineral extraction, subject to a condition which provided that no working should take place except in accordance with a scheme to be agreed with the local planning authority (or, in the absence of agreement, by the Secretary of State). The developers were unable to reach agreement with the authority and carried out work on the site. An enforcement notice was served in relation to the works and the question for the court was whether those works were lawful and, therefore, prevented the permission from expiring.

In the Court of Appeal, Woolf LJ stated:

> "*As I understand the effect of the authorities to which I am about to refer, it is only necessary to ask the single question; are the operations (in other situations the question would refer to the development) permitted by the planning permission read together with its conditions? The permission is controlled by and subject to the conditions. If the operations contravene the conditions they cannot be properly described as commencing the development authorised by the permission. If they do not comply with the permission they constitute a breach of planning control and for planning purposes will be unauthorised and thus unlawful. This is the principle which has now been clearly established by the authorities.*"

The courts have, however, recognised limited exceptions to this general principle. In *Agecrest Ltd v Gwynedd CC* (1998) J.P.L. 325 conditions of a planning permission required a number of infrastructure schemes to be submitted to and approved by the local planning authority before development could commence. Subsequently, however, the local planning authority agreed that the development could commence without full compliance with those conditions. The High Court held that the authority had a discretion in the way in which it dealt with such conditions and that the work did amount to a start of the development.

In *R v Flintshire County Council and Another Ex Parte Somerfield Stores Limited* [1998] P.L.C.R. 336 a permission had been granted for a retail development. A pre-commencement condition in the permission required a study to be made and approved by the Council of projected traffic generation and highway effects of the scheme before the development commenced. The study had been carried out with the full knowledge and co-operation of the Council and the highway authority. However, the developers had made no actual application to the Council for approval of the study, nor was there a record of the Council communicating approval to the developer. A rival retail operator tried to persuade the authority to take enforcement action when the development started and then applied to the High Court to force the issue. Carnwath J refused an application for judicial review to quash the Council's decision not to consider taking enforcement action against the development, holding that the general "*Whitley principle*" had to be applied with common sense and with regard to the facts of the particular case. In the instant case it would have been unreasonable for the Council to have decided that the planning permission had not been implemented.

It is important to place the *Flintshire* case in its proper jurisprudential setting. A local planning authority cannot vary a condition unless it does so in accordance with statute[72] nor can it waive compliance with a condition or vary it. However, it has a discretion as to whether it takes enforcement action in respect of the breach of a condition. Notwithstanding that the statutory mechanism for the issue of a "*breach of condition notice*"[73] does not require that the authority satisfy itself that such enforcement action is "*expedient*", the authority is entitled to ask itself this question and, indeed, is required to do so by legislation and treaty obligations outside the 1990 Act.[74] There will be cases where, on any objective assessment, it would be wrong to take enforcement action. Clearly, it would then be irrational if the disputed development is, nonetheless, declared to be of no worth in law. This has been described as the "*irrationality principle*".

In *Leisure Great Britain plc v Isle of Wight CC* [2000] P.L.C.R. 88 the court considered that any exception to the general *Whitley* principle should be on a clearly identifiable basis and not simply because the court considered it unfair on the merits to apply the general principle.

In *R (on the application of Hart Aggregates Ltd) v Hartlepool BC* [2005] EWHC 840 (Admin) a permission for mineral extraction was granted subject to a condition ("*Condition 10*") which provided that: "*The worked out areas shall be progressively back-filled and the areas restored to levels shown on the submitted plan or to a level to be agreed by the Local Planning Authority in accordance with a restoration scheme to be agreed by the Local Planning Authority before extraction is commenced*".

The issue was whether the 1971 permission had lapsed because Condition 10 had not been complied with, in that a restoration scheme had not been agreed by the local planning authority before extraction commenced. This turned on whether the condition was a "*condition precedent*" and, if so, whether the breach of it meant that the quarrying which purported to rely on the 1971 permission was, in fact, unauthorised.

Sullivan J held that Condition 10 was not a condition precedent. He referred to the "*Whitley principle*" and said:

> [55] *The 1990 Act draws a clear distinction between development without planning permission and development in breach of condition; see s.171(A)(1)(a) and (b). It is important that that distinction is not blurred by an indiscriminate use of the judge-made term "condition precedent".*

---

[72] Normally, following an application under section 96A or 73 of the 1990 Act.
[73] i.e. section 187A of the 1990 Act.
[74] For example, the Human Rights Act 1998.

He concluded:

> *[59] Condition 10 is a "condition precedent" in the sense that it requires something to be done before extraction is commenced, but it is not a "condition precedent" in the sense that it goes to the heart of the planning permission, so that failure to comply with it will mean that the entire development, even if completed and in existence for many years, or in the case of a minerals extraction having continued for 30 years, must be regarded as unlawful.*

> *[60] In my judgment, the principle argued for by the defendant applies only where a condition expressly prohibits any development before a particular requirement, such as the approval of plans, has been met. Condition 10 is not such a condition.*

He added that, even if Condition 10 were a condition precedent, he would have concluded that enforcement action was precluded on the *"irrationality"* principle.

This judgment makes sense to the practitioner; however, a later decision of the Court of Appeal has not assisted in the day to day application of this increasingly complex doctrine.

In *Greyfort Properties Ltd v Secretary of State for Communities and Local Government and Torbay Council* [2011] EWCA Civ 908, the disputed condition (*"Condition 4"*) stated:

> *"Before any work is commenced on the site the ground floor levels of the building hereby permitted shall be agreed with the Local Planning Authority in writing".*

There, a planning inspector had concluded that the condition was a condition precedent and that the failure to settle floor levels was fatal to the validity of access works which had been carried out pursuant to the permission. One could be forgiven for believing that this condition was on all fours with Condition 10 in the *Hart Aggregates* case; however, the Court of Appeal concluded that it was, instead, a condition precedent. The Inspector was entitled to find that those ground floor levels were fundamental to the development permitted and that the condition went to the heart of the permission.

As the then case editor for the J.P.L. (Martin Edwards) commented, this is a *"vexed issue"* which *"simply refuses to go away"*: J.P.L. 2012, 1, 39-51.

The current approach is to deduce the effect of a failure to discharge a pre-commencement condition by asking whether it *"goes to the heart of"* the planning permission. Many such conditions govern merely ancillary matters and would not do so. As is so often the situation with town and country planning, this is a matter of judgement in each case. The lesson which can, however, be derived from this jurisprudence is that, if a local planning authority wishes to put the matter beyond doubt, then it should draft clear and unambiguous conditions.

## 11.12    Scheme conditions

The local planning authority is entitled to impose conditions which provide that the detail of matters not particularised in the application may be settled after the planning permission is determined. For example:

> *"No part of the development shall be begun unless and until a scheme for the provision of the [\*\*\*\*] junction arrangements has been submitted to and approved by the local planning authority. No dwelling forming part of the scheme shall be occupied unless and until the approved junction arrangements have been completed."*

The above example means that the details mentioned in the condition (i.e. the eponymous "*scheme*") must be submitted and approved before any works are commenced pursuant to the planning permission. It will be seen that the condition in this example not only provides for the approval of details but also stipulates when the works have to be completed. However, the condition puts a hold on the actual carrying out of the scheme until a later date – in this case until first residential occupation.

## 11.13    Policy limits on "pre-commencement" conditions

The utility of pre-commencement conditions was restricted by the advice contained in Appendix A to PPG 13: "*Highways Considerations in Development Control*" and paragraph 40 of the Annex to Circular 11/95 that there must be "*at least reasonable prospects of the action in question [i.e. those stipulated in the condition] being performed within the time-limit imposed by the condition*" i.e. within the period allowed for commencement of the development.

Whilst the Circular has been withdrawn, this "*reasonable prospects*" test still appears in the decision letters of some planning inspectors.

This policy advice was not an expression of the law. A local planning authority is entitled, as a matter of law, to grant planning permission notwithstanding that the developer, on the face of it, appears to have insuperable site-assembly problems.

In *British Railways Board v Secretary of State for the Environment* [1994] J.P.L. 32, the British Railways Board applied for outline planning permission to develop land for housing. On appeal, the Inspector recommended approval subject to the condition that:

> *13. The works to provide the main access road shall be completed to base course level prior to the commencement of the construction of the residential development hereby approved, and shall be fully completed prior to the occupation of buildings.*

The site was subject to certain land-assembly problems; the Secretary of State therefore refused planning permission on the basis that he was precluded in law from granting the permission subject to conditions which appeared to have no reasonable prospect of fulfilment within the five year life of the permission. The House of Lords held that he had misdirected himself in law in considering that the proposed condition regarding the access road would be invalid.

The Secretary of State responded by saying that the judgment leaves open the possibility for the Secretary of State to maintain, as a matter of policy, that there should be at least reasonable prospects of the action in question being performed within the time-limit imposed by the permission: see Endnote 3 to Circular 11/95.

The issue was raised again in *Merritt v Secretary of State for the Environment, Transport and the Regions* [2000] J.P.L. 371 where Robin Purchas QC (sitting as a Deputy Judge) quashed the decision of an inspector to dismiss an appeal on the ground that the Inspector had erred in law in rejecting a *Grampian* condition relating to the provision of access to the site because, applying Circular 11/95, the Inspector had not been convinced that there was a reasonable prospect that the condition would be fulfilled within the time-limit imposed on any permission. The Deputy Judge pointed to the danger in promulgating a policy in an absolute form and that a decision-maker may (wrongly) regard himself as bound to follow that policy. The Inspector had simply applied the policy as a mandatory requirement, without considering whether there was scope for the exercise of discretion.

The Office of the Deputy Prime Minister then sent a letter dated 25 November 2002 to all Chief Planning Officers in England[75] which stated:

> As a result of the Judgement in Merritt, paragraph 40 should be amended to read, *"It is the policy of the Secretary of State that such a condition may be imposed on a planning permission. However, <u>when there are no prospects at all</u> of the action in question being performed within the time-limit imposed by the permission, negative conditions should not be imposed. In other words, when the interested third party has said that they have no intention of carrying out the action or allowing it to be carried out, conditions prohibiting development until this specified action has been taken by the third party should not be imposed."*
>
> *The foot note [sic] at the bottom of page 16 should be replaced with: "A policy of refusing permission where there was no reasonable prospect of planning conditions being met could be lawful, but sound planning reasons for the refusal should be given and it should be made clear that this was only a starting point for consideration of cases."*
> (Emphasis as per original).

This appears the final word – at least for now!

### 11.14    Legal limits on "pre-commencement" conditions

Section 14 of the Neighbourhood Planning Act 2017 created a very important limitation on the unfettered use of pre-commencement conditions. From 1 October 2018, a local planning authority must obtain the written agreement of the applicant before imposing such conditions on a planning permission.

---

[75]    Headed *"Circular 11/95: Use of negative conditions"*.

The 2017 Act inserted new section 100ZA into the Town and Country Planning Act 1990. This provides that an <u>outline</u> planning permission for the development of land may not be granted subject to a *"pre-commencement condition"* without the written agreement of the applicant to the terms of the condition: section 100ZA(5). Section 100ZA(6) then adds that the requirement under subsection (5) for the applicant to agree to the terms of a pre-commencement condition does not apply in such circumstances as may be prescribed. The detailed provisions are now set out in the Town and Country Planning (Pre-commencement Conditions) Regulations 2018 (S.I. 2018, No. 566).

A *"pre-commencement condition"* is defined in section 100ZA(8) as a condition imposed on a grant of planning permission (other than a grant of outline planning permission within the meaning of section 92 of the 1990 Act) which must be complied with:

- before any building or operation comprised in the development is begun; or

- where the development consists of a material change of use of any buildings or other land, before the change of use is begun.

References to a condition include a limitation: section 100ZA(13).

The formula in section 100ZA(8)(a) above is odd because, of course, a *Grampian* condition is not a condition "... *which must be complied with ... before any building or operation comprised in the development is begun...*". It is a condition which prohibits that commencement unless and until certain specified events have taken place. The draftsman seems to have fallen into the trap identified by Martin Goodall. See Martin Goodall's Planning Law Blog for 24 June 2011 at http://planninglawblog.blogspot.com/2011/06/pre-commencement-conditions.html. Also, please note the interesting correspondence in the blog.

To take an example:

> *"The [****] scheme shall be agreed prior to the start of the development ...".*

Whilst this can be read as a pre-commencement condition, its more natural meaning is that it is a condition which goes to the matter of timing. If, for example, this formula were used in a contract, then it would be a requirement as to the date of delivery and not some form of embargo on the start of the development. Furthermore, unlike a contractual obligation, this condition cannot bite until the development has commenced; that is to say, after the stipulated date for delivery. Accordingly, the better course is to avoid these contortions and, if a pre-commencement condition is intended, then it should be expressed in clear terms e.g.

> *"No part of the development shall be commenced unless and until the [****] scheme has been submitted to and approved by the local planning authority".*

Goodall has noted that some conditions in this form are, in practice, unenforceable. He gives this example:

> *"A scheme shall be submitted to and approved by the Local Planning Authority before any site clearance or development works commence on site to ensure the retention and protection of all existing trees on the site and to ensure that such trees are not damaged in the course of the development. All works subsequently carried out shall be in strict accordance with the approved scheme."*

He points out that the conditions attached to a planning permission only take effect when the permission is implemented by starting a *"material operation"* under section 56 of the 1990 Act. If the development is not started, then the conditions do not bite. The problem is that the removal of trees or other vegetation is not an activity which falls within the definition of a *"material operation"* because it does not normally amount to *"development"* within the definition in section 55 of the 1990 Act. Thus this clearance work does not implement the planning permission and would not amount to starting the development. So at that point in time, the conditions in the planning permission will not have come into effect and they cannot be enforced.

Be that as it may, rather than trying to distinguish which conditions fall within section 100ZA(8) and which do not, the better course is for the local planning authority to provide the full suite of proposed conditions to the applicant. Indeed, this is good practice in any event, not least because it might save practical difficulties at a later date and, perhaps, appeals which could have been avoided.

Sections 100ZA(5) and 100ZA(8) apply to permissions which arise from relevant grants of planning permission. References to a *"relevant grant of planning permission"* are to any grant of permission to develop land which is granted on an application made under Part III of the 1990 Act and include the modification of any such grant: section 100ZA(13).

Article 2(1) of the 2018 Regulations provides (in effect) that the agreement of the applicant under section 100ZA(5) of the 1990 Act is not needed, in relation to a relevant grant of planning permission where:

(a)    the local planning authority or, as the case may be, the Secretary of State gives notice in writing to the applicant that, if planning permission is granted, the authority or the Secretary of State intends to grant that permission subject to the pre-commencement condition specified in the notice; and

(b)    the applicant does not provide a substantive response to the notice no later than the last day of the period of 10 working days[76] beginning with the day after the date on which the notice is given.

---

[76]    The phrase *"working day"* is defined as meaning *"a day which is not a Saturday, Sunday or public holiday (where "public holiday" means Christmas Day, Good Friday or a day which is a bank holiday in England under the Banking and Financial Dealings Act 1971)"*.

Where notice has been given under paragraph (1)(a), the application for planning permission must not be determined until the period given in the notice for a substantive response to be received has expired unless, before that expiry, the local planning authority or, as the case may be, the Secretary of State receives a substantive response, or written agreement to the terms of the proposed pre-commencement condition: paragraphs 2(2) and 2(3).

## 11.15    *"Wheatcroft"* conditions

A planning condition may modify the development proposed by the application.

In *Kent CC v Secretary of State for the Environment* (1977) 33 P. & C.R. 70 Sir Douglas Frank, QC (sitting as a Deputy Judge in the Queen's Bench Division) upheld a condition which had the effect of removing a proposed access road from a scheme for an oil refinery. The substance of the permission was the construction of the refinery, to which all else was ancillary. The operator's acceptance of the condition imposed was evidence that it was not such as to make the refinery unworkable; and that, accordingly, the condition was not invalid.

Such conditions are often called *"Wheatcroft"* conditions after *Bernard Wheatcroft Ltd v Secretary of State for the Environment* (1982) 43 P. & C.R. 233 where proposals for a housing development were reduced in size by condition, the test for the validity of such a condition being whether or not the proposed modification is so fundamental that to apply it by condition would frustrate the normal public participation processes. Forbes J stated:

> *"I should add a rider. The true test is, I feel sure, that accepted by both counsel: is the effect of the conditional planning permission to allow development that is in substance not that which was applied for? Of course, in deciding whether or not there is a substantial difference the local planning authority or the Secretary of State will be exercising a judgment, and a judgment with which the courts will not ordinarily interfere unless it is manifestly unreasonably exercised. The main, but not the only, criterion on which that judgment should be exercised is whether the development is so changed that to grant it would be to deprive those who should have been consulted on the changed development of the opportunity of such consultation, and I use these words to cover all the matters of this kind with which Part III of the Act of 1971 deals.*
>
> *There may, of course, be, in addition, purely planning reasons for concluding that a change makes a substantial difference."*

In *Breckland District Council v Secretary of State for the Environment and Hill* (1993) 65 P. & C.R. 34 an application for a 16 pitch gipsy caravan site was accompanied by a plan which identified the site as being 0.47 ha. The application was refused by the Council. On appeal, the Inspector accepted an amended plan increasing the site to 0.6 ha. and so bringing it nearer to three dwellings in the vicinity. Mr David Widdicombe, QC (sitting as a Deputy High Court Judge in the Queen's Bench Division) quashed the Inspector's decision on the basis that the result must not be substantially different from the development applied for, the amendment to the plan was substantial and the decision that it was not substantial was perverse. Also, by expressly providing for third parties to be heard on an appeal by written representations, the relevant regulations, by necessary implication, gave them the right to be informed of any amendment to the application which materially affected them.

The approach of Forbes J in *Wheatcroft* was heavily criticised by John Howell QC (sitting as a Deputy High Court Judge in the Queen's Bench Division) in *R (Holborn Studios Limited v The Council of the London Borough of Hackney and GHL (Eagle Wharf Road) Limited* [2017] EWHC 2823 (Admin):

> *[73] In my judgment this conflation of the substantive and procedural constraints on the powers of the local planning authority is flawed. It is quite possible for a person to be deprived of an opportunity of consultation on a change which would not result in a permission for a development that is in substance not that which was applied for. Thus, for example, a proposed change to the external appearance of a new building or to the proposed access to it might be said not to result in a development that is in substance different from that applied for, or not to involve a "substantial difference" or a "fundamental change" to the application, but it may still be a change about which persons other than the applicant may want to make representations and would be deprived of the opportunity to do so if not consulted about it. On the other hand to say that any change about which others may want to make representations is to be classified as one that involves a "fundamental change" or a "substantial difference" to the application, or one which makes the development something that was not in substance what was applied for (as would be the result of using the loss of an opportunity to be consulted as the "main criterion" of whether or not there is such a change), deprives such terms of meaning.*

With respect, this seems to take Forbes J out of context. In *Wheatcroft*, the condition reduced the size of the scheme. It is difficult to see how this could be objectionable to the public. Nor did Forbes J's "*rider*" turn on the matter of substance, in the sense of quantum or scale. The question of substance turns, instead, on that which is important to members of the public. Hence why Forbes J said:

> *"The main, but not the only, criterion on which that judgment should be exercised is whether the development is so changed that to grant it would be to deprive those who should have been consulted on the changed development of the opportunity of such consultation."*

Counter to John Howell QC, it could be equally said that a proposed change to the external appearance of a new building, or to the proposed access to it, might be said to result in a development that is in substance different from that applied for; because it may be a change about which persons other than the applicant may want to make representations.

Subject to these limitations and this note of caution, it would, for example, be possible to modify proposals by condition to change their effects on the highway. Thus:

> *"The development shall be carried out in accordance with the approved drawings save that Drawing XXX (titled "Highway Access") shall be replaced by Drawing YYY (titled "Revised Highway Access")"*

## 11.16    The *Proberun* case

*Medina Borough Council v Proberun Ltd* (1991) 61 P. & C.R. 77 is important because it shows that a local planning authority cannot go back against a grant of an outline planning permission on the retrospective ground that the arrangements for access are not satisfactory.

There, the developer's land was joined to a highway by a narrow lane owned by the developer. The developer did not own any other land surrounding the site. On the refusal of an application to renew an earlier lapsed full planning permission for an extensive housing development on the site, under which access to the highway via the lane had been accepted, the developer appealed to the Secretary of State. The Secretary of State granted an outline planning permission only and attached a condition to the permission providing that details of the design of the buildings, the means of access and landscaping must be submitted to the local authority for approval. Subsequently, the local planning authority refused to approve an access which used the lane only. The authority made it quite clear that the only access which would satisfy them would be over land not in the developer's ownership and an inspector then dismissed the developer's appeal on the grounds that the proposed access contained serious flaws and did not meet required standards.

The Court of Appeal decided that, where permission is granted subject to the details of access being approved and the applicant owns or controls no other land than that set out in the application, then details cannot be turned down simply because the local planning authority deems them to be unsatisfactory. It is enough that they are the best that can be achieved on the application site. To expect the developer to provide access on land outside his control was an abuse of power and unlawful.

In *R v Newbury DC ex. p. Chieveley Parish Council* [1997] J.P.L. 1137 Carnwath J drew a distinction between, on the one hand, the effective nullification of an outline permission, and on the other hand, the refinement of the scheme at the reserved matters stage (@ p.1156):

> *"In my view, while the general approach as explained in Medina is not in doubt, its application must depend on the circumstances. Much will depend on the scope of the matters left open by the outline permission. In Medina the issue was as narrow as the strip within which room for access had to be found. By contrast, if one takes the example, given earlier, of an outline permission for residential development of a defined area, with all matters reserved, including numbers and form of housing, I cannot see how questions of traffic generation can be irrelevant in fixing the acceptable density and the form of access. Medina merely shows that any limitations imposed at that stage cannot be such as to nullify the principle of residential development."*

## 11.17    Effect of invalid conditions

In *Kent CC v Kingsway Investments (Kent) Ltd* [1971] A.C. 72, the House of Lords held that certain conditions were valid. However, the Lords went on to say that if the invalid conditions are unimportant, incidental or merely superimposed on the permission, then the permission might endure. If the conditions are part of the structure of the permission, then the permission falls with it.

In *Fisher v Wychavon District Council* (2001) J.P.L. 694, the Court of Appeal was faced with a decision notice which purported to be the grant of permission for the permanent stationing of a caravan on the one hand, but then included conditions which suggested it was a temporary permission only. Unfortunately, the situation was compounded by a typographical error which masked what the temporary period was intended to be. The Court struck down the permission. They did not seek to correct the permission by the use of a *"blue pencil"* and adopted Wade: *Administrative Law*, 8th ed. (2000) at p.295:

> *"The court may be particularly disinclined to perform feats of surgery where an invalid condition is one of the terms on which a discretionary power is exercised. If an invalid condition is attached to a licence or to planning permission, the permission without the condition may be such as the licensing authority would not have been willing to grant on grounds of public interest. The right course for the court is then to quash the whole permission, so that a fresh application may be made."*

In *R v St Edmundsbury BC ex. p. Investors in Industry Commercial Properties Ltd* [1985] 1 W.L.R. 1168 the court stated that a condition requiring a development to provide for small retail outlets as well as a supermarket had neither been unreasonable nor been imposed for considerations other than those of planning. Alternatively, it was not so fundamental as to render the whole permission void and was, accordingly, severable and the grant of permission was not void on account of the imposition of the condition. The condition related to retail sales, though not necessarily to food retail sales, and envisaged retail entities not forming part of the supermarket activities as such. It was within the general ambit of the permission sought, and the purpose of the condition was to improve the facilities that the development would afford, particularly to the local area.

## 11.18    "Tail-piece" conditions

Many permissions have, over the years, been granted subject to conditions which allow for minor variations to the matters prescribed by them by agreement with the local planning authority. For example:

> *"The development shall be carried out in accordance with the approved layout plan <u>unless otherwise agreed in writing by the local planning authority</u>".*

The underlined words are now known as *"tail-pieces"* and have been found to be objectionable.

The leading case is *R (Midcounties Co-operative Ltd) v Wyre Forest DC* [2009] EWHC 964 (Admin). Whether such a *"tail-piece"* will invalidate a condition depends on its substantive effect. There, two such conditions were challenged; one was held to be defective and the other was not.

One imposed limits on the retail floorspace of a new superstore and continued "*unless otherwise agreed in writing with the Local Planning Authority.*" Ouseley J held that the effect of the tail-piece was to enable development to take place: "*which could be very different in scale or impact from that applied for, assessed or permitted, and it enables it to be created by means wholly outside any statutory process*".

The second condition identified the drawings in accordance with which the development was to be carried out. It added: "*unless other minor variations are agreed in writing after the date of this permission and before implementation with the Local Planning Authority*". Ouseley J stated:

> *[79] I do not regard this tail-piece as unlawful. Its clear scope is to enable "minor variations" to an obligation otherwise to develop "in strict accordance" with plans and drawings. Both those parts of the condition operate to limit the flexibility which the tailpiece provides.*

In the event, Ouseley J held that he could excise the offending tail-piece from the first condition so as to leave the balance (and the permission) intact.

In *R (Warley) v Wealden DC* [2011] EWHC 2083 (Admin) permission was granted for lighting at a tennis court subject to a condition which provided that the court should not be operated outside prescribed times "*without the prior consent in writing of the Local Planning Authority.*" Mr Rabinder Singh QC (as he then was), sitting as a Deputy High Court Judge, concluded that these words were inappropriate and severed them from the permission.

Regardless whether such conditions can be saved by severance, the lesson to be learned is not to use such "*tail-pieces*". Section 96A of the 1990 Act now provides a statutory mechanism for minor variations to planning permissions and this should be used. More significant variations to a scheme should be made via section 73 of the 1990 Act or a new application.

## 11.19    Discharge of conditions

Article 27 of the Town and Country Planning (Development Management Procedure) (England) Order 2015 (S.I. 2015, No. 595) provides that, on an application for any consent, agreement or approval required by a condition or limitation attached to a grant of planning permission, the authority must give notice to the applicant of their decision within a period of eight weeks or such longer period as may be agreed by the applicant and the authority.

Article 28 provides a mechanism for deemed discharge of certain planning conditions where the applicant has given notice in accordance with Article 29 (called a "*deemed discharge notice*"). A condition to which section 74A(2) of the 1990 Act applies is deemed to be discharged where the applicant has given such notice, in relation to that condition, and the period for the authority to give notice to the applicant of their decision on the application has elapsed without the authority giving notice to the applicant of their decision. Deemed discharge takes effect on the date specified in the deemed discharge notice or on such later date as may be agreed by the applicant and the authority, unless the authority has given notice to the applicant of their decision on the application before that date.

A deemed discharge notice may not be given unless at least six weeks have elapsed beginning with the day immediately following that on which the application under Article 27 is received by the local planning authority or such shorter period as may be agreed in writing between the applicant and the authority for serving a deemed discharge notice has elapsed: Article 29(2).

Deemed discharge does not apply where the condition falls within the exemptions listed in Schedule 6 of the 2015 Order or, in relation to that condition, the applicant and the local planning authority have agreed that the provisions of section 74A of the 1990 Act (*deemed discharge of planning conditions*) do not apply: Article 30.

## 11.20    Challenging conditions

If the applicant is unhappy with a planning condition then he has a number of options available to him:

- a High Court challenge if he believes that the condition is *"ultra vires"*;

- an appeal against the condition to the Secretary of State;

- an application for renewal of the permission under the streamlined procedure in regulation 3(3) of the Town and Country Planning (Applications) Regulations 1988;

- an application to *"vary"* the condition under section 73 of the 1990 Act;

- seeking a *"non material amendment"* under section 96A of the 1990 Act; or

- an application for a new planning permission.

Each of these actions is subject to its own limitations:

- a High Court challenge must be started within six weeks of the date of grant of the planning permission;

- an appeal against a condition must be started within three months of the date of grant of the planning permission;

- an application for renewal is not available if the permission has lapsed, the development has begun or if the time-limit for the submission of reserved matters has expired; and

- an application to vary is not available if the permission has lapsed.

A High Court challenge can be precarious because, if the court feels that the condition is fundamental to the permission, it may quash both the condition and the planning permission. There is established authority for the proposition that, if an authority has imposed a wrongful condition, then it is guilty of taking into account an improper consideration thereby vitiating its subsequent decision as a whole: see para. 11.17 above.

Similarly, an appeal to the Secretary of State reopens the question of whether or not the planning permission should have been granted with or without the disputed condition or at all.

By contrast, an application to vary under section 73 is a much safer course because the local planning authority (or the Secretary of State on appeal) must review the condition only and cannot upset the original permission.

# Chapter 12

# Planning Obligations

## 12.1    Introduction

Planning obligations have a significant role to play in the interaction of town and country planning and highways. They can set the scene for a number of actions relatively early in the process. Examples are:

- financial contributions for highway works which arise from the specific impacts of the development;

- site specific traffic management;

- provision and maintenance of sustainable drainage systems;

- arrangements for the private maintenance of estate roads;

- measures to encourage the use of low (or non-emission) motor vehicles; and

- travel plans.

## 12.2    The usual sequence

The usual process is as follows:

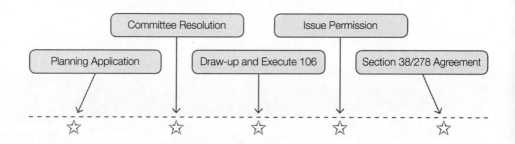

## 12.3    Section 106

It is imperative that the terms of section 106 are borne in mind at all times when negotiating and settling planning obligations because section 106 imposes a number of limitations on what can and cannot be done under its aegis. It is, unfortunately, true to say that many purported Section 106 Agreements fail to meet this basic test.

Section 106(1) states:

> *"Any person interested in land[77] in the area of a local planning authority may, by agreement or otherwise, enter into an obligation (referred to in this section and sections 106A and 106B as "a planning obligation"), enforceable to the extent mentioned in sub-section (3):*
>
> *(a)      restricting the development or use of the land in any specified way;*
>
> *(b)      requiring specified operations or activities to be carried out in, on, under or over the land;*
>
> *(c)      requiring the land to be used in any specified way; or*
>
> *(d)      requiring a sum or sums to be paid to the authority[78] on a specified date or dates or periodically".*

To put it bluntly, if a particular provision does not fall within (a) – (d) above then it does not fall within section 106 at all. So, for example, a requirement that an owner should not apply for parking permits in respect of the highway outside his land is outwith section 106 and cannot be enforced pursuant to section 106. Whilst this requirement might be binding under the law of contract, it is of little use where the title to the land has changed hands (see below).

## 12.4      Agreements and unilateral undertakings

A planning obligation may be created either by a *"Planning Agreement"* (aka *"Section 106 Agreement"*) or a *"Unilateral Undertaking"*. As the name implies, a planning agreement is a bilateral deed which is executed by the persons interested in the land and the local planning authority. By contrast, a unilateral undertaking is a deed which is executed by the person interested in the land only. Both are *"planning obligations"* for the purposes of section 106, viz:

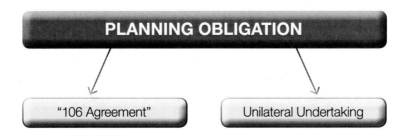

Unilateral undertakings can be very useful in expediting the planning process; however, they are not suited to complex transactions which require covenants from the local planning

---

[77]    In practice, the freeholder will always be the principal party.
[78]    Or, in a case where section 2E applies, the Greater London Authority.

authority (sometimes called *"reciprocal covenants"*) because, of course, the authority is not a signatory party. For example, in a bilateral agreement, covenants which require the developer to pay a financial contribution will normally be subject to a reciprocal covenant by the authority to repay any part of the contribution which they have not spent within a specified period. It is not appropriate to include such *"clawback"* in a unilateral undertaking because the authority is not a party to it and, therefore, is not bound by it. One finds that one of the most common mistakes in respect of unilateral undertakings is where the draftsman mistakenly structures it as a bilateral agreement. That is to say, he provides for covenants on behalf of the local planning authority, notwithstanding the fact that the authority is not a party to the document.

Notwithstanding these drawbacks, unilateral undertakings are well suited to straightforward transactions, such as the payment of money. An example of a short undertaking is included below at Form 3.

## 12.5     The magic of section 106

The obvious question is why should a local planning authority be so keen to enter into a Section 106 Agreement when an ordinary commercial contract would seem to fit the bill? The answer to this question lies in what is known as the common law doctrine of *"privity of contract"*. In essence, this doctrine provides that the only persons who may be bound by a contract are the parties to that contract.[79] Whilst this might be adequate in the ordinary commercial transactions, it is not helpful in connection with planning requirements because, of course, the relevant site can be sold on. If the contract is entered into by the local planning authority and the landowner, then it does not bind successors in title at common law. Thus the developer would escape free from the agreement. This would be a considerable restriction on the utility of such an approach when many planning permissions are granted to owners who then pass their sites on to the actual developers.

Section 106 overcomes this problem by providing a nexus between the council and the successor in title. If the landowner enters into a Section 106 Agreement with the local planning authority and then sells the site, then any person deriving title from him is bound in

---

[79]     Now subject to the Contracts (Rights of Third Parties) Act 1999.

law to the local planning authority and the authority is entitled to enforce the provisions of the agreement against the successor in title.

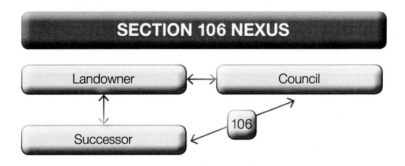

In theory, the original landowner would remain bound to the local planning authority under the law of contract, notwithstanding the sale of the land; however, most Section 106 Agreements contain a release for the original landowner when he sells the site. This type of provision often states that he will remain liable for any breaches of the agreement whilst he was the owner but is released from any future breaches. Most agreements also provide that incoming residential occupiers are excluded from the agreement, the exception being ongoing provisions relating to affordable housing. It would be surprising if an incoming residential occupier were to be bound by provisions relating to major highway infrastructure; however, it might be the case that they might have to assume some liabilities in respect of on-site infrastructure, such as estate roads and drainage.

## 12.6     Section 106(13)

Before moving on to consider section 106 in detail, it is necessary to pause and consider the impact of section 106(13) on sub-clauses (a), (b) and (c), all of which use the word *"specified"*. The word specified has a particular effect within section 106 and it is defined by section 106(13);

> *"In this section "Specified" means specified in the instrument by which the planning obligation is entered into ...".*

The apparent effect of section 106(13) is that a requirement in a planning obligation may be defective if it leaves essential items to be settled by a later document.

All lawyers are familiar with the difficulties associated with *"agreements to agree"* in the law of contract. The same essential principles apply in this case. As such, it is important that, where key matters are left for determination after the date of the agreement, then a mechanism is provided in the agreement which will lead to their crystallisation. In most cases, the point can be resolved by the use of a dispute resolution mechanism.

Thus, an embargo on the commencement of development until a scheme has been settled can be said to restrict *"the development or use of the land in any specified way"* for section 106(1)(a) where the agreement provides that the exact details of the scheme may, if need be, be settled by an independent expert.

## 12.7      Section 106(1)(a)

Section 106(1)(a) allows the imposition of the restrictive covenants. For example *"no buildings on open spaces"*. However, subsection 106(1)(a) can also allow for positive actions if phrased in the negative i.e.:

> *"No part of the Development shall be begun unless Certificate 1 has been issued by the Council in respect of the Highway Works".*

## 12.8      Section 106(1)(b)

Requirements under section 106(1)(b) can underpin the construction of on-site highway works (but not off-site works on land not controlled by any party to the development).

## 12.9      Section 106(1)(c)

Section 106(1)(c) allows requirements that land is being used in a particular positive way.

## 12.10      Section 106(1)(d)

This allows a variety of payment arrangements, for example payments for highways, drainage etc. Section 106(2)(c) allows any payments under this provision to be calculated by reference to a formula. Section 106(1)(d) would also appear to allow payments calculated by reference to enhanced land values resulting from the development. Section 106(1)(d) does not use the word *"specified"*; therefore section 106(13) does not appear to apply (see above).

It is important to note that Section 106(1)(d) provides, in terms, that the sums in question must be paid to the local planning authority. Accordingly, it would be wrong to include a provision which provides that the payment of a contribution should be made directly to any other person. This would appear to preclude direct payments to third parties e.g. a local parish council, etc.

For example, it would be inappropriate for a local planning authority which is not the highway authority to provide that highway contributions should be paid directly to a highway authority which is not a party. This would be outwith section 106 and therefore unenforceable under section 106.

It follows that such a contribution should be paid to the local planning authority in the first instance; or the highway authority may, if it is also a local planning authority, join in the agreement as a party. If the former approach is adopted, then the agreement should make it crystal clear that the local planning authority is simply acting as a conduit and that the money is intended for onward transmission to the highway authority. Otherwise, this could give rise to auditing problems. Arguably, the better approach, in such a situation, is for the local planning authority and the highway authority to enter into an agency arrangement whereby the local planning authority is authorised to settle and collect money on behalf of the highway authority.[80]

## 12.11    The need to observe formalities

Section 106(9) provides that a planning obligation may not be entered into except by an instrument executed as a deed which:

(a)    states that the obligation is a planning obligation for the purposes of this section;

(aa)   if the obligation is a development consent obligation, contains a statement to that effect;

(b)    identifies the land in which the person entering into the obligation is interested;

(c)    identifies the person entering into the obligation and states what his interest in the land is; and

(d)    identifies the local planning authority by whom the obligation is enforceable and, in a case where section 2E applies, identifies the Mayor of London as an authority by whom the obligation is also enforceable.

A failure to comply with these requirements is highly likely to put the document outside section 106 and to render it defective.

To give one example, there have been cases where purported planning obligations have failed where they required that the landowners who were party to them should not apply for parking permits on nearby streets. The laudable objective of such requirements was to reduce congestion which may be caused by on-street parking in connection with the developments; however, they do not fall within section 106. In *Westminster CC v Secretary of State for Communities and Local Government* [2013] EWHC 690 (Admin), Deputy Judge Bucknell QC stated:

> *"The unilateral undertaking entered into by Mr Vok does not meet the requirements of any of sub-paragraphs (1)(a)-(d). In the result it does not have the characteristics required for a planning obligation. In the further result it is not enforceable as provided by sub-paragraphs (3) and (5) and, because it is not a planning obligation but a purely personal undertaking by Mr Vok which does not run with the land, is not capable of being registered as a local land charge within the scope of sub-paragraph (11)."*

This was endorsed by the Court of Appeal in *R (Khodari) v Royal Borough of Kensington and Chelsea Council and Cedarpark Holdings Inc.* [2017] EWCA Civ 333.

---

[80]    Perhaps for a collection and administration fee.

## 12.12　The parties

Section 106(3) provides (inter alia) that a planning obligation is enforceable by the authority identified in accordance with subsection 106(9)(d) -

(a)　against the person entering into the obligation; and

(b)　against any person deriving title from that person.

Section 336(8) of the 1990 Act provides that:

(a)　references to a person from whom title is derived by another person include references to any predecessor in title of that other person;

(b)　references to a person deriving title from another person include references to any successor in title of that other person; and

(c)　references to deriving title are references to deriving title either directly or indirectly.

## 12.13　Some misconceptions

The following can be found on the "*Planning Portal*" website:

> "*Planning obligations, also known as Section 106 Agreements (based on that section of The 1990 Town & Country Planning Act) are private agreements made between local authorities and developers and can be attached to a planning permission to make acceptable development which would otherwise be unacceptable in planning terms. The land itself, rather than the person or organisation that develops the land, is bound by a Section 106 Agreement, something any future owners will need to take into account.*"[81]

This advice leaves a lot to be desired. Taking the mistakes in order:[82]

It is not right to say that planning obligations are "*... also known as Section 106 Agreements ...*" because the phrase "*planning obligation*" includes both bilateral agreements and unilateral undertakings: see para. 12.4 above.

Planning obligations are not "*private agreements*"; they are statutory documents which are subject to a raft of public law requirements and remedies: see para. 12.23 below.

They are not "*... agreements made between local authorities and developers ...*". A planning obligation is made by the persons interested in the land mentioned in it, normally the freeholders. The inclusion of the developer is necessary only where he has a property interest in the land.

---

[81]　https://www.planningportal.co.uk/info/200126/applications/58/the_decision-making_process/7.

[82]　One is left to wonder at the professional qualifications of those who wrote this unhelpful "*advice*". The website is said to be a "*... joint venture between TerraQuest and the Department for Communities and Local Government...*".

It is not right that "... *the land itself, rather than the person or organisation that develops the land, is bound by a Section 106* ...". The current owner of the land will be bound by the planning obligation, as will those deriving title from him. This is particularly the case where the payment of money is secured by the obligation: see para. 12.5 above.[83]

## 12.14     Practical enforcement of planning obligations

Subsections 106(5) and 106(6) provide the statutory enforcement mechanisms:

> *"(5) A restriction or requirement imposed under a planning obligation is enforceable by injunction.*
>
> *(6) Without prejudice to subsection (5), if there is a breach of a requirement in a planning obligation to carry out any operations in, on, under or over the land to which the obligation relates, the authority by whom the obligation is enforceable may-*
>
> *(a) enter the land and carry out the operations; and*
>
> *(b) recover from the person or persons against whom the obligation is enforceable any expenses reasonably incurred by them in so doing."*

It is important to consider the way in which these mechanisms might apply in real-life situations.

An elegantly drafted planning obligation is of little use to a local planning authority if it is either unenforceable or involves the expenditure of a disproportionate amount of powder and shot in the enforcement process. Yet many authorities fail to recognise that the provision of straightforward and efficient enforcement mechanisms is at the heart of the process. Take, for example, the following clause:

> *"If required by the Council by giving to the applicant at any time within three months from the date of the Commencement of Development at least 28 days written notice requiring the Applicant to enter into a contract with the for the transfer of an area of land within the Site of not less that 0.3 hectares ("the Highway Land") to enter into a contract for the transfer of the Highway Land and the following provisions shall apply to such contract and the transfer shall be at no cost to the Council ...".*

This example is fundamentally flawed because:

(a)     it involves the transfer of land, yet such an obligation does not fall within section 106;[84]

(b)     if it is outside section 106 then it is doubtful whether the clause is effective as an ordinary agreement to transfer under conventional property law principles because it does not appear to comply with section 2 of the Law of Property (Miscellaneous

---

[83]     Hence why the local planning authority will require the freeholder to be the principal party.
[84]     See para. 12.3 above.

Provisions) Act 1989;

(c)    even if (a) and (b) can be overcome, the enforcement of such a clause would be time-consuming and difficult because it would involve forcing an unwilling applicant to execute a contract and transfer; and

(d)    nothing in the clause prevents the carrying out of the development whilst the applicant is in breach.

All of these criticisms could be avoided by the simple mechanism of planning an embargo upon progress of the development by way of a negative obligation:

> *"The Development shall not commence until the Highway Land has been transferred to the Council PROVIDED that this clause shall be discharged and cease to be of effect in the event that the Council fails to accept a transfer of the Highway Land when tendered by the Applicant in accordance with the following terms of this clause ...".*

If the Applicant fails to offer the transfer of the Highway Land in accordance with the terms of the planning obligation then the solution is straightforward; the Council can apply for an injunction requiring cessation of all work on the development.

If the planning obligation is designed to secure the payment of money to the Council, then, again, a positive obligation to pay money is not necessarily the most effective approach. For example:

> *"The Applicant shall pay the Highways Contribution to the Council not later than 28 days following Commencement of Development".*

The theoretical enforcement mechanism for a default is by way of a debt action, but this is of no use if the money has been spent or the owner has gone into liquidation with no visible assets. It is possible to cover the matter by way of a negative clause:

> *"The Development shall not be commenced unless and until the Highways Contribution has been paid to the Council".*

But even this approach has limitations in terms of practical enforcement. Consider:

> *"No dwelling forming part of the development shall be occupied unless and until the Highways Contribution has been paid".*

It is difficult to believe that a judge would dispossess a family from their home in order to enforce breach of this obligation by a commercial house-builder. Not only will the enforcing authority have to contend with the Human Rights Act 1998 and Article 8 of the European

Convention on Human Rights; but it will also have to deal with Article 3.1 of the United Nations Convention on the Rights of the Child where children are in residence.[85]

A better approach in this case might be for the Council to require that the payment of the money is secured by a bond or guarantee.[86]

## 12.15  "Planning gain"

It is said to be a fundamental principle that planning permissions should be neither bought nor sold. This principle is often advanced as though it enshrines some deep moral or philosophical tenet - although it could be argued that there is no moral objection to attaching a cash value to the uplift in the value of land following the grant of planning permission in respect of it. The legal objection is, simply, that the town and country planning legislation does not allow permissions either to be sold or to be the subject of an ad hoc local tax or levy. If a developer passes money or some other benefit to the local planning authority when he obtains a planning permission, then that money or benefit must be related to the planning permission. For example, a cash payment may be lawful if it overcomes a highway problem created by the development. But a payment could be unlawful ("*ultra vires*") if it does not address a material issue arising from the development, for example a cash payment to charity not associated with the development. In practice, the line between lawful and unlawful payments and benefits is very difficult to draw.

Although it is an expression which was once in everyday use, the phrase "*planning gain*" is now frowned upon. The now repealed Circular 16/91 ("*Planning and Compensation Act 1991 - Planning Obligations*") stated at paragraph B2 of Annex B:

> "The term "planning gain" has no statutory significance and is not found in the Planning Acts. The whole planning process is intended to operate in the public interest, in that it is chiefly aimed at securing economy, efficiency and amenity in the development and use of land. This is achieved through the normal process of development plan preparation and the exercise of development control. In granting planning permission, or in negotiations with developers and other interests that lead to the grant of planning permission, the local planning authority may seek to secure modifications or improvements to the proposals submitted for their approval. They may grant permission subject to conditions, and where appropriate they may seek to enter into planning obligations with a developer regarding the use or development of the land concerned or of other land or buildings. Rightly used, planning obligations may enhance development proposals".

And paragraph B3 went on to say:

> "By these means the local planning authority can aim to ensure that new development or redevelopment is facilitated while having regard to the interest of the local environment and

---

85   See *Stevens v Secretary of State for Communities and Local Government* [2013] EWHC 792 (Admin).
86   Indeed, any defence advocate who is versed in these matters would be entitled to ask why the authority failed to seek a bond instead of placing his ostensibly innocent residential clients in jeopardy.

*other planning considerations. The term "planning gain" has come to be used very loosely to apply both to this normal and legitimate operation of the planning system and also to attempts to extract from developers payments in cash or in kind for purposes that are not directly related to the development proposed but are sought as "the price of planning permission". Equally, the term "planning gain" has been used to describe offers from developers to a local authority that are not related to their development proposal. The Planning Acts do not envisage that planning powers should be used for such purposes, and in this sense "planning gain" is outside the scope of the planning process. Since the term "planning gain" is imprecise and misleading, it is not used in this policy guidance, which relates to the role of planning obligations in the proper exercise of development control".*

## 12.16    The legal boundaries of "planning benefits": Introduction
It is important to distinguish between two dimensions of this topic:

•    first the boundaries of *"planning benefits"* as material considerations in the determination of planning applications; and

•    secondly, the impact of *"planning benefits"* on the validity of planning obligations which purport to secure them.

These dimensions are often conflated, yet they go to very different points. The first relates to challenges to the validity of the decision which gives rise to the grant of a planning permission, usually with a view to having it quashed by the courts. The second is a challenge to a planning obligation itself, having regard to the terms of section 106 itself. As will be explained below, they are not the same thing.

## 12.17    "Planning benefits" as material considerations
In order to be a proper material consideration in the determination of a planning application, a proposed planning requirement has to pass the legal tests handed down by the House of Lords in *Newbury DC v Secretary of State for the Environment* [1981] A.C. 578 before a decision-maker can legitimately take it into account; that is:

•    it has to be for a planning purpose and not for any ulterior one;

•    it must be fairly and reasonably related to the proposed development; and

•    it must not be so unreasonable that no reasonable planning authority could have imposed it.

It is well established that certain *"enabling development"* can meet the *Newbury* tests. In *R v Westminster City Council ex. p. Monahan* [1989] J.P.L. 107 (aka the *"Royal Opera House Case"*), the Court of Appeal held that the local planning authority had been entitled, in deciding to grant planning permission for the erection of the offices as part of scheme involving the renovation of the Royal Opera House, to balance the fact that improvements to the Opera

House would not be financially viable if the permission for the offices were not granted against the fact that the office development was contrary to the development plan.

The renovation of the Opera House was a matter of land use; however, in respect of the *"fair and reasonable relationship"* test, the court declined to be drawn on the wider question of whether or not there should be a geographical proximity between the *"enabling"* development and the *"enabled"* development. The Opera House was within the same overall area as the office development. Nicholls LJ stated:

> *Mr. Carnwath's strongest point was that if what I have said above is correct, one is on a slippery slope on which there is no stopping short of a conclusion which would embrace and accept as valid other cases from which one instinctively recoils. If the purpose of granting permission for development A is to finance development B, that purpose can equally exist and be fulfilled if the two developments have no physical contiguity at all... All that need be said to decide this appeal is that the sites of the commercial development approved in principle are sufficiently close to the opera house for it to have been proper for the local planning authority to treat the proposed development of the office sites, in Russell Street and elsewhere, and the proposed improvements to the opera house as forming part of one composite development project. [Page 121]*

Staughton LJ was more forthcoming saying (inter alia):

> *...On the first issue, the major difficulty seems to me to lie in drawing a line between obvious extremes. It may be sufficient for the decision in this case to say on which side of the line it lies. But in my view the court ought, if it can, to give some indication where the line should be drawn... The question here is whether a planning authority can permit undesirable development A as a means of securing desirable development B... One extreme is the example given by Kerr LJ of a derelict listed building which the planning authority wishes to see restored. In principle it would be wholly proper to consider partial office development A, if that were the only means by which restoration and partial residential occupation B could be made financially viable.*
>
> *The other extreme arises from the axiom of Lloyd LJ in Bradford City Metropolitan Council v Secretary of State for the Environment [1986] 1 E.G.L.R. 199, 202G that planning permission cannot be bought and sold. Suppose that a developer wished to erect an office building at one end of the town A, and offered to build a swimming-pool at the other end B. It would in my view be wrong for the planning authority to regard the swimming-pool as a material consideration, or to impose a condition that it should be built. That case seems to me little different from the developer who offers the planning authority a cheque so that it can build the swimming-pool for itself - provided he has permission for his office development... Where then is the line to be drawn between those extremes? In my judgment the answer lies in the speech of Viscount Dilhorne in Newbury District Council v. Secretary of State for the Environment [1981] A.C. 578, 599, which Kerr LJ has quoted. Conditions imposed must "fairly and reasonably*

*relate to the development permitted," if they are to be valid. So must considerations, if they are to be material.*

More recent cases have held, as a matter of decided principle, that there must be a geographical or functional connection between the *"enabling"* development and the *"enabled"* development, when considering whether there is a fair and reasonable relationship between the two.

*Tesco Stores Ltd v Secretary of State for the Environment and Others* [1995] 2 All E.R. 636 concerned an application to build a new superstore on the outskirts of Witney in Oxfordshire. Tesco offered to provide funding for a link road which would relieve traffic congestion in the town generally. There was some relationship between the funding of the road and a proposed store because of the slight worsening of traffic conditions attributable to the store, albeit a less than 10% traffic increase. The Secretary of State turned down Tesco's appeal, stating that Tesco's offer of funding failed the *"necessity test"* in Circular 16/91 and could not therefore be treated as a material consideration in deciding whether or not planning permission should be granted. Tesco sought an order that the Secretary of State's decision be quashed on the ground that he had failed to take into account the offer of funding as a material consideration. The House of Lords found in favour of the Secretary of State. They held that if an offered planning obligation had some connection with the proposed development that was not de minimis then it was a relevant consideration and the decision-maker would have to have regard to it. But it was entirely for the decision-maker to attribute to a relevant consideration such weight as he thought fit and, unless he acted unreasonably in doing so, the courts would not interfere with his decision. An offered planning obligation that had nothing to do with the proposed development, apart from the fact that it was offered by the developer, was plainly not a material consideration and could only be regarded as an attempt to buy planning permission. The House of Lords held that, on the facts, the Secretary of State had not disregarded Tesco's offer of funding. On the contrary, he had given it careful consideration. Furthermore, the Secretary of State was entitled, in exercising his discretion, to have regard to his established policy.

Importantly, no challenge was made in the House of Lords, or in the courts below it, to the validity of the planning obligation itself: the question whether the obligation itself regulated the development of Tesco's site within section 106 was not put in issue.

In *R (Sainsbury's) v Wolverhampton CC* [2010] 1 A.C. 437[87] the Supreme Court held that the relationship between Tesco's proposed superstore on the outskirts of Wolverhampton, and the site on which it had offered regeneration benefits in the city centre, was not sufficiently close for the latter to be taken into account as justifying a compulsory purchase order for the former. Again, the speeches went to the question of whether or not the proffered benefits were material considerations and did not deal with the validity of the planning obligations per se.

---

[87]  *Sainsbury's Supermarkets Ltd, R (on the application of) v Wolverhampton City Council & Anor* [2010] UKSC 20.

In *R (Peter Wright) v Forest of Dean District Council v Resilient Energy Severndale Ltd* [2017] EWCA Civ 2102 the Court of Appeal held that the offer of a large amount of money couched as a purported "*community benefit*" as the quid pro quo for permission for a wind farm was an immaterial consideration notwithstanding that there was support for such payments in national policy.

In *Aberdeen City and Shire Strategic Development Planning Authority v Elsick Development Company Limited* [2017] UKSC 66 the Supreme Court held that a planning obligation which purported to require money for off-site highway infrastructure unconnected with the relevant development (the "*Elsick*" development) was invalid. The planning authority adopted a policy in its development plan which in substance required developers to enter into planning obligations with it to make financial contributions to the pooled fund to be spent on highway infrastructure, including interventions at places where a particular development had a trivial impact only. Supplementary Guidance was produced by the local planning authority which explained that the purpose of the pooled fund was to mitigate the cumulative impact of developments at specific "*hotspots*" in the highway network. Elsick challenged the adoption of the guidance under section 238 of the Town and Country Planning (Scotland) Act 1997.

Tables were produced to the court which showed the traffic generated by each development which would use the infrastructure at the identified "*hotspots*" as a percentage of the total traffic generated by that development. A table showed the following in relation to the Elsick site:

| Development Zone | Persley Bridge | A947 | A96 East of AWPR | Kingswells North | A944 | New Bridge of Dee |
|---|---|---|---|---|---|---|
| Elsick | 3.45% | 0.10% | 0.76% | 1.46% | 0.79% | 8.39% |

Thus, according to this table, the traffic impacts on these "*hotspots*" varied between 0.10% and 8.39%. Another table provided:

| Development Zone | Persley Bridge | A947 | A96 East of AWPR | Kingswells North | A944 | New Bridge of Dee |
|---|---|---|---|---|---|---|
| Elsick | 1% | 0% | 1% | 2% | 1% | 7% |

Again, the traffic impacts from the development were, as the Supreme Court concluded, shown to be trivial; namely, between 0% and 7%.

The *Tesco* case above was held to be on the point in connection with planning benefits as material considerations.

As to this issue, Lord Hodge stated:

*[61] First, the requirement imposed on a developer to contribute to the pooled Fund, which is to finance the transport infrastructure needed to make acceptable all of the developments which the development plan promotes, entails the use of a developer's contribution on infrastructure with which its development has no more than a trivial connection and thus is not imposed for a purpose in relation to the development and use of the burdened site as section 75 requires.*

*[63] Secondly, Tesco (above) establishes that for a planning obligation, which is to contribute funding, to be a material consideration in the decision to grant planning permission, there must be more than a trivial connection between the development and the intervention or interventions which the proposed contribution will fund. The planning obligation which Elsick entered into could not be a relevant consideration in the grant of the planning permission. In my view, it was not within the power of the planning authority to require a developer to enter into such an obligation which would be irrelevant to its application for permission as a precondition of the grant of that permission.*

## 12.18 "Planning benefits" and the validity of planning obligations

As noted above, the question of whether a planning obligation itself validly falls within the boundaries of section 106 is a matter separate from any issue as to the obligation as a material consideration in the decision-making process. Surprisingly, there is little juris-prudence on the point.

In the *Aberdeen City* case, Lord Hodge went on to say:

*[52] It is important to recall that the question whether a benefit conferred by a plan-ning obligation is a material consideration in the determination of an application for planning permission is quite separate from the question whether a planning obligation restricts or regulates the development or use of a particular piece of land. Thus, to use the example of the farmer with two farms, A and B. He wishes to develop farm A and is prepared to enter into a planning obligation to restrict the development or use of farm B in the context of his negotiation of a permission for farm A. The legality of the planning obligation in relation to farm B will depend, among other things, on whether it restricts or regulates the development or use of farm B. The relevance of the planning obligation to the determination of the application in relation to farm A depends upon there being a more than trivial connection between the benefit conferred by controlling farm B and the development of farm A, as the Tesco case decided.*

In the *Tesco* case, Beldam LJ (pp.234 to 235) made some obiter dicta comments:

*"In section 106(1) [of the 1990 Act] the obligations referred to in subsections (a), (b) and (c) clearly relate to the land in which the person entering into the obligation is interested. The obligation entered into by a person interested in land under subsection (d) to pay money to the authority is not expressed to be restricted to the payment of money for any particular purpose or object. But all the planning obligations are, by*

> *section 106(3), enforceable not only against the person entering into the obligation but also against his successors in title to the land. Against the background that it is a fundamental principle that planning permission cannot be bought or sold, it does not seem unreasonable to interpret subsection (1)(d) so that a planning obligation requiring a sum or sums to be paid to the planning authority should be for a planning purpose or objective which should be in some way connected with or relate to the land in which the person entering into the obligation is interested."*

The decision of the Supreme Court in the *Aberdeen City* case also turned on this point; however, it is problematic in connection with the law in England.

There Lord Hodge stated (@ para. 21) that he would examine (inter alia) the correct legal test as to the lawfulness of a planning obligation and stated:

> *[33] A planning obligation also is a statutory creation. As with a particular planning condition, the lawfulness of a particular obligation depends upon (i) the wording of the statute, and (ii) the rules of our administrative law.*

He developed the point thus:

> *[44] A planning obligation, which required as a pre-condition for commencing develop-ment that a developer pay a financial contribution for a purpose which did not relate to the burdened land, could be said to restrict the development of the site, but it would also be unlawful. Were such a restriction lawful, a planning authority could use a planning obligation in the context of an application for planning permission to extract from a developer benefits for the community which were wholly unconnected with the proposed development, thereby undermining the obligation on the planning authority to determine the application on its merits. Similarly, a developer could seek to obtain a planning permission by unilaterally undertaking a planning obligation not to develop its site until it had funded extraneous infrastructure or other community facilities unconnected with its development. This could amount to the buying and selling of a planning permission. <u>Section 75, when interpreted in its statutory context, contains an implicit limitation on the purposes of a negative suspensive planning obligation, namely that the restriction must serve a purpose in relation to the development or use of the burdened site. An ulterior purpose, even if it could be categorised as a planning purpose in a broad sense, will not suffice.</u> It is that implicit restriction which makes it both ultra vires and also unreasonable in the Wednesbury sense for a planning authority to use planning obligations for such an ulterior purpose.* (Emphasis added).

*Tesco* was, in part, distinguished on the basis that it dealt with planning benefits as mate-rial considerations in the determination of the relevant appeal, whereas the validity of a planning obligation is judged by reference to the terms of the statute.

The problem in seeking to transpose this decision from Scotland to England on this point is that section 75 of the Town and Country Planning (Scotland) Act 1997 is structured in a way which is materially different to section 106 of the 1990 Act.

Section 75 provides:

(1)     A person may, in respect of land in the district of a planning authority -

    (a)     by agreement with that authority, or

    (b)     unilaterally,

enter into an obligation (referred to in this section and in sections 75A to 75C as a "*planning obligation*") <u>restricting or regulating the development or use of the land,</u> either permanently or during such period as may be specified in the instrument by which the obligation is entered into (referred to in this section and in those sections as the "*relevant instrument*").

(2)     Without prejudice to the generality of subsection (1), the reference in that subsection to restricting or regulating the development or use of land includes -

    (a)     requiring operations or activities specified in the relevant instrument to be carried out in, on, under or over the land, or

    (b)     requiring the land to be used in a way so specified.

(3)     A planning obligation may -

    (a)     be unconditional or subject to conditions,

    (b)     <u>require the payment</u> -

        (i)     of a specified amount or an amount determined in accordance with the relevant instrument, or

        (ii)     of periodical sums either indefinitely or for such period as may be specified in that instrument, and ...

(Emphasis added).

The difference between section 75 and section 106 lies in the fact that the payment of money in section 75(3)(b) applies only where the obligation restricts or regulates the development or use of the land as per section 75(1). In section 75, the payment of money is consequential on an obligation which meets that test. In section 106, by contrast, a requirement to pay money arises from the freestanding and discrete provision in section 106(1)(d).

## 12.19    Planning obligations and composite sites

If the planning obligation relates to matters which fall within a single discrete development site and are part and parcel of the development, then it would be difficult to argue that the geographical nexus described above does not arise, for example the construction of estate roads as part of a residential scheme.

The difficulty arises where the applicant chooses to identify two separate sites as being a single purported development notwithstanding that they might be some distance away from each other and intended for entirely different types of works or uses, for example where a developer is promoting a site for housing and, at the same time, combines an application for highway works some distance from the site within the same application. It might be the case that the developer is offering a planning obligation which secures the funding of those off-site highway works. The developer might argue that this is a *"composite development"*; however, it might also be the case that there are two entirely separate developments which simply share the same application form. If the latter, then it will be necessary to consider whether or not there is a sufficient nexus between those sites. This is not an easy matter because the case law is not as clear as one would like it to be.

In *Derwent Holdings Ltd v Trafford Borough Council* [2011] EWCA Civ 832, the Court of Appeal was concerned with the validity of a planning permission granted by Trafford Borough Council to Tesco Stores and Lancashire County Cricket Club. Their joint application proposed development in two parts: a large superstore on land owned by the Council, and the redevelopment of the nearby Old Trafford Cricket Ground as an improved stadium for international cricket. The two parts were said to be linked by a pedestrian walkway. It was intended that, if permission was granted, the Council would sell their land to Tesco for £21m and the proceeds of sale would then be passed on to LCCC to subsidise their redevelopment. Carnwath LJ stated:

> *[19] "... Derwent, shortly before the committee meeting, had offered to match Tesco's cross-subsidy with its own contribution of £21m to the development of the cricket ground. The members were understandably advised that this was not relevant to the merits of Derwent's proposed retail development, given the lack of any sufficient relationship between the Derwent site and the cricket ground. In the joint application, however, there was a direct relationship. <u>The two elements were in close proximity and physically linked, and they were reasonably included in a single application</u> ... "*[88].
> (Emphasis added).

This dicta would suggest that a purported *"composite development"* can be viewed as such provided that:

- the elements have some form of *"direct relationship"* (for example where the elements have some form of functional or geographical proximity); and

---

[88]    With respect, anyone who has ever visited Old Trafford will know that the purported physical link between the Ground and the Tesco store is somewhat ephemeral.

•     they are reasonably included in a single application.

Whilst the second point was not addressed in terms in *R (Thakeham Village Action Limited) v Horsham District Council* [2014] EWHC 67 (Admin), that decision of the Court of Appeal provides helpful guidance on this topic.

There, a large mushroom growing enterprise flourished on two nearby sites in Thakeham, West Sussex, but, by 2010 that enterprise was failing. Proposals for the re-development of both nurseries were permitted in 2013. One was for the demolition of the existing nursery buildings and the construction of 146 houses on one site. The other was for new buildings on the other site in which mushroom production could continue. The housing development would cross-subsidise the mushroom business. The Claimant challenged the planning permission for the housing development on grounds which included the assertion that the local planning authority had, by taking the benefits in the cross subsidy into account, had regard to an immaterial consideration. That is, the Council acted unlawfully in relying on that proposal as enabling development for the proposed nursery development. The Court of Appeal rejected this argument, in part because it regarded the development of the two sites as being a composite scheme.

The dicta of Lindblom LJ are worth quoting at length:

> [206] As Mr Taylor and Mr Warren submitted, the connection between the two sites was not simply a matter of geography – in that they are adjacent to each other and separated only by a road. It was also a matter of their history – in their combined use over many years as the two parts of a single mushroom growing operation, which had been owned and run by one company, as if on a single site, until the operation began to fail.

> [207] The two proposals were mutually dependent. They were, in effect, a comprehensive scheme for the redevelopment of both sites. The connection between them was a matter of economic reality. The consolidation of the mushroom operation on Site B would not be achieved unless the development proposed on Site A was permitted. This was so when the original proposals were submitted in July 2010. And it was still so after Monaghan Mushrooms had become involved as the operator intending to run the business on Site B once it was redeveloped to accommodate all of the plant. The Council knew that Monaghan Mushrooms was a profitable company, and was prepared to invest in Site B provided the subsidy promised by the development of Site A was released. It knew that there was no prospect of mushroom production continuing in Thakeham unless Monaghan Mushrooms was prepared to make that investment. And it knew that there was no other likely source of the funds required.

> [208] The proposals were also directly linked to each other in a practical way. The proposed redevelopment of Site B depended on the financial contribution from the redevelopment of Site A. The latter would only go ahead once the works it was funding on Site B had been completed. The whole operation, including the activity previously

*undertaken on Site A, could then be located on Site B and would be able to continue in a viable form.*

## 12.20    Community Infrastructure Levy Regulations 2010: Regulation 122

The Community Infrastructure Levy Regulations 2010 now impose limitations on the use of planning obligations with effect from 6 April 2010. They stipulate a set of statutory rules in connection with the permitted relationship between planning obligations and proposed developments.

Regulation 122 provides that a planning obligation may only constitute a reason for granting planning permission for the development if the obligation is:

(a)    necessary to make the development acceptable in planning terms;

(b)    directly related to the development; and

(c)    fairly and reasonably related in scale and kind to the development.

The first question in respect of Regulation 122 is what is meant by the phrase *"development"*. This has to do with the difficult questions relating to whether or not there is a sufficient nexus between the obligations in the agreement and the development. The Regulation is part of a system which has land use planning at its heart and it is difficult to see how a relationship which cannot be expressed in land use planning terms falls within the statutory provision.

Turning to Regulation 122 in detail:

- Regulation 122(a): whether the obligation is necessary to make the development acceptable in planning terms.

- Regulation 122(b): whether the obligation is directly related to the development.

- Regulation 122(c): whether the obligation is fairly and reasonably related in scale and kind to the development.

The position has been complicated by the judgment of Lang J in *Amstel Group Corporation v Secretary of State for Communities and Local Government and North Norfolk District Council* [2018] EWHC 633 (Admin). There the proposed development was for up to 200 houses with, among other things, land for community resources. Permission was refused by the LPA and on appeal. The Inspector found, among other things, that the proposal would cause harm to the setting of a nearby conservation area and to the settings of three listed buildings, but that the cumulative harm would be less than substantial. The Appellant submitted a unilateral undertaking to provide land for community purposes and land for a new primary school and included a commitment by the Norwich Diocesan Board to construct a new primary school. However, he concluded that, whilst they might be desirable, it had not been demonstrated that they were necessary in planning terms and did not meet the tests of the CIL Regulations: "... *I have not therefore taken them into account.*"

Thus, the asserted benefits of this aspect of the unilateral undertaking were not taken into account in the overall balancing exercise. Lang J quashed the Inspector's decision on the basis that he had made a mistake.

The issue for present purposes relates to the effect of Regulation 122. As noted above, the regulation provides that a planning obligation may only constitute a reason for granting planning permission for the development if the obligation is, among other things, necessary to make the development acceptable in planning terms. Lang J stated that the Inspector had acted correctly when he said:

> *"They have evidently been offered as an inducement to make the scheme more attractive but they do not meet the tests of CIL Regulation 122 or comply with Framework 204. I have not therefore taken them into account."*

However, she then went on to find that he should have, nonetheless, taken those asserted benefits into account for the purposes of the balancing tests in the (then extant) NPPF. The difficulty in this approach is that the effect of a breach of Regulation 122 is to make the relevant planning obligation an immaterial consideration. It is, with respect, cutting a fine point to try to separate the benefits secured by the obligation as though they are somehow distinct from the obligation itself, when the whole raison d'être of the obligation is to deliver those benefits. It is arguable that, if the relevant benefits do not meet the regulation, then they are immaterial so far as they may weigh in favour of the grant of a permission. They cannot, somehow, make a re-appearance in a sub-component of the decision-making process. Hence, it is arguable that the Inspector was right to disregard them.

The decision of the Supreme Court in *Aberdeen City and Shire Strategic Development Planning Authority v Elsick Development Company Limited* [2017] (see above) was not cited in *Amstel*; and, arguably, *Amstel* is inconsistent with it.

## 12.21    Community Infrastructure Levy Regulations 2010: Regulation 123
Regulation 123(2) provides that a planning obligation may not constitute a reason for granting planning permission for development to the extent that the obligation provides for the funding or provision of "*relevant infrastructure*".

By Regulation 123(4), "*relevant infrastructure*" means –

(a)    where a charging authority has published on its website a list of infrastructure projects or types of infrastructure that it intends will be, or may be, wholly or partly funded by Community Infrastructure Levy, those infrastructure projects or types of infrastructure, or

(b)    where no such list has been published, any infrastructure.

Regulation 123(3) provides that a planning obligation ("obligation A") may not constitute a reason for granting planning permission to the extent that -

(a)   obligation A provides for the funding or provision of an infrastructure project or type of infrastructure; and

(b)   five or more separate planning obligations that -

   (i)   relate to planning permissions granted for development within the area of the charging authority; and

   (ii)   which provide for the funding or provision of that project, or type of infrastructure,

   have been entered into before the date that obligation A was entered into.

The underlying purpose of Regulation 123 is to ensure that the developer is not, effectively, double charged in respect of common infrastructure which is going to receive a proportion of the Community Infrastructure Levy which is, in any event, attributable to his development. It is, therefore, incumbent upon the local planning authority to show that any contribution from the developer is specific to the development site, as opposed to being a contribution towards common infrastructure.

Regulation 123 can cause a problem where common highway infrastructure is in the CIL list, but will not come forward for some time. The developer is precluded from making a contribution to accelerate the delivery of the infrastructure, yet his scheme could be delayed whilst he waits for it to be delivered.

Whilst not perfect, one interim approach might be for the grant of planning permission which is subject to a planning obligation or planning condition which restricts the occupation of later phases of the scheme until the relevant infrastructure is in place: see *R (Oates) v Wealden District Council* [2018] EWCA Civ 1304. If the scheme is subject to a CIL contribution, then this will, also, have the effect of ensuring some income to the CIL fund for the infrastructure and should, in theory, accelerate it.

## 12.22   The validity of allegedly "ultra vires" planning obligations

There is a theoretical possibility that a planning obligation which is good on its face is nonetheless invalid if it is executed pursuant to a decision which is ultra vires, in the sense that it is the product of an ultra vires decision. This is where the decision is challenged on the basis that the decision-maker has failed to take account of the CIL Regulations or otherwise failed to have regard to the "*Wednesbury*" tests.

The difficulty with this approach is that it amounts to a collateral challenge to the validity of the decision itself and the courts have shown themselves to be reluctant to entertain such challenges. If a person is aggrieved by the provisions of a planning obligation and wishes to raise a point pursuant to the decision-making process itself, there is authority that judicial review is not the correct mode of challenge.

In *McIntosh v Aberdeenshire Council* (1999) S.L.T. 93 the developer entered into an agreement with the local planning authority pursuant to section 50 of the Town and Country Planning (Scotland) Act 1972 whereby he undertook to construct an internal estate road to provide access to any future housing development to the west of the development site. He then sought (inter alia) to invalidate the agreement by way of judicial review. The Outer House of the Court of Session held that the petition was incompetent because judicial review was an inappropriate means by which to challenge what was a contractual agreement between the parties to it. By his signature, the petitioner had made good any defect or want of power on the part of the authority, and once the agreement had been implemented and acted on, he had waived any objection he might have had to a want of power on the part of the authority.

As to the second point (i.e. challenging the planning obligation itself), this, again, does not seem to be a matter for a direct judicial review. Even then, the problem for a challenger who is not a party to the agreement is that administrative law has developed to the point where findings that a statutory document which is regular on its face is "*so much waste paper*" is a rarity.

The modern approach turns on relative invalidity, whereby the validity of such a document is presumed unless it is declared to be a nullity by a court of competent jurisdiction.[89] It follows that, even if a planning obligation has been entered into pursuant to an ultra vires decision or a conflict with section 106 or the CIL Regulations, it would not be a nullity unless the court declares it to be so. In the absence of such a declaration, a planning obligation which is otherwise regular on its face should be as good as the most impeccable of documents. The words of Lord Radcliffe in *Smith v East Elloe UDC* [1956] A.C. 736 have been cited with approval in many modern cases:

> "*An Order, even if not made in good faith, is still an act capable of legal consequences. It bears no brand of invalidity upon its forehead. Unless the necessary proceedings are taken at law to establish the cause of invalidity and to get it quashed or otherwise upset it will remain as effective for its ostensible purpose as the most impeccable of Orders.*"

This analysis would suggest that, once a planning obligation has been executed by all parties, and has come into effect, then it is not open to a third party to seek to set aside the planning obligation. That is to say, those aggrieved by the planning obligation should have sought relief by judicial review at the decision-making stage.

---

[89]   At least, outside the atavistic world of planning enforcement: see "*The Carnwath Report: 30 years on (almost). Reflections on 'nullity' and 'invalidity'*" - The Journal of Planning and Environmental Law, Autumn 2018 @ p.1311.

As to whether or not a failure to comply with Regulation 122 has, by itself, the effect of vitiating a planning obligation the short answer is that (unlike section 106) the regulation does not prescribe the content of planning obligations. It is not an adjunct to section 106. Instead, it limits those matters which a local planning authority may take into account in determining a planning application; hence the words "... *a planning obligation may only constitute a reason for granting planning permission for the development* ...". In the *Aberdeen City* case (see above), Lord Hodge stated:

> *[52] It is important to recall that the question whether a benefit conferred by a planning obligation is a material consideration in the determination of an application for planning permission is quite separate from the question whether a planning obligation restricts or regulates the development or use of a particular piece of land ...*

This distinction must apply equally to the distinction between the effect of Regulation 122 on admissible considerations and the separate validity of a subsequent planning obligation.

## 12.23    Enforcement of planning obligations

The 1990 Act provides a number of powerful enforcement mechanisms.

Section 106(6) provides that, without prejudice to subsection 106(5), if there is a breach of a requirement in a planning obligation to carry out any operations in, on, under or over the land to which the obligation relates, the authority by whom the obligation is enforceable may -

(a)    enter the land and carry out the operations; and

(b)    recover from the person or persons against whom the obligation is enforceable any expenses reasonably incurred by them in doing so.

Before an authority exercises their power under subsection 106(6)(a) they shall give not less than twenty-one days' notice of their intention to do so to any person against whom the planning obligation is enforceable: section 106(7).

Any person who wilfully obstructs a person acting in the exercise of a power under subsection 106(6)(a) shall be guilty of an offence and liable on summary conviction to a fine not exceeding Level 3 on the Standard Scale: section 106(8).

As with many enforcement mechanisms which allow the local planning authority to carry out works in default, the immediate problem is that the planning authority must incur costs before it can reclaim them from the liable party. The harsh truth is that they often do not have the financial resources to do so.

Section 106(5) provides that a restriction or requirement imposed under a planning obligation is enforceable by injunction. This might be a more straightforward approach where the costs of seeking the injunction are not prohibitive.

## 12.24    Release clauses

Section 106(4) provides that the instrument by which a planning obligation is entered into may provide that a person shall not be bound by the obligation in respect of any period during which he no longer has an interest in the land.

It is conventional to exclude individual owner-occupiers of dwellinghouses from the requirements of planning obligations, the obvious exception being on-going affordable housing requirements. However, it might be the case that, if the estate roads are to be maintained by an estate management company, then certain requirements might fall to owner-occupiers, particularly default provisions in respect of any failure of the management company.

## 12.25    The effect of section 73 of the 1990 Act

Section 73 of the 1990 Act allows for applications for planning permission for the development of land without complying with conditions subject to which a previous planning permission was granted. On such an application the local planning authority shall consider only the question of the conditions subject to which planning permission should be granted, and if they decide that planning permission should be granted subject to conditions differing from those subject to which the previous permission was granted, or that it should be granted unconditionally, they shall grant planning permission accordingly.

Whilst an application pursuant to section 73 is often called an application to "*vary conditions*" (or the like), this is not only an incorrect label as a matter of law, but it can produce the false pre-conception that the process merely "*varies*" the original permission; however, this is wrong. The end result of the process is to create an entirely new planning permission which is separate from the original. The section 73 permission should be an entirely new planning permission which is identical to the original save for the varied conditions. That is to say, the developer will then have two permissions in his hands; namely, the original and the new section 73 permission.

In *Pye v The Secretary of State for the Environment and North Cornwall District Council* [1999] P.L.C.R. 28 Sullivan J explained the position as follows:

> "*Whilst Section 73 applications are commonly referred to as applications to "amend" the conditions attached to a planning permission, a decision under section 73(2) leaves the original planning permission intact and unamended. That is so whether the decision is to grant planning permission unconditionally or subject to different conditions under paragraph (a), or to refuse the application under paragraph (b), because planning permission should be granted subject to the same conditions.*
>
> *In the former case the applicant may choose whether to implement the original planning permission or the new planning permission; in the latter case, he is still free to implement the original planning permission. Thus, it is not possible to "go back on the original planning permission" under section 73. It remains as a baseline, whether the application under section 73 is approved or refused, in contrast to the position that previously obtained.*"

This situation can act as trap for the unwary local planning authority.

Whilst not a case on section 73, *R (Robert Hitchins Ltd) v Worcestershire County Council* [2015] EWCA Civ 1060 exemplifies the problem. There a developer obtained a planning permission for a development subject to a planning agreement which required the payment of a transport contribution in three equal payments. The agreement contained the following:

> *"Nothing in this Deed shall be construed as prohibiting or limiting any right to develop any part of the Land in accordance with a planning permission (other than the ... Planning Permission) granted by the City Council or the County Council or by the First Secretary of State on appeal or by reference to him after the date of this Deed."*

The first instalment of the transport contribution had been paid. The developer then obtained a second planning permission on appeal for the same site which was subject to a unilateral undertaking which made no mention of the transport contribution. The central question for the Court of Appeal was whether the developer, having begun the development under the first permission and having thereby become liable for the first instalment of the transport contribution, switched horses following the grant of the second permission and carried out the rest of the development under that second permission, thereby avoiding liability to pay further instalments of the transport contribution. It was held that the developer had so acted and that no further instalments of the transport contribution were payable.

Whilst the facts of this case are unusual, it contains a salutary lesson; namely that where a local planning authority grants a new permission for a site, which is subject to a planning obligation whether by section 73 or otherwise, it should take care that the obligation is not thus excluded by mistake.

The prudent authority will require the execution of a new planning obligation before releasing the new permission. Alternatively, a deed of variation might be executed which extends the original planning obligation to cover both permissions.

It is also open to an authority to draft the original planning obligation in a way which captures any new permissions in respect of the relevant scheme. For example, the definition of "*development*" in it could be drawn widely so as to include not only the scheme permitted by the original planning permission but also any variations to it by way of later planning permissions.

### 12.26    Statutory modification and discharge of existing planning obligations
It is necessary to ensure that any intention to modify or discharge an extant planning obligation does not fall foul of either the terms of the original obligation or the legislation.

Section 106A(1) provides that a planning obligation may not be modified or discharged except:

(a)     by agreement between the authority by whom the obligation is enforceable and the person or persons against whom the obligation is enforceable; or

(b)     in accordance with that section and section 106B.

That is to say, a planning obligation cannot be varied or withdrawn informally (i.e. by an exchange of letters).

If the person seeking a release cannot locate the other liable parties, or they do not agree to the proposed modification or release, then he will need to use the statutory regime under section 106A(1)(b) (see below).

Section 106A(3) provides (in effect) that a person against whom a planning obligation is enforceable may, at any time after the expiry of the *"relevant period"*, apply to the local planning authority by whom the obligation is enforceable for the obligation:

(a)     to have effect subject to such modifications as may be specified in the application; or

(b)     to be discharged.

Section 106A(4) states that the *"relevant period"* means:

(a)     such period as may be prescribed; or

(b)     if no period is prescribed, the period of five years beginning with the date on which the obligation is entered into.

No period has been prescribed by regulation, therefore the five year period in section 106(4)(b) applies.

Section 106A(6) states that where an application is made to an authority under section 106A(3) the authority may determine:

•       that the planning obligation shall continue to have effect without modification;

•       if the obligation no longer serves a useful purpose, that it shall be discharged; or

•       if the obligation continues to serve a useful purpose, but would serve that purpose equally well if it had effect subject to the modification specified in the application, that it shall have effect subject to those modifications.

The making of an application is subject to publicity requirements. The Town and Country Planning (Modification and Discharge of Planning Obligations) Regulations 1992 (S.I. 1992, No. 2832) provide that the applicant must give notice to any other persons against whom the obligation is enforceable (regulation 4) and the authority must publicise the application by site notice, newspaper notice or neighbour notification (regulation 5).

If the authority refuses the application or fails to determine it, then the applicant may appeal to the Secretary of State: section 106B(1).

The statutory regime is available to a single party of a multi-party obligation and those drafting the obligation need to take this into account.

# Chapter 13

# Agreements Under Section 38 Of
# The Highways Act 1980

## 13.1      Introduction

A "*Section 38 Agreement*" is an agreement for the carrying out of highway works made pursuant to section 38 of the Highways Act 1980.

Section 38 Agreements are usually associated with the construction and adoption of estate roads, normally within residential developments. Works which are due to take place on the existing highway network are usually carried out pursuant to a different type of highways agreement (whether by section 278 of the 1980 Act or otherwise).[90] This is the traditional demarcation between section 38 and highways agreements.

The objective of a Section 38 Agreement is to ensure that incoming occupiers are provided with suitable estate roads. The agreement will ensure that the roads are properly constructed and will provide that they will, at an appropriate time, be adopted by the highway authority so as to make them maintainable at the public expense.

## 13.2      Section 38 of the Highways Act 1980

Section 38(3) provides as follows:

> *A local highway authority may agree with any person to undertake the maintenance of a way:*
>
> *(a)*      *which that person is willing and has the necessary power to dedicate as a highway,*
>
> *(b)*      *which is to be constructed by that person, or by a highway authority on his behalf, and which he proposes to dedicate as a highway;*
>
> *and where an agreement is made under this subsection the way to which the agreement relates shall, on such date as may be specified in the agreement become, for the purposes of this Act a highway maintainable at the public expense.*

It will be noted that in section 38(3) the use of the word "*may*" shows that the authority has a discretion as to whether it enters into such an agreement; it is not a duty. Thus it can refuse to enter into such an agreement. Also, the wording goes on to make it clear that the person with whom the highway authority enters into the agreement is the person who "... *is willing and has the necessary power to dedicate as a highway*". The only person with capacity to dedicate land as a highway is the freeholder. It follows that the highway authority's solicitor must check title to the site to ensure that the signatory is, indeed, the freeholder.

Section 38(4) provides that:

---

[90]     See Chapter 15 below.

> *Without prejudice to the provisions of subsection (3) above and subject to the following provisions of this section, a local highway authority may, by agreement with railway, canal or tramway undertakers, undertake to maintain as part of a highway maintainable at the public expense a bridge or viaduct which carries the railway, canal or tramway over such a highway and is to be constructed by those undertakers or by the highway authority on their behalf.*

Section 38(6) provides that:

> *An agreement under this section may contain such provisions as to the dedication as a highway of any road or way to which the agreement relates, the bearing of the expenses of the construction, maintenance or improvement of any highway, road, bridge or viaduct to which the agreement relates and other relevant matters as the authority making the agreement think fit.*

## 13.3    Key considerations

Matters to be considered in respect of, and identified in, a proposed Section 38 Agreement may include:

- connection to the existing highway network;

- land on which carriageways can be built;

- land for footways, if any;

- footpath links to other highways;

- adequate drainage for the highway, including (perhaps) off-site easements;

- a system of lighting;

- turning heads and parking places;

- private accesses;

- landscaping;

- commuted payments; and

- service margins.

In particular, it is important to decide whether or not any of these elements will be maintained by an estate management company.

## 13.4    Common elements of a Section 38 Agreement

These are:

- Payment of the council's charges and costs.

- The execution of the works.

- The issue of a "Part 1 Certificate" on practical completion of the main works.

- The issue of a "Part 2 Certificate" on practical completion of the balance of the works.

- The provision of a maintenance period.

- Final certification of the works when all remedial works arising during the maintenance period have been rectified.

- Adoption of the new street.

- A bond.

- Public liability insurance.

- An indemnity.

- Provision for commuted payments for future maintenance.

## 13.5    Section 38 and trunk roads

Section 38(3A) allows the Minister to enter into a Section 38 Agreement where it is proposed that the way will become part of a trunk road on its completion.

Where an agreement is made under this provision, then the way shall become a highway maintainable at the public expense on the date on which an order under section 10 of the 1980 Act (directing that the way shall become a trunk road) comes into force or, if later, the date on which the way is opened for the purposes of through traffic.

## 13.6    Sequence for a simple Section 38 Agreement

As with any other technical exercise, the use of Section 38 Agreements can have differing degrees of complexity. In many cases, the proposed road works are relatively simple and it follows that the agreement need not be overly sophisticated. This following diagram shows the process which goes with a very simple Section 38 Agreement.

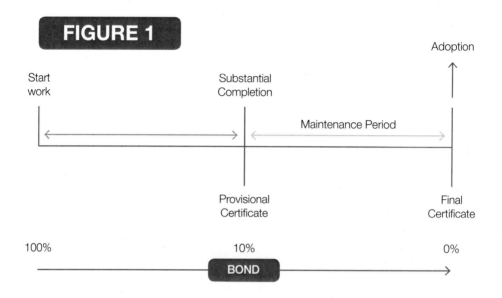

## 13.7    With Part 1 and Part 2 stages

If the scheme is more complex, the provisional certificate stage might, then, be split into two discrete components. These will be called, respectively, the "Part 1 Works" and the "Part 2 Works". The purpose behind this division of the provisional certificate stage is, in the main, driven by the bonding arrangements. As will be explained below, the figure secured by the bond is reduced on a stage by stage basis throughout the section 38 process. If the two part approach is taken, the bond will be reduced on the issue of the "Part 1 Certificate" and then reduced again on the issue of the "Part 2 Certificate". Otherwise, the overall structure is very similar to the process shown in Figure 1: viz.

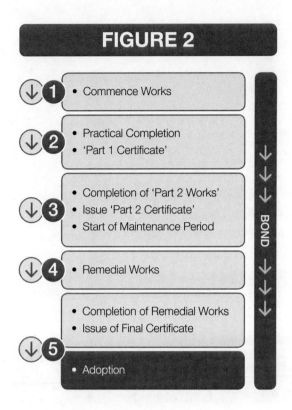

**FIGURE 2**

- ① • Commence Works
- ② • Practical Completion
      • 'Part 1 Certificate'
- ③ • Completion of 'Part 2 Works'
      • Issue 'Part 2 Certificate'
      • Start of Maintenance Period
- ④ • Remedial Works
      • Completion of Remedial Works
      • Issue of Final Certificate
- ⑤ • Adoption

BOND

### 13.8    With an estate management company

It is, nowadays, not unusual to find that some of the common parts within a new estate will be maintained privately by way of an estate management company. Many Section 106 Agreements are, now, drafted on that basis. This might mean that certain of the estate roads will not be adopted but, more likely, the drainage arrangements might not be adopted. This is particularly the case where the drainage arrangements are by way of sustainable drainage systems with relatively high maintenance costs. Clearly, these are matters of concern to the highway authority in relation to the drainage of estate roads. It is, therefore, important to impose a stage within the section 38 process which ensures that those estate roads which are going to be adopted will be adequately drained in perpetuity. This means that the highway authority should examine the arrangements for the estate management company to ensure that it is fit for purpose and will not go bankrupt. Therefore the highway authority should be heavily involved in the process of setting up the estate management company. Unfortunately, it is fair to say that this is not always the case.

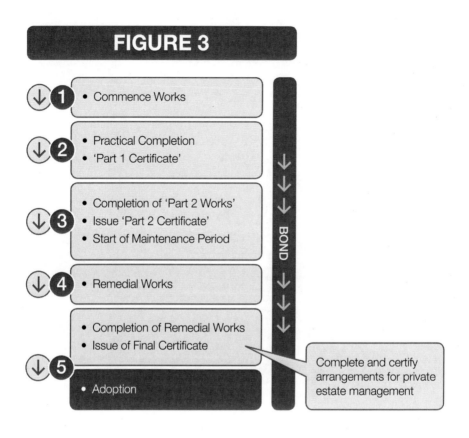

**FIGURE 3**

1 • Commence Works

2 • Practical Completion
  • 'Part 1 Certificate'

3 • Completion of 'Part 2 Works'
  • Issue 'Part 2 Certificate'
  • Start of Maintenance Period

4 • Remedial Works

  • Completion of Remedial Works
  • Issue of Final Certificate

5
  • Adoption

BOND

Complete and certify arrangements for private estate management

### 13.9 Bonding arrangements

The purpose behind the bond will be to ensure that adequate financial security is provided throughout the section 38 process, the objective being to ensure that if the highway authority has to "*step-in*" to complete the works in default, then it can draw down the costs of doing so from the surety.[91]

### 13.10 The description of the Works

The works for the construction of the estate roads and associated infrastructure should be described both verbally in the agreement itself and also by way of appropriate drawings which are attached to the agreement.

If the provisional stage is divided into "*Part 1 Works*" and "*Part 2 Works*", then there will be separate descriptions for each stage.

---

[91] Hence the phrase "*step-in*" rights.

Whichever approach is adopted, the agreement should provide for adjustments to the descriptions and the drawings during the course of the process. It is almost inevitable that detailed changes will take place from time to time as the works are constructed.

### 13.11　Practical completion

Works are generally considered to be practically complete when there are no outstanding defects (except for minor items or "*snagging*") and they can be put to their intended use. Practical completion is referred to as "*substantial completion*" in some forms of contract.

If practical completion follows the common two stage approach, then there will be two certificates; namely, the "*Part 1 Certificate*" and the "*Part 2 Certificate*". In that case, the maintenance period will begin on the issue of the Part 2 Certificate.

### 13.12　Maintenance period

In building contracts the "*maintenance period*" is often called the "*defects liability period*" or the "*rectification period*". The reason for the different terminology in Section 38 Agreements is probably due to the fact that it is important, with highway works, to identify not only who is responsible for rectification of the works but also to appropriate responsibility for day to day maintenance, that is to say, to distinguish the unadopted roads from highways maintainable at the public expense. The maintenance period normally begins upon certification of practical completion or (if completion is in two stages) the issue of the Part 2 Certificate. It typically lasts 12 months but the period should extend automatically to cover any additional time needed to carry out and test works of rectification.

During the maintenance period the developer should carry out such repairs and maintenance as may be necessary to facilitate safe and convenient use by the public of the estate roads. The developer should, also, be responsible for the payment of energy charges in respect of all street lights and illuminated traffic signs.

During this period, the developer should report any defects that arise to the highway authority and the authority will carry out its own inspections.

If the highway authority considers there are defects, then it will issue instructions to the developer to make them good by way of "*remedial works*" within a reasonable time. It is important to note that, whilst the nominal maintenance period will be for a fixed period (normally 12 months), the agreement should provide that that period will be extended in the event that the remedial works are not carried out to the satisfaction of the highway authority. If the remedial works are significant, then it is not unusual to find that the maintenance period can be extended by months or even years.

### 13.13　The Final Certificate

The agreement will provide that the estate roads become highways maintainable at public expense upon the issue of the final certificate. The bond will be released entirely at that stage.

Given that both the developer and the surety will be free of any obligation under the agreement from the date of the final certificate, it follows that the highway authority must be assured that not only is the highway fit for purpose but also that associated infrastructure has been provided to a suitable standard. This is particularly so in connection with the drainage. Accordingly, the release of the final certificate will be dependent upon the developer satisfying the highway authority that all of these measures are in place. Thus, for example, it is highly unlikely that any highway authority will issue a final certificate if those drains which are proposed for adoption are not the subject of an appropriate arrangement under section 104 of the Water Industry Act 1991.

## 13.14    The status of the section 38 land prior to adoption

The land which is subject to a Section 38 Agreement will not undergo an immediate transition from part of a building site to an adopted highway. The transition will normally occur after the passage of some time, during which the way will probably have been opened to traffic, constructed to practical completion and undergone a maintenance period of at least 12 months. It is necessary to consider how these changes will affect the legal status of the land.

One popular theory is that, during this interim period, the way becomes an unadopted highway at common law. The theory is attractive, but it needs to be analysed.

A highway may be created at common law by implied dedication and acceptance. If the landowner allows the public to use a defined corridor across his land for passage and repassage, without licence and "*as of right*", then it is possible that, by his acquiescence, he has allowed the creation of a highway at common law. His dedication of the way, as a highway, might be implied from the circumstances as a whole. If, as in the case of section 38 works, the landowner has constructed a way across his land with the obvious intention that it is to be thrown open to the public as a highway and then he allows public passage and repassage across it, the inference that he intended to dedicate the way would be very strong and the period of public user could be correspondingly short – perhaps a matter of months rather than years. One can see how this might lead the observer to conclude that a way which has been constructed pursuant to a Section 38 Agreement, and then opened to the public for a matter of months or years, could become an unadopted highway at common law.

However, this theory could be questioned where the terms of the Section 38 Agreement make it apparent that this was never the intention of the landowner. The reality will usually be that the agreement makes it clear that the way is to become an adopted highway on the issue of the final certificate and not before. It is, therefore, necessary to ask how it can be implied that the landowner intended to create, or acquiesced in the creation of, an unadopted highway at common law.

The better response to this point is, perhaps, to say that the Section 38 Agreement sets the terms for the creation of a way which is to become a highway maintainable at the public expense, but if it is silent as to the point, it does not preclude the creation of an unadopted highway at common law. It is difficult to see how a developer can build a way so that it is effective for public passage and repassage, install street lighting, drainage, street name plates etc and then meaningfully contend that the opening of it to the public (who then use it for passage and repassage) is devoid of legal meaning.

The situation is, perhaps, clearer if a way is constructed pursuant to a Section 38 Agreement, is then opened to and used by the public and the final certificate is either never issued or is delayed for a period of years. It might be that the courts would, in such a situation, decide that the landowner's original intentions under the Section 38 Agreement (whatever they might have been) have been superceded by the passage of time and that he has acquiesced in the continued user of the way as a highway by the public for so long that his dedication may be implied.

In *Bromley Local Board v Lansbury* (1894)[92], a new road was laid out in 1878, and in 1884, buildings having been erected on each side of the road, an arrangement not under seal was made between the defendant (who was one of the frontagers) and the Local Board that the new road should be made up to the satisfaction of the Board's surveyor, should be kept in repair by the frontagers for six months and that the Board should then adopt the road. This arrangement was carried out, but the Local Board did not, after the expiration of the six months, give the usual notice of adoption under section 152 of the Public Health Act 1875. Subsequently, in consequence of heavy traffic, the road fell into disrepair, and the Local Board paved the road under the provision of section 150 and sought to recover a share of the expenses from the defendant. It was held by a Divisional Court that the Local Board, having accepted the work thus done by the defendant, were bound by the arrangement come to in 1884.

Perhaps the answer to this apparent conundrum is (with new agreements), simply, to provide for the creation of an unadopted highway in the Section 38 Agreement itself, viz:

> *"On the completion of the Part 1 Works in accordance with this Agreement: ...the Engineer shall issue the Part 1 Certificate and from the date thereof: ...the Ways shall become highways maintainable by the Owner ...".*

## 13.15    Dedication for section 38

It should be trite that one of the first questions for the highway authority must go to the capacity of the person who is making a dedication which will have the effect of making the relevant ways into highways. The short answer is that this person must be the freehold owner of the land because only the freeholder has the legal capacity to create a perpetual public interest in his land. Hence, the offer of a leaseholder or a person with an option to purchase will not suffice.

In theory, the fact that the land is held in trust should not be a barrier; however, it is often the case that the constitutions of trusts are not up to date, with the result that one sometimes finds that those being held out as trustees are not duly appointed.

---

[92]    (1894), The Times, December 5th; 16 M.C.C. 574. Courtesy of Pratt & Mackenzie ibid @ p.548. See also *Folkestone Corporation v Marsh* (1906) 70 J.P. 113 and *Folkestone Corporation v Rook* (1907) 71 J.P. 550.

If the land is subject to a mortgage, then the mortgagee should be made a party to the agreement and should consent to the dedication. This will avoid any possible complications in the event that the mortgagee takes possession before the highway status of the ways is perfected. Otherwise, it might be possible to argue that the pre-existing mortgage had the effect of restricting the landowner's power to dedicate.

One can also foresee the potential for a dispute where the proposed way is over a pre-existing private right of way or crosses one. Again, the prudent highway authority lawyer will seek to include those persons as consenting parties to the Section 38 Agreement.

In *Man O'War Station Limited v Auckland City Council (No. 2)* [2002] U.K.P.C. 32, Lord Scott of Foscote stated (on behalf of the Privy Council):

> *[49] The point was taken, on behalf of the appellant, that the consent of third parties with an interest in the land over which the road ran was necessary in order for there to be an effective dedication but was absent. Their Lordships accept the principle that a person with an interest in the land inconsistent with the public right of way must consent to the dedication if the dedication is to be effective. So, if the land is subject to a mortgage, the mortgagee must consent, and, if it is subject to a lease, the lessee cannot dedicate without the consent of the lessor (see Griffith CJ in Narracan at p 864).*

Sauvain's advice on the point is that the test in each case ought to be whether the landowner has sufficient interest in the land to create a permanent right over it or whether the creation of such a right will require the agreement of the party with his own interest in the land.[93]

Section 38(3) provides, where an agreement is made under this subsection, the way to which the agreement relates shall, on such date as may be specified in the agreement, become for the purposes of this Act a highway maintainable at the public expense. It follows that the parties must specify a date upon which the way will become a highway maintainable at the public expense. The agreement will not normally specify a date as such; instead it will normally identify this date as being the day upon which the final certificate is issued. For example:

> *"At the end of the maintenance period the County Surveyor shall satisfy himself that the Street has been kept in good repair and condition and thereupon the County Surveyor shall issue a final certificate and thereafter the Street shall become a highway maintainable at the public expense".*

A Section 38 Agreement does not automatically run with the land – i.e. it does not automatically bind the successors in title of the landowner who originally signed the agreement. This can cause problems with, among other things, dedication of the land as a highway. The agreement might provide that not only the adoption but also the dedication shall occur only upon the date of issue of the final certificate. This has the advantage that the

---

[93]   Ibid @ p.50.

dedication and adoption will be based on the *"as-built"* drawings, thereby absorbing any variations which might have occurred during the construction period. There is, however, a shortcoming to this approach in that the land may have changed hands between the date of execution of the agreement and the issue of the final certificate. If the date of dedication is at the end of the process, then there is the possibility that a change of ownership before the issue of the final certificate might frustrate the dedication. This can be seen from the Court of Appeal decision in *Overseas Investment Services Limited v Simcobuild Construction Limited and Swansea City Council* (1995) 70 P. & C.R. 322.

In the *Overseas Investment Services* case, the Section 38 Agreement was entered into in 1983 to create a highway across one site (*"the front land"*) to serve another (*"the rear land"*). The front land and rear land were in separate ownerships. The rear land was only accessible by passing over the front land and the developer intended to construct an access road across the front land to the rear land. Under the agreement the Council acquired the right to bring about the future construction of a highway maintainable at public expense over a specified part of the front land, either by requiring the developer to build it, or by carrying out the works itself if the developer defaulted. That right was never registered by the Council. The owner of the front land sold it to Overseas Investment Services Limited (*"OISL"*) in 1987 and then went into liquidation. In the event, the developer did not built the road. The Council subsequently issued a default notice under the agreement prior to itself building a road over the front land to the rear land. No final certificate was issued in respect of completion of that road until June 1988. OISL then prevented access to the rear land over the road. The question for the court was whether OISL was entitled to do so. The issue between the parties turned on the meaning to be given to *"public rights"* in section 70(1)(a) of the Land Registration Act 1925, whether the rights created by the agreement were *"public rights"* (even though the road had not been built by the time OISL bought the front land) and, if so, whether by operation of section 70(1)(a) they were overriding and binding on OISL as a subsequent purchaser of the land who was obliged to allow access over the road. The Court of Appeal held that a *"public right"* is a right exercisable by anyone, whether he owns land or not, merely by virtue of the general law. On that test the rights under the agreement were not public rights as no member of the public could exercise any right of way over the front land at the time of its purchase by OISL, there being no highway across it at that time, and no member of the public had any right to require the Council to procure a highway to come into existence on the front land. Accordingly, the rights were not public rights within the meaning of section 70(1)(a) of the Land Registration Act 1925 and OISL took the front land free from them.

Gibson LJ added that the agreement could have been protected by expressing the agreement to have been made under section 33 of the Local Government (Miscellaneous Provisions) Act 1982. He also referred to section 87 of the New Roads and Street Works Act 1991.

These comments do not stand up to critical analysis. As Sauvain pointed out[94], section 33 of the Local Government (Miscellaneous Provisions) Act 1982 cannot be used for the purpose

---

[94]    Ibid @ p.141.

of facilitating or in connection with the development of land – which would almost inevitably be the case with a Section 38 Agreement. Some agreements recite, instead, section 106 of the Town and Country Planning Act 1990, but section 106 does not allow for a positive obligation which can oblige a future owner to dedicate land as a highway or give effect to an undertaking to dedicate. The best that can be achieved is a *"Grampian"* type embargo, within section 106(1)(a) of the 1990 Act, on the carrying out or occupation of parts of the development unless and until the dedication takes place. But it is questionable whether this is realistic because the estate will have been built and, in all probability, occupied long before the maintenance period has run its course. Furthermore, section 106A of the 1990 Act allows for the review of a Section 106 Agreement after five years. If things go slowly or some of the terms of the Section 38 Agreement last a long time, then the rights to modify or discharge the Section 106 Agreement may come into operation irrespective of the state of play on the section 38 part of the agreement.

As to section 87 of the New Roads and Street Works Act 1991, this simply allows for a declaration, by the street authority, that a street will become a maintainable highway in order to regulate undertakers' works. Section 87 does not provide a mechanism which creates such a highway, per se.

It is fair to say that the relevant clause in the *Overseas Investment Services* case left a lot to be desired. Gibson LJ set out the clause as follows:

> *"By clause (15): Upon the issue of the final certificate or certificates as herein provided [R. & K.] hereby give up and dedicate to the public land on which the works are intended to be constructed or such part of such land as shall be covered by the final certificate or certificates TO THE INTENT that the said land shall become a public highway up to and including the boundary of the said land with other land as indicated on the plan."*

His Lordship then commented:

> *"This clause is an unhappy mixture of present and future events. It purports to be a present dedication ("hereby [...] dedicate"), yet it is qualified by the words "Upon the issue of the final certificate or certificates as herein provided", plainly a future and (in view of the provisions for termination of the agreement) contingent event. Further, the land to be dedicated as a highway would not be finally identified until the issue of the final certificate or certificates. To my mind what was intended by the clause was that R. & K. [i.e. the original landowner] would make a dedication in such form as would obviate the necessity of any further act of dedication on its part. To that extent it was a present dedication but could not be effective until the issue of the final certificate, which was the date specified in the agreement for the purposes of section 38(3) for the way to become a highway maintainable at the public expense."*

In *Secretary of State for the Environment, Transport and the Regions v Baylis (Gloucester) Ltd* [2000] 4 W.L.U.K. 463, Mr Kim Lewison QC (sitting as a Deputy Judge of the Chancery

Division) had to consider the effect of the following words in deed between a landowner and a highway authority:

> *"NOW IT IS HEREBY AGREED as follows:*
>
> *1. In pursuance of the said Agreement and in consideration of the sum of Sixty Four pounds now paid by the Council to the Landowners ... and of the Council executing the works hereinafter mentioned the Landowners hereby forthwith GIVE UP AND DEDICATE TO THE PUBLIC for the purpose aforesaid ALL THAT piece of land containing an area of 0.77 of an acre or thereabouts situate on the north side of the Road Number A438 leading from Teddington to Tewkesbury in the Parish of Ashchurch in the County of Gloucester ... TO THE INTENT THAT the said piece of land shall be added to and form part of the highway ...".*

He stated (by reference to the similar clause in the *Overseas Investment Services* case):

> *"In my judgment the clause in the present case is not the same unhappy mixture. It is, in my judgment, consistent only with an immediate dedication. First, the phrase "hereby ... dedicate" is, ... a present dedication. Second, far from qualifying that present dedica-tion, the word "forthwith" reinforces it. Third, although the memorandum contemplates that work will be carried out in the future, there is no linguistic linkage between that obligation and the dedication, except to the extent that the carrying out of the work is part of the consideration for the dedication. ... In so far as an element of futurity is necessary, it is to be found in the notion that the land is to be part of the highway with effect from the dedication. ... Fourth, the land to be dedicated was identified in the memorandum of agreement. Fifth, there were no provisions for the termination of the agreement. I come to the conclusion, therefore, that a present intention to dedicate as a highway is established."*

## 13.16    Acceptance and section 38

It will be recalled that express "*dedication*" occurs where the landowner declares that the public may use his land as a highway[95] and "*acceptance*" occurs where the public accept the landowner's dedication. The highway does not come into being unless and until the terms of both the dedication and acceptance have been satisfied.

In the *Baylis* case (see above), Deputy Judge Lewison was required to consider what amounted to acceptance in the case of an express dedication; in particular, whether actual use by the public of their right to pass and repass is the only way in which acceptance can be proved or whether the way can be accepted by the highway authority on behalf of the public. In other words, actual use by the public is not merely a sufficient condition for establishing acceptance; it is a necessary condition. He noted that, if acceptance by the public in that case can only be established by actual use by the public, then odd results could follow:

---

[95]    See para. 3.6 above.

> *"But suppose that the landowner had expressly dedicated the land for use as a highway. When the first member of the public approached the newly dedicated highway, could the landowner bar his entry? If actual use by the public is necessary before the highway can come into existence, logic would suggest that the answer is "yes". For until the first member of the public has actually used the highway, he has no right to do so. And if he has no right to do so, he would appear to be trespassing on the land. The logical impasse suggests to me that I should look critically at the submission that only actual use by the public can constitute acceptance, even where there is an express dedication."*

Following analysis of the historical case law he concluded that, under modern highways legislation, the highway authority is, so to speak, the representative of the public and has the ability to accept a highway on behalf of the public:

> *"It [the authority] has a statutory duty to assert and protect the rights of the public over highways. ...In my judgment, a highway authority has the ability to accept a highway on behalf of the public. Evidence of acceptance by the highway authority is, therefore, capable of amounting to proof of acceptance by the public. An acceptance could, in my judgment, be proved by showing that the highway authority had agreed in writing to accept the dedication or by showing that an appropriate committee of the highway authority had resolved to do so. It is not invariably necessary to show actual exercise by members of the public of their rights of passage in the case of an express dedication."*

Whilst this was a decision at first instance, it is suggested that it is, with respect, impeccable and it is difficult to see any dissent from it by another court. The only additional point to make is that, of course, a committee may delegate this function to an officer of the authority.

The parties may seek to structure the agreement so that, if the terms of both dedication by the landowner and acceptance by the highway authority stipulate that the highway shall come into being upon the issue of the final certificate, then this will be the way in which the agreement unfolds.

### 13.17    The physical extent of a dedication
*Rowley v Tottenham Urban District Council* [1914] A.C. 95 is instructive. The submitted plan for a proposed housing estate showed a road with a total width of forty feet. The road would connect with two highways. The developer built the houses and made-up the road for one half of its width next to the houses. But the other half width was left unmetalled. The road was then used for the purposes of the estate and as a thoroughfare by pedestrians, cyclists and carts without interruption for about three years, the metalled part being used in preference to the unmetalled part. The House of Lords held that, on the evidence, there had been a dedication of the whole width of the road as a highway. As Sir Herbert Cozens Hardy MR stated:

> *"I think it must be a dedication of the whole or none, and I am satisfied that the latter alternative would do great injustice."*

In the *Baylis* case (see above), Deputy Judge Lewison posed the following question:

*"Can use of part of dedicated land amount to an acceptance of the whole?"*

He concluded that:

*"In my judgment it can. ...To reach any other conclusion would lead to strange results. Suppose that the owner dedicates a road one mile long. If a member of the public used the first quarter of a mile and then turned off the road, could it really be said that the remaining three quarters of a mile were not highway? In my judgment, no. Part of the reason why a land owner dedicated land as a highway (at least before the 1835 Act) was to relieve himself of the burden of repair. It would not be just to allow the public to take the benefit of those parts of the road which were in repair, and to repudiate liability to repair those parts of the road which were not."*

The position becomes more complicated where it transpires that parts of the way which have been constructed pursuant to a Section 38 Agreement do not, in fact, fall within the boundaries of the drawing (if there is one) showing the extent of the dedication land. In most cases, the only answer is to resort to one of the remedies for a *"failed"* agreement mentioned at para. 13.21 below, the most robust being a deed of novation to substitute the original drawings for the *"as-built"* drawings. However, the courts have provided remedies in some cases.

In *Floyd v Redcar & Cleveland Borough Council* [2009] EWCA Civ 1137 the Claimant was injured when he tripped on an uneven area of pavement and claimed that the highway authority was responsible for the area as forming part of the adopted highway, which it was liable to maintain. He contended that the authority had adopted the area pursuant to a Section 38 Agreement entered into in 1982, notwithstanding that it was unclear whether the area fell within the agreement at all. The Court of Appeal held that, nonetheless, the disputed area had been adopted.

The agreement showed a considerable degree of detail as to what was required in relation to the works, including the footways. It appeared that a provisional certificate had been issued which should have certified that the works conformed with the agreement. However, the layout of the development differed from the agreement plan in a number of respects. The relevant area had, so far as was known, always served as a footway. The borough engineer had clearly been satisfied in 1984 that the footway should be adopted pursuant to the agreement. He recommended adoption in 1984 on the footing of the plan that was then prepared. Given all those facts, the local authority had been entitled to regard the agreement as substantially complied with and accordingly to adopt the works.

Whilst instructive, this case turned (as such cases often do) on its particular facts and so, it is suggested, it is not an example of good practice. Indeed, the court went on to make it clear that there might be a case where the distance between the Section 38 Agreement and what was purported to be adopted under it would be so great that there was, in truth, no statutory adoption.[96]

The Court of Appeal was more robust in *Betterment Properties (Weymouth) Limited v James Carthy & Company Limited* [2010] EWCA Civ 1401. This case concerned a purported "*ransom*" strip which lay between a developer's frontage land and a made-up road, access across the strip being essential to the proposed development. A Section 38 Agreement had provided for the construction of the made-up road and its dedication as a highway. The road was constructed and approved by the authority but the disputed strip of land was not included in the dedication. The putative owner of the disputed strip argued that the developer's land lay behind the area marked for adoption on the plan for the agreement and that the agreement thereby excluded the strip for the purposes of adoption. The Court of Appeal agreed and held that the disputed strip had not been adopted. The point of the adoption plan was, in part, to provide precision as to where the road was to be. The only obligation which could be derived from the agreement was to construct a new road up to the line on the plan, which did not cover the entire disputed strip.

### 13.18    The problem of successors in title – again!

Some authorities seek to circumvent the problem of successors in title entirely by requiring the landowner to dedicate the way to be constructed as a highway when the agreement is entered into, but to leave acceptance of that dedication until the issue of the final certificate. A common example as to dedication is:

> "*The Owner dedicates a right of way as a highway to the use of the public for all purposes over the land described in the first schedule and within the limits shown and defined on the plan annexed*".

And as to acceptance:

> "*The Street shall become a highway maintainable at the public expense on the date of issue of the Final Certificate*".

This approach also gives rise to a practical problem; namely, that the landowner will be dedicating the way as specified in the drawings annexed to the agreement. If it later transpires that the way was not constructed in accordance with the drawings, then any deviations will not be covered by the original dedication. It is difficult to see how this problem could be overcome by providing that the dedication relates to such land as is identified when the final certificate is issued, because a landowner cannot, realistically, dedicate land which will be identified at a later date. Furthermore, a covenant which requires the owner to dedicate the way after it has been completed does not run with the land and, as such, would not be binding on successors in title.

---

[96]    By way of a helpful tip, it is often helpful to look out materials which show the area which was in question in a judgment. Close scale maps and aerial photographs are often readily available on the internet, including ancient maps. The author examined this site in good detail via *Google Earth*. The physical character of the *locus in quo* was, perhaps, more compelling than a reading of the judgment alone might suggest.

A "*belt and braces*" approach to the problem of ensuring enforceability against successors in title is evident in the use, in some modern agreements, of clauses which amount to options to purchase. This practice appears to take up some of the further comments made by Gibson LJ in the *Overseas Investment Services* case. Gibson LJ's comments related to the fact that the Section 38 Agreement in that case included, within it, the option for the Council to acquire the freehold to the way. He added that, at the most, there was an option in the agreement existing for the benefit of the public but which was void for want of registration as the Council had failed to take any of the protective measures available to it, whether by registering an estate contract as a land charge, or lodging a caution or notice under the Land Registration Act 1925: see now the Land Registration Act 2002.

There is nothing to prevent a highway authority from adding such an option by way of a safeguard (coupled with a bond) and then protecting its position by registration. If the landowner's successor in title defaults, then the authority will have the ability to exercise the option, obtain the freehold and complete the adoption procedure at the cost of the surety.

If an authority has entered into a Section 38 Agreement without the benefit of such an option, then a failure of the dedication mechanism may have to be met by one of the procedures for rescuing "*failed agreements*" mentioned at para. 13.21 below.

One question which might arise is why have both an option to purchase and a dedication mechanism in the same agreement? If the authority is going to the trouble of requiring an option, then why not simply rely on the option and convey the land when the final certificate is issued? The short answer is that conveying the land to the authority is not normally required (because a dedication is usually enough to create the highway) and carrying out a conveyance involves unnecessary time and costs. The incorporation of the option is, therefore, simply an insurance.

One common example of an option to purchase is:

> "*If and when called upon by the Council to do so within 21 years from the date of this Agreement the Developer shall prove its title to the Land dedicated to the public and shall transfer with full title guarantee to the Council or its nominee the freehold estate in the Land*".

Some critical observations can be made about this draft. The authority has to decide whether it wishes to capture any deviations between the original scheme drawings and the final "*as-built*" drawings. If so, the option would have to be drafted so as to be exercisable against the "*as-built*" drawings. This draft does not cover this point – because the option clause does not contain a mechanism that caters for deviations from the original scheme drawings. As noted above, it is possible to stipulate that the definition of the "*Land*" should include additional land within reasonable limits of deviation. There is, then, no reason why the option clause should not allow for the authority to call for all or part of the land thus defined.

A better example would be:

> *"Definition: the "Option Land" means the Adoption Land and such other land as may be shown as being part of the Ways by the Drawings".*

> *"If and when called upon by the Council to do so within 21 years from the date of this Agreement the Developer shall transfer with full title guarantee to the Council or its nominee the freehold estate free from incumbrances in the Option Land or such part of it as may be nominated by the Council".*

### 13.19    Interface with agreements under the Water Industry Act 1991

The objective is that the drainage system for the new roads will be adopted by the sewerage undertaker before the roads are adopted by the local highway authority.

Section 104 of the Water Industry Act 1991 provides for agreements to adopt sewers, drains or sewage disposal works at a future date by the sewerage undertaker.

Section 104(1) provides that a sewerage undertaker may agree with any person constructing or proposing to construct:

(a)    any sewer;

(b)    any drain which is intended to communicate with a public sewer vested in that undertaker; or

(c)    any sewage disposal works,

that, if the sewer, drain or sewage disposal works is or are constructed in accordance with the terms of the agreement, the undertaker will, upon completion of the work, at some specified date or on the happening of some future event, declare the sewer or such part of the drain as constitutes the lateral drain or the works (as the case may be) to be vested in that undertaker.

In essence the process for a sewer adoption through a Section 104 Agreement generally runs as follows:

- The developer enters into a *"Section 104 Agreement"* with the sewerage undertaker and then begins building the sewers.

- The undertaker's inspection team monitors the works on site and signs off testing, etc.

- The developer supplies drawings showing the sewers *"as-built"*.

- When the sewers are built and the majority of premises are occupied, the developer requests a joint inspection.

- If the sewers are found to be satisfactory, then the sewerage undertaker will issue a provisional certificate and the maintenance period (usually 3 to 12 months) commences. The developer remains liable for the maintenance of the sewers.

- A joint final inspection is arranged just before the end of the maintenance period.

- After any remedial works are completed, the sewerage undertaker will issue a final certificate and adopt the sewers.

- Once adopted the sewers become public sewers and the sewerage undertaker is then responsible for the maintenance and repair of them.

The interface between the Section 38 Agreement and the Section 104 Agreement is achieved by tying the issue of completion certificates under the Section 38 Agreement to the comparable stages under the section 104 process. Thus:

**Stage 1**: The Part 1 Certificate under the Section 38 Agreement should not be issued until the developer has entered into the Section 104 Agreement with the sewerage undertaker.

**Stage 2**: The Part 2 Certificate under the Section 38 Agreement should not be issued until the provisional certificate has been issued under the Section 104 Agreement.

**Stage 3**: The Final Certificate under the Section 38 Agreement should not be issued until the final certificate has been issued under the Section 104 Agreement.

### 13.20 "Failed" Section 38 Agreements

As noted above, the only person who has the capacity to dedicate land for the purposes of a highway is the freeholder. If the developer owns the site but then sells the land over which the way is, or will be, constructed pursuant to the Section 38 Agreement, or a part of it, before he signs the agreement, then the agreement will not be effective to secure the adoption of the way. This can happen where the developer is dilatory in settling the agreement and engages in plot sales before the agreement is executed. If the highway authority fails to spot these plot sales[97], then the land involved in them will not be captured by the agreement and will not form part of the adopted highway.[98] This would suggest that the prudent highway authority would ask for a schedule of plot sales to the date of execution of the agreement.

---

[97] Sometimes by not carrying out last minute Land Registry searches before or, perhaps, because plot sales have taken place but have yet to reach the Land Registry.

[98] Orlik said (in 2001) that the solicitor for the purchaser of a new house on a new estate is able to ask the local authority whether there is a Section 38 Agreement and whether it is supported by a bond: ibid @ p.28. This is true, but one might be forgiven for wondering why those dealing with the conveyancing process on behalf of the buyer sometimes fail to spot this obvious defect in title.

If the way has been constructed to an adoptable standard, then there are two options available to the highway authority which is seeking to retrieve the situation - but neither of them are foolproof.

First, to try to persuade the relevant freeholders to enter into dedication agreements in respect of the sections of way which suffer from defective title. This tactic may work where the consent of only one or two landowners is needed, but it is likely to be unworkable where numerous freeholders are involved.[99]

Secondly, the highway authority may invoke the procedure stipulated by section 228 of the Highways Act 1980 (see para. 13.21 below). Unfortunately, there is a shortcoming in that affected frontagers have certain rights of objection which may delay or even frustrate the procedure.

If the way has not been constructed to an adoptable standard, then the position is even more complicated because the developer no longer has the capacity to enter those parts of the way which have been conveyed and cannot be required to enter them to finish the works. If the consent of the freeholders to the carrying out of the works can be procured then it might be possible to press the developer into service by the threat of legal action. Failing that, the highway authority will have the ability to make up the way under the Private Street Works Code. The authority may think about recharging the frontagers for the costs of doing so, but it might be unwise to do so when the authority was at fault in not spotting the defect in title in the first place.

### 13.21    The section 228 procedure
In essence, section 228 provides that, when any street works have been executed in a private street, the Street Works Authority may, by a notice displayed in a prominent position in the street, declare the street (or part of a street) to be a highway which is a highway maintainable at the public expense. If completed highway works fall within this provision, then it might be possible to adopt them notwithstanding that the landowner has not engaged in formal adoption or dedication procedures.

The procedure under section 228 of the Highways Act 1980 can be engaged only where the way or section of way in question qualifies as a "*private street*" and works have been carried out in respect of it which, in turn, qualify as "*street works*".

As explained in para. 7.5, section 203(2) provides that a "*private street*" means a "*street*" that is not a highway maintainable at the public expense. It is necessary to analyse this less than straightforward definition in some depth.

The word "*street*" is itself defined in section 329(1) of the 1980 Act as having the same meaning as in Part III of the New Roads and Street Works Act 1991. Section 48(1) of the 1991 Act states:

---

[99]    The author speaks from sad experience.

*"In this Part a "street" means the whole or any part of any of the following, irrespective of whether it is a thoroughfare –*

*(a) any highway, road, lane, footway, alley or passage,*

*(b) any square or court, and*

*(c) any land laid out as a way whether it is for the time being formed as a way or not."*

Regardless of whether one can describe a way constructed pursuant to a Section 38 Agreement as a *"highway"*, it is clear that it will comprise a *"road, lane, footway, alley or passage"*. There is nothing in the section 48 definition to suggest that any of these ways has to be a highway. On the other hand, it does not preclude (and, indeed, facilitates) the adoption of currently unadopted highways.

As to *"street works"*, section 203(3) of the 1980 Act provides that *"street works"* means any works for the sewering, levelling, paving, metalling, flagging, channelling and making good of a street, and includes the provision of proper means for lighting a street; and *"paving, metalling and flagging"* includes all methods of making a carriageway or footway. The definition does not stipulate that the works must have been carried out by the Street Works Authority; therefore works executed under a Section 38 Agreement should qualify.

It follows that all of the prerequisites for the engagement of the section 228 procedure should be available where a way has been constructed pursuant to a Section 38 Agreement and one or more of the freeholders was not a signatory party.

One difficulty is that section 228(2) provides that a street shall not become a highway maintainable at the public expense if the owner of the street or, if more than one, the majority in number of the owners of the street, by notice to the authority object; if such an objection is made, then the Street Works Authority may apply to a magistrates' court for an order overruling the objection.

### 13.22    Commuted payments

Sauvain comments[100] that there is an increasing tendency for local highway authorities to seek within Section 38 Agreements a requirement to pay commuted sums and suggests that there is nothing in section 38, or as a matter of principle, to prevent such a term from being included in a Section 38 Agreement. He adds that, however, there are other ways by which roads can become adopted and these do not require the developer to incur any costs in respect of future maintenance of the highway.[101] However, there are three reasons why a developer might be shy of using other approaches. First, it is likely that the Advance Payments Code will then apply to his scheme, with all that entails in terms of financial securities etc. Secondly, each of these alternatives is not available until he has carried out the relevant

---

[100]    Ibid @ p.37.
[101]    I.e. under section 37 (for which see para. 14.1 below) or sections 228 and 229 of the Highways Act 1980.

works and there is no guarantee as to the outcome, in terms of eventual adoption, because the highway authority might be dissatisfied with the standard of workmanship. Thirdly, the absence of a Section 38 Agreement (and bond) might act to deter the occupation or plot sales during the maintenance period. The lawyer acting for the potential purchaser of a plot should check that a Section 38 Agreement or other similar mechanism is in place.

# Chapter 14

# Forced Adoption

It might be the case that a highway authority is not minded to adopt a way but that it is forced into the position of having to do so as the result of the use of section 37 or section 228(7) of the 1980 Act by a developer or frontager.

## 14.1    Section 37 of the Highways Act 1980

Section 37 of the Highways Act 1980 provides a procedure whereby a landowner, that is a landowner who owns the way in question, may procure the adoption of a way by the highways authority. If a way is not currently maintainable at the public expense, then the landowner may, if he desires to seek the adoption of the way, try to do so under section 37. This may occur where the highway authority has, for some reason, refused to enter into a Section 38 Agreement for a new development or where an established highway has, for many years, been maintainable at private expense and the owner wishes to relieve himself of this burden.

Section 37(1) provides that a person who proposes to dedicate a way as a highway and who desires that the proposed highway shall become maintainable at the public expense by virtue of this section shall give notice of the proposal, not less than three months before the date of the proposed dedication, to the local highway authority, describing the proposed highway and the nature of the proposed dedication. Given that section 37 turns on dedication, it follows that all the principles relating to the capacity of the dedicating owner and the involvement of other interested persons, mentioned at para. 13.15 above, apply equally here. Accordingly, those acting for the recipient authority should ask for proof of title.

Some highway authorities and developers enter into what they describe as "*Section 37 Agreements*". It is difficult to see the logic which underpins this affectation because section 37 does not provide for any form of agreement. The statutory procedure is relatively clear; namely, that the authority will either accede to the notice or refuse to do so.

If the authority accede, then section 37(3) provides that, if the authority certify that the way has been dedicated in accordance with the terms of the notice and has been made up in a satisfactory manner, and if;

(a)    the person by whom the way was dedicated, or his successor, keeps it in repair for a maintenance period[102] of 12 months from the date of the authority's certificate, and

(b)    the way has been used as a highway during that period,

---

[102]    The author's term.

then, the way shall, at the expiration of the maintenance period, become a highway maintainable at the public expense.

If the authority refuses to accede to the notice, then it must make a complaint to a magistrates' court and the matter will be determined by the magistrates.

Whilst the statute is not clear as to the considerations which may be taken into account by the magistrates, it is submitted that the first consideration should be the suitability of the proffered way itself. Section 37(4) states that the court must be satisfied that the certificate ought to have been issued. Clearly, this could not be the case if the way is unsuitable, otherwise they could require the adoption of a way which is unsafe.

Be that as it may, the authority can resist on the ground that the proposed highway will not be of "*sufficient utility*" to the public to justify its being maintained at the public expense: section 37(2). The content of the "*public utility*" test in section 37(2) is something of an unknown quantity. There do not appear to be any High Court judgments on the point. Arguably, one example might be where the length of way which is put up for adoption is excessive in relation to the properties served by it. The drafting of this part of the section is strange because it does not say that the application to the court can include the allegation that the way has not been constructed to an appropriate standard; however, this point may be arguable nonetheless.

Whilst the section 37 procedure might appear to be attractive to the developer at first glance, it contains a number of significant shortcomings. First, the Advance Payment Code will apply, therefore the developer will have to provide the requisite security in any event. Secondly, unlike the usual process for a Section 38 Agreement, the developer will not be able to engage in an enforceable iterative process with the highway authority in connection with the design of or specifications for the proposed ways. Thus, the developer may produce works which might, in the event, be seen as flawed by the authority when unveiled to them. Thirdly, a failure to enter into a Section 38 Agreement and bond might have the effect of deterring potential purchasers or occupiers prior to the adoption, if any, of the ways. Fourthly, the authority can, justifiably, argue that the magistrates cannot, on any appeal to them, satisfy themselves that the ways are suitable for adoption without being armed with full inspection reports. Given that those reports would relate to works which have been covered up, one could foresee that the costs of sampling and restoration might well exceed those costs which might have been incurred by way of a conventional Section 38 Agreement.

It might be faintly opined that the use of the section 37 route would lead to the avoidance of potential highway authority inspection fees; however, the works would be subject to the Advance Payments Code and so the authority's proper inspection fees would be recoverable from the security in any event.

**14.2     Section 228(7) of the Highways Act 1980**

Section 228(7) provides that, if all street works (whether or not including lighting) have been executed in a private street to the satisfaction of the Street Works Authority, then, on the application of the majority in rateable value of the owners of premises in the street, the authority shall, within the period of 3 months from the date of the application, by notice displayed in a prominent position in the street, declare the street to be a highway maintainable at the public expense and thereupon the street shall become such a highway.

In this subsection a reference to a "*street*" does not include a reference to a part of a street.

# Chapter 15

# Highway ("Section 278") Agreements

## 15.1 The need for a highways agreement

If a developer wants to carry out works to the highway, then he will need to enter into an agreement with the relevant highway authority to enable him to do so. It will often be the case that the developer's planning permission is subject to a *Grampian* type condition which precludes the commencement of the development unless and until the highway works have been completed.

In most cases, the proposed agreement will be called a *"Section 278 Agreement"*, which is taken to mean an agreement made pursuant to section 278 of the Highways Act 1980. Unfortunately, phraseology is often the manifestation of confusion at a conceptual level, and a misuse of language into the bargain. In reality, many agreements which are labelled *"Section 278"* have nothing to do with section 278.

## 15.2 The ambit of section 278

The starting point with any analysis which is based on a statute is to read the statute itself. This might seem self-evident, but it is clear that section 278 is a provision with a very limited ambit.

Section 278(1) of the Highways Act 1980 provides as follows:

> *(1) A highway authority may, if they are satisfied it will be of benefit to the public, enter into an agreement with any person -*
>
> > *(a) for the execution <u>by the authority</u> of any works which the authority are or may be authorised to execute, or*
> >
> > *(b) for the execution <u>by the authority</u> of such works incorporating particular modifications additions or features, or at a particular time or in a particular manner.*
>
> *on terms that that person pays the whole or such part of the cost of the works as may be specified in or determined in accordance with the agreement. (Emphasis added).*

It will be noted that the statute refers to works <u>by the authority</u>, not by the developer.

Sections 278(2), 278(3) and 278(4) go on to provide that:

> *(2) Without prejudice to the generality of the reference in subsection (1) to the cost of the works, that reference shall be taken to include -*
>
> > *(a) the whole of the costs incurred by the highway authority, in or in connection with -*

(i)     the making of the agreement,

(ii)    the making or confirmation of any scheme or order required for the purposes of the works,

(iii)   the granting of any authorisation, permission or consent required for the purposes of the works, and

(iv)    the acquisition by the authority of any land required for the purposes of the works; and

(b)    all relevant administrative expenses of the highway authority, including an appropriate sum in respect of general staff costs and overheads.

(3)   The agreement may also provide for the making to the highway authority of payments in respect of the maintenance of the works to which the agreement relates and may contain such incidental and consequential provisions as appear to the highway authority to be necessary or expedient for the purposes of the agreement.

(4)   The fact that works are to be executed in pursuance of an agreement under this section does not affect the power of the authority to acquire land, by agreement or compulsorily, for the purposes of the works.

It is important to stress that section 278 is a financial provision. It is not a provision which deals with the making of highway works per se. Not only does it not authorise the carrying out of highway works but also it does not mention highway works at all. That is to say that the provision refers to "*any works which the authority are or may be authorised to execute*" without using the word "*highway*" to limit the word "*works*". Thus, one must seek to discover those powers which enable a highway authority to execute works to the highway.

First, the authority owns the surface of a highway maintainable by it at the public expense by way of what Lord Denning MR once described as a determinable fee simple: see *Tithe Redemption Commissioners v Runcorn UDC* [1954] Ch 383. This means that the authority has all powers of a landowner in respect of such a highway. These include the right to sue in trespass or nuisance and, of course, to carry out works of maintenance: see *Wiltshire County Council v Frazier* (1984) 47 P. & C.R. 69. Given that the authority has a duty to ensure that the highway is fit for the traffic which uses it from day to day, it should follow that it is also required to, and entitled to, upgrade the highway to meet the changing needs of this traffic.[103]

Secondly, reference can be made to the Highways Act 1980 itself. Section 24 is a provision that allows a local highway authority to construct a highway and Part V contains a raft of powers of improvement. These include, by way of examples, a general power of improvement (section 62) and particular powers to improve dual carriageways (section

---

[103]   *Burnside v Emerson* [1968] 1 W.L.R. 1490.

64), construct cycle tracks (section 65), provide footways and fencing (section 66), provide pedestrian refuges, subways and footbridges (sections 68, 69 and 70), to widen highways and vary their widths (sections 72 and 75), to alter levels and cut-off corners (sections 76, 77 and 78) and to fence them (section 80).

Section 278 means that the authority may enter into an agreement with any person to execute any of these works (or modify any such works) on terms that that person pays the whole or such part of the cost of the works as may be specified in or determined in accordance with the agreement. Section 278 then goes on to allow the authority to recover the costs of doing so from another person. It follows that section 278 is a financial provision only.

It is necessary, in order to understand the concepts underlying section 278, to study a mixture of constitutional law and history because the roots to section 278 and all similar charging provisions lie there. They are discussed at some length at para. 15.4 below.

## 15.3    Section 278 and "agency" arrangements
It will be noted that section 278 does not mention the creation of "*agency*" arrangements between local highway authorities and developers, whereby the developer purports to carry out the works at its expense as the "*agent*" of the highway authority. This is a significant practical problem because many purported "*Section 278 Agreements*" are, instead, agency agreements and owe little, if anything, to section 278.

This problem formed the centrepiece of the decision of the Court of Appeal in *O'Connor v Wiltshire County Council* [2007] EWCA Civ 426.

The decision in *O'Connor v Wiltshire County Council* (2007) shows that:

• There is a potential pitfall in the commonly adopted arrangement whereby the developer is deemed to be acting as the agent of the highway authority in the construction of a new highway pursuant to a purported "*Section 278 agreement*".

• A road constructed by or on behalf of a local highway authority pursuant to an agreement which is wrongly purported to be made under section 278 may become maintainable at the public expense once it is opened to the public for passage and without the need for any act of dedication.

The somewhat contrived "*agency*" device is often used, purportedly, to avoid the strictures of section 278(1), which make it clear that the highway authority may enter into an agreement with any person for the execution by the authority of any works which the authority are or may be authorised to execute on terms that that person pays the whole or such part of the cost of the works. Section 278(1) does not provide for reimbursement of the costs of the carrying out of the highway works by the developer, presumably for the simple reason that the developer will be carrying out the works at its own cost in any event.

The *O'Connor* case was an appeal in respect of a decision of the Lands Tribunal. The Claimants were the owners and occupiers of a house affected by noise from a new distributor road. They made a claim under Part 1 of the Land Compensation Act 1973 for compensation for the diminution in the value of their house due to the noise impact. The Council maintained that the claim for compensation was barred because the road, having been constructed by the developers, was not a highway maintainable at the public expense at the date when it was opened to traffic and had not become so maintainable within three years.[104] The road was the subject of an agreement which required the developers to build the road and the Council to adopt it when complete. The Council appointed the developers to act as its agents to let and manage the construction contract for the road and the developers agreed to pay the Council the sums they would have been obliged to pay to construct the road had it been opened but not adopted by the Council. The Council submitted that the road had been built by the developers and not by the Council despite the labelling of the developers as agents of the Council in the agreement. The Lands Tribunal held that the claim was barred by section 19(3) of the 1973 Act, as contended by the Council.

The Court of Appeal held that the road was a highway maintainable at public expense. The road fell within section 36(2)(a) of the Highways Act 1980 because it had been constructed by the Council otherwise than on behalf of some person who was not a highway authority. Although the developers were to enter into the road contract as principals, so that, as between the developers and the contractor, the developers would be liable as principals and not as agents, the position as between the Council and the developers was defined by the agreement which provided for the road to be constructed by the Council through the agency of the developers.

The point is that section 278 does not empower a highway authority to construct new highways. This is the function of section 24(2) of the 1980 Act which provides, simply, that a local highway authority may construct new highways. It follows that, if a highway authority engages a developer as its agent in the construction of a new highway, then the highway is constructed on behalf of the highway authority and pursuant to section 24(2) of the 1980 Act.

Not only may the highway authority construct new highways, but also those new highways will become highways maintainable at the public expense without the need for any dedication from the landowner. Once constructed, pursuant to section 24(2), such a way will become a highway maintainable at the public expense by the operation of section 36(2) without the need for any further documentation. Arguably, the highway authority might have to open the way for public passage before the provisions of section 36(2) come into effect; however, there is no requirement that the way should be dedicated as a highway by the landowner.

Chadwick LJ referred to a statement from the Lands Tribunal to the effect that the question therefore appeared to resolve itself into an inquiry as to whether the Council was

---

[104]   These being the statutory pre-requisites to a valid claim.

exercising its powers to construct a highway under section 24(2) of the Act or under section 278. He then said:

> *"In my view the Tribunal was wrong to think that there is some dichotomy between section 24(2) and section 278 of the Highways Act 1980. It is section 24(2) – in Part III of the Act ("Creation of Highways") – which confers on a local highway authority power to construct a new highway. Section 278 – in Part XIII ("Financial Provisions") – confers no independent power to construct a highway: the section is concerned with the funding of works "which the authority are or may be authorised to execute". Section 278(1)(a) enables the local highway authority to enter into an agreement with someone else under which the authority agrees to construct a highway (under the power conferred by section 24(2) of the Act) upon terms that the other party to the agreement will pay the whole or a part of the cost of those works. In the present case it was section 278(1)(a) of the 1980 Act which enabled the County Council to enter into the acceleration agreement; but it was section 24(2) of that Act which authorised the County Council to perform the obligation – that is to say, to construct the NDR – which it assumed under that agreement."*

## 15.4    The *"Powergen"* case

Local planning authorities, highway authorities and developers normally co-operate in the delivery of a scheme which has the benefit of planning permission. There are very rare cases where that co-operation either breaks down or never comes about in the first place, but it is more often the case that the negotiations which one hopes will lead to a concluded agreement come to an impasse.

The developer might then pray in aid the decision of the Court of Appeal in *R v Warwickshire County Council ex. p. Powergen Plc* (1998) 75 P. & C.R. 89 to bolster his case. Arguably, this approach can be misconceived in many cases because that judgment is of little real import as a precedent. It turned on a very unusual and limited set of facts, the recurrence of which is statistically insignificant.[105]

In *Powergen*, planning permission was refused for a development on highway grounds. The developer appealed and a public inquiry was held, during which the highway reason for refusal was considered by the Inspector. The Inspector granted planning permission subject to a condition requiring that the highway improvements should be carried out before the permitted development was commenced. Subsequently the local highway authority refused to enter into the necessary agreement for carrying out the works under section 278 giving the very reasons which had been rejected by the Inspector. The developer applied for judicial review.

At first instance, Forbes J concluded that the decision to refuse to enter into the agreement was, in the circumstances, unreasonable. The relevant issues having been properly considered

---

[105]   Note the author's recent article: *"The Powergen Case and the Emperor's Old Clothes"* - The Journal of Planning and Environmental Law, June 2018.

and determined at the planning appeal, the local highway authority could not then re-open those issues by refusing to enter into an appropriate agreement. The Court of Appeal then upheld this decision, albeit without adopting the entirety of Forbes J's reasoning.

Forbes J stated:

> *"In my opinion, where the benefit to the public of the proposed highway works, in respect of which an agreement with the highway authority is sought under section 278 of the 1990 Act, has been fully considered and determined in the planning process, because the highway works in question form a detailed and related aspect of the application for development of land in respect of which planning consent has been properly obtained through that planning process, then the highway authority's discretion whether to enter into the section 278 agreement will necessarily be somewhat limited. In such a case, the matters remaining to be considered by the highway authority in the proper exercise of its discretion under section 278, are likely to be relatively minor in nature."*

A number of critical points flow from this statement and an examination of them suggests that these observations have very limited, if any, utility in the day to day practice of settling these agreements.

First, it is highly unlikely that the benefit to the public of highway works, in respect of which an agreement with the highway authority might or might not be sought at some undefined date in the future, will be *"... fully considered and determined in the planning process ..."*. The occasions in which this might occur will be statistically insignificant.

The facts of *Powergen* were unusual in that the details of the proposed highway works had been worked out and were not in dispute. Furthermore, the County Council itself had narrowed the dispute to a single point.

More typically, the parties to an appeal are unlikely to have given much thought to the details of a future agreement in respect of possible future highway works, for the simple reason that it would normally be premature to incur this time, trouble and expenditure before knowing whether planning permission will be granted at all. This is particularly so where there will be multiple parties involved in the arrangements; for example, Highways England, cross-boundary local highway authorities, adjacent landowners etc. The situation would, of course, be complicated if third party land must be acquired and/or there is a potential for claims for disturbance under the Land Compensation Act 1973 and/or it be necessary to divert or close existing highways as part of the works.

Furthermore, the chances of an inspector addressing these matters may be even more remote where the proposed highway works are intended to serve multiple separate development sites and the matter for determination is the planning proposal for one of those sites alone.

In truth, the factual matrix in *Powergen* was something of a rarity and one should bear in mind the axiom that each case must be considered on its own merits.

## 15.5 "... if they are satisfied it will be of benefit to the public ..."

Section 278 contains the pre-condition that the highway authority may enter into a Section 278 Agreement only if they are satisfied it will be of benefit to the public. The words relating to whether the authority is satisfied as to a public benefit are of utmost importance because they provide the threshold test of whether or not the authority has the jurisdiction to enter into an agreement at all. If that threshold is passed, then the authority should go on to consider whether or not it is minded to enter the agreement and, if so, on what terms. Unfortunately, the case law on the point is not particularly clear.

In *Powergen*, the courts appeared to conflate this test with an assessment of the merits of the planning permission itself. Thus Forbes J stated:

> "*In my opinion, where the benefit to the public of the proposed highway works, in respect of which an agreement with the highway authority is sought under section 278 of the 1990 Act, has been fully considered and determined in the planning process, because the highway works in question form a detailed and related aspect of the application for development of land in respect of which planning consent has been properly obtained through that planning process.*"

With respect, and as noted above, it will be surprising if the public benefit in the works themselves will have been fully considered and determined in the planning process.

If one moves the factual basis in *Powergen* forward to 2019, then the question for the planning inspector would, now, be whether any objections on highway safety grounds fall foul of paragraph 109 of the NPPF: see para. 8.10 above.[106] The NPPF does not import a public benefit test and, certainly, does not suggest that highway proposals should be rejected unless they provide a benefit to the public.

The planning authority is not charged with the duty of assessing whether or not the proposed highway works will be of benefit to the public and is not required to reject them if they are not. It has a very different duty in this regard; namely, whether or not the highway impacts of the scheme are adverse and, if so, whether they amount to a freestanding reason for refusal or must be weighed against other benefits of the scheme. If the former, then, far from asking questions about public benefit, the authority must consider whether or not the adverse impacts of the scheme are "*severe*" and, if those impacts are not, then it will be difficult to justify a refusal on highway grounds.

The planning position would be compounded where the relevant development plan is absent or silent or relevant policies are out-of-date, or where the local planning authority cannot demonstrate a five-year supply of deliverable housing sites.[107] Then, according to the NPPF, planning permission should be granted unless (inter alia) any adverse impacts of doing so would significantly and demonstrably outweigh the benefits.

---

[106] Likewise, any local plan policies on highway matters.
[107] Or fails the new housing "*trajectory*" test in the current NPPF.

Section 278 has its roots in section 60 of the Highways Act 1971. In short, section 60 provided that a highway authority proposing to execute any highway works could accept a contribution from any person towards expenses incurred by the authority in executing the highway works with particular modifications, additions or features or where they are executed at a particular time or in a particular manner and that person who would derive a special benefit if those works thus executed.[108]

The application of section 60 was subject to two statutory pre-conditions:

- that that person would derive a special benefit if those works were carried out in a particular time or manner[109]; and

- that the highway authority could not enter into such an agreement unless it was satisfied that it would be of benefit to the public.

Neither pre-condition was a mere aside because they were founded on, and sought to satisfy, the well-known principles of public law which, at that time, imposed stringent controls over the way in which public bodies used public money. In particular, councillors could not use monies derived from their ratepayers to subsidise private transactions. Councillors were seen to be trustees of the public purse. It was axiomatic that a public body which is vested with a statutory power in relation to a public matter cannot utilise that power for purposes outwith the objectives of that statutory power.[110]

The depth of this doctrine can be seen in the famous case where the Westminster Corporation was challenged when it constructed connecting subways under Whitehall pursuant to a power which related to the provision of public toilets only.[111] The House of Lords held that they had acted lawfully. As to the purported public benefit in being able to cross Whitehall in safety, the Earl of Halsbury LC stated: "... *that the public may use it for a purpose beyond which the statute contemplated is nothing to the purpose ...*".[112]

The Court of Appeal applied these principles where Brighton Corporation used its statutory power to make and improve a roadway in order to attract the speed trials of motor cars to its area.[113] The works were needed in their own right and the speed trials merely provided the opportunity to carry out those works at that particular time.[114]

---

[108]   It did not provide for the carrying out of new works at the behest of the developer: see below.

[109]   The "*special benefit*" test was removed in the iteration which appeared in the Highways Act 1980.

[110]   See *Congreve v Home Office* [1976] Q.B. 629.

[111]   *Westminster Corp. v London & North Western Railway* [1905] A.C. 426, the subways being entrances to the toilets, one from each side of Whitehall.

[112]   Per Earl of Halsbury LC @ p.427.

[113]   *R v Brighton Corp. ex. p. Shoosmith* (1907) 96 L.T. 762.

[114]   No doubt the good burghers of Brighton also felt that this event would enhance income from tourism, thereby balancing the books as it were.

These principles have been applied in many cases over many years,[115] and represented the backdrop against which section 60 was cast. If one needs to develop the point further, then it can be seen that the importation of the "*public benefit*" test overcame the strictures evident from the *Westminster* case and provided a statutory foothold for the position adopted by the Court of Appeal in the *Brighton* case.

Whilst the nature and magnitude of this "*public benefit*" was not described in the statute, the test appears to have been included in section 60 as a form of exception to the, then, extant general law, and this would suggest that section 278 should be construed narrowly; that is to say, in accordance with the fact that it had to do with highways, and not wider benefits (e.g. social, economic, environmental etc). Therefore, the relevant benefits should be limited to those concerned with passage and repassage on highways and, *ex necessitate rei*, will be limited to considerations such as highway safety, traffic flows etc. This construction does no violence to mechanisms for the proper consideration of any allied environmental and aesthetic matters because they were, and are, the subject of the separate town and country planning code.

All of this might suggest that the public benefit test is something of an anachronism. Arguably, this is the case; however, it remains a part of the statute unless and until it is removed by Parliament. A highway authority cannot parallel Hamlet and say that the breach of a statute brings more honour than its observance.[116]

## 15.6    The interface with Section 106 Agreements

Where the planning and highways authorities are the same body, the question might be asked whether or not the works could be covered by a combined agreement under section 278 and section 106 of the Town and Country Planning Act 1990.

However, the fundamental objection is that Section 106 Agreements and Section 278 Agreements are special documents that are created and operate under the provisions of, respectively, the Town and Country Planning Act 1990 and the Highways Act 1980. Section 106 contains enforcement mechanisms that are specific to Section 106 Agreements as does section 278 in connection with Section 278 Agreements: see para. 15.8 below. Mixing the two disparate enforcement regimes in one document is a recipe for confusion.

Furthermore, section 106A of the Town and Country Planning Act 1990 allows for the review of a Section 106 Agreement after five years: see para. 12.26 above. If things go slowly or some of the terms of the Section 278 Agreement last a long time, then the rights to modify or discharge the Section 106 Agreement may come into operation irrespective of the state of play on the section 278 part of the agreement.

---

[115]    For example, see *R v Inner London Education Authority ex. p. Westminster City Council* [1986] 1 WLR 28. And generally, Wade & Forsyth, "*Administrative Law*" (11th Edn.) 2014 @ pp.352 and 353 and, for a more socio-political commentary, Loveland, "*Constitutional Law, Administrative Law and Human Rights*" (6th Edn.) 2012 @ pp.446 to 453.

[116]    Hamlet, Act I - Scene IV.

## 15.7 Commuted sums

Section 278 allows for the payment of commuted sums.

A *"commuted sum"* or *"commuted payment"* is a sum of money which, in this context, normally provides for the future maintenance of capital works. For example, a commuted sum might be used to secure the future costs of maintaining street lighting associated with a new highway. The sum will be calculated to cover an agreed period of maintenance; however, since it is a lump sum paid in advance of its expenditure, a discount will be applied to reflect the fact that the recipient authority could, should it wish, invest the money at a rate of compound interest.

## 15.8 Breach of a Section 278 Agreement

A breach of the Section 278 Agreement by the developer is breach of contract and enforceable through the courts in the same way as any other breach of contract. Section 278 also includes its own special remedies as follows:

> *(5) If any amount due to a highway authority in pursuance of an agreement under this section is not paid in accordance with the agreement, the authority may -*
>
> *(a) direct that any means of access or other facility afforded by the works to which the agreement relates shall not be used until that amount has been paid.*
>
> *(b) recover that amount from any person having an estate or interest in any land for the benefit of which any such means of access or other facility is afforded, and*
>
> *(c) declare that amount to be a charge on any such land (identifying it) and on all estates and interests therein.*
>
> *(6) If it appears to the highway authority that a direction under subsection (5)(a) is not being complied with, the authority may execute such works as are necessary to stop up the means of access or deny the facility, as the case may be, and may for that purpose enter any land.*
>
> *(7) Where a highway authority recovers an amount from a person by virtue of subsection (5) (b), he may in turn recover from any other person having an estate or interest in the land for the benefit of which the means of access or other facility was afforded such contribution as may be found by the court to be just and equitable.*

This does not affect the right of any of those persons to recover from the person liable under the agreement the amount which they are made to pay.

If the agreement is secured by a surety, then the highway authority can sue either or both the developer and the surety.

# Chapter 16

# Land Compensation Act 1973

## 16.1 Introduction

Part 1 of the Land Compensation Act 1973 provides compensation for depreciation in the value of an interest in land caused by use of public works including works to provide a new or altered highway.

Section 1(1) provides that where the value of an interest in land is depreciated by physical factors caused by the use of public works, then, if -

(a) the interest qualifies for compensation under Part 1 of the 1973 Act; and

(b) the person entitled to the interest makes a claim after the time provided by and otherwise in accordance with Part 1 of the 1973 Act,

compensation for that depreciation shall (subject to the provisions of Part 1) be payable by the responsible authority to the person making the claim.

In the case of highway works, the appropriate highway authority will be the "*responsible authority*": section 1(4).

## 16.2 The "physical factors"

The "*physical factors*" mentioned in section 1(1) are noise, vibration, smell, fumes, smoke and artificial lighting and the discharge on to the land in respect of which the claim is made of any solid or liquid substance: section 1(2).

Compensation is not payable in respect of physical factors caused by accidents involving vehicles on a highway: section 1(7).

In *Lanceley v Wirral Borough Council* [2011] UKUT 175 (LC) the Upper Tribunal Member, A J Trott, said, in respect of the reference dwelling:

> [21] In his evidence Mr Lanceley referred to the inconveniences associated with the construction of the new road. Part I of the Land Compensation Act 1973, under which this claim is brought, is concerned with the use of public works and not their construction. Mr Lanceley's claim includes a sum in respect of "a reduction in living standards" and the stress and anxiety to the claimant's everyday life (and that of his family) which the use of the new road has caused. Compensation under Part I of the 1973 Act is limited to the deprecation in the value of an interest in land and is not payable for personal losses.

In *Blower v Suffolk County Council* (1994) 67 P. & C.R. 228, a house-owner claimed compensation for depreciation caused to his house by light emanating from a group of low pressure lamps in one group some 600 metres from his house, and from 17 further lamps in a second group some 1,100 metres from his house, all on columns 10 metres in height. The Council contended that a claim only arose under the Act where a house was illuminated by such artificial lighting and not, as here, where the source of light could be viewed from the house but where the amount of light falling on the ground round the house was infinitesimally small. Even if a view of the source of the lights was not to be disregarded the Council still considered that compensation would be nil as a potential purchaser would not be so affected by this as to reduce his bid.

The Lands Tribunal held, awarding compensation of £10,000, that although the surroundings of the house were by no means entirely rural, the presence of orange lights which were surprisingly prominent when viewed from the house would, in the conditions prevailing in July 1990 (the date of the claim) when prices had been dropping for two years and there was a buyer's market, have put off a potential purchaser or been used as a bargaining factor to reduce the price. Although the light was of a very low intensity around the house it still came within *"artificial lighting"* for the purposes of the 1973 Act. The judge emphasised that he had had regard to the circumstances of an unusual property in an unusual market when he had reached this conclusion as to the effect of fairly distant street lighting.

## 16.3 The interests qualifying for compensation.

Section 2(1) provides that an interest qualifies for compensation under Part 1 if it was acquired by the Claimant before the *"relevant date"* in relation to the claim and the requirements of section 2(2) or, as the case may be, section 2(3) are satisfied on the date on which notice of the claim for compensation in respect of that interest is served.

Section 1(9)(a) provides that, subject to section 9, *"the relevant date"* means, in relation to a claim in respect of a highway, the date on which it was first open to public traffic.

Section 2(2) provides that, if and so far as the interest is in land which is a dwelling, the said requirements are -

(a)     that the interest is an owner's interest; and

(b)     where the interest carries the right to occupy the land, that the land is occupied by the Claimant in right of that interest as his residence.

Section 2(3) provides that, if and so far as the interest is not in such land as aforesaid, the said requirements are:

(a)     that the interest is that of an owner-occupier; and

(b)     that the land is or forms part of either -

(i)     a hereditament the annual value of which does not exceed the prescribed amount; or

(ii)    an agricultural unit.

In section 2 "*owner's interest*", in relation to any land, means the legal fee simple therein or a tenancy thereof granted or extended for a term of years certain of which, on the date of service of the notice of claim in respect thereof, not less than three years remain unexpired: section 2(4).

In section 2, "*owner-occupier*", in relation to land in a hereditament, means a person who occupies the whole or a substantial part of the land in right of an owner's interest therein and, in relation to land in an agricultural unit, means a person who occupies the whole of that unit and is entitled, while so occupying it, to an owner's interest in the whole or any part of that land: section 2(5).

Section 2 has effect subject to sections 10(4), 11 and 12: section 2(7).

### 16.4    Claims for compensation

Section 3(1) provides that a claim under Part 1 shall be made by serving on the responsible authority a notice containing particulars prescribed in that section.

Section 3(2) provides that, subject to the provisions of that section and of sections 12 and 14, no claim shall be made before the expiration of twelve months from the date on which the highway was first open to public traffic (i.e. the "*relevant date*"). The day next following the expiration of the said twelve months is referred to as "*the first claim day*".

Section 3(3) provides that subsection 3(2) shall not preclude the making of a claim in respect of an interest in land before the first claim day if:

(a)    the Claimant has during the said twelve months made a contract for disposing of that interest or (in so far as the interest is in land which is not a dwelling) for the grant of a tenancy of that land; and

(b)    the claim is made before the interest is disposed of or the tenancy is granted;

but compensation shall not be payable before the first claim day on any claim made by virtue of this subsection.

Claims under Part 1 are subject to the six year limitation period in section 9 of the Limitation Act 1980. Section 19(2A) of the 1973 Act provides that, for the purposes of the Limitation Act 1980, a person's right of action to recover compensation under Part 1 shall be deemed to have accrued on the first claim day. Given that "*the first claim day*" is the day next following the expiration of the twelve month period, this results in an overall period of seven years from the date on which the works were first open to public traffic.

Section 19(3) provides that, in the application of Part 1 of the 1973 Act to a highway which has not always, since 17 October 1969, been a highway maintainable at the public expense:

(a)     references to its being open to public traffic shall be construed as references to it being so open whether or not as a highway so maintainable;

(b)     for references to the highway authority who constructed it there shall be substituted references to the highway authority for the highway;

and no claim shall be made if the relevant date falls at a time when the highway was not so maintainable and the highway does not become so maintainable within three years of that date." (Emphasis added).

The underlined words were the subject of a decision of the Court of Appeal in *Thomas & Ors v Bridgend County Borough Council* [2011] EWCA Civ 862.

The Claimants in that case all owned houses close to a new relief road in Pencoed, Bridgend. They claimed compensation under Part 1 for alleged depreciation in the value of their houses attributable to noise and other nuisance from the road. The relief road was opened for public use on 9 July 2002, but not adopted by the council until 29 June 2006; that is, more than three years later. On an ordinary reading of the 1973 Act the claim was excluded by section 19(3). The question for the Court of Appeal was whether that result is compatible with the Claimants' rights under the European Convention of Human Rights, and if not, whether the court could provide a remedy.

Article 1 of the First Protocol to the Convention provides:

> *"Every natural or legal person is entitled to the peaceful enjoyment of his possessions. No-one shall be deprived of his possessions except in the public interest and subject to conditions provided for by law. The preceding provisions shall not, however, in any way impair the right of a State to enforce such laws as it deems necessary to control the use of property in accordance with the general interest or to secure the payment of taxes or other contributions or penalties."*

Carnwath LJ gave the leading judgment. He reviewed the arrangements between the developer and the local highway authority, which consisted of a set of planning and highway agreements, and observed:

> *[13] On any view, the practical effect of these arrangements, in their statutory context, is remarkable. On the one hand, under the highways agreement, the opening of the road to traffic could not take place before completion of works as there specified; and, under the planning agreement, there was a limit on the number of houses which could be occupied before that date. However, neither the opening of the road nor the sale and occupation of houses was dependent on completion of the steps required (under the Highways Act agreement) before adoption by the council as a road maintainable at public expense. Thus, once the road was opened, there was little commercial incentive for the developers to hasten progress towards adoption, but rather, on the face of it, good reason to delay it until the expiry of the three year period for claims under section 19(3).*

Turning to the legal arguments, His Lordship said:

> *[28] Mr Weir's case in short is that the use of the road has interfered with the peaceful enjoyment of his clients' houses; and that the provisions designed by Parliament for their protection, and necessary to achieve the fair balance which Article 1 requires, fail to do so because they can be defeated by the unilateral action (or inaction) of those responsible for payment. He submits that the court has power to remedy that defect, under section 3 of the Human Rights Act 1998, by re-interpreting section 19(3) of the Act; or, failing that, to make a declaration of incompatibility.*

He agreed that, on the assumed facts, there was established an interference with the peaceful enjoyment of the Claimants' properties, sufficient to engage Article 1, and went on to conclude that they were entitled to compensation on the basis that section 19(3) had to be construed so as to give way to the Convention notwithstanding its literal meaning.

In *Fallows v Gateshead Metropolitan Borough Council* (1993) 66 P. & C.R. 460, a house-owner claimed compensation for depreciation caused to his house by the use of a new by-pass. This was opposed by the local authority on the ground that the by-pass was under construction when the Claimant's house was built, bought and occupied by him, so that he could be said to have bought an interest which was already depreciated. The Lands Tribunal held, that to arrive at compensation for depreciation caused to a property by the use of a highway, it was mandatory to value it at "*the first claim day*" (i.e. one year from "*the relevant date*" the date on which the road was first open to the public). On the latter date, 11 January 1990, the Claimant was the owner of the property, having bought it in July 1989, so that he was entitled to be compensated for any depreciation in his property caused by the use of the by-pass. The Tribunal awarded £1,800 as compensation.

If a highway is constructed in sections then it is only the section of the highway from which the physical factors actually come that will be relevant in deciding compensation.

In *Price and Others v Caerphilly County Borough Council* [2005] R.V.R. 103, a home-owner claimed compensation for depreciation in the value of his home caused by the construction of a highway. His home was close to an elevated road which had been built in sections during the early 1990's. The Claimant gave notice of reference to the tribunal on 28 March 2003. Preliminary issues arose as to what constituted the highway for the purposes of the claim and the date when it had actually opened. The Claimant submitted, among other things, that the construction of the whole of the highway was relevant to the claim, not just the section nearest his house, and that, for the purpose of calculating time-limits, the highway had opened to public traffic on 1 April 1996 when all sections had been completed.

The Judge, George Bartlett QC, determined the preliminary issues in favour of the local authority. Although the weight of traffic on the whole of a highway could be taken into account, in practical terms it was only the section of the highway from which the noise and nuisance actually came that was relevant in deciding compensation. In the instant case, "*highway*" meant the section nearest to the Claimant's home, which had been completed at a different time to other sections. The local authority had accepted in writing to the contractors that the relevant section had been completed on 8 November 1995. The earliest date for a claim under the Act would have been 8 November 1996. The Claimant's reference to the tribunal on 28 March 2003 was therefore outside the six year time-limit by a matter of just over 4 months.

## 16.5 Alterations to public works and changes of use

Section 9(1)(a) provides that it has effect where, whether before, on or after the commencement date, the carriageway of a highway has been altered after the highway has been open to public traffic.

Section 9(2)(a) and (c) provide that, if and so far as a claim in respect of the highway works relates to depreciation that would not have been caused but for the alterations or change of use, Part 1 shall, subject to section 9(3), have effect in relation to the claim as if the relevant date (instead of being the date specified in section 1(9)) were the date on which the highway was first open to public traffic after completion of the alterations to the carriageway; or the date of the change of use, as the case may be.

Section 9(5) provides that the carriageway of a highway is altered if, and only if, -

(a)    the location, width or level of the carriage way is altered (otherwise than by re-surfacing); or

(b)    an additional carriageway is provided for the highway beside, above or below an existing one;

and the reference in section 9(2) above to depreciation that would not have been caused but for alterations to the carriageway of a highway is a reference to such depreciation by physical factors which are caused by the use of, and the source of which is situated on, the length of carriageway which has been altered as mentioned in section 9(5)(a) or, as the case may be, the additional carriageway and the corresponding length of the existing one mentioned in section 9(5)(b).

In *Williamson v Cumbria County Council* (1994) 68 P. & C.R. 367, the Claimants sought compensation for depreciation in the freehold interest of their dwellinghouse. The house was situated in what was, before the carrying out of the relevant works, a vehicular cul-de-sac with a footbridge over a river at one end. As a result of a traffic management scheme the road outside the house had been widened and improved and a new road bridge had been constructed to replace the existing footbridge. The Council argued that section 9 of the 1973 Act was concerned with alterations to an existing highway rather than with the creation of a new highway. As it was the new road bridge which had resulted in the increase of traffic which had caused depreciation in the Claimants' property, the Claimants could not make a claim under the Act. The Claimants contended that the alteration to the road outside their house came within the definition of alteration in section 9(5)(a) and that it was the use of this road by increased traffic with its attendant noise and fumes, etc, which had caused the depreciation, for which they were entitled to be compensated.

Judge Bernard Marder, QC (President) held that section 9 takes effect where the carriageway of a highway has been altered after the highway has been open to public traffic and as the road in this case had been so altered, section 9 was applicable. It was plain, as a matter of grammatical construction, that physical factors giving rise to compensation (i.e. noise, fumes, etc.), must be caused by the use of the altered carriageway and the source of these factors must be situated on the altered length of carriageway and the Claimant was entitled to be compensated for depreciation caused by these factors.

## 16.6    Further Lands Tribunal/Upper Chamber Decisions

Disputes as to liability for, and amounts of, compensation can be referred to the Upper Tribunal (Lands Chamber) for determination. The body with this jurisdiction before 2008 was the Lands Tribunal.

The Lands Tribunal was abolished in 2008 by the Tribunals, Courts and Enforcement Act 2007, and its duties relating to compensation under Part 1 of the 1973 Act were transferred to the then newly created Upper Tribunal (Lands Chamber). The Upper Tribunal is a superior court of record, giving it equivalent status to the High Court. The Tribunal currently consists of four Chambers. The Lands Chamber decides disputes concerning land, including the purchase of land blighted by the proposals of a public authority, compensation for land compulsorily purchased or the value of which has been affected by public works.

It is possible to access past Lands Chamber decisions via the internet: http://www.lands-tribunal.gov.uk/Aspx/Default.aspx.

In *Horton & Griffin v Worcestershire County Council* (2001) (unreported) the Lands Tribunal awarded compensation in the respective sums of £30,000 and £11,250 where two dwellings suffered noise pollution from a new by-pass.

*Wolff & 15 Others v Transport for London* [2008] 8 W.L.U.K. 52 demonstrates that a series of relatively small claims can add up to a significant sum. This decision is concerned with sixteen references to determine the compensation payable by Transport for London following the coming into operation of a highway improvement scheme in 1999. All the claims had been made on the basis of the effects of noise. Pollution (in its Part 1 sense) had not initially been an issue; it had only been referred to by one Claimant. The Tribunal determined that the amounts of compensation payable in respect of each of the reference properties were as follows:

*   60 Mansfield Road          £4,750

*   50 Mansfield Road          £2,450

*   10 Corbett Road            £4,300

| | | |
|---|---|---|
| • | 128 Gardner Close | £6,000 |
| • | 6 Nadir Court | £5,550 |
| • | 22 Addison Road | £3,100 |
| • | 13 Sydney Road | £1,700 |
| • | 26b Cambridge Road | £500 |
| • | 26 Mansfield Road | Nil |
| • | 6 Chester Road | Nil |
| • | 11 Sydney Road | £1,600 |
| • | 16 Redbridge Lane West | Nil |
| • | 10 Felstead Road | £4,100 |
| • | 10 Hardwick Court | £5,750 |
| • | 8 Corbett Road | £4,050 |
| • | 28 Preston Drive | £4,400 |
| | **Total** | **£48,250** |

In *Anthony Livesey v Lancashire County Council* [2014] UKUT 501 (LC) the Upper Tribunal awarded compensation of £75,000 in respect of a dwelling, the value of which had been depreciated by light and noise impacts arising from the upgrading of adjacent roundabout. N J Rose summarised the facts as follows:

> *[8] The property is located on Preston Road at the roundabout junction of the A6 and the A674, which is the connecting road to the M61 Junction 8.8. The property is located on Preston Road at the roundabout junction of the A6 and the A674, which is the connecting road to the M61 Junction 8 ... .*

> *[9] The subject property is adjacent to the altered carriageway and access is gained directly off it. The approach road to the roundabout from the south was widened by 4m and moved 6.5m closer to the subject property. There are now three lanes on the approach road from the south, whereas there were previously only two. There are now three lanes on that section of the roundabout in front of the claim property (one dedicated lane heading north on the A6 and two lanes navigating the roundabout). There*

> *were previously two lanes around the whole of the roundabout. The nearest point of the building is approximately 41m from the edge of the carriageway.*
>
> *[10] Traffic signals have now been introduced at the entry points to the roundabout and at points on the roundabout itself. Traffic on the roundabout is now stopped for short spells until a change of traffic lights.*

As to the claim itself, Mr Rose said:

> *[47] The third, and most significant issue, is the extent of the diminution in value suffered by the subject property. In the light of the evidence it is clear that by far the most serious of the physical factors resulting from the use of the new road layout are noise and light intrusion.*
>
> *[48] The findings of Jacobs on these factors were accepted by the parties ... .*
>
> *[50] In summary Jacobs concluded that, on a worst case scenario, the noise level increase was minor but potentially perceptible in the short term, and this effect would decline over time. There would be a slight increase in headlight intrusion, but Jacobs were unable to assess the extent of the change in intrusion from the new street lighting system because of the absence of records.*
>
> *[51] As I have said, these conclusions were agreed by the parties and I accept them. I also accept Mr Livesey's evidence that in his perception the changes to the street lighting have resulted in a significant increase in light intrusion to the subject property; that the increased traffic at the junction has led to a much greater use of emergency sirens and corresponding disturbance; and that the extent of sooty deposits on his vegetation has increased significantly.*

## 16.7  Compensation outside the 1973 Act

*Andrews v Reading Borough Council* [2005] EWHC 256 (QB) was a case where compensation under the 1973 Act was not payable, yet Calvert-Smith J made an award in the Queen's Bench Division by reference to the Claimant householder's rights to the enjoyment of his home under Article 8 of the European Convention on Human Rights 1950. The Council implemented a traffic scheme that involved closing one road to vehicular traffic so that the traffic using the road adjacent to the householder's property would increase. He experienced a dramatic rise in the traffic noise levels affecting his house, but was refused a grant to install secondary glazing so as to lessen their impact. The Court awarded him a sum of damages representative of a proportion of the costs of the secondary glazing.

The increase in noise levels had resulted in substantial interference with his Article 8 rights. There was nothing to suggest that a payment was ruled out entirely where compensation was unavailable under the Regulations. The Regulations did not confer immunity on highway authorities from actions by individuals. The local authority had been entitled to take the view, in advance, that the scheme's benefits for the general public outweighed its disadvantages for the residents on the Claimant's road. However, there was no justification for the authority's failure to consider compensating the Claimant for the scheme's impact on him.

# Chapter 17

# Structures Over And Under The Highway

## 17.1    Section 176 of the Highways Act 1980

Section 176 of the Highways Act 1980 provides a restriction on the construction of bridges over highways but enables a highway authority to grant a licence to the owner or occupier of any premises adjoining the highway to construct a bridge over the highway on such terms and conditions and for such period as the authority think fit.[117]

Such licences are granted on the condition that the person to whom the licence is granted is, at his own expense, to remove the bridge or alter it in such manner as the authority may require, if at any time they consider the removal or alteration necessary or desirable in connection with the carrying out of the improvements to the highway.

It is an offence to construct a bridge without a licence under this section.

## 17.2    Section 177 of the Highways Act 1980

Section 177 of the Highways Act 1980 is a restriction on the construction of buildings over highways but allows the highway authority to grant a licence to enable such a building to be constructed. This is commonly known as a licence to "*overhang*" the highway or a "*projection licence*" in that the building is allowed to overhang or project over the highway.

It is an offence to construct or alter a building so that it overhangs the highway without such a licence.

The licence may contain such terms or conditions with respect of the construction (including headway over the highway), maintenance, lighting and use of the building as the highway authority think fit.

The only charge a highway authority can make for such a licence is in respect of their legal fees for the preparation of the licence and an annual fee for administering the licence.

A person aggrieved by the refusal of a highway authority to grant such a licence or by the terms or conditions of the licence may appeal to the Crown Court.

A charge may not be made for a licence, but if the authority owns the highway it may charge for the use of airspace.

No such licence may authorise any interference with the convenience of persons using the highway, or affect the rights of the owners of premises adjoining the highway, or the rights

---

[117]    See a discussion of *Hemel Hempstead Development Corporation v Hemel Hempstead Borough Council* [1962] 1 W.L.R. 1158 at para. 18.4 below.

of statutory undertakers or the operator of a telecommunications code system or a driver information system.

A person aggrieved by the refusal of a highway authority to grant a licence under this section or by a term or condition of the licence may appeal to the Crown Court,

Where a person has constructed or altered a building without such a licence or otherwise than in accordance with the terms and conditions of the licence, the highway authority may require the owner of the building to demolish it.

Where there has been a failure to comply with any terms or conditions of a licence with respect to the maintenance or use of a building, the authority may require the licensee or the owner of the building to execute works or take steps to secure compliance with those terms or conditions. If a person on whom such a notice is served fails to comply with it, the authority may demolish the building or execute such works or take such steps as are necessary to comply with the notice and may recover the expenses reasonably incurred by them in so doing from that person.

### 17.3    Section 178 of the Highways Act 1980

Section 178(1) of the Highways Act 1980 places a restriction on the placing of beams, rails, pipes, cables, wires or other similar apparatus over, along or across a highway and allows a highway authority to licence them on such reasonable terms and conditions as it thinks fit.[118]

A person aggrieved by the refusal of a highway authority to grant such a licence or the terms or conditions of the licence may appeal to the magistrates' court.

If a person contravenes section 178(1), or the terms or conditions of any licence, then he is guilty of an offence: section 178(4).

---

[118]    See a discussion of *Hemel Hempstead Development Corporation v Hemel Hempstead Borough Council* [1962] 1 W.L.R. 1158 at para. 18.4 below.

# Chapter 18

# Cranage Licences

## 18.1 Introduction

The carrying out of construction often involves the use of cranes which swing over (aka "*oversail*") the highway. This should be of concern to local highway authorities because not only does the conveyance of heavy loads over the highway raise obvious safety concerns but also, unfortunately, cranes have been known to malfunction and, in extreme cases, to collapse resulting in injury and fatalities. Sometimes, the collapse of a crane, or the displacement of a load, is over the highway itself.

Whilst the Health and Safety Executive has responsibilities in connection with the safe use of cranes, many, if not most, local highway authorities operate some form of licencing scheme in respect of cranes which oversail the highway, albeit not necessarily with any great consistency of approach.

The highway authority's involvement can stem from either the common law or statute.

## 18.2 Oversailing and the Common Law - highways owned by the highway authority

In *Anchor Brewhouse v Berkley House (Docklands) Developments Ltd* [1987] 1 W.L.U.K. 780 it was held that a trespass occurred where the jibs of cranes oversailed land owned by an adjacent landowner. It was not necessary to show the interference caused any loss or damage to the landowner and an injunction was granted to stop the oversailing: see also *Woolerton & Wilson v Richard Costain Ltd* [1970] 1 WLR 411.

The well-known judgments which apply this principle have involved adjacent land which is in private ownership and the courts have tended to favour the award of damages over the use of injunctions. However, the position might be different where that land is a highway because the material considerations will include the safety of the public. There is an obvious potential for accidents, even when the crane is not carrying loads or is in "*free slew*" because of the possibility of mechanical failure, particularly in high winds.

## 18.3 Oversailing and the Common Law - highways maintainable at the public expense

If a highway is maintainable at the public expense, then the local highway authority has a freehold interest in its surface. This interest is sufficient to enable the authority to initiate proceedings against those who trespass on it and in the airspace above it. Arguably, if those working on adjacent land set up a crane which oversails such a highway, then they are guilty of trespass against the highway authority's airspace over the highway. Unfortunately, the highway authority's freehold is a very limited one. The interest of the highway authority is limited to that area which is required by it for the exercise of its powers and the performance of its statutory duties.

In *Finchley Electric Light Company v Finchley Urban District Council* [1903] 1 Ch 437 the highway authority could not restrain the running of a power cable by the plaintiff at a height of 34 feet above its surface. Romer LJ stated that the law only intended to vest in the highway authority so much as might be necessary for the control, protection and maintenance of a way as a highway.

This principle was recently endorsed by the Supreme Court in *London Borough of Southwark & Anor v Transport for London* [2018] UKSC 63. There, Lord Briggs characterised the highway authority's rights in the airspace over a highway maintained at the public expense as being *"a modest slice of the airspace above it"* sufficient to enable the public to use and enjoy it, and the responsible authority to maintain and repair it, and to supervise its safe operation.

## 18.4    Oversailing and statute

Given that the presence of cranes on construction sites is an everyday occurrence, one could be forgiven for believing that the legislation relating to highways would provide bespoke provisions for the regulation of cranes which oversail the highway. Unfortunately, this is not the case. Accordingly, local highway authorities must seek to utilise provisions which are not best suited to this exercise. It is, therefore, no surprise to find that there is a divergence of approach between authorities. One finds that sections 168, 169, 177 and 178 of the 1980 Act are often cited by them.

Section 168 of the Highways Act 1980 provides a criminal offence where building operations have endangered public safety. The definition of building operation includes direction or dismantling of cranes. However, it is not a licensing provision. Furthermore, it is a reactive provision which has affect only after the safety of the public has been endangered. This is of little use to the highway authority which is seeking to provide controls in order to obviate danger to the public in the first place.

Some local highway authorities seek to provide for the licensing of cranes by way of section 169 of the Highways Act 1980. However, this provision is wholly unsuited to the purpose. Section 169 is concerned with the erection of *"... scaffolding or other structure which obstructs the highway..."*. A crane does not fall within this definition.

Some authorities seek to apply section 178 of the 1980 Act. This provision relates to the fixing or placing of overhead beams, rails, pipes, cables, wires or other similar apparatus over the highway. It can be argued that the jib of a crane is an overhead beam, and that a crane deploys cables and wires by way of that jib, and so section 178 is not necessarily inappropriate; however, *Hemel Hempstead Development Corporation v Hemel Hempstead Borough Council* [1962] 1 W.L.R. 1158 suggests otherwise. There, a company proposed to build a large building on each side of a highway and extending across the highway. It was held that the beams, pipes, cables and other apparatus which would doubtless be incorporated in that part of the structure in question would not exist as separate apparatus for which any separate consent could sensibly be required under a predecessor to section 178. Accordingly, they did not need to be authorised by any consent under either section.

Other highway authorities utilise section 177 of the 1980 Act. This provides controls over the construction of buildings over highways maintainable at public expense. It can be properly argued that a crane is a *"building"* for the purposes of section 177 because a *"building"* is defined as including *"any structure and any part of a building"*, which should include a crane and its jib: see section 177(13). This is reinforced by the use of the words *"... whether it is intended to span the highway or not ..."* in section 177(1). Furthermore, it is provided that, where the land on which a highway is situated is owned by the highway authority, nothing in section 177(3) is to be taken as affecting the rights of that authority as the owner of that land to sell or lease the airspace above the surface of that land or grant any rights in relation to it: section 177(14).

The obvious limitation to section 177 is that it applies to highways maintainable at public expense only.

Irrespective of the applicability of section 176 or section 177 or both, they are limited in so far as they relate to fixed structures. They cannot be applied to control mobile cranes on development sites. This is a significant shortcoming in those provisions.

It follows that, if the relevant highway is maintainable at the public expense, then the prudent local highway authority should utilise such common law rights as it might possess in the airspace in addition to the application of the statutory licensing regime. Thus the licence which is given to the contractor should recite not only the relevant statutory provision in the Highways Act 1980, but also section 111 of the Local Government Act 1972 or section 1 of the Localism Act 2011 or both.

### 18.5    Oversailing licences - key considerations
An example of a simple oversailing licence is provided at Form 9: Cranage Licence below in order to show one way of assembling the various elements. There are a number of key points which need to be observed in drafting such a licence.

First, it is important to focus on the contractor. The contractor should have a record which is acceptable in terms of financial probity, safety and compliance with regulatory regimes. These considerations should go to individual directors within the relevant company and appropriate searches should be carried out at Companies House. Next, either the contractor or the developer or both should be capable of showing that they have the financial resources to meet any obligations which might arise in the event that the highway authority has to rely upon an indemnity in the licence. A bond might be required in a case of uncertainty.

Turning to the licence itself, one of the primary considerations is whether it is appropriate to allow the transverse of a loaded jib over the highway at all. Unless there is a good reason for doing so, the prudent highway authority should lean against allowing this to take place.

The authority should consider whether it is appropriate that the crane should be used to load and unload to and from the highway. If the highway access to the site is suitable for heavy goods vehicles, then this would suggest that such operations could properly be excluded. Otherwise, it might be appropriate to place limits on those times when the jib of the crane can operate over the highway.

## 18.6    Oversailing and planning permission

There is a case for arguing that local planning authorities should consider whether it is appropriate to consider the imposition of conditions on planning permissions which place controls over the use of cranes within development sites.

Whilst the use of fixed tower cranes in the construction process might be obvious in many cases, the use of mobile cranes which oversail the highway might be less predictable. As noted above, the highway authority may find the use of such equipment in this way might pose problems when it comes to licensing. However, that would often be an appropriate topic for a planning condition.

A condition might impose a blanket ban on the oversailing of any highway by any jib or require that no loaded jib will oversail. A more measured approach might allow for the settling of an agreed scheme for cranage operations which oversail the highway, including limits on hours of operation.

# Chapter 19

# Cognate Highway Agreements & Licences

## 19.1    Street works licences

The New Roads and Street Works Act 1991 provides for the granting of *"street works licences"*.

Section 50(1) provides that the street authority may grant a street works licence permitting a person -

   (a)    to place, or to retain, apparatus in the street, and

   (b)    thereafter to inspect, maintain, adjust, repair, alter or renew the apparatus, change its position or remove it,[119]

and to execute for those purposes any works required for or incidental to such works (including, in particular, breaking up or opening the street, or any sewer, drain or tunnel under it, or tunnelling or boring under the street).

Section 50(2) provides that a street works licence authorises the licensee to execute the works permitted by the licence without obtaining any consent which would otherwise be required to be given -

   (a)    by any other relevant authority in its capacity as such, or

   (b)    by any person in his capacity as the owner of apparatus affected by the works;

but without prejudice to the provisions of this Part of the Act as to the making of requirements by any such authority or person or as to the settlement of a plan and section and the execution of the works in accordance with them.

A street works licence does not dispense the licensee from obtaining any other consent, licence or permission which may be required; and it does not authorise the installation of apparatus for the use of which the licence of the Secretary of State is required, unless and until that licence has been granted: section 50(3).

## 19.2    Scaffolding licences

Section 169(1) of the 1980 Act provides that no person shall, in connection with any building or demolition work or the alteration, repair, maintenance or cleaning of any building, erect or retain on or over a highway any scaffolding or other structure which obstructs the highway unless he is authorised to do so by a licence issued by the highway authority and complies with the terms of the licence.

---

[119]    *"Apparatus"*, *"street authority"*, *"street works"* and *"street"* are defined terms: see section 106.

Section 169(2) provides that, if a person applies to a highway authority for such a licence in respect of any relevant structure and furnishes the authority with such particulars in connection with the structure as the authority reasonably demand, it is the duty of the authority to issue a licence to him in respect of the structure unless the authority consider:

(a)    that the structure would cause unreasonable obstruction of a highway; or

(b)    that a relevant structure erected otherwise than as proposed by the applicant would cause less obstruction of a highway than the structure proposed by him and could conveniently be used for the work in question.

If the highway authority refuse to issue a licence, or issue a licence containing terms to which the applicant objects, the applicant may appeal to a magistrates' court: section 169(3).

It is an offence to fail to comply with the terms of a licence without reasonable excuse: section 169(5).

### 19.3    Section 171 licences

Section 171(1) of the 1980 Act provides that a person may, with the consent of the highway authority for a highway maintainable at the public expense, temporarily deposit building materials, rubbish or other things in the street or make a temporary excavation in it. The authority may give its consent subject to such conditions as it thinks fit: section 171(2).

There is a right of appeal to the magistrates' court where a licence is refused or against its conditions: section 171(3).

It is an offence to contravene a condition without reasonable excuse: section 171(6).

The Local Authorities (Transport Charges) Regulations 1998 gives a highway authority power to impose charges for its consideration of an application for a licence under sections 169 or 171.

# PART 2

# ANNOTATED STATUTES

# The Highways Act 1980

**Section 4 - Agreement for exercise by Minister or strategic highways company of certain functions of local highway authority as respects highway affected by construction, etc. of trunk road.**

(1)   The Minister or a strategic highways company, whichever is the highway authority for that trunk road ("the trunk road authority") and a local highway authority may enter into an agreement for providing, in relation to a highway specified in the agreement, being a highway that crosses or enters the route of that trunk road or is or will be otherwise affected by the construction or improvement of that trunk road, that any functions specified in the agreement, being functions of improvement exercisable as respects that highway by the local highway authority, shall be exercisable by the trunk road authority on such terms and subject to such conditions (if any) as may be so specified.

(2)   Where under an agreement made under this section any function of a local highway authority is exercisable by the trunk road authority, then, for the purpose of exercising that function the trunk road authority shall have the same powers under this Act (including highway land acquisition powers) as the local highway authority have for that purpose, and in exercising that function and those powers the trunk road authority shall have the like rights and be subject to the like liabilities as that authority.

(3)   Where for purposes connected with any function exercisable under an agreement made under this section the trunk road authority proposes to construct a new highway, every council (other than the council of a non-metropolitan district) in whose area the proposed highway is situated shall be a party to the agreement and the agreement shall provide for a local highway authority specified in the agreement to become the highway authority for the highway on its completion.

(4)   An agreement under this section made between the trunk road authority and any other highway authority may provide for the payment of contributions -

   (a)   by the trunk road authority to that other authority in respect of any additional liabilities imposed on that other authority in consequence of the provisions of the agreement;

   (b)   to the trunk road authority by that other authority in respect of liabilities so imposed on the trunk road authority, being liabilities which would otherwise have fallen to be discharged by that other authority;

and may also provide for the determination by arbitration of disputes as to the payment of such contributions.

(5)    Any local highway authority who are a party to an agreement made under this section may contribute towards any expenses incurred by the trunk road authority in executing any works to which the agreement relates.

See Text @ para. 2.3.

### Section 5 - Agreement for local highway authority to maintain and improve certain highways constructed or to be constructed by Minister [sic] or a strategic highways company or strategic highways company.

(1)    The local highway authority may by agreement with the Minister undertake the maintenance and improvement of a highway in the local highway authority's area, being a highway (other than a trunk road) which the Minister or the company proposes to construct or has, whether before or after the commencement of this Act, constructed.

(2)    Where an agreement is made under this section the council who are a party to the agreement shall, on such date as may be provided by the agreement, become the highway authority for the highway to which the agreement relates.

See Text @ para. 2.3.

### Section 6 - Delegation etc. of functions with respect to trunk roads.

(1)    The Minister or a strategic highways company may by agreement with a county council, a metropolitan district council, or a London borough council delegate to that council all or any of his or its functions (including functions under a local or private Act) with respect to the maintenance and improvement of, and other dealing with, any trunk road or any land which does not form part of a trunk road but which has been acquired by him or it in connection with a trunk road under section 239(2) or (4) or section 246 below;

(1A)  The Minister or a strategic highways company shall not delegate functions to a council under subsection (1) above -

    (a)    with respect to a trunk road or land outside that council's area but within a non-metropolitan county or London borough, except with the consent of the council of that county or borough;

    (b)    with respect to a trunk road or land outside that council's area but within a metropolitan district except after consultation with the council of that district.

(1B)   The Minister or a strategic highways company shall not delegate functions to a council under subsection (1) above with respect to a trunk road or land outside that council's area but in Wales except after consultation with the Welsh council in whose area it is situated; and subsection (1A) does not apply in relation to a trunk road or land in Wales.

(2)   A council shall, in the exercise of any functions delegated to them under subsection (1) above, act as agents for the Minister or a strategic highways company and in accordance with such conditions as may be attached to the delegation, and among such conditions there shall be included the following -

(a)   that the works to be executed and the expenditure to be incurred by the council in the discharge of the delegated functions shall be subject to the approval of the Minister or a strategic highways company;

(b)   that the council shall comply with any requirement of the Minister or a strategic highways company as to the manner in which any such works are to be carried out, and with any directions of the Minister or a strategic highways company as to the terms of contracts to be entered into for the purposes of the discharge of the delegated functions; and

(c)   that any such works shall be completed to the satisfaction of the Minister or a strategic highways company.

(3)   If at any time the Minister or a strategic highways company is satisfied that a trunk road or land with respect to which functions are delegated under subsection (1) above is not in proper repair and condition, he or the company may give notice to the council requiring them to place it in proper repair and condition within such time as may be specified in the notice, and if the notice is not complied with the Minister or a strategic highways company may do anything that seems to him or the company necessary to place the road or land in proper repair and condition.

(4)   A delegation to a council under subsection (1) above may be determined by notice given by the Minister or a strategic highways company to the council during the first 9 months of any calendar year, or the functions so delegated may be relinquished by a notice given by the council to the Minister or a strategic highways company during any such period; and the notice shall take effect as from 1st April in the calendar year following that in which it is given.

(5)   The Minister or a strategic highways company may enter into an agreement with a county council, a metropolitan district council or a London borough council -

(a)   for the construction of a trunk road, or

(b)   for the carrying out by the council of any work of improvement of, or other dealing with, any trunk road or any such land as is mentioned in subsection (1) above;

and subsection (2) above applies to the discharge of the functions of a council under any such agreement and to the conditions to be included in any such agreement as it applies to the discharge of functions delegated under subsection (1) above to any such council and to the conditions to be attached to any such delegation.

(6)    Where -

    (a)    any functions have been delegated by the Minister or a strategic highways company to a county council under subsection (1) above, or

    (b)    the Minister or a strategic highways company has entered into an agreement with a county council under subsection (5) above,

the county council (the "responsible council") may, with the consent of the Minister or a strategic highways company, enter into arrangements with a district council or Welsh council (the "contracting council") for the carrying out by the contracting council, in accordance with the arrangements, of such of the delegated functions or, as the case may be, of the functions to which the agreement relates as may be specified in the arrangements.

(6A)  No arrangements shall be entered into under subsection (6) above for the carrying out by a contracting council of any functions -

    (a)    with respect to a trunk road or land outside their area but within a non-metropolitan district, except with the consent of the council of the non-metropolitan district;

    (b)    with respect to a trunk road or land outside their area but within a metropolitan district, except after consultation with the council of the metropolitan district;

    (c)    with respect to a trunk road or land in Wales but outside the area -

        (i)    of the responsible council; and

        (ii)   of the contracting council,

    except after consultation with the Welsh council in whose area the trunk road or land is situated.

(7)    Plant or materials belonging to a council by whom functions fall to be exercised by virtue of a delegation, or agreement or arrangements under this section may be used by them for the purposes of those functions subject to the terms of the delegation, or agreement or arrangements.

(8)     Nothing in this section limits the power of the Minister or a strategic highways company to enter into and carry into effect agreements with any person for any purpose connected with the construction, improvement or maintenance of, or other dealing with, a trunk road or otherwise connected with his or the company's functions relating to trunk roads under this or any other Act; but no such agreement shall provide for the delegation of powers or duties of the Minister or a strategic highways company except in accordance with-

(a)     the provisions of this section; or

(b)     the provisions of any order made under section 69 of the Deregulation and Contracting Out Act 1994.

See Text @ para. 2.3.

### Section 24 - *Construction of new highways and provision of road-ferries.*

(1)     The Minister or a strategic highways company may construct new highways; but where he or it proposes to construct a new highway other than -

(a)     a trunk road,

(b)     a special road,

(c)     a highway the construction of which is authorised by an order relating to a trunk road under section 14 above or an order under section 18 above, or

(d)     a highway to be constructed for purposes connected with any function exercisable by him or it under an agreement made under section 4 above,

he or it shall give notice of his or its proposals to, and consider any representations by, every council through whose area the highway will pass.

(1A)    ...

(2)     A local highway authority may construct new highways; but -

(a)     where a new highway to be constructed by such an authority will communicate with a highway for which the Minister or a strategic highways company is the highway authority;

(b)     ...

the communication shall not be made unless the manner in which it is to be made has been approved by the Minister or the company.

(3)    ...

(4)    The Minister or a local highway authority may provide and maintain new road-ferries.

See Text @ paras. 3.2 and 15.3; also, *O'Connor v Wiltshire County Council* [2007] EWCA Civ 426.

### Section 36 - *Highways maintainable at public expense.*

(1)    All such highways as immediately before the commencement of this Act were highways maintainable at the public expense for the purposes of the Highways Act 1959 continue to be so maintainable (subject to this section and to any order of a magistrates' court under section 47 below) for the purposes of this Act.

(2)    Without prejudice to any other enactment (whether contained in this Act or not) whereby a highway may become for the purposes of this Act a highway maintainable at the public expense, and subject to this section and section 232(7) below, and to any order of a magistrates' court under section 47 below, the following highways (not falling within subsection (1) above) shall for the purposes of this Act be highways maintainable at the public expense -

(a)    a highway constructed by a highway authority, otherwise than on behalf of some other person who is not a highway authority;

(b)    a highway constructed by a council within their own area under Part II of the Housing Act 1985, other than one in respect of which the local highway authority are satisfied that it has not been properly constructed, and a highway constructed by a council outside their own area under the said Part II, being, in the latter case, a highway the liability to maintain which is, by virtue of the said Part II, vested in the council who are the local highway authority for the area in which the highway is situated;

(c)    a highway that is a trunk road or a special road;

(d)    a highway, being a footpath, bridleway or restricted byway, created in consequence of a public path creation order or a public path diversion order or in consequence of an order made by the Minister of Transport or the Secretary of State under section 247 of the Town and Country Planning Act 1990 or by a competent authority under section 257 of that Act, or dedicated in pursuance of a public path creation agreement,

(e)     a highway, being a footpath, bridleway or restricted byway, created in consequence of a rail crossing diversion order, or of an order made under section 14 or 16 of the Harbours Act 1964, or of an order made under section 1 or 3 of the Transport and Works Act 1992;

(f)     a highway, being a footpath, a bridleway, a restricted byway or a way over which the public have a right of way for vehicular and all other kinds of traffic, created in consequence of a special diversion order or an SSSI diversion order.

(3)     Paragraph (c) of subsection (2) above is not to be construed as referring to a part of a trunk road or special road consisting of a bridge or other part which a person is liable to maintain under a charter or special enactment, or by reason of tenure, enclosure or prescription.

(3A)     Paragraph (e) of subsection (2) above shall not apply to a footpath, bridleway or restricted byway, or to any part of a footpath, bridleway or restricted byway, which by virtue of an order of a kind referred to in that subsection is maintainable otherwise than at the public expense.

(4)     Subject to subsection (5) below, where there occurs any event on the occurrence of which, under any rule of law relating to the duty of maintaining a highway by reason of tenure, enclosure or prescription, a highway would, but for the enactment which abrogated the former rule of law under which a duty of maintaining highways fell on the inhabitants at large (section 38(1) of the Highways Act 1959) or any other enactment, become, or cease to be, maintainable by the inhabitants at large of any area, the highway shall become, or cease to be, a highway which for the purposes of this Act is a highway maintainable at the public expense.

(5)     A highway shall not by virtue of subsection (4) above become a highway which for the purposes of this Act is a highway maintainable at the public expense unless either -

(a)     it was a highway before 31st August 1835[120]; or

(b)     it became a highway after that date and has at some time been maintainable by the inhabitants at large of any area or a highway maintainable at the public expense;

and a highway shall not by virtue of that subsection cease to be a highway maintainable at the public expense if it is a highway which under any rule of law would become a highway maintainable by reason of enclosure but is prevented from becoming such a highway by section 51 below.

---

[120]    This was the date when the Highways Act 1835 came into effect.

(6) The council of every county, metropolitan district and London borough and the Common Council shall cause to be made, and shall keep corrected up to date, a list of the streets within their area which are highways maintainable at the public expense.

(7) Every list made under subsection (6) above shall be kept deposited at the offices of the council by whom it was made and may be inspected by any person free of charge at all reasonable hours and in the case of a list made by the council of a county in England, the county council shall supply to the council of each district in the county an up to date list of the streets within the area of the district that are highways maintainable at the public expense, and the list so supplied shall be kept deposited at the office of the district council and may be inspected by any person free of charge at all reasonable hours.

See Text @ para. 15.3 and *O'Connor v Wiltshire County Council* [2007] EWCA Civ 426.

## Section 37 - Provisions whereby highway created by dedication may become maintainable at public expense.

(1) A person who proposes to dedicate a way as a highway and who desires that the proposed highway shall become maintainable at the public expense by virtue of this section shall give notice of the proposal, not less than 3 months before the date of the proposed dedication, to the council who would, if the way were a highway, be the highway authority therefor, describing the location and width of the proposed highway and the nature of the proposed dedication.

(2) If the council consider that the proposed highway will not be of sufficient utility to the public to justify its being maintained at the public expense, they may make a complaint to a magistrates' court for an order to that effect.

(3) If the council certify that the way has been dedicated in accordance with the terms of the notice and has been made up in a satisfactory manner, and if -

    (a) the person by whom the way was dedicated or his successor keeps it in repair for a period of 12 months from the date of the council's certificate, and

    (b) the way has been used as a highway during that period,

then, unless an order has been made in relation to the highway under subsection (2) above, the highway shall, at the expiration of the period specified in paragraph (a) above, become for the purposes of this Act a highway maintainable at the public expense.

(4) If the council, on being requested by the person by whom the way was dedicated or his successor to issue a certificate under subsection (3) above, refuse to issue the

certificate, that person may appeal to a magistrates' court against the refusal, and the court, if satisfied that the certificate ought to have been issued, may make an order to the effect that subsection (3) above shall apply as if the certificate had been issued on a date specified in the order.

(5)     Where a certificate has been issued by a council under subsection (3) above, or an order has been made under subsection (4) above, the certificate or a copy of the order, as the case may be, shall be deposited with the proper officer of the council and may be inspected by any person free of charge at all reasonable hours.

See Text @ para. 14.1.

### Section 38 - *Power of highway authorities to adopt by agreement.*

(1)     Subject to subsection (2) below, where any person is liable under a special enactment or by reason of tenure, enclosure or prescription to maintain a highway, the Minister, or a strategic highways company, whichever is the highway authority in the case of a trunk road, or a local highway authority, in any other case, may agree with that person to undertake the maintenance of that highway; and where an agreement is made under this subsection the highway to which the agreement relates shall, on such date as may be specified in the agreement, become for the purposes of this Act a highway maintainable at the public expense and the liability of that person to maintain the highway shall be extinguished.

(2)     A local highway authority shall not have power to make an agreement under subsection (1) above with respect to a highway with respect to which they or any other highway authority have power to make an agreement under Part V or Part XII of this Act.

(3)     A local highway authority may agree with any person to undertake the maintenance of a way -

(a)     which that person is willing and has the necessary power to dedicate as a highway, or

(b)     which is to be constructed by that person, or by a highway authority on his behalf, and which he proposes to dedicate as a highway;

and where an agreement is made under this subsection the way to which the agreement relates shall, on such date as may be specified in the agreement, become for the purposes of this Act a highway maintainable at the public expense.

(3A)   The Minister may agree with any person to undertake the maintenance of a road –

(a)  which that person is willing and has the necessary power to dedicate as a highway, or

(b)  which is to be constructed by that person, or by a highway authority on his behalf, and which he proposes to dedicate as a highway,

and which the Minister proposes should become a trunk road; and where an agreement is made under this subsection the road shall become for the purposes of this Act a highway maintainable at the public expense on the date on which an order comes into force under section 10 directing that the road become a trunk road or, if later, the date on which the road is opened for the purposes of through traffic.

(4)  Without prejudice to the provisions of subsection (3) above and subject to the following provisions of this section, a local highway authority may, by agreement with railway, canal or tramway undertakers, undertake to maintain as part of a highway maintainable at the public expense a bridge or viaduct which carries the railway, canal or tramway of the undertakers over such a highway or which is intended to carry such a railway, canal or tramway over such a highway and is to be constructed by those undertakers or by the highway authority on their behalf.

(5)  ...

(6)  An agreement under this section may contain such provisions as to the dedication as a highway of any road or way to which the agreement relates, the bearing of the expenses of the construction, maintenance or improvement of any highway, road, bridge or viaduct to which the agreement relates and other relevant matters as the authority making the agreement think fit.

See Text @ Chapter 13.

**Notes**

The words "*... which he proposes to dedicate as a highway*" and "*which that person is willing and has the necessary power to dedicate as a highway ...*" effectively limit the person thus dedicating to the freehold owner only. The effect of "*... on such date as may be specified in the agreement ...*" is that such a dedication may include a deferred acceptance which is triggered on the date specified in the agreement and not immediately.

### *Section 59 - Recovery of expenses due to extraordinary traffic.*

(1)  Subject to subsection (3) below, where it appears to the highway authority for a highway maintainable at the public expense, by a certificate of their proper officer, that having regard to the average expense of maintaining the highway or other similar highways

in the neighbourhood extraordinary expenses have been or will be incurred by the authority in maintaining the highway by reason of the damage caused by excessive weight passing along the highway, or other extraordinary traffic thereon, the highway authority may recover from any person ("the operator") by or in consequence of whose order the traffic has been conducted the excess expenses.

(2)   In subsection (1) above "the excess expenses" means such expenses as may be proved to the satisfaction of the court having cognizance of the case to have been or to be likely to be incurred by the highway authority by reason of the damage arising from the extraordinary traffic; and for the purposes of that subsection the expenses incurred by a highway authority in maintaining a highway are (without prejudice to the application of this section to a by-pass provided under this Act for use in connection with a cattle-grid) to be taken to include expenses incurred by them in maintaining a cattle-grid provided for the highway under this Act.

(3)   If before traffic which may cause such damage commences the operator admits liability in respect of such traffic, then -

   (a)   the operator and the highway authority may agree for the payment by the operator to the highway authority of a sum by way of a composition of such liability, or

   (b)   either party may require that the sum to be so paid shall be determined by arbitration;

and where a sum has been so agreed or determined the operator is liable to pay that sum to the highway authority and is not liable to proceedings for the recovery of the excess expenses under subsection (1) above.

(4)   ...

(5)   Proceedings for the recovery of any sums under this section shall be commenced within 12 months from the time at which the damage has been done or, where the damage is the consequence of any particular building contract or work extending over a long period, not later than 6 months from the date of completion of the contract or work.

(6)   In the application of this section to highways for which the Minister is the highway authority the words "by a certificate of their proper officer" in subsection (1) are to be omitted.

## Notes

The expression "*extraordinary traffic*", as distinct from "*excessive weight*" includes all such continuous or repeated user of the road by a person's vehicles as is out of the common order of traffic, and as may be calculated to damage the highway and increase the expenditure on its repair: *Hill v Thomas* [1893] 2 Q.B. 333. It is important to note that traffic which may be judged "*extraordinary*" at one time, might become relatively ordinary if the highway is subject to that traffic year on year. The duty of a highway authority to keep a highway in good repair must keep pace with the changing nature of the traffic using it: see *Henry Butt & Co Ltd v Weston-super-Mare* U.D.C. 1 A.C. 340. The most famous dictum on the point comes from Diplock LJ in *Burnside v Emerson* [1968] 1 W.L.R. 1490; namely, that the authority's duty is not merely to keep the highway in such a state or repair as it is at a particular time, but to put it into such good repair as renders it reasonably passable for the ordinary traffic of the neighbourhood at all seasons of the year. That is, the duty to repair must evolve over time.

### Section 62 - General power of improvement.

(1)   The provisions of this Part of this Act have effect for the purpose of empowering or requiring highway authorities and other persons to improve highways.

(2)   Without prejudice to the powers of improvement specifically conferred on highway authorities by the following provisions of this Part of this Act, any such authority may, subject to subsection (3) below, carry out, in relation to a highway maintainable at the public expense by them, any work (including the provision of equipment) for the improvement of the highway.

(3)   Notwithstanding subsection (2) above, but without prejudice to any enactment not contained in this Part of this Act, work of any of the following descriptions shall be carried out only under the powers specifically conferred by the following provisions of this Part of this Act, and not under this section -

(a)   the division of carriageways, provision of roundabouts and variation of the relative widths of carriageways and footways;

(b)   the construction of cycle tracks;

(c)   the provision of subways, refuges, pillars, walls, barriers, rails, fences or posts for the use or protection of persons using a highway;

(d)   the construction and reconstruction of bridges and alteration of level of highways;

(e)   the planting of trees, shrubs and other vegetation and laying out of grass verges;

(f)   the provision, maintenance, alteration, improvement or other dealing with cattle-grids, by-passes, gates and other works for use in connection with cattle-grids;

(ff)   the construction, maintenance and removal of road humps;

(fg)    the construction and removal of such traffic calming works as may be specially authorised by the Secretary of State under section 90G below or prescribed by regulations made by him under section 90H below;

(g)    the execution of works for the purpose of draining a highway or of otherwise preventing surface water from flowing on to it;

(h)    the provision of barriers or other works for the purpose of affording to a highway protection against hazards of nature.

(4)    A highway authority may alter or remove any works executed by them under this section.

## Section 72 - Widening of highways.

(1)    A highway authority may widen any highway for which they are the highway authority and may for that purpose agree with a person having power in that behalf for the dedication of adjoining land as part of a highway.

(2)    A council have the like power to enter into a public path creation agreement under section 25 above, or to make a public path creation order under section 26 above, for the purpose of securing the widening of an existing footpath, bridleway or restricted byway as they have for the purpose of securing the creation of a footpath, bridleway or restricted byway, and references in those sections to the dedication or creation of a footpath, bridleway or restricted byway are to be construed accordingly.

(3)    The council of a parish or community have the like power to enter into an agreement under section 30 above for the purpose of securing the widening of an existing highway in the parish or community or an adjoining parish or community as they have for the purpose of securing the dedication of a highway, and references in that section to the dedication of a highway are to be construed accordingly.

### Notes

The words "... *a person having power in that behalf for the dedication of adjoining land* ..." effectively limit the person thus dedicating to the freehold owner only. It is not necessary for actual use by the public to be proved in order to constitute acceptance for the purposes of section 72 because the section envisages that the dedicated land will become highway before the public actually uses it: see *Secretary of State for the Environment, Transport and the Regions v Baylis (Gloucester) Ltd* [2000] 4 W.L.U.K. 463.

### Section 80 - Power to fence highways.

(1)    Subject to the provisions of this section, a highway authority may erect and maintain fences or posts for the purpose of preventing access to -

    (a)    a highway maintainable at the public expense by them,

    (b)    land on which in accordance with plans made or approved by the Minister or a strategic highways company they are for the time being constructing or intending to construct a highway shown in the plans which is to be a highway so maintainable, or

    (c)    land on which in pursuance of a scheme under section 16 above, or of an order under section 14 or 18 above, they are for the time being constructing or intending to construct a highway.

(2)    A highway authority may alter or remove a fence or post erected by them under this section.

(3)    The powers conferred by this section shall not be exercised so as to -

    (a)    interfere with a fence or gate required for the purpose of agriculture; or

    (b)    obstruct a public right of way; or

    (c)    obstruct any means of access for the construction, formation or laying out of which planning permission has been granted under Part III of the Town and Country Planning Act 1990 (or under any enactment replaced by the said Part III) and, in the case of a trunk road, consent has been given under section 175B (consent of highway authority required for trunk road access); or

    (d)    obstruct any means of access which was constructed, formed or laid out before 1st July 1948, unless it was constructed, formed or laid out in contravention of restrictions in force under section 1 or 2 of the Restriction of Ribbon Development Act 1935.

(4)    As respects -

    (a)    a highway that is a trunk road, and

    (b)    land on which the Minister or a strategic highways company is for the time being constructing or intending to construct a highway that is, or is to be, a trunk road, either in accordance with plans made by him or it in which the road is shown or in pursuance of a scheme under section 16 above, the powers under this section may be exercised not only by the Minister or a strategic highways company but also, where the road or land is outside Greater London, by the council of the county or metropolitan district in which it is situated, or where the road or land is in Greater London, by the council of the London borough in which it is situated.

See Discussion @ Chapter 4.

**Notes**

See *Cusack v London Borough of Harrow* [2013] UKSC 40.

## Section 81 - Provision of highway boundary posts.

A highway authority may erect and maintain, in a highway for which they are the highway authority, posts or stones to mark the boundary of the highway and may alter or remove any post or stone erected by them under this section.

**Notes**

The principle in the *Cusack* decision (see above) applies to this provision as well.

## Section 124 - Stopping up of private access to highways.

(1)    Subject to subsection (3) below, where the highway authority for a highway consider that a private means of access from the highway to any premises is likely to cause danger to, or to interfere unreasonably with, traffic on the highway, they may be authorised by an order made in accordance with this section to stop up the means of access.

(2)    An order under this section shall be made by the highway authority for the highway in question and, if they are a strategic highways company or a local highway authority, shall be confirmed either by the Minister or, where subsection (5) below allows, by the highway authority themselves.

(3)    No order under this section relating to an access to any premises shall be made by the Minister or, in the case of an order made by any other highway authority, confirmed either by the Minister or by that authority unless the Minister or, as the case may be, the confirming authority is or are satisfied -

(a)    that no access to the premises from the highway in question is reasonably required, or

(b)    that another reasonably convenient means of access to the premises is available or will be provided by the Minister or, as the case may be, the other highway authority.

(4)    Subject to subsection (5) below, the Minister may make regulations for prescribing the procedure to be followed in connection with the making and confirmation of orders under this section, and such regulations shall in particular make provision -

(a)    for the publication in such manner as may be prescribed by the regulations of notice of the order proposed to be made or confirmed and for service on such persons as may be so prescribed of a copy of that notice and of such other documents, if any, as may be so prescribed;

(b)    as to the content of that notice;

(c)    for objections to the making of an order by the Minister received within such period as may be so prescribed and not withdrawn, to be considered by him;

(d)    for objections to the confirmation of an order made by a highway authority to be considered by the Minister if any of the objections to the confirmation of the order received within such period as may be so prescribed and not withdrawn was made by an owner, lessee or occupier of any premises with a private means of access which the order would authorise the highway authority to stop up;

(e)    for objections to the confirmation of an order made by a highway authority received within such period as may be so prescribed and not withdrawn to be considered by the highway authority if there is no objection received within that period from an owner, lessee or occupier such as is mentioned in paragraph (d) above or if all such objections so received are withdrawn before the order is referred to the Minister for confirmation;

(f)    for the making of modifications in the order, whether in consequence of any objections or otherwise, before the order is made or confirmed.

(5)    In the case of an order made by a strategic highways company or a local highway authority under this section -

(a)    if no objection to the confirmation of the order is received within the period prescribed by regulations under subsection (4) above; or

(b)    if every such objection so received is withdrawn; or

(c)    if every such objection so received from an owner, lessee or occupier of any premises with a private means of access which the order would authorise the highway authority to stop up is withdrawn, the highway authority may themselves confirm the order, with or without modifications.

(6)    Before confirming an order with modifications the highway authority, if they consider that the proposed modifications will make a substantial change in the order, shall inform every such owner, lessee or occupier as is mentioned in subsection (5)(c) above and every other person who appears to them to be likely to be affected by the modifications to the order -

(a)    of their intention to make the order; and

(b)    of the form in which they propose to make it.

(7)    The highway authority shall give every such person as is mentioned in subsection (6) above an opportunity to make representations with regard to the order, and shall consider any representations with regard to it which any such person makes.

(8)    Schedule 2 to this Act has effect as to the validity and date of operation of any order under this section.

### Section 125 - *Further powers to stop up private access to premises.*

(1)    Subject to subsection (2) below an order under section 14 or 18 above (orders for certain purposes connected with trunk, classified or special roads) and an order under section 248 of the Town and Country Planning Act 1990 (order by Minister or London Borough to stop up or divert highway that crosses etc. a main highway) may authorise the appropriate authority -

(a)    to stop up any private means of access to premises adjoining or adjacent to land comprised in the route of the relevant road, or forming the site of any works authorised by the order or by any previous order made under the same enactment;

(b)    to provide a new means of access to any such premises.

(2)    For the purposes of subsection (1) above -

(a)    the appropriate authority in the case of an order under section 248 of the Town and Country Planning Act 1990 is the highway authority for the main highway, and in any other case is the authority by whom the order is made; and

(b)    the relevant road is the trunk road, classified road, special road or, as the case may be, main highway to which the order relates.

(3)    No order authorising the stopping up of a means of access to premises shall be made or confirmed by the Minister by virtue of subsection (1)(a) above unless he is satisfied -

(a)    that no access to the premises is reasonably required, or

(b)    that another reasonably convenient means of access to the premises is available or will be provided in pursuance of an order made by virtue of subsection (1) (b) above or otherwise.

(4)    Section 252 of the Town and Country Planning Act 1990 (procedure for making certain orders) in its application to an order under section 248 of that Act which by virtue of subsection (1)(a) above authorises the stopping up of a private means of access to premises has effect as if the persons on whom the Minister or, as the case may be, the council of a London borough is required by section 252(2), (3), (10) and (11) to serve certain documents relating to the order included the owner and the occupier of those premises.

In this subsection "owner" in relation to any premises, means a person, other than a mortgagee not in possession, who is for the time being entitled to dispose of the fee simple in the premises, whether in possession or in reversion, and includes also a person holding or entitled to the rents and profits of the premises under a lease the unexpired term of which exceeds 3 years.

### Section 138 - Penalty for erecting building, etc., in highway.

If a person, without lawful authority or excuse, erects a building or fence, or plants a hedge, in a highway which consists of or comprises a carriageway he is guilty of an offence and liable to a fine not exceeding level 3 on the standard scale.

### Notes

This would also be a public nuisance.

### Section 143 - Power to remove structures from highways.

(1)    Where a structure has been erected or set up on a highway otherwise than under a provision of this Act or some other enactment, a competent authority may by notice require the person having control or possession of the structure to remove it within such time as may be specified in the notice.

For the purposes of this section the following are competent authorities -

(a)    in the case of a highway which is for the time being maintained by a non-metropolitan district council by virtue of section 42 or 50 above, that council and also the highway authority, and

(b)    in the case of any other highway, the highway authority.

(2)    If a structure in respect of which a notice is served under this section is not removed within the time specified in the notice, the competent authority serving the notice may, subject to subsection (3) below, remove the structure and recover the expenses reasonably incurred by them in so doing from the person having control or possession of the structure.

(3)    The authority shall not exercise their power under subsection (2) above until the expiration of one month from the date of service of the notice.

(4)    In this section "structure" includes any machine, pump, post or other object of such a nature as to be capable of causing obstruction, and a structure may be treated for the purposes of this section as having been erected or set up notwithstanding that it is on wheels.

### Notes

Finding out who has control or possession of a structure can be very problematic in practice.

Query whether "*on a highway*" means that the provision does not apply where the structure is over the highway but does not touch its surface?

### Section 165 - Dangerous land adjoining street.

(1)    If, in or on any land adjoining a street, there is an unfenced or inadequately fenced source of danger to persons using the street, the local authority in whose area the street is situated may, by notice to the owner or occupier of that land, require him within such time as may be specified in the notice to execute such works of repair, protection, removal or enclosure as will obviate the danger.

(2)    A person aggrieved by a requirement under subsection (1) above may appeal to a magistrates' court.

(3)    Subject to any order made on appeal, if a person on whom a notice is served under this section fails to comply with the notice within the time specified in it, the authority by whom the notice was served may execute such works as are necessary to comply with the notice and may recover the expenses reasonably incurred by them in so doing from that person.

(4)    Where the power conferred by subsection (1) above is exercisable in relation to land adjoining a street and has not been exercised by the local authority empowered to

exercise it, then, if that authority are not the highway authority for the street, the highway authority for the street may request the local authority to exercise the power.

(5)    If the local authority refuse to comply with a request made under subsection (4) above or fail within a reasonable time after the request is made to them to do so, the highway authority may exercise the power (and where they do so subsections (2) and (3) above apply accordingly).

### Definitions

"*Street*" – see section 329(1).

### Notes

The phrase "... *any land adjoining a street* ..." is open to wide interpretation. The words "*source of danger*" suggest that this provision applies where there is a risk of injury, albeit this leaves open the question of how the risk assessment is carried out and then evaluated.

The notion of a "*person aggrieved*" is well known to public law. Plainly it must include a person on whom a notice is served, but leaves open the possibility that another person interested in the land could appeal.

### Section 168 - Building operations affecting public safety.

(1)    If in the course of the carrying out of any building operation in or near a street there occurs an accident which -

(a)    gives rise to the risk of serious bodily injury to a person in the street, whether or not the death or disablement of any person is caused thereby; or

(b)    would have given rise to such risk but for the fact that a local authority or highway authority had in the exercise of their powers under section 78 of the Building Act 1984 (emergency measures to deal with dangerous buildings) or any other enactment taken steps to ensure that if an accident occurred it would not give rise to such risk,

then, subject to the provisions of this section, the owner of the land or building on which the building operation is being carried out is, without prejudice to any liability to which he or any other person may be subject apart from this section, guilty of an offence and liable to a fine not exceeding level 5 on the standard scale.

(2)    Where the commission by any person of an offence under this section is due to the act or default of some other person, that other person is guilty of the offence, and a person may be charged with and convicted of the offence by virtue of this subsection whether or not proceedings are taken against the first-mentioned person.

(3)    In any proceedings for an offence under this section it is a defence, subject to subsection (4) below, for the person charged to prove -

   (a)    that he took all reasonable precautions to secure that the building operation was so carried out as to avoid causing danger to persons in a street; or

   (b)    that the commission of the offence was due to the act or default of another person and that he took all reasonable precautions and exercised all due diligence to avoid the commission of such an offence by himself or any person under his control.

(4)    A person charged with an offence under this section is not, without leave of the court, entitled to rely on the defence provided by subsection (3)(b) above unless, within a period ending 7 clear days before the hearing, he has served on the prosecutor a notice in writing giving such information identifying or assisting in the identification of that other person as was then in his possession.

(5)    In this section "building operation" means the construction, structural alteration, repair or maintenance of a building (including re-pointing, external re-decoration and external cleaning), the demolition of a building, the preparation for, and laying the foundations of, an intended building and the erection or dismantling of cranes or scaffolding.

### Section 169 - Control of scaffolding on highways.

(1)    Subject to subsection (6) below no person shall, in connection with any building or demolition work or the alteration, repair, maintenance or cleaning of any building, erect or retain on or over a highway any scaffolding or other structure which obstructs the highway (hereafter in this section referred to as a "relevant structure") unless he is authorised to do so by a licence in writing issued for the purposes of this section by the highway authority (hereafter in this section referred to as "a licence") and complies with the terms of the licence; and a licence may contain such terms as the authority issuing it thinks fit.

(2)    If a person applies to a highway authority for a licence in respect of any relevant structure and furnishes the authority with such particulars in connection with the structure as the authority reasonably demand, it is the duty of the authority to issue a licence to him in respect of the structure unless the authority consider -

   (a)    that the structure would cause unreasonable obstruction of a highway; or

(b)    that a relevant structure erected otherwise than as proposed by the applicant would cause less obstruction of a highway than the structure proposed by him and could conveniently be used for the work in question.

(3)    If on an application for a licence in connection with a highway the highway authority refuse to issue a licence or issue a licence containing terms to which the applicant objects, the applicant may appeal to a magistrates' court against the refusal or terms; and on such an appeal the court may -

(a)    in the case of an appeal against a refusal, direct the highway authority to issue a licence in pursuance of the application;

(b)    in the case of an appeal against the terms of the licence, alter the terms.

(4)    Subject to subsection (6) below, it is the duty of a person to whom a licence is issued by a highway authority in respect of a relevant structure -

(a)    to ensure that the structure is adequately lit at all times between half an hour after sunset and half an hour before sunrise;

(b)    to comply with any directions given to him in writing by the authority with respect to the erection and maintenance of traffic signs in connection with the structure; and

(c)    to do such things in connection with the structure as any statutory undertakers reasonably request him to do for the purpose of protecting or giving access to any apparatus belonging to or used or maintained by the undertakers.

In this subsection and in section 171(2) below "statutory undertakers" means any of the following, namely, any body who are statutory undertakers within the meaning provided by section 329(1) below, any universal service provider in connection with the provision of a universal postal service, any licensee under a street works licence and the operator of an electronic communications code network or a driver information network.

(5)    A person who contravenes the provisions of subsection (1) above otherwise than by failing to comply with the terms of a licence or who fails without reasonable excuse to comply with the terms of a licence or to perform a duty imposed on him by subsection (4) above, is guilty of an offence and liable to a fine not exceeding level 5 on the standard scale.

(6)    Nothing in the preceding provisions of this section applies to a relevant structure erected before 14th February 1977 or erected or retained by the British Railways Board, Canal & River Trust or Transport for London or any of its subsidiaries (within the meaning of the Greater London Authority Act 1999) in the exercise of powers

conferred on the body in question by any enactment; and nothing in paragraph (a) or (b) of subsection (4) above applies to a relevant structure if no part of it is less than 18 inches in a horizontal direction from a carriageway of the relevant highway and no part of it over a footway of the relevant highway is less than 8 feet in a vertical direction above the footway.

(7)  No civil or criminal proceedings lie in respect of any obstruction of a highway which is caused by a relevant structure if the structure is on or over the highway in accordance with a licence and the person to whom the licence is issued performs the duties imposed on him in respect of the structure by subsection (4) above; and a highway authority by whom a licence is issued do not incur any liability by reason of the issue of the licence.

See Text @ para. 19.2.

**Notes**

The description of a *"relevant structure"* as *"... scaffolding or other structure which obstructs the highway ..."* means that the provision is not (as is commonly thought) limited to scaffolding only.

### Section 176 - Restriction on construction of bridges over highways.

(1)  The highway authority for a highway may grant to the owner or occupier of any premises adjoining the highway a licence to construct a bridge over the highway on such terms and conditions, and to use it for such period and on such terms and conditions, as the authority think fit.

(2)  No fine, rent or other sum of money, except a reasonable sum in respect of legal or other expenses, is payable in respect of a licence under this section.

(3)  A licence under this section shall not authorise any interference with the convenience of persons using the highway, or affect the rights of owners of premises adjoining the highway, or the rights of tramway, railway, dock, harbour or electricity undertakers.

(4)  It shall be a condition of every licence under this section that the person to whom it is granted is, at his own expense, to remove the bridge or alter it in such manner as the authority may require, if at any time they consider the removal or alteration necessary or desirable in connection with the carrying out of improvements to the highway.

The decision of the authority that the removal or alteration is necessary or desirable in that connection shall be final, and the condition shall be enforceable by the authority against the owner for the time being of the premises.

(5)     Subject to subsection (6) below, a person aggrieved by the refusal of an authority to grant a licence under this section or by the period for which the licence is granted or by a term or condition of the licence (other than the condition mentioned in subsection (4) above) may appeal to the Crown Court.

(6)     No appeal lies under subsection (5) above against any term or condition of a licence granted by the Minister under this section if he declares the term or condition to be necessary for the purpose of securing the safety of persons using the highway or of preventing interference with traffic on it.

(7)     If a person, except in the exercise of statutory powers -

(a)     constructs a bridge over a highway without a licence under this section, or

(b)     constructs or uses a bridge otherwise than in accordance with the terms and conditions of such a licence, or

(c)     fails to remove or alter a bridge when required to do so in accordance with any condition of the licence or within one month from the date of the expiration of the licence,

he is guilty of an offence and is liable to a fine not exceeding level 2 on the standard scale, and if the offence is continued after conviction he is guilty of a further offence and is liable to a fine not exceeding £5 for each day on which the offence is so continued.

(8)     In this section "bridge" means a structure the sole purpose of which is to provide a way over a highway.

See Text @ Chapter 18.

**Notes**

The reference to "*a bridge*" was a source of confusion in the earlier version of this provision. See *Hemel Hempstead Development Corporation v Hemel Hempstead Borough Council* [1962] 1 W.L.R. 1158.

### Section 177 - Restriction on construction of buildings over highways.

(1)     No person shall -

(a)     except in the exercise of statutory powers, construct a building over any part of a highway maintainable at the public expense (whether it is intended to span the highway or not), or alter a building so constructed, without a licence granted under this section by the highway authority for that highway or otherwise than in accordance with the terms and conditions of a licence so granted;

(b)    use a building so constructed or altered in pursuance of a licence so granted otherwise than in accordance with the terms and conditions thereof:

and any person who contravenes any provision of this subsection is guilty of an offence and liable to a fine not exceeding level 5 on the standard scale; and if the offence is continued after conviction, he is guilty of a further offence and liable to a fine not exceeding £50 for each day on which the offence is so continued.

(2)    Subject to subsections (3) and (4) below, a licence under this section may contain such terms and conditions, including terms and conditions with respect to the construction (including the headway over the highway), maintenance, lighting and use of the building, as the highway authority think fit; and, any such term or condition is binding on the successor in title to every owner, and every lessee and occupier, of the building.

(3)    No fine, rent or other sum of money is payable in respect of a licence granted under this section except -

(a)    a reasonable sum in respect of legal or other expenses incurred in connection with the grant of the licence; and

(b)    an annual charge of a reasonable amount for administering the licence;

and any sum payable by virtue of paragraph (a) above is recoverable from the applicant for the licence and any sum payable by virtue of paragraph (b) above is recoverable from the owner of the building.

(4)    No such licence shall authorise any interference with the convenience of persons using the highway, or affect the rights of the owners of premises adjoining the highway, or the rights of statutory undertakers or the operator of an electronic communications code network or a driver information network.

(5)    Where a licence under this section makes provision for the execution of any works or the provision of any facilities which in the opinion of the highway authority require to be executed or provided by them in connection with the building or its construction or alteration, the authority may execute those works or, as the case may be, provide those facilities and may recover the expenses reasonably incurred by them in so doing from the licensee or from the owner of the building.

(6)    A person aggrieved by the refusal of a highway authority to grant a licence under this section or by a term or condition of the licence may appeal to the Crown Court, except that no such appeal lies -

(a)    if the land on which the highway in question is situated is owned by the highway authority, or

(b)    against any term or condition which the highway authority declare to be necessary for the purpose of securing the safety of persons using the highway or of preventing interference with traffic thereon.

(7)    Where a person has constructed or altered a building for the construction, or, as the case may be, alteration, of which a licence is required by this section without such a licence or otherwise than in accordance with the terms and conditions of the licence, the highway authority may by notice served on the licensee or the owner of the building require him to demolish the building within such time as may be specified in the notice or, as the case may be, to make such alterations therein and within such time as may be so specified.

(8)    Where there has been a failure to comply with any terms or conditions of a licence under this section with respect to the maintenance or use of a building, the highway authority may by notice served on the licensee or the owner of the building require him to execute such works or take such steps as are necessary to secure compliance with those terms or conditions within such time as may be specified in the notice.

(9)    If a person on whom a notice is served under subsection (7) or (8) above fails to comply with the notice within the time specified in it, the highway authority may demolish the building or, as the case may be, execute such works or take such steps as are necessary to comply with the notice and may recover the expenses reasonably incurred by them in so doing from that person.

(10)   Where by virtue of subsection (9) above a highway authority demolish a building, they may dispose of the materials resulting from the demolition.

(11)   In relation to any prohibition or restriction on the use of a building imposed by the Minister by virtue of any term or condition contained in a licence granted by him under this section, section 1(1)(c) of the Local Land Charges Act 1975 has effect as if the references to the date of the commencement of that Act were references to 1st November 1971.

(12)   Part 10 of Schedule 3A to the Communications Act 2003 (the electronic communications code) (which provides a procedure for certain cases where works involve the alteration of electronic communications apparatus) shall apply, for the purposes of works authorised or required by a licence under this section to be executed, to the licensee.

(13)   This section does not apply to a building which constitutes a bridge within the meaning of section 176 above, but subject to that in this section "building" includes any structure and any part of a building.

(14)   Where the land on which a highway is situated is owned by the highway authority, nothing in subsection (3) above is to be taken as affecting the rights of that authority as the owner of that land to sell or lease the air-space above the surface of that land or grant any rights in relation to it.

See Text @ Chapter 18.

**Notes**

The phrase "*a building*" is open to interpretation. Arguably, it may include structures which are not intended to be permanent and may include cranes which oversail the highway and this is reinforced by "... *whether it is intended to span the highway or not* ...". See discussion of cranage licences at Chapter 18 above. The provision is limited to highways maintainable at the public expense.

### Section 178 - Restriction on placing rails, beams etc. over highways.

(1)   No person shall fix or place any overhead beam, rail, pipe, cable, wire or other similar apparatus over, along or across a highway without the consent of the highway authority for the highway, and the highway authority may attach to their consent such reasonable terms and conditions as they think fit.

(2)   Subject to subsection (3) below, a person aggrieved by the refusal of a consent under subsection (1) above, or by any terms or conditions attached to such a consent, may appeal to a magistrates' court.

(3)   No appeal lies under subsection (2) above against any term or condition attached by the Minister to a consent given by him under this section if he declares the term or condition to be necessary for the purpose of securing the safety of persons using the highway to which the consent relates or of preventing interference with traffic on it.

(4)   If a person contravenes subsection (1) above, or the terms or conditions of any consent given under that subsection, he is guilty of an offence and liable to a fine not exceeding level 1 on the standard scale; and if the offence is continued after conviction he is guilty of a further offence and liable to a fine not exceeding £1 for each day on which the offence is so continued.

(5)   This section does not apply to any works or apparatus belonging to any statutory undertakers, and for this purpose the Civil Aviation Authority, a person who holds a licence under Chapter I of Part I of the Transport Act 2000 (to the extent that the person is carrying out activities authorised by the licence), a universal service provider in connection with the provision of a universal postal service and the operator of an

electronic communications code network or a driver information network are to be deemed to be statutory undertakers.

See Text @ Chapter 18.

**Notes**

See discussion of *Hemel Hempstead Development Corporation v Hemel Hempstead Borough Council* [1962] 1 W.L.R. 1158 at para. 18.4.

### Section 179 - Control of construction of cellars etc. under street.

(1)  No person shall construct works to which this section applies under any part of a street without the consent of the appropriate authority, and the authority may by notice served on a person who has constructed such works in contravention of this section require him to remove them, or to alter or deal with them in such a manner as may be specified in the notice.

For the purposes of this section the appropriate authority is -

      (i)    in relation to a street outside Greater London which is a highway, the highway authority for the street; and

      (ii)   in relation to any other street, the local authority in whose area the street is situated.

(2)  A person aggrieved by the refusal of a consent, or by a requirement of a notice, under subsection (1) above may appeal to a magistrates' court.

(3)  A person who constructs works to which this section applies in contravention of this section is guilty of an offence and is liable to a fine not exceeding level 1 on the standard scale; and, subject to any order made on appeal, if he fails to comply with a requirement of a notice served on him under subsection (1) above he is guilty of a further offence and is liable to a fine not exceeding £2 for each day during which the failure continues.

(4)  The appropriate authority may also cause works to which this section applies constructed in contravention of this section to be removed, altered or otherwise dealt with as they think fit, and may recover the expenses reasonably incurred by them in so doing from the offender.

(5)     As soon as may be after an authority consent to the construction of works to which this section applies under a street they shall give notice of their consent to any public utility undertakers having any apparatus under the street.

(6)     Subject to subsection (7) below, the works to which this section applies are -

    (a)     any part of a building; and

    (b)     without prejudice to the generality of paragraph (a) above, a vault, arch or cellar, whether forming part of a building or not.

(7)     This section does not apply to street works within the meaning of Part III of the New Roads and Street Works Act 1991.

### Section 203 - Interpretation of Part XI.

(1)     In this Part of this Act (and elsewhere in this Act) "the private street works code" means sections 205 to 218 below; and "the advance payments code" means sections 219 to 225 below.

(2)     In this Part of this Act "private street" means a street that is not a highway maintainable at the public expense, and -

    (a)     includes any land that is deemed to be a private street by virtue of a declaration made under section 232 below, and

    (b)     for the purpose of the application of the advance payments code or section 229 below in relation to any building, includes -

        (i)     any land shown as a proposed street on plans deposited with respect to that building either under building regulations or on an application for planning permission under the Town and Country Planning Act 1990, and

        (ii)     ...

but the fact that a part of a street is a highway maintainable at the public expense does not prevent any other part of it from being a part of a private street for the purposes of this Part of this Act.

(3)     In this Part of this Act-

"fronting" includes adjoining, and "front" is to be construed accordingly;

"industrial premises" means premises used or designed or suitable for use for the carrying on of any such process or research as is specified in section 66(1) of the Town and Country Planning Act 1971, and includes premises used for purposes ancillary to the carrying on of any such process or research;

"paving, metalling and flagging" includes all methods of making a carriageway or footway;

"street works" means any works for the sewering, levelling, paving, metalling, flagging, channelling and making good of a street, and includes the provision of proper means for lighting a street;

"street works authority" means -

(a)    as respects a street outside Greater London, the council of the county or metropolitan district in which the street is situated,

(b)    as respects a street in a London borough, the council of the borough, and

(c)    as respects a street in the City, the Common Council.

(4)    For the purposes of the advance payments code and of section 229 below, the frontage of a building or proposed building on a street shall be deemed to be the frontage that the building itself and any land occupied or, as the case may be, proposed to be occupied, with the building and for the purposes of it has or will have on the street.

(5)    In ascertaining a majority in number of owners for the purposes of any provision of this Part of this Act, joint owners are to be treated as one owner.

### Section 204 - Purposes and application of private street works code and advance payments code.

(1)    The private street works code has effect for securing the execution of street works in private streets anywhere in England or Wales.

(2)    The advance payments code has effect for securing payment of the expenses of the execution of street works in private streets adjacent to new buildings, and applies -

(a)    in all outer London boroughs;

(b)    in all areas in counties in which the advance payments code in the Highways Act 1959 (which is replaced by the advance payments code in this Act) was in force immediately before 1st April 1974; and

(c)    in any parish or community in which the advance payments code in the Highways Act 1959 was, after 1st April 1974, adopted in accordance with Schedule 14 to that Act, or in which the advance payments code is adopted in accordance with Schedule 15 to this Act.

(3)    ...

> See Text @ Chapter 7.

### Section 219 - Payments to be made by owners of new buildings in respect of street works.

(1)    Subject to the provisions of this section, where -

    (a)    it is proposed to erect a building for which plans are required to be deposited with the local authority in accordance with building regulations, and

    (b)    the building will have a frontage on a private street in which the street works authority have power under the private street works code to require works to be executed or to execute works,

no work shall be done in or for the purpose of erecting the building unless the owner of the land on which it is to be erected or a previous owner thereof has paid to the street works authority, or secured to the satisfaction of that authority the payment to them of, such sum as may be required under section 220 below in respect of the cost of street works in that street.

(2)    If work is done in contravention of subsection (1) above, the owner of the land on which the building is to be erected and, if he is a different person, the person undertaking the erection of the building is guilty of an offence and liable to a fine not exceeding level 3 on the standard scale, and any further contravention in respect of the same building constitutes a new offence and may be punished accordingly.

Proceedings under this subsection shall not be taken by any person other than the street works authority.

(3)    Where the person undertaking the erection of the building is not the owner of the land on which it is to be erected and is charged with an offence under subsection (2) above, it shall be a defence for him to prove that he had reasonable grounds for believing that the sum required under section 220 below had been paid or secured by the owner of the land in accordance with subsection (1) above.

### Definitions

For "*private street*", "*street works authority*" and "*private street works code*" see section 203.

### Notes: Section 219(1-3)

One question in respect of section 219(1)(a) is whether the reference to the deposit of plans with the local authority is affected by the fact that external approved inspectors may be involved in checking plans as opposed to in-house local authority inspectors. There are three responses. First, section 219(1) does not say that the Advance Payments Code applies only where plans are, in fact, deposited with the local authority. The words "... *a building for which plans are required to be deposited* ..." (Emphasis added) do not describe a process, they describe a type of proposed building; namely, a building which is subject to building regulation control before its construction. Secondly, an external approved inspector does not usurp all of the local authority's functions. His role is that of notification and certification subject to the ultimate control of the local authority. Thirdly, section 16 of the Building Act 1984 still requires the deposit of plans albeit that they may be accompanied by an approved inspector's certificate of satisfaction.

Section 219(1)(b) applies the Advance Payments Code to proposed new buildings which will have a frontage on a private street; therefore it is important to understand what "*frontage*" means in this context. Section 203(3) states that "*fronting*" includes "*adjoining*" and section 329(1) states that "*adjoining*" includes "*abutting on*". Section 203(4) adds that, for the purposes of the Advance Payments Code and of section 229, the frontage of a building or proposed building on a street shall be deemed to be the frontage that the building itself and any land occupied or, as the case may be, proposed to be occupied, with the building and for the purposes of it has or will have on the street.

The current position appears to be that there must be measurable boundary contact between the relevant property and the private street.

In *Buckinghamshire County Council v Trigg* [1963] 1 All E.R. 403, it was held that a first floor maisonette which was separated from a street by a garden did not front the street for the purposes of the Private Street Works Code.

If there is no common boundary, then there might be exceptional cases where a very small gap between the boundaries is discounted. In *Wakefield Local Board of Health v Lee* (1876) 1 Ex. D. 336, it was held that a property fronted a street for the purposes of the Private Street Works Code where they were separated by a small stream.

Section 219(2) provides a criminal sanction for breach of the Advance Payments Code. It is notable that section 219(2) does not stipulate in terms that the service of an APC Notice is a condition precedent to the operation of it. It is arguable that the offence occurs where work is done in contravention of section 219(1) regardless of whether an APC Notice has been served beforehand.

Section 219(1) states: "... *[the relevant owner] thereof has paid to the street works authority, or secured to the satisfaction of that authority the payment to them of, such sum as may be required under section 220* ..." (Emphasis added). Clearly, it is possible to argue that if the Street Works Authority has not "*required*" a sum under section 220 until the APC Notice has been served, then it would follow that the commencement of the works in the absence of such a requirement is not in contravention of section 219(1). However, this argument appears to suffer from two fatal flaws; first, that it does not deal with the fact that the Street Works Authority is given six weeks to thus require the said sum. If this construction is applied, then the owner could start work during this six week period without fear of any criminal sanction; secondly, the APC Notice served by the authority will not set out the sum as may be required under section 220 where the Secretary of State has imposed a sum following an appeal under section 220(6) and, again, one has to question whether it could be said that the owner could start work during the appeal period without fear of any criminal sanction. Ergo, this construction of section 219(1) would undermine the Advance Payments Code as a whole.

(4)  This section does not apply -

(a)  where the owner of the land on which the building is to be erected will be exempt, by virtue of a provision in the private street works code, from liability to expenses incurred in respect of street works in the private street in question;

(b)  where the building proposed to be erected will be situated in the curtilage of, and be appurtenant to, an existing building;

(c)  where the building is proposed to be erected in a parish or community and plans for the building were deposited with the district council or, according to the date of deposit, the rural district council before the date on which the New Streets Act 1951, or the advance payments code (either in this Act or in the Highways Act 1959) was applied in the parish or community or, as the case may require, in the part of the parish or community in which the building is to be erected;

(d)  where an agreement has been made by any person with the street works authority under section 38 above providing for the carrying out at the expense of that person of street works in the whole of the street or a part of the street comprising the whole of the part on which the frontage of the building will be, and for securing that the street or the part thereof, on completion of the works, will become a highway maintainable at the public expense;

### Notes: The exemption under section 219(4)(d)

The Advance Payments Code does not apply where the developer has entered into a Section 38 Agreement. However, that exemption applies only where such an agreement has been executed; it does not apply to a proposal to enter into a Section 38 Agreement in the future. As such, it is important that the highway authority does not prejudice its position by failing to issue an APC Notice against the promise of a Section 38 Agreement which might or might not materialise in the future.

The highway authority has only six weeks to serve the APC Notice, starting from the date that building regulation approval is given. Unless the developer is unusually proactive in these matters, it is unlikely that the agreement will be concluded by the conclusion of this six-week period. Accordingly, the prudent approach is to serve the APC Notice regardless of whether or not an agreement is promised or is in the course of discussion. Otherwise, the authority might lose its opportunity to do so. Once the APC Notice is served, it will then be up to the developer to claim the benefit of the exemption as and when the agreement is entered into.

(e)     where the street works authority, being satisfied that the whole of the street or such a part thereof as aforesaid is not, and is not likely within a reasonable time to be, substantially built-up or in so unsatisfactory a condition as to justify the use of powers under the private street works code for securing the carrying out of street works in the street or part thereof, by notice exempt the building from this section;

### Notes: The exemption under section 219(4)(e)

Section 219(4)(e) separates into two different situations:

**Case (1)**: where the Street Works Authority are satisfied that the whole or the part of the street is not, and is not likely within a reasonable time to be, substantially built up; or

**Case (2)**: where the Street Works Authority are satisfied that the whole or the part of the street is not, and is not likely within a reasonable time to be, in so unsatisfactory a condition as to justify the use of powers under the Private Street Works Code for securing the carrying out of street works in the street or part thereof.

On this construction, Case (1) would relate to the typical situation where a building is, or a group of buildings are, served or to be served by a long access, the frontage of which is not otherwise built up and will not become so within a reasonable time.

One example might be where planning permission is given for the construction of an agricultural dwelling which is accessed from a long farm track.

Case (2) would be relevant where the authority is satisfied that a proposed private estate road will be constructed and maintained in a manner which would preclude the need to resort to the Private Street Works Code for a reasonable period of time. It would also be relevant where a new building is proposed on an existing street which is already of a satisfactory condition.

If this construction is taken, then an exemption can be justified if either of the two Cases apply.

However, obiter[121] dicta statements by *Burton J in R v Local Government Ombudsman ex parte Hughes* (2001) have the potential to cause confusion in the construction of the exemption.

The *Hughes* case related to the judicial review of the manner in which the "Ombudsman" had investigated a complaint about the alleged failure of a Street Works Authority, Hartlepool Borough Council, to apply the APC properly. A developer had promoted a housing development and the houses in it were to be served by a private estate road which was to be constructed by the developer. The developer did not make an advance payment or provide the appropriate security and then went into liquidation. The Claimants had purchased houses on the site only to find that the estate road was never completed. The Council had not applied the APC to the development, had not issued an exemption under section 219(4)(e) and had not taken any criminal proceedings against the developer. The works that were done to the road were carried out unsatisfactorily and at least the sum of £42,000, if not more, was required to bring the roads into a satisfactory condition. The Ombudsman concluded that there was maladministration by Hartlepool Council, but that there was no injustice resulting, and consequently no order or recommendation was made by the Ombudsman. Burton J held that the finding of no injustice was wrong and ordered the Ombudsman to revisit her decision.[122]

One of the issues related to the exemption in section 219(4)(e).

The Claimants argued that, on the proper construction of section 219(4)(e), an exemption notice cannot be issued in respect of a private street that has not yet been constructed. Thus, the only course open to the Street Works Authority was to apply the APC and require a security, which they had failed to do.

Part of their argument was that:

---

[121]  (2001) EWHC Admin 349; (2001) 3 L.G.L.R. 50; [2001] A.C.D. 89; (2001) 98(20) L.S.G. 45.

[122]  [71] *"This is a case which I have found difficult, simply because if I were the Local Ombudsman deciding this matter I would have no doubt whatever that there has been gross maladministration and very serious injustice, ..."*

Section 219(4)(e) sets out a two stage test: is the street at present in a certain condition, whether it is built up or in a condition which is not (or will not be) unsatisfactory; or is it likely within a reasonable time to fall within one or other of those categories? If either of those two are not satisfied, then it would not be appropriate to issue the exemption notice.

Consequently the word *"and"* is conjunctive and not disjunctive in the sense that these are not alternatives; they are two different and necessary tests, both of which have to be applied before it can be seen whether a notice is or is not appropriate.[123]

When considering the first part of the section, namely the question of whether a street which is or is not to be exempted is not and is not likely within a reasonable time to be *"substantially built up"*, that interpretation is all the clearer.

The Claimants' objective in seeking to make this point was to show that, as a matter of statutory construction, the exemption cannot apply to streets which are not yet constructed or are in the course of being made up. As such, on this basis, the only course available to the Street Works Authority would have been to apply the APC and to require a deposit or a security from the developer – which they had failed to do.

The common flaw in the arguments of both parties lies in a failure to deal with the meaning of the word *"street"* in the context of the exemption.

One of the counter-arguments on behalf of the Defendant related to the provisions of section 203(2), which provides that, for the purposes of the APC, the definition of *"private street"* also includes *"... any land shown as a proposed street on plans deposited with respect to any building either under building regulations or on an application for planning permission under the Town and Country Planning Act 1990."*

Counsel for the Defendant submitted that the definition of *"private street"* in section 203(2) imports into sections 219 and 220 the consideration not only of an existing street, but also a proposed street, in the sense of a street which is shown on the plans. Thus, when it comes to section 219(4)(e), the words *"proposed street"* must be read into the reference to *"street"*.

The Claimants responded by pointing out that, within section 219(4)(e), the word that is used is *"street"* and not *"private street"*, and consequently that the definition in section 203(2) which indicates what is to be meant by *"private street"* should not be imported into section 219(4)(e), in which subparagraph the use of the word *"street"* rather than *"private street"* is used.

---

[123] By way of interjection, the word *"and"* is the *"and"* which appears underlined in the following extract from section 219(4)(e): *"... being satisfied that the whole of the street ... is not __and__ is not likely within a reasonable time to be ..."*.

Counsel for the Defendant further contended that section 219(4)(e) has to be taken in its context and that section 219(1) refers to "*private street*"; therefore section 219(4) (e) is then a reference back to "*private street*" by way of exclusion of the otherwise applicable provisions of section 219.

It is notable that no mention was made of the definition of a "*street*" in section 329, which adopts the definition in section 48 of the New Roads and Street Works Act 1991 and includes "*... any land laid out as a way whether it is for the time being formed as a way or not.*" This includes ways which have yet to be constructed and, it is submitted, clearly counters the Claimants' argument that the use of the word "*street*" in section 219(4)(e) limits it to existing ways.

So far as the Claimants' reliance on the omission of the word "*private*" in connection with the word "*street*" is concerned, the reality is that it makes no difference as to whether it is in or out. This is because the only type of "*street*" within the compass of section 219(4)(e) is a private street. A private street is, inter alia, a street which is not a highway maintainable at the public expense. Section 219(4)(e), patently, has nothing to do with ways which are already highways maintainable at the public expense. Ergo, its application is limited to private streets, whether or not the whole phrase is used.

Accordingly, it is submitted that Exemption (e) can be applied to ways which are in the course of construction, or which are proposed, provided that any such way or proposed way falls within the definition in section 48 of the 1991 Act.

The Claimants also argued for a "*purposive construction*" of the statute; namely, that it makes a nonsense to have a situation in which the Street Works Authority can issue an exemption notice where a street is not yet constructed, because it is impossible for them to consider, never mind be "*satisfied*", that a street that is not yet built is likely within a reasonable time to be in an unsatisfactory condition. Accordingly, they argued that the most that can be done is to look at the plans, but the plans will already have been required to be looked at for the purpose of granting planning regulations approval, and consequently the provision would give carte blanche to an authority to issue an exemption notice in every case, and cannot have anything to do with the question which really lies behind this section, which is ensuring carrying out of works which a developer will only have said he is going to carry out, by including them in the approved plans.

Burton J stated:

> *[52] I find both arguments extremely persuasive and, particularly in these days of purposive construction, it may be that Mr Pennock's [the Claimants'] construction is right. I do not, however, propose to decide this question on this application, not least on an application where it is agreed that I am to quash the decision by the Local Ombudsman on other grounds.*

One answer to the Claimants' "*purposive construction*" point is that the purported uncertainty as to the promised construction of the way is eliminated in cases where the way is to be constructed to a specification and within a period of time stipulated in a suitable contract. In the *Hughes* case, Burton J stated:

> "*The inevitable conclusion of Mr Corner's arguments about the proper construction of section 219(4)(e), if they be right, would be that, in relation to a proposed street, if there had been consideration by the Council, it would have had to have been an unusual and difficult one. It would plainly not have been enough for them simply to have looked at the plans, because that would not have assisted them in any way to consider whether the plans were going to be complied with, which, of course, is the whole reason for considering whether or not to enforce any obligation by a bond. If the Council on consideration was, assuming it carried out the exercise, satisfied, and thus, on a hypothetical reconstruction would have been satisfied, on the evidence before it that the road was "not likely within a reasonable time to be in an unreasonable condition", the only basis, it seems to me, on which it could have been so satisfied would have been not simply by reference to the plans, but by reference to some evidence that the plans would be complied with. Thus, assuming that the construction for which Mr Corner contends is right (and he may be wrong, as I have indicated), some consideration of the past record of the developer and its financial solvency and competence might have been relevant. Further, or in the alternative, some consideration as to whether there was some other reason why the Council could be satisfied that the road would not within a reasonable time be in a reasonable condition; for example, if some security was not offered of a financial kind, some other kind of security, perhaps involving regular inspections by the Council, so that its own surveyor would have the opportunity to inspect, intervene and supervise.*"

With respect, Burton J's following comment does not show any appreciation of day to day practice within local highway authorities: "*... in relation to a proposed street, if there had been consideration by the Council, it would have had to have been an unusual and difficult one.*" Far from being "*unusual and difficult*", the assessment of whether or not a proposed way will be suitable is part of the bread and butter of a local authority highways department. As to securing that proposed ways will be constructed properly, local highway authorities throughout the country enter agreements providing for street works under sections 38 and 278 of the Highways Act 1980 on a regular basis.

One way of absorbing Burton J's comments is for the developer to enter into a planning agreement pursuant to section 106 of the Town and Country Planning Act 1990 with the Street Works Authority, which agreement could set out the specifications for the estate road, provide for inspections and provide some form of security to ensure that the works are carried out. The agreement would also contain the exemption notice for the purposes of section 219(4)(e). The difficulty here is in understanding why this more complicated approach would confer any advantage over use of the Advance Payments Code. Arguably there are three advantages:

1) the agreement can set out a bespoke specification for the construction of the estate road;

2) the "*security*" might be a bond but, perhaps with a large development, an alternative might be to dispense with a bond on the basis that the agreement provides an alterative enforcement mechanism, for example an embargo on the balance of a phased development; and

3) the use of a planning agreement can be coupled with the creation of a management company which would then be responsible for future maintenance of the way.

As to point 3), the Advance Payments Code is limited in that it provides for the construction of the way but does not provide for its future maintenance - this is left to the Private Street Works Code. Thus, providing for future maintenance does confer an advantage over the use of the Advance Payments Code only.

Taking into account the foregoing, it is submitted that the position is as follows:

• The application of the Advance Payments Code does not mean that the relevant way must necessarily become a highway or a highway maintainable at the public expense;

• An exemption under section 219(4)(e) can be granted if either of the two following cases apply:

a) where the Street Works Authority are satisfied that the whole or the part of the private street is not, and is not likely within a reasonable time to be, substantially built up; or

b) where the Street Works Authority are satisfied that the whole or the part of the private street is not, and is not likely within a reasonable time to be, in so unsatisfactory a condition as to justify the use of powers under the Private Street Works Code for securing the carrying out of street works in the street or part thereof.

• Section 219(4)(e) can be applied to ways which are either in the course of construction or are to be constructed in the future so long as the proposed way falls within the definition of a "*street*" in section 48 of the New Roads and Street Works Act 1991.

Overall, it is probably more straight forward to apply the Advance Payments Code to the development in the first instance. However, if the Street Works Authority is minded to take a different course, then an exemption could be justified as part of a section 106 agreement provided that the agreement and/or associated legal mechanisms provide reasonable assurance that the ways will be made up to an appropriate standard and then maintained in the future.

(f)    where the street works authority, being satisfied that the street is not, and is not likely within a reasonable time to become, joined to a highway maintainable at the public expense, by notice exempt the building from this section;

(g)    where the whole street, being less than 100 yards in length, or a part of the street not less than 100 yards in length and comprising the whole of the part on which the frontage of the building will be, was on the material date built-up to such an extent that the aggregate length of the frontages of the buildings on both sides of the street or part constituted at least one half of the aggregate length of all the frontages on both sides of the street or part;

### Notes: The exemption under section 219(4)(g)

As to ground (g) of section 219(4), an automatic exemption would appear to arise in two cases:

- If the street is not less than 100 yards long and at least 50% of it was built up at the *"material date"*; or

- If the street is more than 100 yards long and the proposed building will be sited in any length of street which is not less than 100 yards long and was at least 50% built up at the *"material date"*. The *"material date"* is defined by section 219(6) (see below).

If ground (g) does not apply, then the authority may grant an exemption by notice under ground (h) if they are satisfied that, in any event, the whole of the street was substantially built up at the material date (see below).

(h)    where (in a case not falling within paragraph (g) above) the street works authority, being satisfied that the whole of the street was on the material date substantially built-up, by notice exempt the building from this section;

(i)    where the building is proposed to be erected on land belonging to, or in the possession of -

        (i)    the British Railways Board, Canal & River Trust, Transport for London any wholly-owned subsidiary (within the meaning of the Transport Act 1968) or joint subsidiary (within the meaning of section 51(5) of that Act) of any of those bodies other than Transport for London, or any of its subsidiaries (within the meaning of the Greater London Authority Act 1999);

(ii)    the council of a county, district or London borough or the Common Council;

(iii)    the new towns residuary body or a new town development corporation;

(j)    where the building is to be erected by a company the objects of which include the provision of industrial premises for use by persons other than the company, being a company the constitution of which prohibits the distribution of the profits of the company to its members, and the cost of the building is to be defrayed wholly or mainly by a government department;

(k)    where the street works authority, being satisfied -

(i)    that more than three-quarters of the aggregate length of all the frontages on both sides of the street, or of a part of the street not less than 100 yards in length and comprising the whole of the part on which the frontage of the building will be, consists, or is at some future time likely to consist, of the frontages of industrial premises, and

(ii)    that their powers under the private street works code are not likely to be exercised in relation to the street, or to that part of it, as the case may be, within a reasonable time,

by resolution exempt the street, or that part of it, from this section.

### Notes: The exemption under section 219(4)(k)

If the developer is bringing forward an industrial estate, then he can apply for an exemption under section 219(4)(k). Unfortunately, this exemption is an anachronism. The term "*industrial premises*" is defined in section 203(3) by reference to section 66(1) of the now revoked Town and Country Planning Act 1971 and are, quite simply, long out of date. Section 66(1) in turn referred to buildings which were used for industrial processes and for commercial scientific research. Such a building falls within the exemption if it is used for, designed for or suitable for such purposes or for ancillary purposes. This would seem to exclude business parks which are to be used exclusively for offices, but could include estates with more flexible accommodation on the basis that they are designed for, or are suitable for, such purposes. Premises constructed for uses within class B1 of the Town & Country Planning (Use Classes) Order 1987 can cater for light industry, office use and research. It is notable that an exemption under ground (k) is not by way of notice but by way of a resolution that exempts not just the proposed building but the street or a part of it.

> In subsection 219(4)(c), "*district council*" is to be read in relation to plans deposited on or after 1 April 1996 for a building to be erected in Wales as "*Welsh council*": section 219(4A).

(4A) In subsection (4)(c) above, "district council" is to be read in relation to plans deposited on or after 1st April 1996 for a building to be erected in Wales as "Welsh council".

(4B) In subsection (4)(i)(iii) "new towns residuary body" means -

    (a) in relation to England, the Homes and Communities Agency so far as exercising functions in relation to anything transferred (or to be transferred) to it as mentioned in section 52(1)(a) to (d) of the Housing and Regeneration Act 2008 or the Greater London Authority so far as exercising its new towns and urban development functions; and

    (b) in relation to Wales, the Welsh Ministers so far as exercising functions in relation to anything transferred (or to be transferred) to them as mentioned in section 36(1)(a)(i) to (iii) of the New Towns Act 1981.

(5) Where a sum has been paid or secured under this section by the owner of the land in relation to a building proposed to be erected on it, and thereafter a notice is served under subsection (4) above exempting the building from this section, or a resolution is passed under paragraph (k) of that subsection exempting the street or part of a street on which the building will have a frontage from this section, the street works authority shall refund that sum to the person who is for the time being owner of the land or shall release the security, as the case may be.

Where the said sum was paid, and after the payment but before the service of the said notice or the passing of the said resolution, as the case may be, the land in respect of which it was paid was divided into 2 or more parts each having a frontage on the private street in question, the sum is to be treated for the purposes of this subsection as apportioned between the owners of the land according to their respective frontages.

(6) For the purposes of this section "the material date" is -

    (a) in relation to a building proposed to be erected in an area which before 1st April 1974 was a rural district or a contributory place within a rural district, the date on which the New Streets Act 1951 or the advance payments code (either in this Act or in the Highways Act 1959) was applied in that area;

    (b) in relation to a building proposed to be erected anywhere else, 1st October 1951.

## Section 220 - Determination of liability for, and amount of, payments.

(1)   In a case to which section 219 above applies the street works authority shall, within 6 weeks from the passing of any required plans relating to the erection of a building deposited with them or, in a case to which subsection (2) or (2A) below applies, with the district council or Welsh council, serve a notice on the person by or on whose behalf the plans were deposited requiring the payment or the securing under section 219 above of a sum specified in the notice.

In this subsection and subsections (2) and (2A) below "required plans" means plans required to be deposited with the local authority in accordance with building regulations.

(2)   Where (outside Greater London) the advance payments code is in force in the whole or any part of a non-metropolitan district, the district council, in any case to which section 219 above may be applicable, shall within one week from the date of the passing of any required plans deposited with them relating to the erection of a building in an area in which that code is in force inform the street works authority that the plans have been passed.

(2A)  Where any required plans which -

(a)   are deposited with a Welsh council; and

(b)   relate to the erection of a building in an area -

(i)    in which the advance payments code is in force; but

(ii)   which is treated as being within the area of a street works authority other than that Welsh council,

are passed, the Welsh council shall, in any case to which section 219 above may be applicable, within one week inform the street works authority of that event.

(3)   Subject to the provisions of this section, the sum to be specified in a notice under subsection (1) above is such sum as, in the opinion of the street works authority, would be recoverable under the private street works code in respect of the frontage of the proposed building on the private street if the authority were then to carry out such street works in the street as they would require under that code before declaring the street to be a highway which for the purposes of this Act is a highway maintainable at the public expense.

In this subsection a reference to a street does not include a reference to a part of a street, except to a part which the street works authority think fit to treat as constituting a separate street for the purposes of this subsection and which comprises the whole of the part on which the frontage of the building will be.

(4)     If, at any time after the service of a notice under subsection (1) above, the street works authority -

    (a)     are of opinion that the sum specified in the notice exceeds such sum as in their opinion would be recoverable as mentioned in subsection (3) above if they were then to carry out such street works as are so mentioned, or

    (b)     are of opinion that no sum would be so recoverable,

they may, by a further notice, served on the person who is for the time being owner of the land on which the building is to be, or has been, erected, substitute a smaller sum for the sum specified in the notice served under subsection (1) above or, as the case may be, intimate that no sum falls to be paid or secured.

This subsection does not apply where a sum has been paid or secured in compliance with a notice served under subsection (1) above and the case is one in which the authority have power to make a refund or release under section 221(1)below.

(5)     Where, under a local Act, the erection of buildings on land having a frontage on a new street is prohibited until works for the construction or sewering of the street have been carried out in accordance with byelaws, the amount of the sum to be specified in a notice served under this section shall be calculated as if those works had been carried out.

(6)     Where a notice is served on any person under this section (other than a notice intimating that no sum falls to be paid or secured) that person or, if he is a different person, the owner of the land on which the building is to be, or has been, erected, may, not later than one month from the date of the service of the notice, appeal to the Minister and the Minister may substitute a smaller sum for the sum specified by the street works authority.

On an appeal under this subsection, the Minister shall give the appellant an opportunity of being heard before a person appointed by the Minister.

(7)     Where a sum has been paid or secured in compliance with a notice served under subsection (1) above and a notice is subsequently served under subsection (4) above substituting a smaller sum for the sum specified in the first-mentioned notice or intimating that no sum falls to be paid or secured, the street works authority -

    (a)     if the sum was paid, shall refund the amount of the excess or, as the case may be, the whole sum to the person who is for the time being owner of the land on which the building is to be, or has been, erected;

(b)    if the sum was secured and the person whose property is security for the payment of it is for the time being owner of that land, shall release the security to the extent of the excess or, as the case may be, the whole security;

(c)    if the sum was secured and the person whose property is security for the payment of it is not for the time being owner of that land, shall pay to that owner an amount equal to the excess or, as the case may be, the whole sum, and are entitled to realise the security for the purpose of recovering the amount so paid.

(8)    Where land in respect of which a sum has been paid or secured in compliance with a notice under subsection (1) above is subsequently divided into 2 or more parts so that 2 or more owners would, if street works were carried out, incur liability in respect of it, the sum is to be treated as apportioned between those owners according to their respective frontages and, if the sum was secured and the security is the property of one only of those owners, the street works authority -

(a)    are required under subsection (7)(b) above to release the security only to the extent of the amount apportioned to that owner, and

(b)    are entitled to realise the security for the purpose of recovering the amount or amounts paid to the other owner or owners under subsection (7)(c) above.

(9)    Where a security is realised for the purpose of recovering an amount paid by a street works authority under subsection (7)(c) above, and the sum produced by realising the security exceeds the amount so paid, the amount of the excess shall be held by the authority and dealt with under the advance payments code as if it had been an amount paid under section 219 above on the date on which the security was realised.

### Notes: Section 220(1) - The 'six week' rule.

Section 220(1) provides that, in a case to which section 219 applies, the Street Works Authority shall, within 6 weeks from the passing of any required plans relating to the erection of a building deposited with them or, in a case to which subsection 220(2) or 220(2A) applies, with the district council or Welsh council, serve a notice on the person by or on whose behalf the plans were deposited requiring the payment or the securing under section 219 of a sum specified in the notice. The words "... *within 6 weeks from the passing of any required plans relating to the erection of a building deposited with them ...*" is the provenance for the so-called "*six week rule*".

This situation is complicated when the Street Works Authority is not the body which deals with Building Regulation approvals. Section 220(2) provides that, where (outside Greater London) the Advance Payments Code is in force in the whole or any part of a non-metropolitan district, the district council shall, within one week from the date of the passing of any required plans deposited with them relating to the erection of a building in an area in which that code is in force, inform the Street Works Authority that the plans have been passed. Thus, in these cases, the six weeks period is reduced, in practice, to five weeks.

### Section 221 - Refunds etc. where work done otherwise than at expense of street works authority.

(1)    Where -

    (a)    a sum has been paid or secured under section 219 above by the owner of land in respect of the cost of street works to be carried out in the private street on which that land has a frontage, and

    (b)    any street works are subsequently carried out in the private street in respect of that frontage to the satisfaction of but otherwise than at the expense of the street works authority,

the authority may refund to the person at whose expense the works are carried out the whole or such proportion of that sum or, as the case may be, release the whole or such part of the security, as in their opinion represents the amount by which the liability of the owner of that land in respect of street works has been reduced as a result of the carrying out of the street works in question.

Where the person at whose expense the works are carried out is not the person who is for the time being owner of that land no refund or release shall be made under this subsection unless the owner has been notified of the proposal to make the refund or release and has been afforded an opportunity of making representations to the street works authority in relation to it.

(2)    Where any land which has a frontage on a private street, and in respect of which a sum has been paid or secured under section 219 above, is subsequently divided into 2 or more parts each having a frontage on that private street, the sum is to be treated as apportioned between the owners thereof according to their respective frontages, and subsection (1) above has effect accordingly.

(3)    Where -

    (a)    a sum has been paid or secured under section 219 above by the owner of land in respect of the cost of street works to be carried out in the private street on which that land has a frontage, and

    (b)    thereafter the street works authority enter into an agreement with any person under section 38 above providing for the carrying out at the expense of that person of street works in respect of that frontage, that agreement may also provide for the refund of the said sum or a part of it either without interest or with interest at such rate as may be specified in the agreement, or for the release of the whole or a part of the security, as the case may be.

### Section 222 - Sums paid or secured to be in discharge of further liability for street works.

(1)    Where a sum has been paid or secured under section 219 above by the owner of land in respect of the cost of street works to be carried out in the private street on which that land has a frontage, the liability of that owner or any subsequent owner of that land in respect of the carrying out of street works in that street under the private street works code ("the street works liability") is, as respects that frontage, to be deemed to be discharged to the extent of the sum so paid or secured.

(2)    If, when the street is declared to be a highway which for the purposes of this Act is a highway maintainable at the public expense, the said sum is found to exceed the total street works liability in respect of that frontage or there is no such liability because the street was not made up at the expense of the street works authority, the street works authority -

(a)    if the sum was paid, shall refund the amount of the excess or, as the case may be, the whole sum to the person who is for the time being owner of the land;

(b)    if the sum was secured and the person whose property is security for the payment of it is for the time being owner of the land, shall release the security to the extent of the excess or, as the case may be, the whole security;

(c)    if the sum was secured and the person whose property is security for the payment of it is not for the time being owner of the land, shall pay to that owner an amount equal to the excess or, as the case may be, the whole sum, and are entitled to realise the security for the purpose of recovering the amount so paid.

(3)    Where land in respect of which a sum has been paid or secured under section 219 above is subsequently divided into 2 or more parts so that 2 or more owners incur or would incur the street works liability, the sum is to be treated as apportioned between those owners according to their respective frontages, and if the sum was secured and the security is the property of one only of those owners the street works authority -

(a)    are required under subsection (2)(b) above to release the security only to the extent to which the amount apportioned to that owner exceeds his street works liability or, as the case may be, to the extent of the whole of that amount, and

(b)    are entitled to realise the security for the purpose of recovering the amount or amounts paid to the other owner or owners under subsection (2)(c) above.

(4)     Where any refund, release or payment has been made under section 220(7) above, or under section 221 above, the foregoing provisions of this section have effect as if for references therein to a sum paid or secured there were substituted references to any sum remaining paid or secured.

### Section 223 - Determination to cease to have effect when plans not proceeded with.

(1)     Where, on the occasion of the deposit of plans for the erection of a building, the amount to be paid or secured under section 219 above has been determined under section 220 above, and subsequently -

    (a)     the local authority, under section 32 of the Building Act 1984, declare the deposit of the plans to be of no effect, or

    (b)     before any work has been done in or for the purpose of erecting the building the owner gives notice to the local authority of his intention not to proceed with the building,

the said determination and any payment made or security given in accordance with it are, unless there have already been carried out or commenced in the street under the private street works code street works in respect of which the owner of the land on which the building was to be erected is liable, of no effect for the purposes of this Part of this Act.

(2)     Where by virtue of subsection (1) above a determination is of no effect and a sum has been paid or security given in accordance with it, the street works authority -

    (a)     if the sum was paid, shall refund it to the person who is for the time being owner of the land;

    (b)     if the sum was secured and the person whose property is security for the payment of it is for the time being owner of the land, shall release the security;

    (c)     if the sum was secured and the person whose property is security for the payment of it is not for the time being owner of the land, shall pay to that owner an amount equal to the said sum, and are entitled to realise the security for the purpose of recovering the amount so paid.

(3)     Where land in respect of which a sum has been paid or secured as mentioned in subsection (2) above is subsequently divided into 2 or more parts so that 2 or more owners would, if street works were carried out, incur liability in respect thereof, the sum is to be treated as apportioned between those owners according to their respective frontages and, if the sum was secured and the security is the property of one only of those owners, the street works authority -

    (a)    are required under subsection (2)(b) above to release the security only to the extent of the amount apportioned to that owner, and

    (b)    are entitled to realise the security for the purpose of recovering the amount or amounts paid to the other owner or owners under subsection (2)(c) above.

(4)    Where any refund, release or payment has been made under section 220(7) above, or under section 221 above, subsections (2) and (3) above have effect as if for references in those subsections to a sum paid and security given there were substituted references to, respectively, any sum remaining paid and any remaining security.

(5)    Where -

    (a)    a person notifies the local authority in accordance with subsection (1)(b) above of his intention not to proceed with the building and by reason thereof a determination is of no effect, and

    (b)    subsequently notice is given to the local authority by the owner of the land that he intends to proceed with the building in accordance with the plans as originally deposited,

the notice to be served under subsection (1) of section 220 above by the street works authority shall, in lieu of being served as required by that subsection, be served on him within one month from the date of the service of the notice of his intention to proceed with the building, and section 220 has effect accordingly.

(6)    Where the advance payments code is in force in the whole or any part of a non-metropolitan district, the district council, in any case to which this section may be applicable, shall within one week inform the county council of the happening of any of the following events: -

    (a)    the making of any declaration that the deposit of plans relating to the erection of a building is of no effect,

    (b)    the giving of any notice by an owner of his intention not to proceed with a building, and

    (c)    the giving of any notice by an owner of his intention to proceed with the building in accordance with the plans as originally deposited.

(7)    In any case -

    (a)    to which this section may be applicable; and

(b)     which relates to plans for the erection of a building in any part of a street in Wales which is treated as being in the area of a street works authority other than the Welsh council for the county or county borough in which it is situated,

the Welsh council shall within one week inform the street works authority of the happening of any event of a kind described in paragraphs (a) to (c) of subsection (6) above.

### Section 224 - Certain matters to be local land charges.

(1)     The matters specified in subsection (2) below are local land charges.

(2)     The matters referred to in subsection (1) above are: -

(a)     notices served by a street works authority under section 220(1) or (4) above;

(b)     determinations by the Minister under section 220(6) above;

(c)     payments made and securities given under section 219 above;

(d)     notices served under subsection (4)(e), (f) or (h) of section 219 above exempting a building from that section;

(e)     resolutions passed under subsection (4)(k) of section 219 above exempting a street or a part of a street from that section; and

(f)     refunds made and releases of securities granted under section 221, 222 or 223 above.

(3)     As respects any matter that is a local land charge by virtue of this section, the street works authority for the street concerned are, notwithstanding anything in section 5(4) of the Local Land Charges Act 1975, to be treated as the originating authority for the purposes of that Act.

### Section 225 - Interest on sums paid under advance payments code.

(1)     Any sum paid by the owner of land to a street works authority under section 219 above, in so far as it continues to be held by the authority, carries simple interest at the appropriate rate from the date of payment until such time as the sum or a part of it remaining so held -

(a)     falls to be set off under section 222 above against the liability of the owner of the land in respect of the carrying out of street works; or

(b)     falls to be refunded in full under the provisions of the advance payments code;

and the interest shall be held by the authority until that time and dealt with under those provisions as if it formed part of the said sum.

This subsection does not apply to any sum in so far as it is repaid under any such agreement as is referred to in section 221(3) above.

(2)    For the purposes of the advance payments code interest on any sum held by a street works authority shall be calculated in respect of each financial year during which it accrues at the appropriate rate prevailing at the commencement of that financial year.

(3)    In this section "the appropriate rate" means the rate at the material time determined by the Treasury in respect of local loans for periods of 10 years on the security of local rates (being a determination under section 6(2) of the National Loans Act 1968, and subject to any relevant direction under the said section 6(2)).

### Section 228 - Adoption of private street after execution of street works.

(1)    When any street works have been executed in a private street, the street works authority may, by notice displayed in a prominent position in the street, declare the street to be a highway which for the purposes of this Act is a highway maintainable at the public expense, and on the expiration of one month from the day on which the notice was first so displayed the street shall, subject to subsections (2) to (4) below, become such a highway.

(2)    A street shall not become a highway maintainable at the public expense by virtue of subsection (1) above if, within the period there mentioned, the owner of the street or, if more than one, the majority in number of the owners of the street, by notice to the authority object; but within 2 months from the expiration of that period the street works authority may apply to a magistrates' court for an order overruling the objection.

(3)    If an order overruling an objection under subsection (2) above is made pursuant to an application under that subsection and no appeal against the order is brought within the time limited for such an appeal, the street or part in question shall become a highway maintainable at the public expense on the expiration of that time.

(4)    Where such an order is made or refused and an appeal, or an appeal arising out of that appeal, is brought against or arises out of the order or refusal, then -

(a)    if the final determination of the matter is in favour of the authority, or

(b)    the appeal is abandoned by the objectors,

the street shall become a highway maintainable at the public expense on that final determination or, as the case may be, on the abandonment of the appeal.

(5)     Notwithstanding anything in any other enactment or provision, for the purposes of this section the time for bringing or seeking leave for any appeal (including an application for certiorari) is 2 months from the date of the decision or of the conclusion of the proceedings appealed against, unless apart from this subsection the time is less than that period; and no power, however worded, to enlarge any such time is exercisable for the purposes of this section.

(6)     Where street works have been executed in a part only of a street (other than a part extending for the whole of the length of the street), subsections (1) to (4) above have effect as if for references in those subsections to the street there were substituted references to the length of the street which constitutes or comprises that part.

(7)     If all street works (whether or not including lighting) have been executed in a private street to the satisfaction of the street works authority, then, on the application of the majority in rateable value of the owners of premises in the street, the street works authority shall, within the period of 3 months from the date of the application, by notice displayed in a prominent position in the street, declare the street to be a highway which for the purposes of this Act is a highway maintainable at the public expense and thereupon the street shall become such a highway.

In this subsection a reference to a street does not include a reference to a part of a street.

### Definitions

For "*street works*" and "*private street*" see section 203(3).

### Notes

The section 228 procedure is useful where a potential access to a development scheme is an unadopted way which is in unknown ownership or the ownership of someone other than the developer. The highway authority has the ability to use the procedure to unlock the site without the need to use powers of compulsory purchase. Also, as noted above @ paras. 13.20 and 13.21, the procedure can be used to rescue ways which should have been adopted by the action of failed Section 38 Agreements.

Section 228(1) requires the posting of a notice in a prominent position in the private street but it does not stipulate the contents of the notice. It is therefore necessary to compose appropriate guidelines for the practical application of the procedure. If the private street to be adopted is of some length, then it is prudent to place two notices, one at each end of the section of way to be adopted. It would be wise to describe the relevant section of the street with some particularity, giving the length in metres and it would do no harm to show it on a plan.

A particular difficulty arises where only a very short length of private street is nominated for adoption by way of the section 228 procedure. It would not, in such a situation, be appropriate to place notices some distance from the nominated section of way. To do so could be misleading to those frontagers who might be minded to object. The notice should be placed on the short section of way only and this short section should be described in the notice. Otherwise it might be the case that confusion could arise as to whether the notice is referring to the private street or the adopted highway abutting it. This is important because a frontager's right to object (see section 228(2) below) relates to his ownership of the private street or a part of it and he could be misled if the notice inadvertently misdescribes the whole private street.

Section 228(2) provides that a street shall not become a highway maintainable at the public expense if the owner of the street or, if more than one, the majority in number of the owners of the street, by notice to the authority object. This begs the question of why any owner or frontager would object when the procedure is designed to relieve them of the liability to maintain in perpetuity. Orlik observes (@ p.131) as follows:

> "It may be thought that there would be little benefit in the residents objecting to a proposal that their road should become a highway maintainable at the public expense once it has been made up. However, it must be remembered that private streets are not necessarily highways when the street works are carried out. Although the street works authority can require a street to be made up to adoption standards, they cannot require the owners to dedicate it as a highway except under the section 228 procedure. If the residents want to keep the general public out of the road, they may decide that it is in their best interest that the road remain private. One advantage to the residents is that they can erect gates across the road and keep them shut in order to deter housebreakers. Another is that they can build ramps in the road to slow down traffic in situations where the highway authority may not be willing to exercise the power to construct ramps or where the residents may want to build more substantial ramps than those allowed by the regulations in maintainable highways. The disadvantage to the residents is that the highway authority will not maintain the road in the future and, if residents allow it to deteriorate, it is quite possible for the highway authority to repeat the street works procedure and again resolve, under section 205, that the road should be made good to adoption standards at the expense of the frontagers."

There is the added problem that the owners/frontagers will be liable to any person who is injured as a result of defects in the unadopted way. It would be surprising if they habitually carry public liability insurance.

Sauvain has observed[124] that, as the section 228 declaration creates a new right of property in the surface of the highway in favour of the highway authority, and restricts

---

[124]    Ibid @ p.413

the rights of the owner of the street - all without the payment of any compensation - there is an untested question whether section 228 is compatible with Article 1 of the First Protocol to the European Convention on Human Rights 1950. He opined:

> *"The Courts have, however, held that it is necessary to look at the reality of the situation in order to determine whether there has been de facto expropriation or whether the action in question amounts to the control of the use of land. If it is the latter then the absence of compensation may not be critical although the lack of compensation will always be weighed in the balance between the public interest and the rights of the landowner. If it is the former then the absence of compensation will only be justified in exceptional circumstances. In practice, in most cases the landowner's rights may not be affected significantly as his rights in the subsoil remain and he has not been deprived of any property interest as such-although he has lost control over the surface of the road. He is also relieved of any burden in respect of maintenance. Loss of control, however, where a road provides the only access to a development site, could be regarded as the deprivation of a valuable asset. Ultimately, there is a balance to be struck between the interests of the landowner and the public interest in securing the long term public maintenance of the street."*

### Section 229 - Power of majority of frontagers to require adoption where advance payment made.

(1)     Where a majority in number of the owners of land having a frontage on a built-up private street, or as many of those owners as have between them more than half the aggregate length of all the frontages on both sides of the street, by notice request the street works authority to exercise their powers under the private street works code so as -

    (a)     to secure the carrying out of such street works in that street as the street works authority require under that code before declaring the street to be a highway which for the purposes of this Act is a highway maintainable at the public expense, and

    (b)     to declare the street to be such a highway,

the street works authority shall proceed to exercise their powers accordingly.

(2)     Subsection (1) above does not apply unless, in at least one case, a payment has been made or security has been given under section 219 above by the owner of land having a frontage on the street and the payment has not been refunded, or the security released or realised, under subsection (5) of that section, or under section 223 above.

(3)     For the purposes of this section a street is to be deemed to be built-up if the aggregate length of the frontages of the buildings on both sides of the street constitutes at least one half of the aggregate length of all the frontages on both sides of the street.

(4)    This section does not apply in relation to a part of a street unless it is a part not less than 100 yards in length which the owners of land having a frontage on that part of the street elect to treat as constituting a street for the purposes of this section.

---

**Definitions**

For "*frontage*" and "*private street*", "*street works authority*" and "*private street works code*" see section 203. The phrase "*built-up*" is defined by section 229(3).

---

### Section 263 - Vesting of highways maintainable at public expense.

(1)    Subject to the provisions of this section, every highway maintainable at the public expense, together with the materials and scrapings of it, vests in the authority who are for the time being the highway authority for the highway.

(2)    Subsection (1) above does not apply -

   (a)    to a highway with respect to the vesting of which, on its becoming or ceasing to be a trunk road, provision is made by section 265 below, or

   (b)    to a part of a trunk road with respect to the vesting of which provision is made by section 266 below, or

   (c)    to a part of a special road with respect to the vesting of which provision is made by section 267 below.

(3)    Where a scheme submitted to the Minister jointly by two or more highway authorities under section 16 above determines which of those authorities are to be the special road authority for the special road or any part of it ("the designated authority") and the designated authority are not the highway authority for the road or that part of it, the road or that part of it vests in the designated authority.

(4)    Where -

   (a)    the responsibility for the maintenance of a bridge or other part of a highway is transferred to a highway authority by means of an order under section 93 above, but the property in it is not so transferred, or

   (b)    the responsibility for the maintenance of a part of a highway is transferred to a highway authority in pursuance of an agreement made under section 94 above, but the property in that part is not so transferred, the part of the highway in question does not by virtue of subsection (1) above vest in that highway authority.

(5)  Notwithstanding anything in subsection (1) above, any such material as is referred to in that subsection which is removed from a highway by a non-metropolitan district council in exercise of their powers under section 42, 50 or 230(7) above vests in the district council and not in the highway authority.

See Text @ para. 4.3.

### Section 264 - Vesting of drains etc. of certain roads.

(1)  The drains belonging to a road for which the council of a county or metropolitan district are the highway authority vest in the council of the county or metropolitan district in which the road is situated and where any other drain or any sewer was at the material date used for any purpose in connection with the drainage of such a road, that council continue to have the right of using the drain or sewer for that purpose.

For the purposes of this subsection the material date is -

(a)  in the case of any highway which first became maintainable at the public expense before the commencement of this Act, the date on which it first became so maintainable or 1st April 1974, whichever date was later; and

(b)  in the case of any highway which first becomes maintainable at the public expense after the commencement of this Act, the date on which it first becomes so maintainable.

(2)  The drains belonging to a highway -

(a)  which immediately before the date of the abolition of the Greater London Council under the Local Government Act 1985 was a metropolitan road; and

(b)  which did not become a trunk road on that date by virtue of an order made under paragraph 53 of Schedule 4 to that Act,

vest in the council of the London borough in which the highway is situated or, if it is situated in the City in the Common Council, and where any other drain or sewer was, at the date when the highway became a metropolitan road, used for any purpose in connection with the drainage of that highway, that council shall have the right of using the drain or sewer for that purpose.

(3)  Any difference arising under this section -

    (a)    between a county council and a non-metropolitan district council -

        (i)    as to the council in whom a drain is vested, or

        (ii)    as to the use of a drain or sewer;

    (b)    ...

    (c)    between a county council, metropolitan district council or London borough council or the Common Council, on the one hand, and a sewerage undertaker, on the other, as to the use of a sewer;

shall, if either party to the dispute so elect, be referred to and determined by the Secretary of State.

(4)    Subsection (3)(a) above does not apply in Wales.

### Section 278 - Agreements as to execution of works.

(1)    A highway authority may, if they are satisfied it will be of benefit to the public, enter into an agreement with any person -

    (a)    for the execution by the authority of any works which the authority are or may be authorised to execute, or

    (b)    for the execution by the authority of such works incorporating particular modifications, additions or features, or at a particular time or in a particular manner,

on terms that that person pays the whole or such part of the cost of the works as may be specified in or determined in accordance with the agreement.

(2)    Without prejudice to the generality of the reference in subsection (1) to the cost of the works, that reference shall be taken to include -

    (a)    the whole of the costs incurred by the highway authority in or in connection with -

        (i)    the making of the agreement,

        (ii)    the making or confirmation of any scheme or order required for the purposes of the works,

        (iii)    the granting of any authorisation, permission or consent required for the purposes of the works, and

> (iv)   the acquisition by the authority of any land required for the purposes of the works; and
>
> (b)   all relevant administrative expenses of the highway authority, including an appropriate sum in respect of general staff costs and overheads.

(3)   The agreement may also provide for the making to the highway authority of payments in respect of the maintenance of the works to which the agreement relates and may contain such incidental and consequential provisions as appear to the highway authority to be necessary or expedient for the purposes of the agreement.

(4)   The fact that works are to be executed in pursuance of an agreement under this section does not affect the power of the authority to acquire land, by agreement or compulsorily, for the purposes of the works.

(5)   If any amount due to a highway authority in pursuance of an agreement under this section is not paid in accordance with the agreement, the authority may -

> (a)   direct that any means of access or other facility afforded by the works to which the agreement relates shall not be used until that amount has been paid,
>
> (b)   recover that amount from any person having an estate or interest in any land for the benefit of which any such means of access or other facility is afforded, and
>
> (c)   declare that amount to be a charge on any such land (identifying it) and on all estates and interests therein.

(6)   If it appears to the highway authority that a direction under subsection (5)(a) is not being complied with, the authority may execute such works as are necessary to stop up the means of access or deny the facility, as the case may be, and may for that purpose enter any land.

(7)   Where a highway authority recovers an amount from a person by virtue of subsection (5)(b), he may in turn recover from any other person having an estate or interest in land for the benefit of which the means of access or other facility was afforded such contribution as may be found by the court to be just and equitable.

This does not affect the right of any of those persons to recover from the person liable under the agreement the amount which they are made to pay.

(8)   The Local Land Charges Act 1975 applies in relation to a charge under subsection (5)(c) in favour of the Secretary of State as in relation to a charge in favour of a local authority.

See Text @ Chapter 15, Form 5: Section 278 Agreement and Form 6: Highway Works Agreement.

### Section 328 - Meaning of "highway".

(1) In this Act, except where the context otherwise requires, "highway" means the whole or a part of a highway other than a ferry or waterway.

(2) Where a highway passes over a bridge or through a tunnel, that bridge or tunnel is to be taken for the purposes of this Act to be a part of the highway.

(3) In this Act, "highway maintainable at the public expense" and any other expression defined by reference to a highway is to be construed in accordance with the foregoing provisions of this section.

See Text @ Chapter 1.

### Notes

In *London Borough of Southwark & Anor v Transport for London* [2018] UKSC 63, Lord Briggs stated:

> *31. The Court of Appeal concluded that "highway" as used in article 2 and section 265 had a clear common law meaning, ... I respectfully disagree. The word "highway" is not a defined term, either in the 1980 Act, in the Transfer Order, or in the GLA Act. There is a limited explanation, in section 328 of the 1980 Act that:*
>
> > *"In this Act, except where the context otherwise requires, "highway" means the whole or a part of a highway other than a ferry or waterway."*
>
> *This is largely circular so far as concerns the core meaning of "highway" and, in any event, subject to context. It does not follow that the interpreter is therefore required to find some uniform meaning of the word "highway" wherever it is used, either in the relevant legislation or, as the Court of Appeal thought, at common law.*
>
> *32. There is in my view no single meaning of highway at common law. The word is sometimes used as a reference to its physical elements. Sometimes it is used as a label for the incorporeal rights of the public in relation to the locus in quo. Sometimes, as here, it is used as the label for a species of real property. When used within a statutory formula, as here, the word necessarily takes its meaning."*

The somewhat Delphic phrase "... *the incorporeal rights of the public in relation to the locus in quo* ..." appears to mean, in non-technical language, public rights of passage, whether on foot, on horseback or in (or on) vehicles over the way (ibid para. 6).

As to "... *a reference to its physical elements*", this appears to mean the physical fabric of the way, including its surface structures, bridges etc.

### Other definitions

It is necessary to distinguish between different definitions which may or may not include highways. Unfortunately, highway law suffers from the paradox of, on the one hand, being driven by expressions and concepts which are closely defined yet, on the other hand, being bedeviled by inconsistent terminology. In many cases, these terminological problems arise from the fact that the Highways Act 1980 and other statutes consolidate or incorporate much older statutes (some going back to the 19th Century) and, to be blunt, the result is, often, that the ends fail to meet up in the middle.

The word "*road*" is used in a number of statutes and has a meaning which includes not only highways but also ways which are not highways.

Section 142 of the Road Traffic Regulation Act 1984 defines "*road*", for the purposes of that Act, thus: "*in England and Wales, means any length of highway or of any other road to which the public has access, and includes bridges over which a road passes* ...".

The use of the phrase "*any other road*" in addition to the preceding word "*highway*" can be construed to mean that this definition is not limited to highways only.

Similarly, section 192(1) of the Road Traffic Act 1988 defines "*road*", for the purposes of that Act, thus: "*in relation to England and Wales, means any highway and any other road to which the public has access, and includes bridges over which a road passes* ...".

In *Bugge v Taylor* [1941] 1 K.B. 198, it was held that a hotel forecourt was a "*road*"; likewise a slaughterhouse yard in *Lister v Romford Ice and Cold Storage Co Ltd* [1957] 1 All E.R. 125.

The word "*road*" is used in other settings in the Highways Act 1980, such as "*principal road*" (section 12), "*trunk road*" and "*classified road*" (section 14), and "*special roads*" (section 16). The term "*classified road*" is mentioned in some modern legislation, but it was an historical designation which was made for grant purposes prior to 1975. Such roads were "*classified*" as Class I, Class II or declared to be not inferior to these classes. The concept of the "*principal road*" was introduced for grant purposes by the Local Government Act 1966.

The New Roads and Street Works Act 1991 re-created the statutory concept of a toll road. The Birmingham Northern Relief Road and part of the M6 are toll roads.

Section 48(1) of the New Roads and Street Works Act 1991 defines a "*street*" as follows:

In this Part a "*street*" means the whole or any part of any of the following, irrespective of whether it is a thoroughfare -

a)   any highway, road, lane, footway, alley or passage,

b)   any square or court, and

c)   any land laid out as a way whether it is for the time being formed as a way or not.

In section 48(1)(a), the use of the phrase "*road, lane, footway, alley or passage ...*" in addition to the preceding word "*highway*" can be construed to mean that this part of the definition is not limited to highways only – otherwise the words following "*highway*" would be redundant. The word "*footway*" in this phrase is odd because a "*footway*" is a form of highway in any event (see above) and should, therefore, be subsumed in the word "*highway*". The reference to "*any land laid out as a way whether it is for the time being formed as a way or not*", in section 48(1)(c), clearly encompasses ways which are in the course of construction.

For the purposes of the Private Street Works Code and the Advance Payments Code, section 203(2) provides that a "*private street*" means a "*street*" that is not a highway maintainable at the public expense. The word "*street*" is itself defined in section 329(1) as having the same meaning as in the New Roads and Street Works Act 1991: see above.

The word "*road*" is used in a number of statutes and has a meaning which includes not only highways but also ways which are not highways.

In *Clarke v Kato and Others* [1998] 1 W.L.R. 1647 the House of Lords considered whether the phrase "*road*" could include public car parks for the purposes of section 145(3)(a) Road Traffic Act 1988. Lord Clyde stated:

> "*But it is also necessary to consider the function of the place in order to see if it qualifies as a road. Essentially a road serves as a means of access. It leads from one place to another and constitutes a route whereby travellers may move conveniently between the places to which and from which it leads. It is thus a defined or at least a definable way intended to enable those who pass over it to reach a destination. Its precise extent will require to be a matter of detailed decision as matter of fact in the particular circumstances. Lines may require to be drawn to determine the point at which the road ends and the destination has been reached. Where there is a door or a gate the*

*problem may be readily resolved. Where there is no physical point which can be readily identified, then by an exercise of reasonable judgment an imaginary line will have to be drawn to mark the point where it should be held that the road has ended. Whether or not a particular area is or is not a road eventually comes to be a matter of fact ...*

*In the present case the question is raised whether one or other or both of the car parks qualifies as a road. In the generality of the matter it seems to me that in the ordinary use of language a car park does not so qualify. In character and more especially in function they are distinct. It is of course possible to park on a road, but that does not mean that the road is a car park. Correspondingly one can drive from one point to another over a car park, but that does not mean that the route which has been taken is a road. It is here that the distinction in function between road and car park is of importance. The proper function of a road is to enable movement along it to a destination. Incidentally a vehicle on it may be stationary. One can use a road for parking. The proper function of a car park is to enable vehicles to stand and wait. A car may be driven across it; but that is only incidental to the principal function of parking. A hard shoulder may be seen to form part of a road. A more delicate question could arise with regard to a lay-by, but where it is designed to serve only as a temporary stopping place incidental to the function of the road it may well be correct to treat it as part of the road. While I would accept that circumstances can occur where an area of land which can be reasonably described as a car park could qualify as a road for the purposes of the legislation I consider that such circumstances would be somewhat exceptional."*

## Section 329 - Further provision as to interpretation.

(1)     In this Act, except where the context otherwise requires -

"adjoining" includes abutting on, and "adjoins" is to be construed accordingly;

"advance payments code" has the meaning provided by section 203(1) above;

"apparatus" includes any structure constructed for the lodging therein of apparatus;

"approach", in relation to a bridge or tunnel, means the highway giving access thereto, that is to say, the surface of that highway together with any embankment, retaining wall or other work or substance supporting or protecting the surface;

"bridge" does not include a culvert, but, save as aforesaid, means a bridge or viaduct which is part of a highway, and includes the abutments and any other part of a bridge but not the highway carried thereby;

"bridleway" means a highway over which the public have the following, but no other, rights of way, that is to say, a right of way on foot and a right of way on horseback or leading a horse, with or without a right to drive animals of any description along the highway;

"by-pass" has the meaning provided by section 82(6) above;

"carriageway" means a way constituting or comprised in a highway, being a way (other than a cycle track) over which the public have a right of way for the passage of vehicles;

"cattle-grid" has the meaning provided by section 82(6) above;

"City" means the City of London;

"classified road" means a highway or proposed highway which is a classified road in accordance with section 12 above;

"Common Council" means the Common Council of the City of London;

"council" means a county council or a local authority;

"cycle track" means a way constituting or comprised in a highway, being a way over which the public have the following, but no other, rights of way, that is to say, a right of way on pedal cycles (other than pedal cycles which are motor vehicles within the meaning of the Road Traffic Act 1988) with or without a right of way on foot;

"footpath" means a highway over which the public have a right of way on foot only, not being a footway;

"footway" means a way comprised in a highway which also comprises a carriageway, being a way over which the public have a right of way on foot only;

"functions" includes powers and duties;

"GLA road" shall be construed in accordance with section 14D(1) above;

"highway maintainable at the public expense" means a highway which by virtue of section 36 above or of any other enactment (whether contained in this Act or not) is a highway which for the purposes of this Act is a highway maintainable at the public expense;

"improvement" means the doing of any act under powers conferred by Part V of this Act and includes the erection, maintenance, alteration and removal of traffic signs, and the freeing of a highway or road-ferry from tolls;

"inland navigation undertakers" means persons authorised by any enactment to carry on an inland navigation undertaking;

"land" includes land covered by water and any interest or right in, over or under land;

"local authority" means the council of a district or London borough or the Common Council but, in relation to Wales, means a Welsh council;

"local highway authority" means a highway authority other than the Minister or a strategic highways company;

"local planning authority" has the same meaning as in the Town and Country Planning Act 1990;

"made-up carriageway" means a carriageway, or a part thereof, which has been metalled or in any other way provided with a surface suitable for the passage of vehicles;

"maintenance" includes repair, and "maintain" and "maintainable" are to be construed accordingly;

"the Minister", subject to subsection (5) below, means as respects England, the Minister of Transport and as respects Wales, the Secretary of State; and in section 258 of, and paragraphs 7, 8(1) and (3), 14, 15(1) and (3), 18(2), 19 and 21 of Schedule 1 to, this Act, references to the Minister and the Secretary of State acting jointly are to be construed, as respects Wales, as references to the Secretary of State acting alone;

"owner", in relation to any premises, means a person, other than a mortgagee not in possession, who, whether in his own right or as trustee or agent for any other person, is entitled to receive the rack rent of the premises or, where the premises are not let at a rack rent, would be so entitled if the premises were so let;

"premises" includes land and buildings;

"private street works code" has the meaning provided by section 203(1) above;

"proposed highway" means land on which, in accordance with plans made by a highway authority, that authority are for the time being constructing or intending to construct a highway shown in the plans;

"public utility undertakers" means persons authorised by any enactment to carry on any of the following undertakings, that is to say, an undertaking for the supply of gas, or hydraulic power;

"rack rent", in relation to any premises, means a rent which is not less than two-thirds of the rent at which the premises might reasonably be expected to let from year to year, free from all usual tenant's rates and taxes, and deducting therefrom the probable average annual cost of the repairs, insurance and other expenses (if any) necessary to maintain the same in a state to command such rent;

"railway" includes a light railway;

"railway undertakers" means persons authorised by any enactment to carry on a railway undertaking;

"restricted byway" has the same meaning as in Part II of the Countryside and Rights of Way Act 2000;

"special road" means a highway, or a proposed highway, which is a special road in accordance with section 16 above or by virtue of an order granting development consent under the Planning Act 2008;

"special road authority" has the meaning provided by section 16(4) above;

"statutory undertakers" means persons authorised by any enactment to carry on any of the following undertakings: -

(a) a railway, tramway, road transport, water transport, canal, inland navigation, dock, harbour, pier or lighthouse undertaking, or

(b) an undertaking for the supply of hydraulic power,

and "statutory undertaking" is to be construed accordingly;

"strategic highways company" means a company for the time being appointed under Part 1 of the Infrastructure Act 2015;

"street" has the same meaning as in Part III of the New Roads and Street Works Act 1991;

"street works licence" means a licence under section 50 of the New Roads and Street Works Act 1991, and "licensee" in relation to such a licence, has the meaning given by subsection (3) of that section;

"traffic" includes pedestrians and animals;

"transport undertakers" means persons authorised by any enactment to carry on any of the following undertakings, that is to say, a railway, canal, inland navigation, dock, harbour or pier undertaking, and "transport undertaking" is to be construed accordingly;

"trunk road" means a highway, or a proposed highway, which is a trunk road by virtue of section 10(1) or section 19 above or by virtue of an order or direction under section 10 above or an order granting development consent under the Planning Act 2008, or under any other enactment;

"universal service provider" has the same meaning as in Part 3 of the Postal Services Act 2011; and references to the provision of a universal postal service shall be construed in accordance with that Part 36;

"water undertakers" means the Environment Agency, the Natural Resources Body for Wales or a water undertaker;

"Welsh council" means the council of a Welsh county or county borough.

(2) A highway at the side of a river, canal or other inland navigation is not excluded from the definition in subsection (1) above of "bridleway", "footpath" or "restricted byway", by reason only that the public have a right to use the highway for the purposes of navigation, if the highway would fall within that definition if the public had no such right thereover.

# The Town & Country Planning Act 1990

*Section 55 - Meaning of "development" and "new development".*

(1) Subject to the following provisions of this section, in this Act, except where the context otherwise requires, "development" means the carrying out of building, engineering, mining or other operations in, on, over or under land, or the making of any material change in the use of any buildings or other land.

(1A) For the purposes of this Act "building operations" includes -

    (a)    demolition of buildings;

    (b)    rebuilding;

    (c)    structural alterations of or additions to buildings; and

    (d)    other operations normally undertaken by a person carrying on business as a builder.

(2) The following operations or uses of land shall not be taken for the purposes of this Act to involve development of the land -

    (a)    ...

    (b)    the carrying out on land within the boundaries of a road by a highway authority of any works required for the maintenance or improvement of the road but, in the case of any such works which are not exclusively for the maintenance of the road, not including any works which may have significant adverse effects on the environment ;

    (c)    the carrying out by a local authority or statutory undertakers of any works for the purpose of inspecting, repairing or renewing any sewers, mains, pipes, cables or other apparatus, including the breaking open of any street or other land for that purpose;

    ...

    (f)    in the case of buildings or other land which are used for a purpose of any class specified in an order made by the Secretary of State under this section, the use of the buildings or other land or, subject to the provisions of the order, of any part of the buildings or the other land, for any other purpose of the same class.

### Definitions

For *"building"*, *"highway"*, *"local authority"*, *"local highway authority"* and *"use"* see section 336(1).

For *"statutory undertaker"* see section 262.

For *"road"* see pages 220 to 222 above.

### Notes

Lord Denning M.R. observed in Parkes v Secretary of State for the Environment [1979] 1 All E.R. 211 at 213, that:

> *"the first half, 'operations,' comprises activities which result in some physical alteration to the land, which has some degree of permanence to the land itself, whereas the second half, 'use,' comprises activities which are done in, alongside or on the land but do not interfere with the actual physical characteristics of the land."*

There is no definition of *"engineering operations"* except to extend it to include *"the formation or laying out of means of access to highways"*; and *"means of access"* includes *"any means of access, whether private or public, for vehicles or for foot passengers, and includes a street"* (section 336(1)).

As to (2)(f), The Town and Country Planning (Use Classes) Order 1987 (S.I. 1987, No. 764) provides that where a building or other land is used for a purpose of any class specified in the Schedule to the Order, then the use of that building or that other land for any other purpose of the same class shall not be taken to involve development of the land (Article 3(1)).

### Section 57 - *Planning permission required for development.*

(1) Subject to the following provisions of this section, planning permission is required for the carrying out of any development of land.

...

(3) Where by a development order, a local development order, a Mayoral development order or a neighbourhood development order planning permission to develop land has been granted subject to limitations, planning permission is not required for the use of that land which (apart from its use in accordance with that permission) is its normal use.

## Section 58A - Permission in principle: general.

(1)   Permission in principle may be granted for housing-led development of land in England as provided in section 59A.

(2)   Permission in principle may not be granted for development consisting of the winning and working of minerals.

(3)   For the effect of permission in principle, see section 70(2ZZA) to (2ZZC) (application for technical details consent must be determined in accordance with permission in principle, except after a prescribed period).

(4)   ...

### Definitions

For "*permission in principle*" see sections 336(1) and 58A.

### Notes

This was added by the Housing and Planning Act 2016 with effect from 12 July 2016.

See also Housing and Planning Act 2016 (Permission in Principle etc) (Miscellaneous Amendments) (England) Regulations 2017.

## Section 59 - Development orders: general.

(1)   The Secretary of State shall by order (in this Act referred to as a "development order") provide for the granting of planning permission.

(2)   A development order may either -

(a)   itself grant planning permission for development specified in the order or for development of any class specified; or

(b)   in respect of development for which planning permission is not granted by the order itself, provide for the granting of planning permission by the local planning authority (or, in the cases provided in the following provisions, by the Secretary of State or) on application to the authority (or, in the cases provided in the following provisions, on application to the Secretary of State) in accordance with the provisions of the order.

## Section 59A - Development orders: permission in principle

(1)    A development order may either -

    (a)    itself grant permission in principle, in relation to land in England that is allocated for development in a qualifying document (whether or not in existence when the order is made) for development of a prescribed description; or

    (b)    provide for the granting by a local planning authority in England, on application to the authority in accordance with the provisions of the order, of permission in principle for development of a prescribed description.

(2)    In this section -

"prescribed" means prescribed in a development order;

"qualifying document" means a document, as it has effect from time to time, which -

    (a)    falls within subsection (3),

    (b)    indicates that the land in question is allocated for development for the purposes of this section, and

    (c)    contains prescribed particulars in relation to the land allocated and the kind of development for which it is allocated.

### Section 61A - *Local development orders.*

(1)     ...

(2)     A local planning authority may by order (a local development order) grant planning permission -

    (a)     for development specified in the order;

    (b)     for development of any class so specified.

(3)     A local development order may relate to -

    (a)     all land in the area of the relevant authority;

    (b)     any part of that land;

    (c)     a site specified in the order.

(4)     ...

(7)     Schedule 4A makes provision in connection with local development orders.

### Section 70 - *Determination of applications: general considerations.*

(1)     Where an application is made to a local planning authority for planning permission -

    (a)     subject to section 62D(5) and sections 91 and 92, they may grant planning permission, either unconditionally or subject to such conditions as they think fit; or

    (b)     they may refuse planning permission.

(1A)   Where an application is made to a local planning authority for permission in principle -

    (a)     they may grant permission in principle; or

    (b)     they may refuse permission in principle.

(2)     In dealing with an application for planning permission or permission in principle the authority shall have regard to -

    (a)     the provisions of the development plan, so far as material to the application,

    (aza) a post -examination draft neighbourhood development plan, so far as material to the application, (aa)   ...

(b)    any local finance considerations, so far as material to the application, and

(c)    any other material considerations.

(2ZZA)    The authority must determine an application for technical details consent in accordance with the relevant permission in principle.

This is subject to subsection (2ZZC).

(2ZZB)    An application for technical details consent is an application for planning permission that -

(a)    relates to land in respect of which permission in principle is in force,

(b)    proposes development all of which falls within the terms of the permission in principle, and

(c)    particularises all matters necessary to enable planning permission to be granted without any reservations of the kind referred to in section 92.

(2ZZC)    Subsection (2ZZA) does not apply where -

(a)    the permission in principle has been in force for longer than a prescribed period, and

(b)    there has been a material change of circumstances since the permission came into force.

"Prescribed" means prescribed for the purposes of this subsection in a development order.

(2ZA)  ...

(2A)  ...

(3)   Subsection (1) has effect subject to section 65 and to the following provisions of this Act, to sections 66, 67, 72 and 73 of the Planning (Listed Buildings and Conservation Areas) Act 1990 and to section 15 of the Health Services Act 1976.

(3C)  For the purposes of subsection (2)(aza) (but subject to subsections (3D) and (3E)) a draft neighbourhood development plan is a "post examination draft neighbourhood development plan" if -

(a) a local planning authority have made a decision under paragraph 12(4) of Schedule 4B with the effect that a referendum or referendums are to be held on the draft plan under that Schedule,

(b) the Secretary of State has directed under paragraph 13B(2)(a) of that Schedule that a referendum or referendums are to be held on the draft plan under that Schedule,

(c) an examiner has recommended under paragraph 13(2)(a) of Schedule A2 to the Planning and Compulsory Purchase Act 2004 (examination of modified plan) that a local planning authority should make the draft plan, or

(d) an examiner has recommended under paragraph 13(2)(b) of that Schedule that a local planning authority should make the draft plan with modifications.

(3C) In the application of subsection (2)(aza) in relation to a post examination draft neighbourhood development plan within subsection (3B)(d), the local planning authority must take the plan into account as it would be if modified in accordance with the recommendations.

(3D) A draft neighbourhood development plan within subsection (3B)(a) or (b) ceases to be a post-examination draft neighbourhood development plan for the purposes of subsection (2)(aza) if -

(a) section 38A(4)(a) (duty to make plan) or (6) (cases in which duty does not apply) of the Planning and Compulsory Purchase Act 2004 applies in relation to the plan,

(b) section 38A(5) (power to make plan) of that Act applies in relation to the plan and the plan is made by the local planning authority,

(c) section 38A(5) of that Act applies in relation to the plan and the local planning authority decide not to make the plan,

(d) a single referendum is held on the plan and half or fewer of those voting in the referendum vote in favour of the plan, or

(e) two referendums are held on the plan and half or fewer of those voting in each of the referendums vote in favour of the plan.

(3E) A draft neighbourhood development plan within subsection (3B)(c) or (d) ceases to be a post-examination draft neighbourhood development plan for the purposes of subsection (2)(aza) if -

(a) the local planning authority make the draft plan (with or without modifications), or

(b)    the local planning authority decide not to make the draft plan.

(3F)   The references in subsection (3B) to Schedule 4B are to that Schedule as applied to neighbourhood development plans by section 38A(3) of the Planning and Compulsory Purchase Act 2004.

(4)    In this section -

"local finance consideration" means -

(a)    a grant or other financial assistance that has been, or will or could be, provided to a relevant authority by a Minister of the Crown, or

(b)    sums that a relevant authority has received, or will or could receive, in payment of Community Infrastructure Levy;

"Minister of the Crown" has the same meaning as in the Ministers of the Crown Act 1975;

"relevant authority" means -

(a)    a district council;

(b)    a county council in England;

(c)    the Mayor of London;

(d)    the council of a London borough;

(e)    a Mayoral development corporation;

(f)    an urban development corporation;

(g)    a housing action trust;

(h)    the Council of the Isles of Scilly;

(i)    the Broads Authority;

(j)    a National Park authority in England;

(k)    the Homes and Communities Agency; or

(l)    a joint committee established under section 29 of the Planning and Compulsory Purchase Act 2004.

**Definitions**

For "*development*", see section 55 (above) and section 336(1) (below).

For "*building*", "*conservation area*", "*development plan*", "*local planning authority*", "*planning permission*" and "*use*" see section 336(1) below.

For "*permission in principle*" see sections 336(1) and 58A.

**Notes**

Section 38(6) of the Planning and Compulsory Purchase Act 2004 provides that, if regard is to be had to the development plan for the purpose of any determination to be made under the planning Acts the determination must be made in accordance with the provisions of the development plan unless material considerations indicate otherwise.

## Section 72 - Conditional grant of planning permission.

(1)  Without prejudice to the generality of section 70(1), conditions may be imposed on the grant of planning permission under that section -

   (a)  for regulating the development or use of any land under the control of the applicant (whether or not it is land in respect of which the application was made) or requiring the carrying out of works on any such land, so far as appears to the local planning authority to be expedient for the purposes of or in connection with the development authorised by the permission;

   (b)  for requiring the removal of any buildings or works authorised by the permission, or the discontinuance of any use of land so authorised, at the end of a specified period, and the carrying out of any works required for the reinstatement of land at the end of that period.

...

(6)  See also section 100ZA, which makes provision about restrictions on the power to impose conditions by virtue of this section on a grant of planning permission in relation to land in England.

See Text @ Chapter 11.

### Definitions

For *"local planning authority"*, *"minerals"*, *"planning permission"*, *"planning permission granted for a limited period"* and *"use"*, see section 336(1) below. For *"development"*, see section 55 (above) and section 336(1)(below).

### Notes

The principles for construing planning conditions were summarised by Beatson LJ in *Telford and Wrekin Council v Secretary of State for Communities and Local Government* [2013] EWHC 79 (Admin) and include:

- As a general rule a planning permission is to be construed within the four corners of the consent itself, i.e. including the conditions in it and the express reasons for those conditions unless another document is incorporated by reference or it is necessary to resolve an ambiguity in the permission or condition.

- Conditions should be interpreted benevolently and not narrowly or strictly and given a common-sense meaning.

- A condition will be void for uncertainty only if it can be given no meaning or no sensible or ascertainable meaning, and not merely because it is ambiguous or leads to absurd results.

See now the judgments of the Supreme Court in *Trump International Golf Club Scotland Ltd v The Scottish Ministers* [2015] UKSC 74 and the Court of Appeal in *R (Skelmersdale Limited Partnership) v West Lancashire BC* [2016] EWCA Civ 1260; *Dunnett Investments Ltd v Secretary of State for Communities and Local Government* [2017] EWCA Civ 192 and *Lambeth LBC v Secretary of State* [2018] EWCA Civ 844.

A condition may have the effect of modifying the development proposed by the application, provided that it does not constitute a fundamental alteration in the proposal: see, e.g. *Kingston-upon-Thames LBC v Secretary of State for the Environment* [1974] 1 All E.R. 193 (condition relating to off-street car-parking upheld); *Hildenborough Village Preservation Association v Secretary of State for the Environment* [1978] J.P.L. 708 (condition requiring suitable visibility splays upheld); *Kent CC v Secretary of State for the Environment* (1977) 33 P. & C.R. 70 (condition deleting a proposed means of access upheld). In *Suburban Property Investment Ltd v Secretary of State for Communities and Local Government* [2011] EWCA Civ 112 it was held as a matter of construction that a condition tied the use of parking in a block of flats to that block.

## Conditions interfering with land ownership

The courts have tended to lean against conditions which interfere with rights of land ownership, particularly when a condition has the effect of expropriating land without the compensation which would otherwise be payable.

In *Colonial Sugar Refining Company Limited v Melbourne Harbour Trust Commissioners* [1927] A.C. 343, Lord Warrington of Clyffe, in delivering the judgment of the Privy Council, said:

> *"In considering the construction and effect of this Act, the board is guided by the well known principle that a statute should not he held to take away private rights of property without compensation unless the intention to do so is expressed in clear and unambiguous words."*

In *Hall & Co Ltd v Shoreham by Sea Urban District Council* [1964] 1 W.L.R. 240, the plaintiffs obtained planning permission to develop land for industrial purposes. The main road was overloaded with traffic, and in the interests of highway safety, the local planning authority granted permission subject to conditions, that provided, among other things, that the plaintiffs *"shall construct an ancillary road over the entire frontage of the site at their own expense and as and when required by the local planning authority, and shall give right of passage over it to and from such ancillary roads as may be constructed on adjoining land"* and that *"the new access shall be temporary for a period of five years initially but the local planning authority will not enforce its closure until the ancillary roads ... have been constructed and alternative access to the main road is available."*

The conditions were struck down by the Court of Appeal. Willmer LJ said:

> *"I turn now to consider what I regard as the main point in the case, namely, the contention that conditions 3 and 4 are ultra vires. It is contended that the effect of these conditions is to require the plaintiffs not only to build the ancillary road on their own land, but to give right of passage over it to other persons to an extent that will virtually amount to dedicating it to the public, and all this without acquiring any right to recover any compensation whatsoever. This is said to amount to a violation of the plaintiffs' fundamental rights of ownership which goes far beyond anything authorised by the statute... Under the conditions now sought to be imposed, on the other hand, the plaintiffs must construct the ancillary road as and when they may be required to do so over the whole of their frontage entirely at their own expense... The defendants would thus obtain the benefit of having the road constructed for them at the plaintiffs' expense, on the plaintiffs' land, and without the necessity for paying any compensation in respect, thereof.*
>
> *Bearing in mind that another and more regular course is open to the defendants, it seems to me that this result would be utterly unreasonable and such as Parliament cannot possibly have intended... I can certainly find no clear and unambiguous words*

*in the Town and Country Planning Act 1947 authorising the defendants in effect to take away the plaintiffs' rights of property without compensation by the imposition of conditions such as those sought to be imposed...*

*In these circumstances, although I have much sympathy with the object sought to be achieved by the defendants, I am satisfied that conditions 3 and 4 are so unreasonable that they must he held to be ultra vires."*

In *Minister of Housing and Local Government v Hartnell* [1965] A.C. 1134, the House of Lords confirmed that the law ordinarily entitles a person whose land is taken for a highway to compensation unless the statutory intention to eschew compensation is expressed in clear and unambiguous terms.

In *M J Shanley Ltd (in Liquidation) v Secretary of State* [1982] J.P.L. 380 the developer had proposed that, if it was granted planning permission for a housing development, it would donate 40 acres as public open space. Again, the ensuing condition was held to be void.

In *Westminster Renslade Ltd v Secretary of State for the Environment and Another* (1984) 48 P. & C.R. 255, the High Court quashed a planning inspector's refusal of planning permission where he held, among other things, that the developer should have made a contribution to off-site public car parking. There was no complaint that the scheme failed to provide enough on-site parking for its own needs. The Inspector, however, took the view that there were insufficient car parking spaces provided for what he called "public control" and that that was a serious demerit of the scheme which indicated that the appeal should be dismissed. Forbes J said:

> *"Of course, it is perfectly simple to provide off-street car parking that is under public control: the local authority can acquire the land to do so. It is, however, wholly illegitimate to try to seek to do that by imposing conditions on the planning consent."*

In *Bradford City Council v Secretary of State for the Environment and McLean Homes Northern Ltd* [1986] 1 E.G.L.R. 199; [1986] J.P.L. 598 the developers applied for planning permission to build 200 houses. The planning authority were concerned that the existing road was inadequate to cope with the likely increase in traffic. They wished to have the existing road widened. Part of the land affected by the proposal to widen the road was owned by the developers and part at that stage was not. As a result of negotiations with the authority, the developers submitted amended plans showing the widening of the road over the whole length. The planning authority granted permission for the building of the houses subject to a condition requiring the widening of the roadway as shown in the amended plans.

There was a dispute over the proposed widening and the matter was referred to the Secretary of State who discharged the condition on the ground that it was unlawful. The Court of Appeal held that he was right to do so.

In considering the validity of a condition requiring the applicant to carry out works at his own expense such as road widening which were the responsibility of the planning authority, the true test was whether the conditions imposed were manifestly unreasonable. If so, then it was beyond the powers of the planning authority to impose it even if the developer consented to the condition. The fact that an applicant had suggested or consented to a condition was likely to be powerful evidence that the condition was not unreasonable, as the parties were usually likely to be the best judges of what was reasonable. It was possible, however, that even where an applicant consented to a condition, the condition was not in the general public interest and might still be held to be unreasonable and so unlawful. For in addition to the interests of the "parties," there is the public interest in securing the fair imposition of planning control as between one developer and another: per Wills J in *R v Bowman* [1898] 1 Q.B. 663 (see below).

The National Planning Practice Guidance website states that no payment of money or other consideration can be positively required when granting planning permission, and then adds:

> *"However, where the 6 tests will be met, it may be possible use a negatively worded condition to prohibit development authorised by the planning permission until a specified action has been taken (for example, the entering into of a planning obligation requiring the payment of a financial contribution towards the provision of supporting infrastructure)."* (Emphasis added).

(Paragraph: 005, Reference ID: 21a-005-20140306 - Revision date: 06 03 2014).

No authority is cited for this latter proposition and it is difficult to see how such a condition would be lawful and it is not to be commended: see discussion of *R v Bowman*, the Bill of Rights 1689 etc below. The alleged distinction between positive and negative conditions is, in this context, a misuse of the concepts and an illusion. Whichever way one cuts it, the flaw is the same; namely, that a monetary payment is being sought without the benefit of legislation.

A further dimension is now added by the influence of the European Convention of Human Rights. Article 8 of the Convention provides a right to respect for one's "private and family life, his home and his correspondence", subject to certain restrictions that are "in accordance with law" and "necessary in a democratic society". The courts have held that the Convention must be taken into account in the context of planning conditions: see *R (Gosbee) v First Secretary of State & Anor* [2003] EWHC 770 (Admin).

### Conditions seeking financial contributions

It might seem to be that a local authority which seeks a financial contribution by way of a condition is acting laudably if that money is going to be used to benefit the public. However, the UK subscribes to a constitutional principle known as the "*rule of law*", and has done so for many centuries. This means that executive bodies (which includes local planning authorities) cannot obtain money from the public unless authorised to do so by Parliament. No pecuniary burden can be imposed upon the public, except under clear and distinct legal authority. Not surprising, this concept is often called the doctrine of "*Sovereignty of Parliament*".

The background can be traced back to the struggles between the Crown and Parliament which culminated in historical supremacy of Parliament over the monarchy in the 19th Century. This was reflected in the Bill of Rights 1689. The Bill of Rights established the principles of frequent parliaments, free elections, and freedom of speech within Parliament and the principle that the executive could no longer levy money without the approval of Parliament. It declared, among many other things, that "... *levying money for or to the use of the Crown by pretence of prerogative, without grant of Parliament, for longer time, or in other manner than the same is or shall be granted, is illegal ...*". This principle of "no taxation without legislation" still forms one of the United Kingdom's fundamental constitutional principles.

In *R v Bowman* [1898] 1 Q.B. 663 it was held that justices who were charged with issuing liquor licences were acting unlawfully in requiring applicants to make payments for public purposes; namely, that the applicant should pay £1,000 in reduction of the rates. Wills J, in giving the leading judgment of the Divisional Court, said:

> "*If the attachment of such a condition were allowed to pass without objection there would soon grow up a system of putting licences up to auction; a system which would be eminently mischievous and would open the door to the gravest abuses.*"

*Attorney General v Wilts United Dairies Ltd* (1921) 37 T.L.R. 884 is important in the context of both planning conditions and Section 278 Agreements and so it is set out at some length.

There the Food Controller had imposed a charge of two pence per gallon as a condition of the grant of a licence to purchase milk in certain areas for which no authority had been given by Parliament. He purported to do so under the Defence of the Realm Acts. The case proceeded on the basis that the sums were to be paid into the National Exchequer. The Court of Appeal and the House of Lords held that he had no power to do so. In the Court of Appeal, Atkins LJ referred to the Bill of Rights 1689 and said (@ p.886):

> "*Though the attention of our ancestors was directed especially to abuses of the prerogative, there can be no doubt that this statute declares the law that no money shall be levied for or to the use of the Crown except by grant of Parliament. We know how strictly Parliament has maintained this right - and, in particular, how jealously the House of Commons has asserted its predominance in the power of raising money.... In these circumstances, if an officer of the executive seeks to justify a charge upon the subject*

*made for the use of the Crown (which includes all the purposes of the public revenue), he must show, in clear terms, that Parliament has authorized the particular charge."*

He added (@ p.887):

*"It makes no difference that the obligation to pay the money is expressed in the form of an agreement. It was illegal for the Food Controller to require such an agreement as a condition of any licence. It was illegal for him to enter into such an agreement. The agreement itself is not enforceable against the other contracting party; and if he had paid under it he could, having paid under protest, recover back the sums paid, as money had and received to his use."*

Scrutton LJ said (@ p.885):

*"It is conceivable that Parliament, which may pass legislation requiring the subject to pay money to the Crown, may also delegate its powers of imposing such payments to the executive, but in my view the clearest words should be required before the courts hold that such an unusual delegation has taken place. As Wilde C.J. said in Gosling v. Veley, 12 Q.B., at p. 407: 'The rule of law that no pecuniary burden can be imposed upon the subjects of this country, by whatever name it may be called, whether tax, due, rate or toll, except under clear and distinct legal authority, established by those who seek to impose the burden, has been so often the subject of legal decision that it may be deemed a legal axiom, and requires no authority to be cited in support of it."*

In the House of Lords, Lord Buckmaster said that the imposition could only be properly described as a *"tax"*, which could not be levied except by direct statutory means: per (1922) 38 T.L.R. 781.

These principles were affirmed by the House of Lords in *O'Brien v Independent Assessor* [2007] UKHL 10 and *Total Network SL v Commissioners of Customs and Excise* [2008] UKHL 19.

If a local planning authority is seeking a financial contribution from a developer, then the best course is to consider whether the use of an agreement under section 106 of the Town and Country Planning Act 1990 might be possible: see Chapter 12.

### Positive conditions and actions outside developer's control

A local planning authority is not entitled to impose a condition which the developer plainly will not be able to discharge. It can only relate to matters over which the developer has control.

A positive condition which requires the developer to carry out works on land outside his control is invalid because he does not have the immediate ability to comply with the condition. Thus a condition requiring the developer to carry out works on the highway outside his site is invalid, viz:

*"The off-site highway works shown on drawing X shall be constructed within one year following the commencement of the development".*

In *Birnie v Banff CC* [1954] S.L.T. (Sh. Ct.) 90 planning permission had been granted for the erection of a house, subject to a condition requiring the construction of an access over land not belonging to the applicant. The access was not constructed, and the local planning authority took enforcement action. It was held that the authority had no power to impose as a condition of a grant of planning permission the carrying out of works on land other than land under an applicant's control, and the enforcement notice was quashed.

In *British Airports Authority v Secretary of State for Scotland* [1980] J.P.L. 260, a condition was imposed concerning the flight path of aircraft taking off and landing at Aberdeen airport. The condition was void because it related to matters over which the applicants had no control. Only the Civil Aviation Authority could control the directions of aircraft.

In *Mouchell Superannuation Trust Fund Trustees v Oxfordshire CC* [1992] 1 W.L.U.K. 212, it was held that a condition requiring that "Vehicles shall travel to and from the site via the A57 and the M1 only" was invalid because it was unenforceable. Obviously, the landowner would have no control over the movements of vehicles owned or operated by others on the A57 or M1 and could not comply with the condition.

These cases should be contrasted with *Davenport v Hammersmith & Fulham LBC* [1999] J.P.L. 1122. There, planning permission had been granted for the use of land for motor vehicle repairs. A condition prohibited vehicles which had been left with or in the control of the applicant being parked on the highway adjacent to the premises; namely, *"no vehicles which have been left with or are in the control of the applicant shall be stored or parked in Tasso Road"*. Following non-compliance with the condition, the Council served a breach of condition notice and then prosecuted the owners for non-compliance with the notice. The owners challenged the validity of the condition; however, the Divisional Court upheld the condition. Whilst the highway was outside the control of the owners, the condition did not require them to have control of the land in question. They were able to comply with it because the vehicles were left with them and were within their control. That is to say, the vehicle owners handed in their car keys when leaving their cars at the garage.

In *Andrews and Andrews v Secretary of State for the Environment, Transport and the Regions and North Norfolk District Council* [2000] P.L.C.R. 366 a condition imposed by a planning inspector in respect of a taxi office was struck down by the High Court.

The condition provided:

> *"No taxis or mini-cabs belonging to the applicant, nor those belonging to freelance drivers operating through the radio control at the premises, shall call at the office hereby permitted for the purposes of waiting, taking orders and instructions, collecting clients or for taking refreshment."*

The court held that it was not convinced that the Inspector had properly considered whether such a condition would solve the planning objections about on-street parking. However, it is arguable that the condition was flawed by the fact that it sought to make the operator responsible for the actions of freelance drivers.

In *R v Rochdale MBC ex. p. Tew* [2000] J.P.L. 54 Sullivan J held that even if a condition was theoretically enforceable it would be invalid if it was not reasonably enforceable. The enforceability of any planning condition had to be considered in the light of the particular facts. A condition which is not reasonably enforceable is not a reasonable condition for the purpose of the *Newbury* tests. Enforceability should be considered in a pragmatic and not in a theoretical manner, and should be considered by reference to the terms of the particular conditions, the specific development, and the particular site in question.

### Section 106 - Planning obligations.

(1)     Any person interested in land in the area of a local planning authority may, by agreement or otherwise, enter into an obligation (referred to in this section and sections 106A to 106C as "a planning obligation"), enforceable to the extent mentioned in subsection (3) -

    (a)     restricting the development or use of the land in any specified way;

    (b)     requiring specified operations or activities to be carried out in, on, under or over the land;

    (c)     requiring the land to be used in any specified way; or

    (d)     requiring a sum or sums to be paid to the authority (or, in a case where section 2E applies, to the Greater London Authority) on a specified date or dates or periodically.

(1A)   In the case of a development consent obligation, the reference to development in subsection (1)(a) includes anything that constitutes development for the purposes of the Planning Act 2008.

(2)     A planning obligation may -

(a)     be unconditional or subject to conditions;

(b)     impose any restriction or requirement mentioned in subsection (1)(a) to (c) either indefinitely or for such period or periods as may be specified; and

(c)     if it requires a sum or sums to be paid, require the payment of a specified amount or an amount determined in accordance with the instrument by which the obligation is entered into and, if it requires the payment of periodical sums, require them to be paid indefinitely or for a specified period.

(3)     Subject to subsection (4) a planning obligation is enforceable by the authority identified in accordance with subsection (9)(d) -

(a)     against the person entering into the obligation; and

(b)     against any person deriving title from that person.

(4)     The instrument by which a planning obligation is entered into may provide that a person shall not be bound by the obligation in respect of any period during which he no longer has an interest in the land.

(5)     A restriction or requirement imposed under a planning obligation is enforceable by injunction.

(6)     Without prejudice to subsection (5), if there is a breach of a requirement in a planning obligation to carry out any operations in, on, under or over the land to which the obligation relates, the authority by whom the obligation is enforceable may -

(a)     enter the land and carry out the operations; and

(b)     recover from the person or persons against whom the obligation is enforceable any expenses reasonably incurred by them in doing so.

(7)     Before an authority exercise their power under subsection (6)(a) they shall give not less than twenty one days' notice of their intention to do so to any person against whom the planning obligation is enforceable.

(8)     Any person who wilfully obstructs a person acting in the exercise of a power under subsection (6)(a) shall be guilty of an offence and liable on summary conviction to a fine not exceeding level 3 on the standard scale.

(9)     A planning obligation may not be entered into except by an instrument executed as a deed which -

(a)     states that the obligation is a planning obligation for the purposes of this section;

(aa) if the obligation is a development consent obligation, contains a statement to that effect;

(b) identifies the land in which the person entering into the obligation is interested;

(c) identifies the person entering into the obligation and states what his interest in the land is; and

(d) identifies the local planning authority by whom the obligation is enforceable and, in a case where section 2E applies, identifies the Mayor of London as an authority by whom the obligation is also enforceable.

(10) A copy of any such instrument shall be given to the local planning authority so identified and, in a case where section 2E applies, to the Mayor of London.

(11) A planning obligation shall be a local land charge and for the purposes of the Local Land Charges Act 1975 the authority by whom the obligation is enforceable shall be treated as the originating authority as respects such a charge.

(12) Regulations may provide for the charging on the land of -

(a) any sum or sums required to be paid under a planning obligation; and

(b) any expenses recoverable by a local planning authority or the Mayor of London under subsection (6)(b),

and this section and sections 106A to 106BC shall have effect subject to any such regulations.

(13) In this section "specified" means specified in the instrument by which the planning obligation is entered into and in this section and section 106A "land" has the same meaning as in the Local Land Charges Act 1975.

(14) In this section and section 106A "development consent obligation" means a planning obligation entered into in connection with an application (or a proposed application) for an order granting development consent.

See Text @ Chapter 12.

**Definitions**

For "*development consent obligation*" see section 106(14).

For "*local planning authority*" and "*use*", see section 336(1) below. For "*development*", see section 55 (above) and section 336(1)(below). For "*land*" and "*specified*", see section 106(13).

## Notes

As to "*person interested in land*", Eveleigh LJ, in *Pennine Raceway Ltd v Kirklees Metropolitan Council (No. 1)* [1983] Q.B. 382, stated that:

> "*I cannot read [subs.(3)] as saying that a person can only be interested in land under subsection (1) if it is possible for someone to derive title under him. I read it as saying that if in a particular case the person interested had such an interest which was transferable and had transferred it, then the agreement may be enforced against the transferee. I cannot read [subs.(3)] as limiting the meaning of subsection (1) so as to make subsection (1) apply only to persons who have an interest in land in a strict conveyancing sense. We are dealing with a statute which controls use and operations on land and provides compensation. It is not a conveyancing statute.*"

However, in *Southampton City Council v Halyard Ltd* [2009] 1 P. & C.R. 5, Morgan J differed from Eveleigh LJ. Morgan J regarded subsections (1), (3), (4), (9), (11) and (12) taken together as being "strongly indicative" of a requirement for a covenantor to have a proprietary interest in the land.

A local authority was unable to enforce a section 106 obligation against a successor in title where the agreement failed to specify the original covenantor's interest in the land: *Southampton City Council v Hallyard Ltd* [2009] ante.

A copy of any planning obligation proposed or entered into in connection with a planning or reserved matters application must be included in the local planning authority's planning register: Article 40 of the Town and Country Planning (Development Management Procedure) (England) Order 2015.

## Section 106ZA - Resolution of disputes about planning obligations.

Schedule 9A (resolution of disputes about planning obligations) has effect.

## Section 106A - Modification and discharge of planning obligations.

(1)  A planning obligation may not be modified or discharged except -

    (a)  by agreement between the appropriate authority (see subsection (11)) and the person or persons against whom the obligation is enforceable; or

    (b)  in accordance with -

      (i)    this section and section 106B, or

      (ii)   sections 106BA and 106BC.

(2)    An agreement falling within subsection (1)(a) shall not be entered into except by an instrument executed as a deed.

(3)    A person against whom a planning obligation is enforceable may, at any time after the expiry of the relevant period, apply to the appropriate authority for the obligation -

    (a)    to have effect subject to such modifications as may be specified in the application; or

    (b)    to be discharged.

(4)    In subsection (3) "the relevant period" means -

    (a)    such period as may be prescribed; or

    (b)    if no period is prescribed, the period of five years beginning with the date on which the obligation is entered into.

### Definitions

For "*appropriate authority*" see section 106A(11).

### Notes

Prior to the expiry of "*the relevant period*" an obligation may only be modified or discharged by agreement although a refusal to agree may be the subject of judicial review (see *R (on the application of Batchelor Enterprises Ltd) v North Dorset* [2004] J.P.L. 1222 (above)).

The High Court held in *R (Garden and Leisure Group Limited) v North Somerset Council* [2004] 1 P. & C.R. 39 that an application to modify an obligation was an "*all or nothing*" decision. It was not open to the authority to accept some of the proposed modifications and not others. If it found some of the proposed modifications unacceptable it may invite the application to submit a fresh or amended application but they must deal with the present application in its entirety.

(5)    An application under subsection (3) for the modification of a planning obligation may not specify a modification imposing an obligation on any other person against whom the obligation is enforceable.

(6) Where an application is made to an authority under subsection (3), the authority may determine -

    (a) that the planning obligation shall continue to have effect without modification;

    (b) if the obligation no longer serves a useful purpose, that it shall be discharged; or

    (c) if the obligation continues to serve a useful purpose, but would serve that purpose equally well if it had effect subject to the modifications specified in the application, that it shall have effect subject to those modifications.

(7) The authority shall give notice of their determination to the applicant within such period as may be prescribed.

(8) Where an authority determine under this section that a planning obligation shall have effect subject to modifications specified in the application, the obligation as modified shall be enforceable as if it had been entered into on the date on which notice of the determination was given to the applicant.

(9) Regulations may make provision with respect to -

    (a) the form and content of applications under subsection (3);

    (b) the publication of notices of such applications;

    (c) the procedures for considering any representations made with respect to such applications; and

    (d) the notices to be given to applicants of determinations under subsection (6).

(10) Section 84 of the Law of Property Act 1925 (power to discharge or modify restrictive covenants affecting land) does not apply to a planning obligation.

(11) In this section "the appropriate authority" means -

    (a) the Mayor of London, in the case of any planning obligation enforceable by him;

    (aa) the Secretary of State, in the case of any development consent obligation;

    (ab) ...

    (b) in the case of any other planning obligation, the local planning authority by whom it is enforceable.

(12)   The Mayor of London must consult the local planning authority before exercising any function under this section.

### Section 106B - Appeals in relation to applications under section 106A.

(1)   Where an authority (other than the Secretary of State) -

   (a)   fail to give notice as mentioned in section 106A(7); or

   (b)   determine under section 106A that a planning obligation shall continue to have effect without modification,

   the applicant may appeal to the Secretary of State.

(2)   For the purposes of an appeal under subsection (1)(a), it shall be assumed that the authority have determined that the planning obligation shall continue to have effect without modification.

(3)   An appeal under this section shall be made by notice served within such period and in such manner as may be prescribed.

(4)   Subsections (6) to (9) of section 106A apply in relation to appeals to the Secretary of State under this section as they apply in relation to applications to authorities under that section.

(5)   Before determining the appeal the Secretary of State shall, if either the applicant or the authority so wish, give each of them an opportunity of appearing before and being heard by a person appointed by the Secretary of State for the purpose.

(6)   The determination of an appeal by the Secretary of State under this section shall be final.

(7)   Schedule 6 applies to appeals under this section.

(8)   In the application of Schedule 6 to an appeal under this section in a case where the authority mentioned in subsection (1) is the Mayor of London, references in that Schedule to the local planning authority are references to the Mayor of London.

### Section 248 - Highways crossing or entering route of proposed new highway, etc.

(1)   This section applies where -

   (a)   planning permission is granted under Part III for constructing or improving, or the Secretary of State or a strategic highways company proposes to construct or improve, a highway ("the main highway"); and

(b)    another highway crosses or enters the route of the main highway or is, or will be, otherwise affected by the construction or improvement of the main highway.

(2)    Where this section applies and the place where the other highway crosses or enters the route of the main highway or is otherwise affected is outside Greater London, if it appears to the Secretary of State expedient to do so -

(a)    in the interests of the safety of users of the main highway; or

(b)    to facilitate the movement of traffic on the main highway,

he may by order authorise the stopping up or diversion of the other highway.

(2A)    Where this section applies and the place where the other highway crosses or enters the route of the main highway or is otherwise affected is within a London borough, if it appears to the council of that borough expedient to do so -

(a)    in the interests of the safety of users of the main highway; or

(b)    to facilitate the movement of traffic on the main highway,

it may by order authorise the stopping up or diversion of the other highway.

(3)    Subsections (2) and (2B) to (6) of section 247 shall apply to an order under this section as they apply to an order under that section, taking the reference in subsections (2) and (2B) of that section to any other highway as a reference to any highway other than that which is stopped up or diverted under this section and the references in subsection (3) to a highway provided or improved by virtue of an order under that section as including a reference to the main highway.

### Definitions

For "*highway*", "*improvement*", "*land*", "*use*" and "*planning permission*", see section 336(1) below.

### Section 254 - Compulsory acquisition of land in connection with highways.

(1)    The Secretary of State, or a local highway authority or a strategic highways company on being authorised by the Secretary of State to do so, may acquire land compulsorily -

(a)    for the purpose of providing or improving any highway which is to be provided or improved in pursuance of an order under section 247, 248 or 249 or for any other purpose for which land is required in connection with the order; or

(b) for the purpose of providing any public right of way which is to be provided as an alternative to a right of way extinguished under an order under section 251.

(2) The Acquisition of Land Act 1981 shall apply to the acquisition of land under this section.

### Definitions

For "*land*" and "*local highway authority*", see section 336(1) below.

## Section 336 - Interpretation.

(1) In this Act, except in so far as the context otherwise requires and subject to the following provisions of this section and to any transitional provision made by the Planning (Consequential Provisions) Act 1990 -

"acquiring authority", in relation to the acquisition of an interest in land (whether compulsorily or by agreement) or to a proposal so to acquire such an interest, means the government department, local authority or other body by whom the interest is, or is proposed to be, acquired;

"bridleway" has the same meaning as in the Highways Act 1980;

"the Broads" has the same meaning as in the Norfolk and Suffolk Broads Act 1988;

"building" includes any structure or erection, and any part of a building, as so defined, but does not include plant or machinery comprised in a building;

"buildings or works" includes waste materials, refuse and other matters deposited on land, and references to the erection or construction of buildings or works shall be construed accordingly and references to the removal of buildings or works include demolition of buildings and filling in of trenches;

"building operations" has the meaning given by section 55;

"development" has the meaning given in section 55, and "develop" shall be construed accordingly;

"development consent" means development consent under the Planning Act 2008;

"development order" has the meaning given in section 59;

"development plan" must be construed in accordance with section 38 of the Planning and Compulsory Purchase Act 2004;

"engineering operations" includes the formation or laying out of means of access to highways;

"footpath" has the same meaning as in the Highways Act 1980;

"highway" has the same meaning as in the Highways Act 1980;

"improvement", in relation to a highway, has the same meaning as in the Highways Act 1980;

"land" means any corporeal hereditament, including a building, and, in relation to the acquisition of land under Part IX, includes any interest in or right over land;

"lease" includes an underlease and an agreement for a lease or underlease, but does not include an option to take a lease or a mortgage, and "leasehold interest" means the interest of the tenant under a lease as so defined;

"local authority" (except in section 252 and subject to subsection (10) below and section 71(7) of the Environment Act 1995) means -

(a)     a billing authority or a precepting authority (except the Receiver for the Metropolitan Police District), as defined in section 69 of the Local Government Finance Act 1992 or the Mayor's Office for Policing and Crime;

(aa)    a fire and rescue authority in Wales constituted by a scheme under section 2 of the Fire and Rescue Services Act 2004 or a scheme to which section 4 of that Act applies;

(ab)    the London Fire Commissioner;

(b)     a levying body within the meaning of section 74 of the Local Government Finance Act 1988; and

(c)     a body as regards which section 75 of that Act applies;

and includes any joint board or joint committee if all the constituent authorities are local authorities within paragraph (a), (b) or (c);

"local highway authority" means a highway authority other than the Secretary of State or a strategic highways company;

"local planning authority" shall be construed in accordance with Part I;

"London borough" includes the City of London, references to the council of a London borough or the clerk to such a council being construed, in relation to the City, as references to the Common Council of the City and the town clerk of the City respectively;

"means of access" includes any means of access, whether private or public, for vehicles or for foot passengers, and includes a street;

"Minister" means any Minister of the Crown or other government department;

"owner", in relation to any land, means a person, other than a mortgagee not in possession, who, whether in his own right or as trustee for any other person, is entitled to receive the rack rent of the land or, where the land is not let at a rack rent, would be so entitled if it were so let;

"permission in principle" means permission of the kind referred to in section 58A;

"planning decision" means a decision made on an application under Part III or section 293A;

"planning permission" means permission under Part III or section 293A but does not include permission in principle;

"prescribed" (except in relation to matters expressly required or authorised by this Act to be prescribed in some other way) means prescribed by regulations under this Act;

"relevant local planning authority" is to be construed in accordance with section 61DB(9);

"restricted byway" has the same meaning as in Part 2 of the Countryside and Rights of Way Act 2000;

"statutory undertakers" and "statutory undertaking" have the meanings given in section 262;

"strategic highways company" means a company for the time being appointed under Part 1 of the Infrastructure Act 2015;

"tenancy" has the same meaning as in the Landlord and Tenant Act 1954;

"use", in relation to land, does not include the use of land for the carrying out of any building or other operations on it;

...

(2)     If, in relation to anything required or authorised to be done under this Act, any question arises as to which Minister is or was the appropriate Minister in relation to any statutory undertakers, that question shall be determined by the Treasury.

(3)     If any question so arises whether land of statutory undertakers is operational land, that question shall be determined by the Minister who is the appropriate Minister in relation to those undertakers.

### Schedule 9A - Resolution of disputes about planning obligations - Section 106ZA.

(Note: Added by Housing and Planning Act 2016 c. 22 Schedule 13 para. 1 but not yet in force).

# PART 3

# DRAFTING EXAMPLES

# Form 1: Boilerplate (Standard) Clauses

### *[Form 1.1] - The Parties*

BETWEEN:

1) *[****]* (the "Council") of *[****]*.

(2) *[****]* LTD (Company number *[****]*) (the "Developer") (which expression shall include the Developer's successors in title and assigns) whose registered office is *[****]*.

(3) *[****]* (the "Owner") (Company Number *[****]*) (which expression shall include the Owner's successors in title and assigns) whose registered office is *[****]*.

(4) *[****]* (Company number *[****]*) (the "Surety") (which expression shall include the Surety's successors in title and assigns) whose registered office is *[****]*.

> **Commentary**
>
> If a party is a company, then carry out a search at Companies House to verify both the company and details of directors. If the developer is a trust, then ask to see the current constitution of the trust. Check that the "owner" is the freeholder free from incumbrances. If there is a charge, then the chargee should be a party. Also, check that the Surety is good for the bond.

### *[Form 1.2] - Definitions*

In this Agreement where the context so admits:

**"As Built Drawings"** means three sets of drawings in hard copies and one copy in an original editable electronic format showing (to a scale of 1:500) the completed Works to the satisfaction of the Engineer and the drawings must include:

- by means of a colour code set out below (or such other colour code required by the Engineer);

    ○ red edging - the highway boundary;

    ○ pink solid - all new highway land;

    ○ red hatched - any highway land the use of which has changed (for example verge to carriageway);

    ○ blue dotted - all existing drainage;

- ○ blue solid - all new drainage;

- and (unless otherwise agreed by the Engineer) must show (both existing and proposed):

  - ○ the positions of all Statutory Undertakers' apparatus;

  - ○ any additional levels boreholes records or other information which may be required by the Engineer;

  - ○ the location, the direction of flow and the construction materials of all and existing drainage ditches and the location of outfalls or soakaways;

  - ○ all street lighting illuminated signs and cables;

  - ○ all shrub areas and grass areas including area measurements;

  - ○ those Buildings which will be maintained by or on behalf of the Council and those permanently maintained by or on behalf of the Developer;

  - ○ signs and road markings on the highway and location and details of sign face[s]; and

  - ○ all completed finishes on the highway that is (but without limitation) high friction surfacing, wearing course, tactile paving, carriageway, footway finishes and kerb types.

**"First Occupation"** means the first time that Occupation occurs;

**"First Schedule"** means the First Schedule to this Agreement;

**"Second Schedule"** means the Second Schedule to this Agreement;

**"Bond"** means the sum of *(£ [****] ([****] Pounds)* provided as security for this Agreement, as may be reduced from time to time in accordance with the provisions of this Agreement;

**"Building"** includes (without limitation) any structure or erection or any part of a building, structure or erection;

**"Charge"** means the *[legal charge] [mortgage]* dated *[****]* and registered at the Land Registry under title number *[****]*;

**"Clear day"** means 24 hours from midnight following the relevant event;

**"Completion Periods"** means the periods specified in Clause *[****]* of this Agreement;

**"Costed Risk Analysis"** means a costed risk analysis in respect of Part 1 Claims under the Land Compensation Act 1973 that may occur as a result of the Works within 7 years of the issue of the Final Certificate;[125]

**"Day"** means 24 consecutive hours unless otherwise specifically stated;

**"Developer's Contractor"** means [****];

**"Due Date"** means the date on which any payments under this Agreement are due to be paid;

**"Engineer"** means [****];

**"Expert"** means an expert appointed pursuant to Clause [****];

**"Force Majeure Event"** means an act of God including but not limited to fire, flood, earthquake, windstorm or other natural disaster; act of any sovereign including but not limited to war, invasion, act of foreign enemies, hostilities (whether war be declared or not), civil war, rebellion, revolution, insurrection, military or usurped power or confiscation, nationalisation, requisition, destruction or damage to property by or under the order of any government or public or local authority or imposition of government sanction embargo or similar action; law, judgment, order, decree, embargo, blockade, labour dispute including but not limited to strike, lockout or boycott; interruption or failure of utility service including but not limited to electric power, gas, water or telephone service; failure of the transportation of any personnel equipment, machinery supply or material required for the discharge of this Agreement, breach of contract by any essential personnel; any other matter or cause beyond the control of the relevant Party;

**"Health and Safety File"** means [****] and (without limitation) shall include:

- a report summarising the construction phase of the Works;

- details of the design options selected by the Developer (including the Developer's Contractor), any significant design changes and the reasons for the changes;

- a section describing all materials used in the Works, their source of supply and their level of performance together with the name and address of the manufacturer and shall describe any problems encountered;

- a report summarising details of the hand over walk through with the officer nominated by the Council to undertake that function (amongst others) together with the date of that activity, the names of the attendees, a summary of the issues raised and consequential actions; and

---

125 See para. 16.4 of the Text as to the calculation of the 7 year period.

shall report any significant problems encountered during the construction phase and describe how those problems were overcome;

**"Index"** means increased by a percentage equal to the percentage increase of the *[RPI Index]* from the *[RPI Index]* last published before the date of this Agreement to the *[RPI Index]* last published before the Due Date;

**"Interest"** means, in relation to any payment due under this Agreement or, where the context requires and where payable in instalments, an instalment thereof, an amount calculated in accordance with Clause *[****]*;

**"Land Compensation Acts"** means the Land Clauses Consolidation Act 1945, the Land Compensation Act 1961, the Compulsory Purchase Act 1965, the Land Compensation Act 1973 and the Planning and Compensation Act 1991 and includes the Human Rights Act 1998 and any statute enacted on a date on or after the date of execution of this Agreement which confers a right of compensation to any person for the compulsory acquisition of land and/or the diminution in value of land as a result of the carrying out of the Works or use of the Works as public works and "Land Compensation Act" shall be construed accordingly;

**"Land Compensation Claim"** means:

(a) any claims (howsoever arising) pursuant to the Land Compensation Acts relating to the use of any street, highway or road following the carrying out and attributable to the Works;

(b) any claims (howsoever arising) made in respect of or arising from the acquisition or use of any land whether by way of compulsory purchase powers or otherwise including (but not limited to) claims for injurious affection or relocation; and

(c) any claims (howsoever arising) made in respect of or arising from the acquisition or making of any drainage arrangements for the Works.

**"Land Compensation Costs"** means all payments in respect of any Land Compensation Claim including (without prejudice to generality) all compensation payments and all costs and fees incurred by the Council in negotiating, paying and settling such claims including (but not limited to) counsel's fees and charges, surveyors' fees and charges, valuation fees and charges and legal fees and charges, and all costs and fees incurred in connection with any proceedings in any mediation, tribunal or court in respect of such claims;

AND, for the purposes of this definition, *"land"* includes any estate or interest in or right over land;

**"Maintain"** includes inspect, repair, adjust, alter, remove or reconstruct and any derivative of *"maintain"* is to be construed accordingly;

**"Month"** means calendar month unless otherwise specifically stated;

***"Occupied"*** means occupation for the purposes permitted by the Planning Permission but not including occupation by personnel engaged in construction, fitting out or decoration or occupation for marketing or display or occupation in relation to security operations and *"Occupy"*, *"Occupier"* and *"Occupation"* shall be construed accordingly;

***"Party"*** means each and any of the Council, the *[Owner] [Developer] [Chargee]* and the *[Surety]*;

***"Parties"*** means (collectively) the Council, the *[Owner] [Developer] [Chargee]* and the *[Surety]*;

***"Planning Permission"*** means the planning permission granted by the Council dated *[****]* for the proposed erection of *[****]* *[and associated infrastructure including open space and sustainable urban drainage system]* under reference numbers *[****]*;

***"Road Safety Audits"*** means (collectively) the Stage 1 Safety Audit, Stage 2 Safety Audit, Stage 3 Safety Audit and the Stage 4 Safety Audit;[126]

***"Site"*** means land at *[****]*, which is shown edged *[****]* on the plan annexed hereto and registered at the Land Registry under Title Numbers *[****]*;

***"Stage 1 Safety Audit"*** means a "Stage 1: completion of preliminary design" audit carried out in accordance with the Design Manual for Roads and Bridges, GG 119 - "Road safety audit";

***"Stage 2 Safety Audit"*** means a "Stage 2: completion of detailed design stage" audit carried out in accordance with the Design Manual for Roads and Bridges, GG 119 - "Road safety audit";

***"Stage 3 Safety Audit"*** means a "Stage 3: completion of construction" audit carried out in accordance with the Design Manual for Roads and Bridges, GG 119 - "Road safety audit";

***"Stage 4 Safety Audit"*** means a "Stage 4: monitoring" audit carried out in accordance with the Design Manual for Roads and Bridges, GG 119 - "Road safety audit";

***"Statutory Undertaker"*** means a person or body authorised by enactment to carry on any of the statutory undertakings or the public utility undertakings mentioned in Section 329(1) of the 1980 Act or the operator of a telecommunications core system or a driver information system;

***"Street"*** means a *"street"* within the meaning of section 48 (*streets, street works and undertakers*) of the 1991 Act, together with land forming the verge of a Street or between two carriageways, and (where the context requires) includes part of a street;

---

[126] See Chapter 10 for Road Safety Audits.

**"Street Authority"**: in relation to a Street, has the same meaning as in Part 3 of the 1991 Act;

**"Street Works"** means *"street works"* as defined by Section 48 of the 1991 Act;

**"Traffic"** means all classes of traffic including (without limitation) vehicular traffic, cyclists, pedestrians, animals and persons on horseback;

**"Traffic Regulation Order"** means an order made pursuant to the Road Traffic Regulation Act 1984 or any similar order which has the effect of controlling any or all types of Traffic (as the case may be), either permanently or temporarily (as the case may be);

**"Working Day"** means a day of the week but excluding Saturdays, Sundays, Bank Holidays and any other day of national holiday;

**"Year"** means calendar year unless otherwise specifically stated.

## *[Form 1.3] - Interpretation*

In this Agreement where the context so admits:

• References to any Party shall include the successors in title to that party and to any person deriving title through or under that Party and in the case of the Council the successors to its statutory functions.

• Reference to any statute or statutory provision includes a reference to that statute or statutory provision as from time to time amended, extended, re-enacted or consolidated; and all statutory instruments or orders made pursuant to it.

• Words denoting the singular number only shall include the plural and vice versa and words denoting any gender include all genders.

• References to persons include firms, companies and corporations and vice versa and shall include bodies of persons whether corporate or incorporate.

• Any and all schedules, annexures and exhibits attached to it or incorporated by reference to this Agreement are and shall be construed as being part of this Agreement.

• Clauses and schedules are references to clauses of, and schedules to, this Agreement, and references to this Agreement include its schedules.

• The headings in this document are inserted for convenience only and shall not affect the construction or interpretation of this Agreement.

- Any reference in this Agreement to any statute or statutory provision shall be construed as referring to that statute or statutory provision as the same may from time to time be amended, modified, extended, re-enacted or replaced (whether before or after the date of this Agreement) and including all subordinate legislation made under it from time to time.

- The words *"highway"*, *"highway authority"*, *"carriageway"*, *"cycletrack"*, *"footpath"* and *"footway"* have the same meaning as in the 1980 Act.

- Where a Street or highway passes over a bridge or through a tunnel, that bridge or tunnel is to be taken for the purposes of this Act to be a part of the Street or highway.

- The words *"public path"*, *"footpath"*, *"bridleway"*, *"byway open to all traffic"* and *"restricted byway"* shall have the same meanings as in the Wildlife and Countryside Act 1981.

### [Form 1.4] - Extent of liabilities

- Where any obligation is undertaken by two or more persons jointly they are to be jointly and severally liable in respect of that obligation.

- Where this Agreement is signed by or on behalf of a partnership any liability arising under it shall be deemed to be the joint and several liability of the partners.

- References in this Agreement to anything which any Party is required to do or not to do shall include that Party's acts, defaults and omissions, whether direct or indirect, on its own account, or for or through any other person, and those which it permits or suffers to be done or not done by any other person.

### [Form 1.5] - Agreement in counterparts

This Agreement shall be executed in *[number]* counterparts or duplicates each of which shall be an original but such counterparts or duplicates shall together constitute one and the same Agreement.[127]

### [Form 1.6] - Survival of rights up to termination

Termination of this Agreement shall not affect any rights of the Parties accrued up to the date of termination.

---

[127] This has been added for completeness but local authorities are normally very reluctant to use counterparts in practice.

### [Form 1.7] - Entire and final Agreement

This Agreement shall constitute the entire agreement and understanding between the Parties with respect to all matters which are referred to and shall supersede any previous agreement(s) between the Parties in relation to the matters referred to in this Agreement.

### [Form 1.8] - Severance

If any provision of this Agreement shall be prohibited by law or adjudged by a court to be unlawful, void or unenforceable such provision shall to the extent required be severed from this Agreement and rendered ineffective as far as possible without modifying the remaining provisions of this Agreement and shall not in any way affect any other circumstances of or the validity or enforcement of this Agreement.

### [Form 1.9] - Specific obligations

The effect of all obligations affecting any Party under this Agreement is cumulative and no obligation shall be limited or modified by any other of those obligations unless there is in this Agreement an express limitation or modification.

### [Form 1.10] - Council's statutory duties

Nothing contained in or implied by this Agreement shall prejudice or affect the rights, discretions, powers, duties and obligations of the Council under all statutes, by-laws, statutory instruments, orders and regulations in the exercise of its functions as a local authority.

### [Form 1.11] - No partnership or agency

This Agreement shall not constitute or imply any partnership, joint venture, agency, fiduciary relationship or other relationship between the Parties other than the contractual relationship expressly provided for in this Agreement and neither Party shall have, nor represent that it has, any authority to make any commitments on the other Party's behalf.

### [Form 1.12] - Payments

- Time for payment of all money payable by [****] under this Agreement shall be of the essence.

- The [Developer] [Owner] shall pay the Council such sums required by this Agreement within 20 Working Days of the Council issuing a written demand.

- If any sum payable under this Agreement shall not be paid when due, then the indebted Party shall pay Interest on such overdue sum calculated on a daily basis and compounded quarterly from the Due Date until payment at the rate of [****]% per annum over the [****] Bank plc base rate from time to time in force.

### *[Form 1.13] - Approvals, consents etc*

- Where, under any of the requirements in this Agreement, the approval, consent, or agreement of the Council is required the matter which requires approval, consent or agreement must be submitted in writing for such approval or agreement; and the approval, consent or agreement must be given in writing.

- Where any requirement provides that the Works are to be carried out in accordance with details, or a scheme, plan or other document approved or agreed by the Council, the approved or agreed details, scheme, plan or other document is taken to include any amendments or revisions subsequently approved or agreed by the Council.

### *[Form 1.14] - Costs of Agreement*

The *[Developer] [Owner]* shall pay the Council's reasonable costs of preparation of this Agreement in the sum of £*[****]* (*[****]* Pounds).

### *[Form 1.15] - Assignment*

This Agreement shall not be assigned by any Party without the written consents of all of the other Parties.

### *[Form 1.16] - Dispute provisions*

- In the event of any dispute or difference arising between the Parties (or any of them) in respect of any matter contained in this Agreement such dispute or difference shall be referred to an independent and suitable person (the "Expert") holding appropriate professional qualifications to be appointed (in the absence of an agreement) by or on behalf of the president for the time being (or his deputy) of the professional body chiefly relevant in England with such matters as may be in dispute and the Expert shall act as an expert whose decision shall be final and binding on the parties to the dispute (in the absence of manifest error) and any costs shall be payable by the said parties in such proportion as the Expert shall determine and failing such determination shall be borne by the said parties in equal shares.

- In the absence of agreement as to the appointment or suitability of the Expert or as to the appropriateness of the professional body then such question may be referred by any party to the dispute to the president for the time being of the Law Society (or his deputy) for him to appoint a solicitor to determine the dispute such solicitor acting as an expert and his decision shall be final and binding on all parties to the dispute in the absence of manifest error and his costs shall be payable by the said parties in such proportion as he shall determine and failing such determination shall be borne by the parties in equal shares.

- The Expert shall be subject to the express requirement that a decision was reached and communicated to all Parties within the minimum practicable timescale allowing for the nature and complexity of the dispute and in any event not more than Twenty-Eight (28) Working Days after the conclusion of any hearing that takes place or Twenty-Eight (28) Working Days after he has received any file or written representation.

- The Expert shall be required to give notice to each of the said parties to the dispute requiring them to submit to him within Ten (10) Working Days of notification of his appointment written submissions and supporting material and the other party to the dispute will be entitled to make a counter written submission within a further Ten (10) Working Days.

### [Form 1.17] - Waiver

No waiver (whether expressed or implied) by any Party of any breach or default in performing or observing any of the covenants terms or conditions of this Agreement shall constitute a continuing waiver and no such waiver shall prevent the enforcement of any of the relevant terms or conditions or from action upon any subsequent breach or default.

### [Form 1.18] - Third parties

None of the terms of this Agreement should be enforceable by virtue of the Contracts (Rights of Third Parties) Act 1999.

### [Form 1.19] - Service of notices

Any notice required to be given by the Council to the *[Developer] [Owner] [Chargee] [Surety]* under this Agreement shall be deemed to have been properly served if it is sent by the Council by pre-paid recorded delivery post to the *[Developer] [Owner] [Chargee] [Surety]* at the addresses given in this Agreement.

Any notice required to be given by the *[Developer] [Owner] [Chargee] [Surety]* to the Council shall be deemed to be properly served if sent by pre-paid recorded delivery post to the Chief Executive of the Council at the address given in this Agreement.

### [Form 1.20] - Chargee's consent

The Chargee acknowledges and declares that this Agreement has been entered into by the Owner with its consent and that the Site shall be bound by the obligations contained in this Agreement and that the security of the Charge shall take effect subject to this Agreement PROVIDED THAT the Chargee shall otherwise have no liability under this Agreement unless it takes possession of the Site in which case it too will be bound by the obligations as if it were a person deriving title from the Owner.

### *[Form 1.21] - Jurisdiction*

This Agreement is governed by and interpreted in accordance with the laws of England.

### *[Form 1.22] - Force majeure*

- A Party will not be liable for any delay in performing or failure to perform any of its obligations under this Agreement caused by a Force Majeure Event.

- The Party claiming the Force Majeure Event will promptly notify the other in writing of the reasons for the delay or stoppage (and the likely duration) and will take all reasonable steps to overcome the delay or stoppage.

- If the Party claiming the Force Majeure Event has complied with clause *[****]* its performance under this Agreement will be suspended for the period that the Force Majeure Event continues and the Party will have an extension of time for performance which is reasonable.

### *[Form 1.23] - Value Added Tax*

All consideration given in accordance with the terms of this Deed shall be exclusive of any value added tax properly payable.

# Form 2: Planning Obligation By Agreement

THIS AGREEMENT is made the *[****]* day of *[****]*

BETWEEN:

(1) *[****]* (the "Council")

(2) *[****]* (the "Owner")

(3) *[****]* (the "Chargee")

(4) *[****]* (the "Surety")

See *[Form 1.1] - The Parties*

## Introduction

A. The Council is both the local planning authority for the purposes of the Act and is the local highway authority for the area in which the Site is situated.

B. The Owner is the freehold owner of the Site.

C. The Chargee is interested in the Site by a legal charge over the Site dated *[****]*.

D. The Owner has submitted the Application to the Council and the Parties have agreed to enter into this Deed in order to secure the planning obligations contained in this Deed.

E. The Council has resolved to grant the Planning Permission subject to the prior completion of this Deed.

NOW THIS DEED WITNESSES AS FOLLOWS:

## OPERATIVE PART

### 1      DEFINITIONS

For the purposes of this Deed the following expressions shall have the following meanings:

**"1980 Act"** means the Highways Act 1980;

**"1990 Act"** means the Town and Country Planning Act 1990;

**"Application"** means the application for planning permission dated *[****]* submitted to the Council for the Development and allocated reference number *[****]*;

**"*Commencement of Development*"** means the date on which any material operation (as defined in section 56(4) of the 1990 Act) forming part of the Development begins to be carried out[128] *[other than (for the purposes of this Deed and for no other purpose) operations consisting of site clearance, demolition work, archaeological investigations, investigations for the purpose of assessing ground conditions, remedial work in respect of any contamination or other adverse ground conditions, diversion and laying of services, erection of any temporary means of enclosure, the temporary display of site notices or advertisements[129] ]* and *"Commence"* and *"Commence Development"* shall be construed accordingly and *"Commencement of Phase"* shall (*mutatis mutandis*) be construed in like manner;

**"*Commencement Date*"** means the date of Commencement of Development;

**"*Completion*"** means in relation to a building or such part as may be specified, the issue of a certificate of practical completion by the Owner's architect or other project consultant appointed by the Owner and otherwise practical completion of the relevant part of the Development and *"Complete"* and *"Completed"* shall be construed accordingly;

**"*Expert*"** See *[Form 1.2] - Definitions*

**"*First Occupation*"** means the first day that any Dwelling is Occupied;

**"*Development*"** means the development of the Site with *[insert description of the development]* as set out in the Application;

**"*Dwelling*"** means any dwelling (including a house, flat or maisonette) to be constructed pursuant to the Planning Permission;

**"*Index*"** See *[Form 1.2] - Definitions*

**"*Interest*"** means, in relation to any payment due under this Deed or, where the context requires and where payable in instalments, an instalment thereof, an amount calculated in accordance with Clause *[****]*;

**"*Occupation*"**, **"*Occupied*"** and **"*Occupier*"** See *[Form 1.2] - Definitions*

**"*Plan*"** means the plan attached to this Deed;

---

[128] Some drafts use the phrase "... *the date on which any material operation ... forming part of the Development is carried out* ..." or "... *forming part of the Development is implemented* ...", but both are ambiguous. They seem to turn on the completion of the material operations, which can be very difficult to detect and date. Also, this begs the question whether the trigger is engaged if the material operation is started but then halted. Ergo, it is preferable to tie commencement to when the material operation is first started. Also, beware of the affectation "*Commencement of the Development*" because one often finds that the "*the*" is then lost in the narrative of the agreement.

[129] These tend to be conventional boilerplate exclusions; however, it is arguable that they go too far into the construction process. For example, some of these activities might generate significant traffic flows.

**"Planning Permission"** means the planning permission to be granted by the Council pursuant to the Application;

**"Site"** means the land against which this Deed may be enforced as shown (for the purposes of identification) edged red on the Plan and registered with the Land Registry under title number *[****]*;

**"Street"** means a street as defined by section 48(3) of the New Roads and Street Works Act 1991; and

**"Working Day"** See *[Form 1.2] - Definitions*

## 2    CONSTRUCTION OF THIS DEED

See *[Form 1.3] - Interpretation*

## 3    LEGAL BASIS

3.1     This Deed is made pursuant to section 106 of the 1990 Act so as to bind the Owner and the Site *[and section 111 of the Local Government Act 1972]* and *[section 1 of the Local Government Act 2000]*.

3.2     The obligations, covenants, restrictions and requirements imposed upon the Owner under this Deed create planning obligations pursuant to section 106 of the 1990 Act and are enforceable by the Council as the local planning authority against the Owner and in respect of the Site.

## 4    CONDITIONALITY

*[4.1     This Deed is conditional upon:*

*(i)      the grant of the Planning Permission; and*

*(ii)     the Commencement of Development*

*save for the provisions of Clauses [****] and [****] [add any other relevant provisions which shall come into effect immediately upon completion of this Deed.]]*[130]

## 5    THE OWNER'S COVENANTS

5.1     The Owner covenants with the Council as set out in the *[****]* and *[****]* Schedules.

---

[130]  This provision is a tiresome affectation which adds nothing but the potential for confusion i.e. when the cross-references are not properly tracked through the agreement. Unfortunately, some draftsmen insist that it adds something to the draft.

## 6      THE COUNCIL'S COVENANTS

6.1      The Council covenants with the Owner as set out in the *[\*\*\*\*]* Schedule.

## 7      MISCELLANEOUS

7.1      This Deed shall be registrable as a local land charge by the Council.

7.2      This Deed shall cease to have effect (insofar only as it has not already been complied with) if the Planning Permission shall be quashed, revoked or otherwise withdrawn or (without the consent of the Owner) it is materially modified by any statutory procedure or expires prior to the Commencement of Development.

7.3      No person shall be liable for any breach of any of the planning obligations or other provisions of this Deed after it shall have parted with its entire interest in the Site but without prejudice to liability for any subsisting breach arising prior to parting with such interest.

*[7.4      This Deed shall not be enforceable against individual owner-occupiers or tenants of Dwellings nor against those deriving title from them.]*[131]

7.5      Nothing in this Deed shall prohibit or limit the right to develop any part of the Site in accordance with a planning permission (other than the Planning Permission) granted (whether or not on appeal) after the date of this Deed.

And see:

*[Form 1.3]* - *Interpretation*

*[Form 1.4]* - *Extent of liabilities*

*[Form 1.8]* - *Severance*

*[Form 1.10]* - *Council's statutory duties*

## 9      CHARGEE'S CONSENT

See *[Form 1.20]* - *Chargee's consent*

## 10      WAIVER

See *[Form 1.17]* - *Waiver*

---

[131]   Whilst this is conventional, it is important to ask whether it is appropriate where the agreement deals with those highway matters which should bear on all properties in a development.

## 11    CHANGE IN OWNERSHIP

11.1    The Owner agrees with the Council to give the Council immediate written notice of any change in ownership of any of its interests in the Site occurring before all the obligations under this Deed have been discharged such notice to give details of the transferee's full name and registered office (if a company or usual address if not) together with the area of the Site or unit of occupation purchased by reference to a plan.[132]

## 12    PAYMENTS

12.1    Any sum referred to in the *[****]* Schedule[s] shall be increased by an amount equivalent to the increase in the Index from the *[date hereof]* until the date on which such sum is payable.

See *[Form 1.12] - Payments*

## 13    INTEREST

See *[Form 1.12] - Payments*

## 14    VAT

See *[Form 1.23] - Value Added Tax*

## 15    DISPUTE PROVISIONS

See *[Form 1.16] - Dispute provisions*

## 16    JURISDICTION

See *[Form 1.21] - Jurisdiction*

## 18    DELIVERY

18.1    The provisions of this Deed (other than this clause which shall be of immediate effect) shall be of no effect until this Deed has been dated.

IN WITNESS whereof .........

---

[132]    Note that this clause is outwith section 106(1) and is not binding on successors in title without an agreement of substitution.

---

FIRST SCHEDULE

*[Details of the Owner's title, and description of the Site]*

---

SECOND SCHEDULE

The Owner's Covenants with the Council as follows:

### *HIGHWAY CONTRIBUTION*

*New Definition:*

**"Highway Contribution"** means the sum of £*[****]* (*[****]* Pounds) being a financial contribution to the carrying out of junction improvements to the *[****]* Road;

*Operative clauses:*

*[i]* Not to Commence Development unless and until the Owner has paid to the Council the sum of £*[****]* (*[****]* Pounds) being part of the Highways Contribution.

*[ii]* That no part of the Development shall be Occupied unless and until the Owner has paid to the Council the sum of £*[****]* (*[****]* Pounds) being the balance of the Highways Contribution.

### *MAINTENANCE OF ESTATE ROADS*

*New Definitions:*

**"Advance Payments Code"** means the code provided by sections 219 to 225 of the Highways Act 1980;

**"Management Company"** means either:

- an existing company appointed for the purposes of carrying out the Maintenance of the Estate Roads; or

- a new company incorporated for the purposes of carrying out the Maintenance of the Estate Roads

and which has been approved by the Council for the purposes of this Agreement;

**"Estate Roads"** means:

(a) all Streets within the Site which are not maintainable at the public expense and are not the subject of an agreement made under section 38 of the Highways Act 1980 or a security deposited pursuant to the Advance Payments Code (as defined in section 203(1) of the Highways Act 1980);

(b) highway verges and areas of landscaping; and

(c) all drains, sewers, drainage systems and street drainage in respect of the Estate Roads (including all water storage and attenuation connected with the drainage of the Estate Roads) which are not maintainable at the public expense and are not the subject of an agreement made under section 104 of the Water Industry Act 1991

as more particularly shown and described in the Management Scheme;

**"Management Scheme"** means a scheme approved by the Council in writing and setting out detailed descriptions of the Estate Roads (including such drawings or plans as the Council may reasonably require) and detailed specifications and requirements for the Maintenance of the Estate Roads including arrangements for the management, administration and financing of the Maintenance of the Estate Roads including such variations to the scheme as may (from time to time) be agreed in writing by the Council;

**"Maintenance of the Estate Roads"** shall include (without limitation) the carrying out of street works (as defined in section 48(3) of the New Roads and Street Works Act 1991);

**"Service Charges"** means charges or expenses levied on residential occupiers of Dwellings by the Management Company in respect of the Maintenance of the Estate Roads and the administration and management of the same.

*Operative clauses:*

*[i]* No part of the Development shall be Commenced unless and until the Owner has submitted the proposed Management Scheme to the Council and the Council has approved it in writing.

*[ii]* If the Management Scheme provides that the Maintenance of the Estate Roads shall be the responsibility of a Management Company, then no part of the Development shall be Commenced unless and until the Council has approved the Management Company PROVIDED THAT the Council may (without limitation) withhold its approval unless satisfied that the Articles and Memorandum of Association of the company are (or will be) fit for purpose and are reasonable in respect of future residential occupiers of the Development and that the proposed company will be appropriately managed and financed.

*[iii]*   If the proposed Management Scheme provides that a Management Company or other body shall levy any charges on future residential occupiers of the Development for the Maintenance of the Estate Roads the Council may (without limitation) withhold its approval of it unless satisfied that mechanisms are shown which ensure that Service Charges will be reasonable and will remain reasonable in perpetuity.

*[iv]*   If the proposed Management Scheme provides that an Estate Management Company shall be responsible for the Maintenance of the Estate Roads then no Dwelling shall be Occupied unless and until the Management Company has delivered to the Council a deed (duly executed by or on behalf of the said company) which provides that:

- the constitution of the Management Company shall not be altered without the prior written consent of the Council unless the whole of the Development shall have been demolished or unless otherwise first agreed in writing by the Council;

- the Management Company shall carry out the Maintenance of the Estate Roads in accordance with the Management Scheme;

- the Management Company shall provide to the Council such information as to any Service Charges as the Council may reasonably require and that such Service Charges shall at all times be reasonable;

- any dispute between the Council and the Management Company as to whether the terms or quanta of Service Charges is/are reasonable may be referred to an expert for determination and the Service Charges shall then be in accordance with the expert's determination; and

- that the provisions of the said deed shall be enforceable by the Council against the Management Company

and the said deed shall be in a form reasonably required by the Council.

*[v]*   In the event that any appointed Management Company ceases operating and/or Maintaining the Estate Roads, the Owner will maintain or will procure the Maintenance of the Estate Roads in accordance with the approved Management Scheme and the provisions set out in clauses *[****]* above shall apply (mutatis mutandis) until such time as a new Management Company has been engaged to undertake the future Maintenance of the Estate Roads.

*[vi]*   In the event that the Owner or (as the case may be) the Management Company (if any) shall fail to Maintain the Estate Roads then the Council may (without prejudice to any other remedy which it may have) enter the Site and carry out such works to the Estate Roads as it may deem to be necessary and the Owner shall reimburse to the Council the costs of those works (which may include the costs of an estate

manager or contractor commissioned by the Council) and the Council's administrative expenses within Ten (10) Working Days of the service of a notice requiring the same.

[vii]  If any Street within the Site is subject of an agreement made under section 38 of the Highways Act 1980 or a security deposited pursuant to the Advance Payments Code or any drain or sewer within the Site is the subject of any an agreement made under section 104 of the Water Industry Act 1991, then the Owner shall be responsible for all maintenance of the said Streets, drains or sewers (as the case may be) until the date that they become maintainable at the public expense unless otherwise provided in the said agreement or security or otherwise agreed in writing by the Council.

## TRANSPORT FACILITIES

*New Definition:*

**"Transport Facilities"** means *[describe any facilities required].*

*Operative clauses:*

[i]  To carry out and complete the Transport Facilities to the satisfaction of the Council prior to Occupation of *[insert number] [any]* Dwelling[s].

[ii]  No Dwelling shall be Occupied unless and until the Transport Facilities have been completed to the satisfaction of the Council.

## BUS SERVICE CONTRIBUTIONS (Version 1)

*New Definition:*

**"Phase"** means a phase of the Development approved pursuant to Condition *[****]* of the Planning Permission and *"Phase 1", "Phase 2"* and *"Phase 3"* shall be construed accordingly.

*Operative clauses:*

[i]  The Owner shall within two months of Completion of Phase 1, Phase 2 and Phase 3 procure the carrying out of a proper survey of the Site's public transport accessibility levels and shall serve *[****]* copies of the same upon the Council within four months on each such completion.

[ii]  The following corresponding Bus Service Contributions shall be paid to the Council prior to the Commencement of the Phase in question:

| Phase 1 | £[****] ([****] Pounds) |
|---------|------------------------|
| Phase 2 | £[****] ([****] Pounds) |
| Phase 3 | £[****] ([****] Pounds) |

No works shall take place on a Phase unless and until the corresponding Bus Service Contribution referred to in paragraph [****] has been paid to the Council.

........................................................................................................................................

## VEHICLE TRIP MONITORING

*New Definitions:*

**"Trip Monitoring Equipment"** means an automated system to monitor and record vehicle trips to and from the Development;

**"Trip Mitigation Sum"** means a sum calculated by reference to the number of trips in excess of [****], and by the following formula [****].

*Operative clauses:*

[i]   No part of the Development shall be Commenced unless and until the Council has approved the specifications, locations and other details of the Trip Monitoring Equipment.

[ii]   No part of the Development shall be Occupied unless and until the Trip Monitoring Equipment has been installed on the Site and is operating to the satisfaction of the Council.

[iii]   The Trip Monitoring Equipment shall be operated at all times between the dates [****] and [****].

[iv]   In the event that the vehicle trips to and from the Site as recorded by the Trip Monitoring Equipment exceed [****] in any calendar year between the dates [****] and [****] the Owner will within 28 Days of receipt of notice of the number of vehicle trips exceeding [****] pay to the Council the Trip Mitigation Sum.

........................................................................................................................................

## BUS SERVICE CONTRIBUTION (Version 2)

*New Definition:*

**"Bus Service Contribution"** means the sum of £*[****] ([****]* Pounds) to be paid by the Owner to the Council and to be applied by the Council to provide *[****]*.

*Operative clauses:*

*[i]*     The Owner will pay the Bus Service Contribution to the Council in the following instalments:

    (a)    no later than 3 months after Commencement the sum of £*[****] ([****]* Pounds);

    (b)    no later than *[the first anniversary of the payment of the instalment required by paragraph [i] (a)] [Occupation by more than 25% of the Dwellings]* the sum of £*[****] ([****]* Pounds); and

    (c)    no later than *[the second anniversary of the payment of the instalment required by paragraph [i] (a)] [Occupation by more than 75% of the Dwellings]* the sum of £*[****] ([****]* Pounds).

*[ii]*    Without prejudice to Paragraph *[****]* no Dwelling shall be Occupied unless and until the first instalment of the Bus Service Contribution has been paid to the Council together with Interest on any balance outstanding at the date of payment.

---

## RECOVERY OF EXPENSES DUE TO EXTRAORDINARY TRAFFIC

*Operative clauses:*

*[i]*    Where it appears to the Council in respect of a highway maintainable at the public expense, by a certificate of their *[****]* that, having regard to the average expense of maintaining the highway or other similar highways in the neighbourhood of the Development, extraordinary expenses will be incurred by the Council in maintaining the highway by reason of the damage caused by excessive weight passing along the highway, or other extraordinary traffic thereon, in consequence of the conduct of the Development, the Council may recover from the Owner the Excess Expenses.

*[ii]*    In Paragraph *[\*\*\*\*]* above *"Excess Expenses"* means such expenses as have been or to be likely to be incurred by the Council by reason of the damage to the highway arising from the traffic to and from the Development.[133]

*[iii]*    These provisions are without prejudice to any remedies which the Council may have pursuant to section 59 of the 1980 Act.

........................................................................................................................................................

## TRAFFIC REGULATION ORDERS

*New Definition:*

**"Traffic Regulation Order"** means an order made pursuant to the Road Traffic Regulation Act 1984 or any similar order which has the effect *[of controlling] [\*\*\*\*]* or *[all types of Traffic]* on the *[\*\*\*\*]* Road by *[outline the controls]*.

*Operative clauses:*

*[i]*    No part of the Development shall be Commenced unless and until the Traffic Regulation Order has been made and (if needed) confirmed which provides that *[\*\*\*\*]*.

*[ii]*    The Council shall use reasonable endeavours to make and confirm the Traffic Regulation Order and the Owner shall pay to the Council the Council's costs in doing so PROVIDED that the Council shall not be obliged to initiate or pursue any Traffic Regulation Order unless and until the Owner has paid to or secured to the satisfaction of the Council a sum equivalent to the estimated costs of making and confirming any such Order and also provided the Council with an indemnity in respect of any costs which might arise from or be incurred in respect of any such proceedings (including, without limitation, legal or court proceedings), whether the Order is completed or confirmed or not.

THIRD SCHEDULE

## TRAVEL PLANNING

*Additional definitions:*

**"Additional Amount"** means the additional amount payable in the event of an increase in the Index, as calculated in accordance with Clause *[\*\*\*\*]* thereof;

---

[133]   In practice, the parties would be well advised to prepare "before" and "after" schedules of condition.

**"Action Plan"** means a plan approved by the Council (which may be varied from time to time with the written approval of the Council) which includes a series of time-bound actions that are identified and implemented by the Occupier so that the Travel Plan's Modal Shift targets can be achieved;

**"Baseline Survey"** means a travel survey to be undertaken within 6 months of First Occupation of the Site or when *[**** %]* of the *[****]* units have been Occupied/or staff are employed on Site exceeds *[****]* [134], whichever is first, being the first survey against which Travel Plan is measured;

**"Car"** means a four wheeled motor vehicle other than one powered by solely by electricity[135];

**"Car Club"** means a car sharing scheme operated by a company, community group or not-for-profit organisation which residents of the development and members of the general public may join and which makes cars available to hire to members either on a commercial or part-subsidised basis;

**"Independent Fieldwork Company"** means a suitably qualified, experienced and independent company/person approved to undertake TRICS surveys;

**"Modal Shift"** means an increase in the proportion of persons travelling to and from the Site using modes of transport other than Cars;

**"Modal Split"** means the proportion of trips made by different modes of transport, expressed as a percentage of the all trips made by employees, visitors and occupiers;

**"Monitoring Period"** means the period of *[defined number of years]* beginning on the date of First Occupation and ending *[****]* during which period the Travel Plan will be monitored;

**"Monitoring Report"** means a Report approved by the Council which summarises the implementation progress of the Travel Plan including details of measures implemented, survey results compared to previous surveys and targets, and a revised Action Plan for future years;

**"Monitoring Survey"** means a survey of persons accessing the Site concerning their travel behaviour to and from the Site, against which target achievement can be measured;

**"Parking Management Plan"** means a scheme approved by the Council pursuant to Paragraph *[****]* below;

**"Remedial Measures"** means measures intended to achieve Modal Shift when Travel Plan targets have not been achieved;

---

[134]   Query whether monitoring levels of occupation or staff numbers is practical.
[135]   Query whether hybrid cars should be excluded as well.

**"Transport Improvements Contribution"** means the sum of £*[****] ([****]* Pounds) being a financial contribution towards improving transport facilities in the locality of the Site;

**"Travel Plan"** means a long-term management strategy for the Site that has been approved by the Council and which seeks to deliver sustainable transport objectives through positive action, including details of outcomes and a package of measures aimed at encouraging a beneficial Modal Shift and includes the particulars listed in Paragraphs *[****]* of this Schedule together with such variations as may be agreed by the Council;

**"Travel Plan Bond"** means a bond in the sum of £*[****] ([****]* Pounds) to secure the obligations in this schedule in a form first approved by the Council in writing;

**"Travel Plan Coordinator"** means a person appointed by the Owner to act as coordinator of the Travel Plan who shall be responsible for the implementation, monitoring and progress reporting of the Travel Plan;

**"Travel Plan Monitoring Cost"** means the Council's costs for administering the requirements for surveys, providing guidance to the Travel Plan Coordinator, and for reviewing the Monitoring Surveys and the Owner's compliance with the terms of the Travel Plan;

**"TRICS"** means TRICS Consortium Limited, Office 20.

The Owner's Covenants with the Council as follows:

*Travel plan submission and site occupation*

(1)    Not to *[Occupy the Development/any Dwelling] [cause or permit First Occupation]* until the Travel Plan has been submitted to and approved in writing by the Council.

(2)    No part of the Development shall be Occupied unless any measures scheduled by the Travel Plan to be implemented before such Occupation have been carried out to the satisfaction of the Council.

*Travel plan minimum requirements*

(3)    The Travel Plan shall provide as a minimum:

(a)    a timetable for the implementation of measures, identifying timescales and responsibilities for ensuring implementation;

(b)    a schedule of Travel Plan monitoring, which includes both surveys and Monitoring Reports to be submitted to the Council. The length of the Monitoring Period shall not be less than *[****]* years from the date of Occupation of the Development;

(c)     an initial Baseline Survey to be undertaken within 6 months of First Occupation of the Development, or when *[[****] % of units are occupied] [[****] % of staff are on Site]*;

(d)     the methods of carrying out the surveys for the purposes of Monitoring to include details of the equipment to be used, the methods of collecting the data and the methods for calculating the Modal Shift; and

(e)     a budget for the implementation of measures and carrying out of surveys, and provisions to ensure the expenditure of this budget.

(4)     The Travel Plan shall include the following targets, to be approved by the Council:

(a)     implementation of actions on-time and to an agreed quality;

(b)     the Modal Split; and

(c)     absolute numbers of vehicles on-site at any one time/arriving on site between *[time]* and *[time]*.

(5)     The Travel Plan shall set targets for and monitor the following users of the Development:

(a)     residents;

(b)     staff commuters;

(c)     staff business travel;

(d)     students;

(e)     visitors / customers / guests / patients; and

(f)     deliveries.

(6)     The Development shall not be *[First Occupied] [Occupied by more than [****]]* unless and until any measures scheduled by the Travel Plan to be implemented before such Occupation have been carried out.

*Travel Plan Coordinator*

(7)     No more than *[****] [Units]* shall be Occupied unless and until a Travel Plan Coordinator has been appointed.

*Travel plan implementation*

(8)   The Owner shall fully carry out the Travel Plan approved by the Council in accordance with the timescales contained in the Travel Plan (or as amended by the agreement between the Council and the Owner in writing).

(9)   The Owner shall use all reasonable endeavours to ensure that the Travel Plan is complied with and that each of the targets contained in the Travel Plan are met.

(10)  The Owner shall continue to implement and observe the requirements and obligations set out in the Travel Plan for a period of not less than *[[****] years following First Occupation/Occupation of the Development]* or if later, for a period commencing on the date of First Occupation and ending on the date being ten years from the date that *[****]*% of the Development is Occupied.

(11)  The Owner shall use all reasonable endeavours to secure compliance with the Travel Plan by its tenants, agents, licensees, workmen, employees and other persons using or Occupying Site or the Development with the Owner's consent.

*Travel plan monitoring*

(12)  A Baseline Survey shall be undertaken by the Owner within *[[****] months [****] years]* following *[First Occupation/Occupation of the Development] [in either April/May or October/November]* and further Monitoring Surveys shall thereafter be undertaken during the corresponding calendar month of each following year for a period of not less than *[**** years]* in the *[**rd and **th]* years from *[First Occupation/Occupation of the Development]*.

(13)  Within *[****]* months of carrying out each of the Monitoring Surveys, the Owner shall submit a Monitoring Report to the Council.

(14)  The Owner undertakes that it will each year submit a Monitoring Report to the Council which shall:

(a)   demonstrate how the Travel Plan has been implemented during the previous 12 month period to include:

(i)   measures introduced and actions taken to promote the Travel Plan; and

(ii)  a statistical summary of the Modal Split of employees/residents/users disclosed by the Monitoring Surveys.

(b)   show the performance in seeking to achieve the targets of the Travel Plan; and

(c)   in the event that targets as set out in the Travel Plan are not achieved, identifying any proposed amendments to the Travel Plan together with a plan for future actions to be implemented

and any measures identified in part (b) shall be submitted to the Council for agreement.

(15)  The Owner shall co-operate with the Council in such manner on such occasions as the Council reasonably require in the verification of the accuracy of any data used to assess the extent to which the objectives of the Travel Plan have been achieved.

(16)  The Council may convene a meeting with the Owner or Travel Plan Coordinator in order to discuss the progress of action implementation, target achievement, or other issues and the Owner or Travel Plan Coordinator shall attend the meeting which shall take place within 21 days of such a request being made and shall be on a date and at a place determined by the Council.[136]

(17)  If the Owner shall fail to carry out any of the requirements set out at *[****]* above, then the Council shall be entitled to carry out those actions and the Owner shall reimburse to the Council the Council's reasonable costs of doing so.

(18)  The Owner is responsible for all the costs of monitoring and reviewing.

*The Bond*

(19)  The Development shall not be Commenced unless and until the Owner has provided the Council with a Bond (in a form and with a surety to be approved by the Council) in the sum of £*[****]* (*[****]* Pounds) for a period of not less than *[****]* years to guarantee the Council the following sums:

(a)   the estimated costs of the Council in exercising its rights pursuant to Clause [17] above;

(b)   *[****]*;

(c)   *[****]*; and

(d)   *[****]*.

*Parking management plan*

(20)  No part of the Development shall be Occupied unless and until a Parking Management Plan has been submitted to and approved by the Council, such plan to set out

---

[136]   NB: This clause is outside section 106.

arrangements for the way in which the car parking spaces on the Site shall be managed during the Occupation of the Development (including the making of a charge for use of a car parking space in excess of *[****]* hours such charge to be not less than the fixed penalty charge for parking without a permit in *[***** Street]* provided that the Parking Management Plan may be varied by written agreement of the Owner and the Council by reference to the results of the Surveys.

(21)  The Owner covenants with the Council to ensure that all of the Car Parking Spaces provided as part of the Development on the Site are used and made available for use only by Occupiers of the *[Dwellings] [or [****]]* and by no other persons.

*[CLAUSES RELATED TO RESIDENTIAL SITES]*

*[****]* No Dwelling shall be Occupied unless the proposed resident of the Dwelling has been informed of the existence of the Travel Plan.

*[****]* No part of the Development shall be Occupied unless and until a scheme for the operation of a Car Club including:

(a)  the number of car parking spaces in the Development to be reserved for Car Club parking to be made available by the Owner to residents of the Development;

(b)  the timing of the start of the operation of the Car Club on the Site; and

(c)  a strategy to support take-up of the Car Club to include incentives and marketing

has been submitted to and approved by the Council, such scheme in its approved form being referred to herein as the *"Car Club Scheme"*.

*[****]* The Travel Plan shall provide that throughout the Occupation of the Development *[****]* surface car parking spaces shall be reserved and maintained for use by the Car Club and not used for any other purpose unless it is demonstrated to the satisfaction of the Council that such a parking space is not required.

*[****]* The Owner shall secure that *[****]* Car Parking Spaces are reserved for the use of the Car Club on the Site and shall provide and retain those spaces as for this purpose for the lifetime of the Development.

*[****]* The Owner shall pay to the Car Club the sum of £*[****]* (*[****]* Pounds) being the membership fee and a contribution towards future usage of the Car Club by the resident referred to in any written notice served on the Owner by the Car Club operator confirming that such resident has joined the Car Club Scheme within 28 days of such notice provided

that the Owner shall not be required to pay more than £*[X times [D (the number of dwellings in the Development)]]* in aggregate.[137]

*[****]* In the event of any Owner failing to pay the sums specified to the Car Club the Owner shall pay the same to the Council and the Council shall apply the same to the Car Club.

---

FOURTH SCHEDULE

## *PARKING SURVEY AND CONTROLLED PARKING ZONES*

*Additional Definitions:*

**"Anticipated Opening Date"** means *[****]*;

**"Baseline Parking Survey"** means a survey to establish the level of vehicle parking on the CPZ Roads prior to the Opening Date conducted in accordance with the methodology settled pursuant to Paragraphs *[****]* of this Schedule;

**"CPZ"** means a Council administered permit controlled zone providing for the restriction of vehicle parking within the highway introduced pursuant to an order made under the Traffic Regulation Act 1984 or any legislation to similar effect;

**"CPZ Consultation Contribution"** means the sum quantified in accordance with Paragraphs *[****]* of this Schedule and to be paid by the Owner to the Council on receipt of a CPZ Consultation Notice from the Council, such sum to be applied by the Council to the cost of carrying out consultation on whether to implement a CPZ in the CPZ Roads;

**"CPZ Consultation Notice"** means a written notice from the Council to the Owner confirming that the Council:

(a)     considers that the results of the Baseline Parking Survey and the Post Opening Parking Survey indicate that a CPZ may be required in the CPZ Roads;

(b)     intends to commence consultation on whether to implement such a CPZ; and

(c)     confirmation that it requires the Owner to pay the CPZ Consultation Contribution;

**"CPZ Implementation Contribution"** means the sum quantified in accordance with Paragraphs *[****]* of this Schedule and to be paid by the Owner to the Council on receipt

---

[137]   This clause falls outside section 106(1)(d) but is "rescued" by the following clause which requires payment to the Council.

of a CPZ Implementation Notice from the Council, such sum to be applied by the Council to implementing a CPZ in the CPZ Roads;

***"CPZ Implementation Notice"*** means a notice from the Council to the Owner confirming that in response to the results of public consultation Council has determined that a CPZ should be implemented in the CPZ Roads;

***"CPZ Roads"*** means those roads shown shaded in orange on Plan *[****]*;

***"Opening Date"*** means the first date upon which any *[Unit] [Dwelling]* is Completed and the terms *"Open"* and *"Opened"* shall be construed accordingly;

***"Parking Surveys"*** means collectively the Baseline Parking Survey and the Post Opening Parking Survey;

***"Post Opening Parking Survey"*** means a survey to establish the level of vehicular parking on the CPZ Roads after the Opening Date conducted in accordance with the methodology settled pursuant to Paragraphs *[****]* of this Schedule;

***"Survey Submission Date"*** means the date on which the Owner submits the Baseline Parking Survey and the Post Opening Parking Survey results to the Council in accordance with Paragraphs *[****]* of this Schedule.

The Owner's Covenants with the Council as follows:

*[i]*     The Owner will notify the Council in writing of the following:

    (a)     *[****]* before the Owner's anticipated Commencement Date, notification of such date;

    (b)     within Ten (10) Working Days of the Commencement Date, confirmation of the actual date;

    (c)     12 months before the Anticipated Opening Date, notification of such anticipated date;

    (d)     within Ten (10) Working Days of the Opening Date occurring, confirmation of the actual date.

*[ii]*    No part of the Development shall Open unless and until the Owner has provided to the Council the notifications required by paragraphs *[i](a), [i](b) and [i](c)* of this Schedule and no more than 1 (one) *[Unit] [Dwelling]* shall be Occupied unless and until the Owner has provided to the Council the notification required by paragraph *[i](d).*

*[iii]* The Council shall provide proposals for the methodologies for the Baseline Parking Survey and the Post Opening Parking Survey to the Owner not later than *[****]* months before the Anticipated Opening Date and no part of the Development shall Open.

*[iv]* The methodologies for the Baseline Parking Survey and the Post Opening Parking Survey shall (as a minimum) provide for:

    (a)    survey periods of not less than one week;

    (b)    12 hour vehicle registration surveys to be carried out on the CPZ Roads and surrounding roads;

    (c)    surveys to be carried out on a minimum of 3 separate days, being a Tuesday, Wednesday and Saturday (or such other days as may be agreed between the Council and the Owner); and

    (d)    surveys to establish level of residential and commuter occupancy;

and/or such other particulars as may be agreed between the Council and the Owner.

*[v]* If the Owner and the Council fail to agree the methodologies for the Baseline Parking Survey and the Post Opening Parking Survey (or both) by the date which is *[****]* months before the Anticipated Opening Date, then either party may refer the matter to an Expert pursuant to Clause *[****]*.

*[vi]* The Owner will carry out the Baseline Parking Survey no earlier than Two (2) months prior to the Anticipated Opening Date and not later than the Opening Date.

*[vii]* The Owner will carry out the Post Opening Parking Survey no earlier than six Months after and not later than *[****]* Months after the Opening Date.

*[viii]* The Owner will submit the results of the Baseline Parking Survey and the Post Opening Parking Survey to the Council no later than Twelve (12) Months from the Opening Date.

*[ix]* The Council shall, within 3 Months of receipt of the Parking Surveys, provide to the Owner estimates of the quanta of the CPZ Consultation Contribution and the CPZ Implementation Contribution and the Owner may provide responses to the said estimates not later than 1 month following receipt of them.

*[x]* The Council shall take into account any responses from the Owner in setting the CPZ Consultation Contribution and the CPZ Implementation Contribution and

provide written notification of the quanta of the CPZ Consultation Contribution and the CPZ Implementation Contribution as settled by the Council.

*[xi]*    If the Owner disputes the quantum of the CPZ Consultation Contribution or the CPZ Implementation Contribution as settled by the Council (or both), then the Owner may refer the matter to a Expert pursuant to Clause *[****]* within the period of Ten (10) Working Days commencing with the date of the notification mentioned in Paragraph *[****]* above.

*[xii]*    If the Owner receives a CPZ Consultation Notice from the Council within six Months of the Survey Submission Date, the Owner will pay the Council the CPZ Consultation Contribution within 20 (Twenty) Working Days of receipt of such notice.

*[xiii]*    Subject to receipt of a CPZ Consultation Notice from the Council, if the Owner receives a CPZ Implementation Notice from the Council within 12 Months of the Survey Submission Date the Owner will pay the CPZ Implementation Contribution to the Council.

*[xiv]*    In the event that the Owner shall fail to comply with Paragraphs *[****]* of this Schedule the Owner shall pay to the Council a sum equal to the Council's reasonable estimate of the CPZ Implementation Contribution.[138]

---

FIFTH SCHEDULE

The Council's Covenants with the Owner

*Repayment of contributions*

(1)    The Council hereby covenants with the Owner to use all sums received from the Owner under the terms of this Deed for the purposes specified in this Deed for which they are to be paid *[or for such other purposes for the benefit of the Development as the Owner and the Council shall agree]*.

(2)    The Council covenants with the Owner that it will pay to the Owner such amount of any payment made by the Owner to the Council under this Deed which has not been expended in accordance with the provisions of this Deed (and money shall be deemed to be expended if the Council has properly entered into a contract for the expenditure of the money for the purpose for which it is paid which is reasonably likely to result in the fulfilment of that purpose) within *[****]* years of the date of receipt by the Council of such payment *[together with interest at the [insert name of bank] base rate from time to time for the period from the date of payment to the date of refund]*.

---

[138]   Again, a default provision designed to bring section 106(1)(d) into play.

(3)    The Council shall provide to the Owner such evidence, as the Owner shall reasonably require in order to confirm the expenditure of the sums paid by the Owner under this Deed.

*Discharge of obligations*

(4)    At the written request of the Owner the Council shall provide written confirmation of the discharge of the obligations contained in this Deed when satisfied that such obligations have been performed.

(5)    Following the performance and satisfaction of all the obligations contained in this Deed the Council shall forthwith effect the cancellation of all entries made in the Register of Local Land Charges in respect of this Deed.

# Form 3: Planning Obligation By Unilateral Undertaking

THIS UNDERTAKING is made the *[****]* day of *[****]*

By: *[****]* of *[****]* (the *"Owner"*)

IN FAVOUR OF: The *[****]* Council (the *"Council"*).

See **[Form 1.1] - The Parties**

### Recitals

A. This undertaking is a planning obligation for the purposes of Section 106(1) of the Town and Country Planning Act 1990 (the "1990 Act").

B. This undertaking relates to land at *[****]* shown for identification edged red on the attached plan (the "Land").

C. The Owner is registered at the Land Registry as the Proprietor of the land with absolute title under title number *[****]*.

D. This undertaking is enforceable by the Council as the Local Planning Authority for the purposes of the 1990 Act for the area within which the Land is situate.

E. The Council has passed a resolution to grant planning permission in respect of the Land for the construction of *[****]* under reference *[****]* (the "Development") subject to the Owner providing a contribution towards highway improvements necessitated by the Development.

### Operative Provisions

(1)  This deed is made as a planning obligation pursuant to section 106 of the 1990 Act so as to bind the Owner and those deriving title from the Owner and the Land.

(2)  The Owner hereby covenants that upon delivery of this deed to the Council the Owner shall pay to the Council the sum of £*[****]* (*[****]* Pounds) as a contribution towards the *[describe the works/facility]*.

IN WITNESS whereof .........

# Form 4: Section 38 Agreement

THIS AGREEMENT is made the *[****]* day of *[****]*

BETWEEN:

(1) *[****]* (the "Council")

(2) *[****]* (the "Owner")

(3) *[****]* (the "Chargee")

(4) *[****]* (the "Surety")

See *[Form 1.1] - The Parties*

### RECITALS

A. The Council is the local highway authority for highways in the County of *[****]* pursuant to the Highways Act 1980.

B. Main Road is a highway maintainable at the public expense vested in the Council.

C. The Owner is the registered proprietor with title absolute of the Site registered at the Land Registry under Title Number *[****]*.

D. The Site is the location of a proposed development pursuant to the Planning Permission where the Developer intends to erect Buildings for which plans are required to be deposited in accordance with Building Regulations.

E. The Site will include the proposed Ways on which some or all of the said Buildings will have frontages.

F. The Developer is desirous of constructing the Ways and the Owner intends to dedicate the Ways as highways so that the same shall, upon issue of the Final Certificate, become highways maintainable at the public expense.

G. The Owner and the Developer have requested that when the Works have been executed and maintained as hereinafter appearing the Council shall thereafter undertake the maintenance of the Ways as highways maintainable at the public expense, which the Council has agreed to do upon the terms and conditions hereinafter appearing.

H. The CDM Regulations apply to and in relation to the construction of the Works.

IT IS HEREBY AGREED AND DECLARED by and between the Parties hereto as follows:-

## 1    DEFINITIONS

In this Agreement where the context so admits:

*"1980 Act"* means the Highways Act 1980;

*"1991 Act"* means the New Roads and Street Works Act 1991;

*"First Schedule"* means the First Schedule to this Agreement;

*"Second Schedule"* means the Second Schedule to this Agreement;

*"As Built Drawings"* See *[Form 1.2] - Definitions*

*"Bond"* means the sum of £*[****]* (*[****]* Pounds) provided as security for this Agreement, as may be reduced from time to time in accordance with the provisions of this Agreement;

*"Building"* includes (without limitation) any structure or erection or any part of a building, structure or erection;

*"Completion Periods"* means the periods specified in Clause *[****]* of this Agreement;

*"Construction Period"* means the period beginning with the date that the Works are commenced and ending when the Part 2 Certificate is issued;

*"CDM Client"* means a "Client" as defined by Regulation 2 of the CDM Regulations;

*"CDM Regulations"* means the Construction (Design and Management) Regulations 2015;

*"Drainage System"* means all of the drains and sewers (excluding any natural water courses private drains and sewers) which will drain the Ways;

*"Drawing"* means the drawing entitled "*[****]*" and marked *[****]* annexed hereto and any amended, substituted or additional drawing approved by or on behalf of the Engineer;

*"Engineer"* means the *[****]* of the Council for the time being or his deputy or any officer of the Council authorised to discharge his duties;

*"Final Certificate"* means the Certificate to be issued by the Engineer in accordance with Clause *[****]* of this Agreement;

*"Final Drawings"* means the As Built Drawings, drainage drawings and other drawings as the Engineer may require in such form as may be required by the Engineer;

**"Health and Safety File"** means a file prepared under regulation 12(5) of the CDM Regulations;

**"Junction"** means the junction between the Ways and Main Road as shown on the Drawing;

**"Land Compensation Acts"** See *[Form 1.2] - Definitions*

**"Land Compensation Claim"** See *[Form 1.2] - Definitions*

**"Land Compensation Costs"** See *[Form 1.2] - Definitions*

**"Maintain"** includes inspect, repair, adjust, alter, remove or reconstruct and any derivative of *"maintain"* is to be construed accordingly;

**"Maintenance Period"** means the period of not less than Twelve (12) Months:

(a)    beginning on:

   (i)    the date of issue of the Part 2 Certificate; or

   (ii)   the date on which the Ways are open to Traffic after the issue of the Part 2 Certificate,

   (whichever is the later); and

(b)    ending on the date of issue of the Final Certificate;

**"Occupied"** and **"Occupier"** See *[Form 1.2] - Definitions*

**"Parties"** See *[Form 1.2] - Definitions*

**"Part 1 Certificate"** means the certificate to be issued by the Engineer pursuant to Clause *[****]*;

**"Part 2 Certificate"** means the certificate to be issued by the Engineer pursuant to Clause *[****]*;

**"Part 1 Works"** means the part of the Works specified in the First Schedule of this Agreement;

**"Part 2 Works"** means the part of the Works specified in the First Schedule of this Agreement;

**"Planning Permission"** means the planning permission granted by the Council dated *[****]* for the proposed erection of *[****]* new dwellings and associated infrastructure including open space and sustainable urban drainage system under reference numbers *[****]*;

*"**Principal Contractor**"* means "principal contractor" as defined by the CDM Regulations;

*"**Principal Designer**"* means "principal designer" as defined by Regulation 2 of the CDM Regulations;

*"**Remedial Works**"* means the remedial works required by the Engineer pursuant to Clauses *[\*\*\*\*]* of this Agreement (including any remedial works in connection with the *[\*\*\*\*]* Road Works);

*"**Road Safety Audits**"* See *[Form 1.2] - Definitions*;

*"**Statutory Undertaker**"* See *[Form 1.2] - Definitions*;

*"**Site**"* means land at *[\*\*\*\*]* which is shown *[edged red]* on the plan annexed hereto and registered at the Land Registry under Title Numbers *[\*\*\*\*]*;

*"**Stage 3 Safety Audit**"* See *[Form 1.2] - Definitions*;

*"**Stage 4 Safety Audit**"* See *[Form 1.2] - Definitions*;

*"**Street**"* See *[Form 1.2] - Definitions*;

*"**Street Authority**"* See *[Form 1.2] - Definitions*;

*"**Street Works**"* See *[Form 1.2] - Definitions*;

*"**Traffic**"* See *[Form 1.2] - Definitions*;

*"**Traffic Regulation Order**"* See *[Form 1.2] - Definitions*;

*"**Ways**"* means the proposed carriageways, footways, footpaths shown on the Drawing or (if different) the Final Drawings together with the associated street lights and all other things ancillary thereto PROVIDED THAT if there is any difference between the Final Drawings and the Drawing, then the Final Drawings shall prevail;

*"**Works**"* means the works comprising the Part 1 Works and the Part 2 Works listed generally in the First Schedule for the construction and making up of the Ways together with any Remedial Works which the Engineer may have required to be executed prior to the issue of the Final Certificate;

*"**Working Day**"* See *[Form 1.2] Definitions*;

*"**Year**"* See *[Form 1.2] - Definitions*.

## 2 INTERPRETATION

See *[Form 1.3] - Interpretation*.

## 3 ENABLING LEGISLATION

3.1 This Agreement is made in pursuance of powers contained in Section 38 of the 1980 Act, Section 111 of the Local Government Act 1972 and Section 1 of the Localism Act 2011 and all other enabling provisions.

3.2 This Agreement does not authorise any interference with the convenience of persons using any Street or affect the rights of the owners of premises adjoining any highway or Street or the rights of Statutory Undertakers.

3.3 Nothing in this Agreement shall operate to take away or prejudice the right of the Council to exercise the powers conferred upon it by the Private Street Works Code contained in Part XI of the 1980 Act in respect of the Ways or other powers available to the Council if the Developer Owner or the Surety shall fail to perform all or any of their obligations under this Agreement.

## 4 APPROVALS, CONSENTS ETC

See *[Form 1.13] - Approvals, consents etc.*

## 5 COMPLETION PERIODS

5.1 The Developer shall carry out and complete the Works (at the Developer's expense) in a good and workmanlike manner and with proper materials in accordance in all respects with the CDM Regulations and the Drawing to the satisfaction of the Engineer within the following periods of time:

(a) the Part 1 Works to be completed within a maximum period of Twelve (12) Months from the date of this Agreement; and

(b) the Part 2 Works to be completed within a maximum period of Twenty Four (24) Months from the date of this Agreement

PROVIDED that the Council may in its discretion agree to extend the Completion Periods subject to being satisfied that the Bond covers any extension of time and that the Developer pays to the Council the Council's costs in settling such an extension of time (including legal costs).

5.2 In the event that the Works have not been completed within Six (6) Years from the date of this Agreement (or such extended period as the Council may have agreed pursuant to Clause *[****]* above) then (without limitation) the Council shall be entitled to enforce this Agreement by way of the provisions of Clause *[****]* below.

## 6     OBLIGATIONS DURING CONSTRUCTION PERIOD

6.1     Throughout the Construction Period the Developer shall:

(a)     erect and maintain on Main Road such signs as the Engineer may reasonably require including (without limitation) direction signs and warning signs; and

(b)     provide and maintain on the access and egress points of the Site, such wheel washing equipment as the Engineer may reasonably require and take such other measures as the Engineer may reasonably require to ensure that Main Road is kept free of mud, debris and other detritus arising from or in connection with the Works.

## 7     DECLARATION

7.1     The Owner and the Developer hereby declare and warrant to the Council that:

(a)     they have, and throughout the duration of this Agreement will maintain, full right liberty and consent to carry out all of the Works and any additional works as may be necessary to connect the Ways to Main Road as shown on the Drawing; and

(b)     the consent of the Environment Agency or other appropriate drainage body has been obtained in connection with any proposed alteration or use of any existing watercourse or land drainage or other works within the Site and vested in or under the control of the said Agency or other drainage body.

## 8     STATUTORY UNDERTAKERS

8.1     The Developer shall before connecting the Ways to the Main Road give notice to each and every Statutory Undertaker for the time being of any service or services laid in upon or under Main Road of the proposal to make such connection as if the connection was work or works for road work purposes as described in Sections 83 and 86 of the 1991 Act.

## 9     INDEMNITIES

9.1     The Owner and the Developer hereby indemnify the Council in respect of all actions, claims, demands, expenses and proceedings arising out of or in connection with or incidental to the carrying out of, or use of, the Works or Ways including any claims under the Land Compensation Act 1973 other than those arising out of or in consequence of any act, neglect, default or liability of the Council.

9.2     The Owner and the Developer hereby undertake and agree with the Council that in the event of any claim or claims arising in connection with or incidental to or in consequence of the carrying out of the Works or use of the Ways and being made against the Council for any one or more of the following payments:

(a)     compensation, including (without limitation) any Land Compensation Costs;

(b)     damages;

(c)     costs;

(d)     charges;

(e)     the cost of any works or measures considered necessary by any Statutory Undertaker in consequence of the making of any connection to its system or apparatus; and

(f)     any other payment arising in connection with or incidental to or in consequence of the carrying out of the Works

and the Owner and the Developer will hold the Council fully indemnified from and against each and every said claim and shall indemnify the Council in respect of the same.

## 10     PUBLIC LIABILITY INSURANCE

10.1     The Developer shall at all times during the period of this Agreement maintain full comprehensive public liability insurance in the sum of not less than £[****] ([****] Pounds) for any one occurrence or series of occurrences arising out of one event against liability to any person arising from the construction, operation or maintenance of the Works or the exercise of any rights granted by the Council and shall allow the Council to inspect the certificate of insurance at all reasonable times.

## 11     COUNCIL'S COSTS AND CHARGES

11.1     The Developer shall pay to the Council the sum of £[****] ([****] Pounds), (the "Council's Costs and Charges") within Twenty Eight (28) Working Days of the date of this Agreement, which sum shall be applied towards the expenses of the Council in respect of the inspection of the Works as they proceed, the testing of materials used or intended for use therein and the administration and monitoring of arrangements pursuant to this Agreement.

11.2     The Works shall not commence unless and until the Developer shall have paid the Council's Costs and Charges in full.

11.3    In the event that the Works have not been completed within Two (2) years from the date of this Agreement (or such extended period as the Council may have agreed pursuant to Clause *[****]* above) then a further fee of £*[****]* (*[****]* Pounds) *[[****] % of the total estimated cost of the Works]* shall be paid to the Council upon demand to cover inspection and administration between years 2 and 4.

11.4    In the event that the Works have not been completed within Four (4) years from the date of this Agreement (or such extended period as the Council may have agreed pursuant to Clause *[****]* above) then a further fee of £*[****]* (*[****]* Pounds) *[[****] % of the total estimated cost of the Works]* shall be paid to the Council upon demand to cover inspection and administration after year 4.

## 12    OCCUPATION OF BUILDINGS

12.1    No Building fronting, adjoining or abutting on or served by the Ways shall be Occupied until the Engineer has issued a Part 1 Certificate in respect of the Ways or such length or lengths of the Ways as will provide the Occupier(s) of the said Building with access (including appropriate operational and energised street lighting) over the Ways to their junction with Main Road and where a surface has been provided by the Developer to the satisfaction of the Engineer.

## 13    LIMITS OF DEVIATION

13.1    The Council may (in its absolute discretion) allow the Developer to deviate vertically or laterally from the levels, lines or situations shown in the Drawing in carrying out the Works PROVIDED that all necessary consents or permissions to such deviations have been obtained, the proposed adoption of the Ways is not prejudiced, the Council is paid its costs in assessing and administering such deviations and that the Bond covers such deviations.

## 14    PART 1 CERTIFICATE

14.1    On the completion of the Part 1 Works in accordance with this Agreement to the satisfaction of the Engineer in all respects including (without limitation):

(a)    the lighting has been installed, tested, energised and is operational and any corrective works to the lighting which have been required by the Engineer have been completed by the Developer to the satisfaction of the Engineer;

(b)    the Works have been inspected and any corrective works to the Works which have been required by the Engineer have been completed by the Developer to the satisfaction of the Engineer;

(c)    the provision of the proposed Drainage System has been secured either:

(i)    by way of an agreement or agreements with *[****]* Water Company (or such organisation which may discharge the functions of *[****]* Water Company) under Section 104 of the Water Industry Act 1991;

(ii)    or pursuant to appropriate arrangements under Section 42 of the Floods and Water Management Act 2010;

(d)    the Ways are connected to Main Road in accordance with the Drawing;

(e)    the Council has granted such street works licences as may be required by Section 50 of the 1991 Act in respect of any apparatus (including private drains or sewers) constructed in, on, over or under the Ways;

the Engineer shall issue the Part 1 Certificate to the Developer and from the date thereof:

(a)    the Ways shall become highways maintainable by the Owner;

(b)    the Owner shall be the Street Manager for the purposes of the 1991 Act until such time as the Ways shall become highways maintainable at the public expense; and

(c)    the liability of the Surety pursuant to this Agreement shall be reduced to £*[****]* (*[****]* Pounds).

## 15    *PART 2 CERTIFICATE*

15.1    On the completion of the Part 2 Works in accordance with this Agreement to the satisfaction of the Engineer in all respects including (without limitation) that:

(a)    associated landscaping works have been completed to the satisfaction of the Engineer;

(b)    the Part 2 Works have been inspected and all corrective works or reinstatement have been completed by the Developer to the satisfaction of the Engineer;

(c)    all corrective works or reinstatement arising in connection with the Part 1 Works or other works have been completed by the Developer to the satisfaction of the Engineer;

(d)    the provision of the Drainage System been secured either:

(i)    by way of an agreement or agreements with *[****]* Water Company (or such organisation which may discharge the functions of *[****]* Water Company) under Section 104 of the Water Industry Act 1991 and a provisional certificate in accordance with such agreement has been issued in respect of the Drainage System;

(ii)    or pursuant to appropriate arrangements under Section 42 of the Floods and Water Management Act 2010 and in respect of the Drainage System then subject to maintenance by the Developer or Owner in accordance with such arrangements;

(e)    the Stage 3 Safety Audit has been completed and any actions arising from it and which the Engineer has required to be carried out have been completed to the satisfaction of the Engineer; and

(f)    all construction works have been completed in respect of the Works;

the Engineer shall issue the Part 2 Certificate to the Developer and from the date thereof:

(a)    the liability of the Surety pursuant to the Bond shall be reduced to £[****] ([****] Pounds);

(b)    the Ways shall remain highways maintainable by the Owner; and,

(c)    the Owner shall remain the Street Manager for the purposes of the 1991 Act until such time as the Ways shall become highways maintainable at the public expense.

## 16    OBLIGATIONS DURING MAINTENANCE PERIOD

16.1    During the Maintenance Period:

(a)    the Developer (at its own expense) shall maintain the Works and carry out such repairs and maintenance as may be necessary to facilitate the safe and convenient use by the public of the Ways and the junction with Main Road;

(b)    the Developer shall at its own expense undertake the routine maintenance of, and be responsible for, the payment of energy charges in respect of all street lights and illuminated traffic signs erected in respect of the Ways and energised in accordance with this Agreement;

(c)    the Developer shall forthwith at its own expense reinstate and make good any defect in or damage to the Works which may have arisen from any cause whatsoever or have been discovered during the Maintenance Period (including any defect in or damage to the street lighting system and the Drainage System) of which the Developer has been notified in writing by the Engineer so that the Works comply with the Drawing; and

(d)    neither the Owner nor the Developer shall place or erect on any part of the Ways or Main Road (or the highway verges thereof) any structure, advertisement or notice or plant any tree or vegetation thereon without the consent of the Council.

## 17    EASEMENTS AND WAYLEAVES

17.1    The Owner shall not after the execution of this Agreement grant without the consent of the Council any wayleave easement or right which could not be exercised or enjoyed without the consent of the Council if the Way were a highway maintainable at the public expense or would interfere with the convenient use of the Ways by Traffic.

## 18    FINAL CERTIFICATE

18.1    The Engineer shall issue the Final Certificate to the Developer and the liability of the Surety pursuant to the Bond shall be released when all of the following conditions are satisfied:

(a)    not less than Twelve (12) Months have passed since either the issue of the Part 2 Certificate or the date on which the Ways are open to traffic after the issue of the Part 2 Certificate (whichever is the later);

(b)    any necessary Remedial Works have been completed by the Developer to the satisfaction of the Engineer;

(c)    the Works have been inspected by the Engineer and no defects been identified by him;

(d)    the Council has received all monies due to the Council under the provisions of this Agreement;

(e)    the Drainage System has been adopted (so as to be maintainable at the public expense) either:

(i)    by way of an agreement or agreements with [****] Water Company (or such organisation which may discharge the functions of Water Company) under Section 104 of the Water Industry Act 1991 and a final certificate pursuant to that agreement has been issued; or

(ii)    or pursuant to appropriate arrangements under Section 42 of the Floods and Water Management Act 2010;

(f)    the Stage 4 Safety Audit has been completed and any actions arising from it and which the Engineer has required to be carried out have been completed to the satisfaction of the Engineer;

(g)    where a Health and Safety File must be prepared pursuant to Regulation 12(5) of the CDM Regulations, the Developer has delivered a copy of the Health and Safety File to the Engineer; and

(h)    the Developer has delivered to the Engineer the Final Drawings.

## 19    PROCEDURE FOR ISSUE OF CERTIFICATES

19.1    The Developer shall apply in writing to the Engineer in the first instance for the issue of certificates pursuant to this Agreement.

19.2    Within Fourteen (14) Working Days of receipt of a written application from the Developer for the issue of the Part 1 Certificate or Part 2 Certificate or Final Certificate (as the case may be) the Engineer shall inspect the Works and, where necessary, provide the Developer with a list in writing of any Remedial Works or other actions required to be carried out before the issue of that Certificate.

19.3    Any such Remedial Works and other actions shall be subject to the same inspection procedure detailed in this Agreement for the Works until such time as they shall be completed to the satisfaction of the Engineer who shall within Twenty-Eight (28) Working Days thereafter issue the relevant Certificate.

## 20    ADOPTION

20.1    Upon the date of issue of the Final Certificate the Ways shall become highways maintainable at the public expense to the extent shown in the Final Drawings and the liability of the Owner to maintain the Ways shall be extinguished.

20.2    The date of issue of the Final Certificate shall be the date "*specified in the agreement*" for the purposes of Section 38(3) of the 1980 Act.

20.3    The Owner hereby covenants that if and when called upon so to do by the Council within a period of Twenty One (21) Years from the date of this Agreement it will prove title to the Ways to the extent shown in the Final Drawings and transfer title absolute to the said Ways (or such parts of the Ways as may be specified by the Council) to the Council free of charge for an estate in fee simple absolute in possession free from incumbrances.

## 21    TRAFFIC REGULATION ORDERS

21.1    The Council shall use reasonable endeavours to make and confirm any Traffic Regulation Order required to carry out the Works and the Developer shall pay to the Council the Council's costs in doing so PROVIDED that the Council shall not be obliged to initiate or pursue any Traffic Regulation Order unless and until the Developer has paid to or secured to the satisfaction of the Council a sum equivalent to the estimated costs of making and confirming any such Order and also provided the Council with an indemnity in respect of any costs which might arise from or be incurred in respect of any such proceedings, whether the Order is completed or confirmed or not.

## 22    *NOTICES TO ENGINEER*

22.1    The Developer shall give to the Engineer not less than Seven (7) Working Days' notice in writing of its intention to set out or commence each stage of the Works and the Developer shall, immediately on the completion of any such stage of construction, give notice to the Engineer.

## 23    *INSPECTION BY ENGINEER*

23.1    The Developer shall during the progress of setting out, constructing and maintaining the Works give to the Engineer (and any person authorised by him) free access to every site of such operations and permission to inspect them and all materials used or intended for use in them and shall (if required by the Engineer to do so) uncover or open up any work to enable it to be inspected and if so required shall remove any structure or materials which are not in accordance with the Drawing or which in the opinion of the Engineer are defective and the Developer shall (at its own expense) re-execute any such work and substitute proper and suitable structures or materials to the satisfaction of the Engineer.

23.2    The Council shall not be liable for any loss damage or injury which the Owner or the Developer may sustain by reason of no or insufficient or faulty inspection of the Works by the Council.

## 24    *SAMPLES AND TESTS*

24.1    The Developer shall at its own expense provide such samples of materials used or intended to be used in the Works as may be required by the Engineer from time to time for the purposes of testing their quality and suitability and for the purpose of ascertaining whether the Works are being or have been constructed to his satisfaction.

24.2    Such sampling and testing shall be in accordance with the current editions of the 'Design Manual for Roads and Bridges' and the "Manual of Contract Documents for Highway Works".

## 25    *DETERMINATION*

25.1    If at any time:

    (a)    the Developer fails to perform or observe any of the conditions stipulations or obligations on its part contained in this Agreement; or

    (b)    if a receiving order in bankruptcy is made against the Developer or the Developer's business is being wound up or dissolved or if the Developer is insolvent or enters into a composition or scheme of arrangement (otherwise than for the purpose of amalgamation or reconstruction),

THEN the Council may (without prejudice to any of its rights claims or remedies against the Developer and the Surety in respect of any non-performance or non-observance of this Agreement) determine this Agreement (except for Clauses *[****]* of this Agreement) by notice in writing delivered to the Developer and send a copy of any such notice to the Surety.

## 26     POWER TO EXECUTE THE WORKS IN DEFAULT

26.1     If at any time:

(a) the Developer fails to perform or observe any of the conditions stipulations or obligations on its part contained in this Agreement; or

(b) a receiving order in bankruptcy is made in respect of the Developer's legal estate or if the Developer's business is being wound up or dissolved or if the Developer is insolvent or enters into a composition or scheme of arrangement (otherwise than for the purpose of reconstruction or amalgamation),

the Council may without prejudice to any of its statutory rights or powers or any other right claim or remedy under this Agreement send to the Developer notice in writing (hereinafter referred to as the "Default Notice").

26.2     The Default Notice shall:

(a) specify the works ("the Default Works") to be carried out in order that the Works may be executed or completed (as the case may be) in accordance with this Agreement; and

(b) contain an estimate by the Engineer of the costs of carrying out the Default Works (whether by the Council or by a contractor appointed by the Council) including (without limitation) the costs of preparation (including any necessary survey) of the Final Drawings; the costs of maintaining the Ways prior to the Ways becoming maintainable at the public expense; and, the usual establishment and inspection charges of the Council (together hereinafter referred to as the "Default Sum") AND the amount of any such costs and charges shall be that certified by the Engineer, whose certificate shall be final and binding upon all Parties.

26.3     If the Default Works are not completed within the period required by the Council in the Default Notice or within such further period as may be agreed by the Council the Council may carry out the Default Works mentioned in the Default Notice and apply the Default Sum (together with interest accrued thereon) to the cost of carrying out any Default Works not carried out by the Developer or to the cost of maintaining the Ways prior to the Ways becoming highways maintainable at the public expense as may be the case (or as being the cost of both) and also retain the amount determined by the Engineer as being the amount of the appropriate usual establishment charges of the Council.

## 27     SURETY'S OBLIGATIONS

27.1     Without prejudice to the right of the Council to exercise any of its rights and powers under this Agreement or any statutory provision, the Surety shall:

(a)     in the event of non-observance or breach of any of the terms of the covenants, conditions, stipulations or obligations on its part of the Developer contained in this Agreement; or

(b)     if a receiving order in bankruptcy is made against the Developer or the Developer's business is being wound up or dissolved or if the Developer is insolvent or enters into a composition or scheme of arrangement (otherwise than for the purpose of amalgamation or reconstruction),

pay to the Council within Twenty Eight (28) days of receiving notice in writing from the Engineer such sum of money as the Engineer may certify to be necessary to perform the obligations of the Developer under this Agreement PROVIDED that the sum payable by the Surety shall not exceed the sum of £*[****]* *([****]* Pounds).

27.2.     The Surety shall not be discharged or released from this Agreement by any arrangement between the Developer and the Council or by any alteration in the Developer's obligations or by any forbearance whether as to payment, performance, time or otherwise whether made with or without the assent of the Surety.

## 28     PARTIAL COMPLETION

28.1     Notwithstanding anything in this Agreement:

(a)     the Developer may from time to time during the currency of this Agreement apply to the Engineer for a Part 1 Certificate or Part 2 Certificate or a Final Certificate in respect of any length of the Ways (being the whole width of any length of the Ways between points to be defined in the application) and if the Engineer shall be satisfied that the length so defined is in all respects suitable to be treated as a separate Way for the purposes of construction and adoption in accordance with the provisions contained in this Agreement then he shall issue a separate Part 1 Certificate or Part 2 Certificate or a Final Certificate (as the case may be) in respect of that length of the Ways; and

(b)     thereafter the same proceedings may be taken in respect of the said length of the Ways as if the said length was the subject of a separate Agreement under which the terms of this Agreement applied to the said length separately from the remainder of the Ways and (without prejudice to the application of this Agreement to the remainder of the Ways) the liability of the Surety pursuant to the Bond may be reduced by the Council.

## 29    HEALTH AND SAFETY

29.1    The Owner hereby confirms that it is a CDM Client in respect of the Works and is aware of the provisions of the CDM Regulations and shall comply and procure compliance with them.

29.2    The Developer and the Owner warrant that:

(a)    *[****]* Limited (Company Number *[****]*) of *[****]* (Registered Office) is the Principal Contractor; and

(b)    *[****]* Limited (Company Number *[****]*) of *[****]* (Registered Office) is the Principal Designer,

and that *[****]* Limited and *[****]* Consulting Engineers Limited are both aware of the provisions of the CDM Regulations and shall procure compliance with them.

29.3    Where a Health and Safety File must be prepared pursuant to Regulation 12(5) of the CDM Regulations, the Developer shall make the Health and Safety File available to the Engineer on request during the carrying out of the Works.

## 30    COSTS OF AGREEMENT

30.1    The Developer shall pay to the Council the costs of preparation of this Agreement in the sum of £*[****]* (*[****]* Pounds).

## 31    ASSIGNMENT

31.1    This Agreement shall not be assigned by any Party without the written consents of all of the other Parties.

## 32    REGISTRATION

32.1    The Parties agree that after completion of this Agreement the Council will arrange for an entry relating to the covenants contained in Clauses *[****]* to be made in the appropriate register/s of title no(s) *[****]*.

## 33    CHARGEE CONSENT

*[33.1    The Chargee joins herein to consent to the terms of this Agreement but without liability save in the event that the Chargee becomes successor in title to the Owner / Developer at any time before the obligations on the part of the Owner / Developer contained in this Agreement have been performed in full.]*

## *34*     *PAYMENTS TO COUNCIL*

34.1     Receipt by the Council of the payment of sums pursuant to this Agreement shall not create any contractual relationship between the Council and the Owner or the Developer nor absolve the Owner or the Developer from any liability or obligation imposed upon them by the terms of this Agreement or by statute or at common law.

See *[Form 1.12] - Payments*

ALSO SEE:

*[Form 1.10] - Council's statutory duties*

*[Form 1.11] - No partnership or agency*

*[Form 1.15] - Assignment*

*[Form 1.16] - Dispute provisions*

*[Form 1.17] - Waiver*

*[Form 1.18] - Third parties*

*[Form 1.19] - Service of notices*

*[Form 1.21] - Jurisdiction*

*[Form 1.22] - Force majeure*

IN WITNESS whereof ...............

# FIRST SCHEDULE - THE WORKS

## *Part 1 Works:*

1.1.     All surface water drains of the Ways.

1.2.     All other drains and services contained within the Ways.

1.3.     All kerb foundations and where appropriate kerbs including lowering at vehicle crossings and pedestrian dropped kerbs.

1.4.     All ironwork and covers to be set flush with top of binder course level.

1.5.     Carriageway sub-base, road base and any supporting structures.

1.6.     Carriageway binder course.

1.7.     For concrete block paving the binder course of shared-use accessways.

1.8.     Street lights erected and energised.

1.9.     Demarcation of sight lines and clearance of vision splays.

1.10.    All pedestrian ways.

1.11.    Street furniture.

1.12.    Street name plates.

1.13.    Grit bin bases and grit bins.

## *Part 2 Works:*

2.1.     All kerbing and verges not completed in Part 1.

2.2.     All ironwork and covers to be raised to finished levels immediately prior to surface course being laid.

2.3.     Carriageway surface course and/or carriageway block paving surfacing.

2.4.     All other works shown in the Drawing.

## SECOND SCHEDULE – LIST OF ATTACHMENTS

• Location Plan

• The drawing entitled "*[****]*" and marked *[****]*.

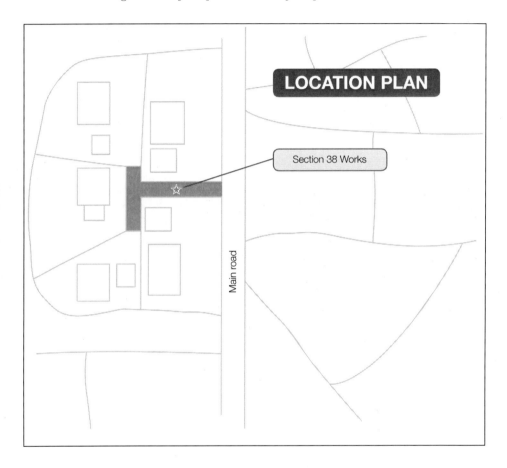

# Form 5: Section 278 Agreement

*Minor works by highway authority at developer's expense including junction with developer's estate roads.*[139]

*Payments in arrears*[140]

THIS AGREEMENT is made the *[****]* day of *[****]*

BETWEEN:

(1) *[****]* (the "Council")

(2) *[****]* (the "Developer")[141]

(3) *[****]* (the "Chargee")

(4) *[****]* (the "Surety")[142]

See *[Form 1.1] - The Parties*

## RECITALS:

A. The Council is the local highway authority for highways in *[****]* pursuant to the Highways Act 1980.

B. Main Road is a highway maintainable at the public expense vested in the Council.[143]

C. The Developer is the registered proprietor with title absolute of the Site.

D. The Site is the location of a proposed housing development where the Developer intends to construct the Estate Roads.

E. The Developer has requested that when the Main Road Works have been executed as hereinafter appearing the Council shall thereafter undertake the maintenance of them as highways maintainable at the public expense, which the Council has agreed to do upon the terms and conditions hereinafter appearing.

---

[139] If the estate roads are being constructed pursuant to a 'Section 38 Agreement', then it might be appropriate to deal with the junction arrangements in that agreement.

[140] Query whether the highway authority would prefer to receive payments on account in advance of carrying out any work.

[141] Will need to add the freehold owner of the Site if different to the Developer.

[142] Query whether a surety is necessary with a minor works agreement.

[143] In this example "*Main Road*" is the existing all purpose highway shown on the Drawing and the "*Main Road Works*" are some straightforward accommodation works at the junction.

F. The Council confirms that the Main Road Works will be of benefit to the public.

G. The CDM Regulations apply in relation to the construction of the Main Road Works.

**IT IS HEREBY AGREED AND DECLARED** by and between the Parties hereto as follows:-

## 1     *DEFINITIONS & INTERPRETATION*

1.1     In this Agreement where the context so admits:

**"1980 Act"** means the Highways Act 1980;

**"Building"** includes (without limitation) any structure or erection or any part of a building, structure or erection;

**"CDM Client"** See **[Form 1.2] - Definitions**;

**"CDM Regulations"** See **[Form 1.2] - Definitions**;

**"Commuted Sum"** means the sum of £[****] being a contribution towards the costs of future maintenance of the Main Road Works;

**"Completion Certificate"** means the certificate to be issued by the Engineer in accordance with Clause [****] of this Agreement;[144]

**"Completion Payment"** means the sum of £[****];

**"Design Fee"** means the sum of [****];[145]

**"Drainage System"** means all of the drains and sewers (excluding any natural water courses, private drains and sewers) which drain Main Road Works;

**"Drawing"** means the drawing entitled "[****]" and marked [****] annexed hereto and any amended, substituted or additional drawing approved by or on behalf of the Engineer;

**"Due Date"** means the date when a sum of money is (according to the provisions of this agreement) due to be paid by the Developer to the Council;

**"Engineer"** means the [****] of the Council for the time being or his deputy or any officer of the Council authorised to discharge his duties;

---

[144]   Given that the works are minor, the draft does not break them down into "*Phase 1*" and "*Phase 2*" works and does not include a "*maintenance period*".

[145]   It is unlikely that minor works will require a sophisticated design; however, if so, then it might be appropriate to require a payment from the developer to cover the costs.

**"Estate Roads"** means the proposed carriageways, footways and footpaths on the Site and shown as such on the Drawing together with the associated street lights and all other things ancillary thereto;

**"Estate Road Works"** means the provision of new roads and associated works to form the Estate Roads as more particularly shown on the Drawing including the Junction Works;

**"Interest"** means interest at 4 per cent above the base lending rate of *[****]* Bank plc from time to time;

**"Junction Works"** means works to form a junction between the Estate Roads and Main Road as more particularly shown on the Drawing;

**"Land Compensation Acts"** See *[Form 1.2] - Definitions*;

**"Land Compensation Claim"** See *[Form 1.2] - Definitions*;

**"Land Compensation Costs"** See *[Form 1.2] - Definitions*;

**"Main Road Works"** means the provision of a new footway (including all associated works and traffic control measures) at Main Road as more particularly shown on the Drawing and described in the Specification;

**"Maintain"** includes inspect, repair, adjust, alter, remove or reconstruct and any derivative of *"maintain"* is to be construed accordingly;

**"Occupied"** See *[Form 1.2] - Definitions*;

**"Parties"** means (collectively) the Council and the Developer;

**"Planning Permission"** means the planning permission granted by the Council dated *[****]* for the proposed erection of *[****]* under reference numbers *[****]*;

**"Road Safety Audits"** See *[Form 1.2] - Definitions*;

**"Statutory Undertaker"** See *[Form 1.2] - Definitions*;

**"Site"** means land at *[****]*, which is shown *[edged red]* on the plan annexed hereto and registered at the Land Registry under Title Numbers *[****]*;

**"Specification"** means the particulars set out in the *[****]*;

**"Stage 3 Safety Audit"** See *[Form 1.2] - Definitions*;

**"Stage 4 Safety Audit"** See *[Form 1.2] - Definitions*;

**"Traffic"** See *[Form 1.2]* - **Definitions**;

**"Traffic Regulation Order"** See *[Form 1.2]* - **Definitions**;

**"Working Day"** See *[Form 1.2]* - **Definitions**.

## 2    INTERPRETATION

See *[Form 1.3]* - *Interpretation*

## 3    ENABLING LEGISLATION

3.1    This Agreement is made in pursuance of powers contained in Section 278 of the 1980 Act and Section 111 of the Local Government Act 1972 and Section 1 of the Localism Act 2011 and all other enabling provisions.[146]

3.2    Nothing in this Agreement shall operate to take away or prejudice the right of the Council to exercise the powers conferred upon it by the Private Street Works Code contained in Part XI of the 1980 Act in respect of the Estate Roads or other powers available to the Council if the Developer or the Surety shall fail to perform all or any of their obligations under this Agreement.

## 4    APPROVALS, CONSENTS ETC

See *[Form 1.13]* - *Approvals, consents etc*

## 5    COMPLETION PERIOD

5.1    The Council shall use *[reasonable endeavours]*[147] to carry out and complete the Main Road Works (at the Developer's expense) in a good and workmanlike manner and with proper materials in accordance in all respects with the CDM Regulations, the Specifications and the Drawing within *[****]* Months from the date of this Agreement (the "Completion Period") PROVIDED that the Council and the Developer may agree to extend the Completion Period subject to being satisfied that the Bond covers any extension of time.

5.2    The Council shall not be liable to the payment of any damages or recompense (whether for loss of profits or income or otherwise) in favour of the Developer in the event that the Main Road Works or Junction Works (or any part thereof) are not completed in accordance with the Completion Period.

---

[146]    The references to Section 111 of the Local Government Act 1972 and the Localism Act 2011 cover ancillary matters and also the overlap with the Estate Road Works.

[147]    Those acting for the Council need to be sure that they wish to attract the liabilities which go with such an undertaking. An alternative might be a "due diligence" clause. The exclusion clause at Clause 5.2 is intended to mitigate any potential damages, but is subject to the rules for such clauses in contract law.

## 6    DECLARATION

6.1    The Developer hereby declares and warrants to the Council that:

(a)    it has, and throughout the duration of this Agreement will maintain, full right, liberty and consent to carry out all of all works as may be necessary to connect the Estate Roads to Main Road as provided by the Drawing and the Specification.[148]

(b)    the consent of the Environment Agency or other appropriate drainage body has been obtained in connection with any proposed alteration or use of any existing watercourse or land drainage or other works within the Site and vested in or under the control of the said Agency or other drainage body.

## 7    STATUTORY UNDERTAKERS

7.1    The Developer covenants that it shall before connecting the Estate Roads to the Main Road give notice to each and every Statutory Undertaker for the time being of any service or services laid in upon or under Main Road of the proposal to make such connection.

## 8    INDEMNITIES

8.1    The Developer hereby indemnifies the Council in respect of all actions, claims, demands, expenses and proceedings arising out of or in connection with or incidental to the carrying out of the Main Road Works or Estate Road Works including (without limitation) any claims under any Land Compensation Act other than those arising out of or in consequence of any act neglect default or liability of the Council.

8.2    The Developer hereby undertakes and agrees with the Council that in the event of any claim or claims arising in connection with or incidental to or in consequence of the carrying out of the Main Road Works or the Estate Road Works and being made against the Council for any one or more of the following payments:

(a)    compensation, including (without limitation) any Land Compensation Costs;

(b)    damages;

(c)    costs;

(d)    charges;

---

[148]   In this example, the Estate Roads fall outside the current highway and so it is essential that provisions are made to ensure that the junction arrangements fall into place at the appropriate time.

(e)     the cost of any works or measures considered necessary by any Statutory Undertaker in consequence of the making of any connection to its system or apparatus; and

(f)     any other payment arising in connection with or incidental to or in consequence of the carrying out of the Main Road Works and/or the Estate Road Works

and the Developer will hold the Council fully indemnified from and against each and every said claim and shall indemnify the Council in respect of the same.

## 9     PUBLIC LIABILITY INSURANCE

9.1     The Developer shall at all times during the period of this Agreement maintain full comprehensive public liability insurance in the sum of not less than £[****] ([****] Pounds) in respect of the Estate Road Works or any one occurrence or series of occurrences arising out of one event against liability to any person arising from the construction, operation or maintenance of the Estate Road Works or the exercise of any rights granted by the Council and shall allow the Council to inspect the certificate of insurance at all reasonable times.[149]

## 10     INTEREST

10.1     If any payment due to the Council under this Agreement is not paid by the Due Date then Interest then will be payable from the due date to the actual date of payment.

## 11     ADMINISTRATION AND INSPECTION COSTS

11.1     The Developer shall within Twenty Eight (28) Working Days of the date of this Agreement, pay to the Council:

(a)     The Design Fee; and

(b)     the sum of £[****] ([****] Pounds) (the *"Administration and Inspection Costs"*)[150] which sum shall be by way of a non refundable contribution towards the expenses of the Council in respect of the inspection of the Main Road Works and/or the Junction Works, the testing of materials used or intended for use therein and the administration and monitoring of arrangements pursuant to this Agreement.

11.2     The Main Road Works shall not commence unless and until the Developer shall have paid the Design Fee and the Administration and Inspection Costs in full.

---

[149]  This is appropriate to ensure that the Council is not caught up in litigation if the Developer proves to be impecunious. Ask to be provided with a certified copy of the insurance certificate.

[150]  This will normally be a percentage of the total estimated cost of the works. At the time of writing, this tends to be between 5% and 10%. This payment is in advance of, and additional to, any ad hoc costs which arise during the course of the works.

11.3    The Developer shall pay or repay (as the case may be) all the Council's legal and administrative costs reasonably incurred in negotiating, settling and executing this Agreement no later than *[****].*[151]

## 12    OCCUPATION OF BUILDINGS

12.1    The Developer covenants that no Building fronting, adjoining or abutting on or served by the Estate Roads shall be Occupied until the said Building has been provided with access (including appropriate operational and energised street lighting) over the Estate Roads to their junction with Main Road and until suitable surface has been provided by the Developer to the satisfaction of the Engineer.

## 13    LIMITS OF DEVIATION

13.1    The Council may (in its absolute discretion) deviate vertically or laterally from the levels, lines or situations shown by the Drawing and Specification in carrying out the Main Road Works PROVIDED that the proposed adoption of the Estate Roads is not prejudiced and that the Council is paid its costs in assessing and administering such deviations before they are incorporated into the Works.[152]

## 14    COMPLETION

14.1    The Engineer shall issue the Completion Certificate when all of the following conditions are satisfied:

(a)    the Main Road Works have been completed in accordance with the Drawing and the Specification;

(b)    the Main Road Works have been inspected by the Engineer and no defects been identified by him or (as the case may be) any necessary remedial works have been completed to the satisfaction of the Engineer;

(c)    the Council has received all monies due to that date to the Council under the provisions of this Agreement;

(d)    *[the Drainage System has been adopted (so as to be maintainable at the public expense)]*; and

(e)    the Safety Audits have been completed and any actions arising from them and which the Engineer has required to be carried out have been completed to the satisfaction of the Engineer.

---

[151]    This will normally be a fixed figure for a minor works agreement. Otherwise, consider whether the developer should enter into a formal abortive costs undertaking before the Council commences drafting and settling the agreement. If not, then, at the least, the developer's solicitor should provide an undertaking to cover these costs whether the agreement is concluded or not.

[152]    It is important that any deviations are caught by the "as-built" drawings.

14.2     Upon the issue of the Completion Certificate the Developer shall pay the Completion Payment, the Commuted Sum and any other monies which remain due under this Agreement to the Council in full not later than 15 Working Days following the issue of the Completion Certificate (together with Interest from the Due Date) and from the date that all the said payments have been made in full the liability of the Surety pursuant to this Agreement shall come to an end.

14.3     Without prejudice to the Council's powers of enforcement pursuant to section 278 of the Highways Act 1980, the Estate Roads shall not be used for access and egress of any Traffic to or from Main Road unless and until the Council has received all monies due to it under the provisions of this Agreement.[153]

## 15     TRAFFIC REGULATION ORDERS

15.1     The Council shall use reasonable endeavours to make and confirm any Traffic Regulation Order required to carry out the Main Road Works PROVIDED that the Council shall not be obliged to initiate or pursue any Traffic Regulation Order unless and until the Developer has paid to or secured to the satisfaction of the Council a sum equivalent to the estimated costs of making and confirming any such Order and also provided the Council with an indemnity in respect of any costs which might arise from or be incurred in respect of any such proceedings, whether the Order is completed or confirmed or not.

## 16     INSPECTION OF JUNCTION WORKS BY ENGINEER

16.1     The Developer shall during the progress of setting out, constructing and maintaining the Junction Works give to the Engineer (and any person authorised by him) free access to those parts of the Site upon which Junction Works are being, or are proposed to be, carried out so as to inspect them and all materials used or intended for use in them and shall if required by the Engineer to do so uncover or open up any work to enable it to be inspected and if so required shall remove any structure or materials which are not in accordance with the Drawing or Specification or which, in the opinion of the Engineer, are defective and the Developer shall (at its own expense) re-execute any such work and substitute proper and suitable structures or materials to the satisfaction of the Engineer.

## 17     SAMPLES AND TESTS

17.1     The Developer shall at its own expense provide such samples of materials used or intended to be used in the Estate Roads within /****/ metres of the Junction Works as may be required by the Engineer from time to time for the purposes of testing their quality and suitability.

---

[153]   This parallels the statutory enforcement mechanism in section 278.

17.2    Such sampling and testing shall be in accordance with the current editions of the 'Design Manual for Roads and Bridges' and the 'Manual of Contract Documents for Highway Works'.

17.3    All sampling and testing shall be at the cost of the Developer.

## 18    DETERMINATION

18.1    If at any time:

(a)    the Developer fails to perform or observe any of the conditions stipulations or obligations on its part contained in this Agreement; or

(b)    if a receiving order in bankruptcy is made against the Developer or the Developer's business is being wound up or dissolved or if the Developer is insolvent or enters into a composition or scheme of arrangement (otherwise than for the purpose of amalgamation or reconstruction),

THEN the Council may (without prejudice to any of its rights claims or remedies against the Developer and the Surety in respect of any non-performance or non-observance of this Agreement) determine this Agreement (except for Clauses [****] of this Agreement) by notice in writing delivered to the Developer and send a copy of any such notice to the Surety.

## 19    SURETY'S OBLIGATIONS

19.1    Without prejudice to the right of the Council to exercise any of its rights and powers under this Agreement or under any statutory provision, the Surety agrees that it shall:

(a)    in the event of non-observance or breach of any of the terms of the covenants conditions stipulations or obligations on the part of the Developer contained in this Agreement; or

(b)    if a receiving order in bankruptcy is made against the Developer or the Developer's business is being wound up or dissolved or if the Developer is insolvent or enters into a composition or scheme of arrangement (otherwise than for the purpose of amalgamation or reconstruction),

pay to the Council within Twenty Eight (28) days of receiving notice in writing from the Engineer such sum of money as the Engineer may certify to be necessary to perform the obligations of the Developer under this Agreement PROVIDED that the sum payable by the Surety shall not exceed the sum of £[****] ([****] Pounds).

19.2    The Surety shall not be discharged or released from this Agreement by any arrangement between the Developer and the Council or by any alteration in the Developer's obligations or by any forbearance whether as to payment, performance, time or otherwise whether made with or without the assent of the Surety.

## 20    HEALTH AND SAFETY

20.1    The Council hereby confirms that it is a "client" for the purpose of the Construction (Design and Management) Regulations 2015 in respect of the Main Road Works and is aware of the provisions of the CDM Regulations and shall comply and procure compliance with them.

ALSO SEE:

*[Form 1.10] - Council's statutory duties*

*[Form 1.11] - No partnership or agency*

*[Form 1.15] - Assignment*

*[Form 1.16] - Dispute provisions*

*[Form 1.17] - Waiver*

*[Form 1.18] - Third parties*

*[Form 1.19] - Service of notices*

*[Form 1.21] - Jurisdiction*

*[Form 1.22] - Force majeure*

IN WITNESS whereof ...............

## FIRST SCHEDULE - THE MAIN ROAD WORKS

(List)

## SECOND SCHEDULE - LIST OF ATTACHMENTS

* Location Plan;

* The drawing entitled "*[****]*" and marked *[****]*;

* The Specification.

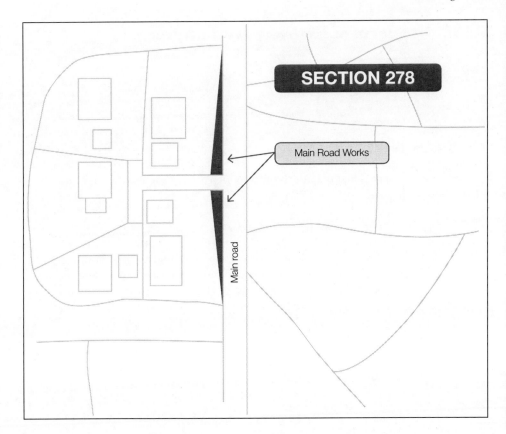

# Form 6: Highway Works Agreement

### Commentary

This is an example showing highway works by a developer as agent for the highway authority at the developer's cost. It includes areas of land which will form part of the highway and which are in private ownership and, therefore, they must be drawn into and adopted as part of the highway network. Whilst not a general practice, one way of ensuring that the title to the adoption areas is secured is beyond doubt to require the transfer of title to them before the Works begin.

It is important to stress that the effect of these arrangements is that the works are treated, at Law, as being the actions of the highway authority. The agreement must reflect this reality. For example, the works will be maintainable at the public expense from the date that they are opened to traffic and so the provisions for the 'maintenance period' must be predicated on the basis that the primary responsibility is that of the Council and that the developer is the agent of the authority only.

THIS AGREEMENT is made the *[****]* day of *[****]*

BETWEEN:

(1) *[****]* (the "Council")

(2) *[****]* (the "Owner")[154]

(3) *[****]* (the "Chargee")

[(4) *[****]* (the "Surety")[155]

See *[Form 1.1] - The Parties*

### RECITALS:

A. The Council is the local highway authority for highways in *[****]* pursuant to the 1980 Act.

B. Main Road is a highway maintainable at the public expense vested in the Council.[156]

C. The Developer is the registered proprietor with title absolute of the Site.

---

[154]  Necessary if the adoption areas are not owned by the developer.
[155]  In order to provide a variety of drafting approaches in these examples, this example is on the basis that the Surety will become involved at a later stage by the execution of a bond in the form shown by Form 7 below.
[156]  In this example "Main Road" is the existing all purpose highway and will be the principal site of the Works.

D. The Site is the location of a proposed housing development.

E. The Council has agreed to enter into this Agreement with the Developer for the purpose of securing the carrying out of the Works by the Developer as the agent of and at no cost to the Council.

F. The Developer has agreed to carry out the Works in accordance with terms of this Agreement.

G. The CDM Regulations apply in relation to the construction of the Works.

H. The Owner is the owner of Adoption Areas and enters this agreement with the intent that they shall be transferred to the Council as the local highway authority.

I. The Chargee is the Registered Proprietor of the Charge dated *[****]* in respect of the Adoption Areas and has agreed to enter into and consent to this Agreement.

## 1    DEFINITIONS & INTERPRETATION

1.1      In this Agreement the following expressions shall have the meanings set out below:

**"1980 Act"** means the Highways Act 1980;

**"1991 Act"** means the New Roads and Street Works Act 1991;

**"First Schedule"** means the First Schedule to this Agreement;

**"Second Schedule"** means the Second Schedule to this Agreement;

**"As-Built Drawings"** See *[Form 1.2]* - **Definitions**;[157]

**"Adopted"** means maintained at the public expense by the Council;

**"Adoption Areas"** means the land shown *[edged in red]* on the Land Transfer Plan;

**"Bond"** means *[the sum of [****] Pounds (£[****]) ([****] Pounds) provided as security for this Agreement, as may be reduced from time to time in accordance with the provisions of this Agreement;[158]] [the bond referred to in Clause [****]]*;

**"Bond Figure"** means the sum of *[****]* pounds (£*[****]*) adjusted in accordance with the movements in the Index between *[insert date Bond Figure agreed]* and a date being Ten

---

[157]  It is important to obtain *"as-built"* drawings to ensure that the adoption process relates to the right land (i.e. includes any deviations) and so that there is an accurate record in the event of any dispute.

[158]  The initial bond figure will be the estimated costs of providing the ways to an adoptable standard.

(10) Working Days prior to commencement of the Works to the intent that the adjusted figure shall constitute the Bond Figure;

**"CDM Client"** See **[Form 1.2] - Definitions**;

**"CDM Regulations"** See **[Form 1.2] - Definitions**;

**"Certificate of Practical Completion"** means the certificate to be issued by the Engineer pursuant to Clause *[****]*;

**"Costed Risk Analysis"** See **[Form 1.2] - Definitions**;

**"Development"** means the development permitted by the Planning Permission;

**"Development Site"** means land at *[****]*, which is shown *[edged red]* on the plan annexed hereto and registered at the Land Registry under Title Numbers *[****]*;

**"Drainage System"** means all of the drains and sewers (excluding any natural water courses private drains and sewers) which drain the Works including those situate outside the limits of the highway Adopted or to be Adopted;

**"Drawing"** means the drawing entitled "*[****]*" and marked *[****]* annexed hereto and any amended, substituted or additional drawing approved by or on behalf of the Engineer;

**"Engineer"** means the *[****]* of the Council for the time being or his deputy or any officer of the Council authorised to discharge his duties;

**"Final Certificate"** means the Certificate to be issued by the Engineer in accordance with Clause *[****]* of this Agreement;

**"Final Drawings"** means the As-Built Drawings, drainage drawings and other drawings as the Engineer may require in such form as may be required by the Engineer;

**"Health and Safety File"** See **[Form 1.2] - Definitions**;

**"Highway(s)"** means Main Road and each and all other highways affected by the Works (whether by traffic movements or otherwise) including any highway to be constructed as part of the Works whether Adopted or to be Adopted;

**"Index"** See **[Form 1.2] - Definitions**;

**"Land Transfer Plan"** means the drawing entitled "*[****]*" and marked *[****]* annexed hereto;

**"Land Compensation Acts"** See **[Form 1.2] - Definitions**;

*"Land Compensation Claim"* See *[Form 1.2]* - **Definitions**;

*"Land Compensation Costs"* See *[Form 1.2]* - **Definitions**;

*"Maintain"* includes inspect, repair, adjust, alter, remove or reconstruct and any derivative of *"maintain"* is to be construed accordingly;

*"Maintenance Period"* means the period of not less than 12 (Twelve) Months:

    (a)    beginning on the date of issue of the Certificate of Practical Completion or if later the date when the Works are used by Traffic; and

    (b)    ending on the date of issue of the Final Certificate;[159]

*"Occupied"* See *[Form 1.2]* - **Definitions**;

*"Parties"* means (collectively) the Council, the Owner and the Developer;

*"Planning Permission"* means the planning permission granted by the Council dated *[****]* for the proposed erection of *[[****] new dwellings and associated infrastructure including open space and sustainable urban drainage system]* under reference numbers *[****]*;

*"Programme"* means a statement approved by the Council describing the sequence in which the Works are to be carried out with a description of the arrangements and methods of construction which the Developer proposes to adopt therefor together with an estimate of the amount of time to be spent by the Developer in carrying out and completing the Works and the expression "Programme" shall include such variations as may from time to time be agreed by the Council;

*"Remedial Works"* means the remedial works required by the Engineer pursuant to Clauses *[****]* prior to the issue of the Final Certificate (including any remedial works in connection with the *[****]* Road Works);

*"Road Safety Audits"* means (collectively) the Stage 1 Safety Audit, Stage 2 Safety Audit, Stage 3 Safety Audit and the Stage 4 Safety Audit;[160]

*"Specification"* means the detailed specification for the Works approved by the Council and attached to this agreement;

*"Statutory Undertaker"* See *[Form 1.2]* - **Definitions**;

---

[159] This open end is designed to cover any overrun arising from the extended rectification of faults found in the maintenance period.

[160] See Chapter 10 for an explanation of road safety audits.

**"Structure"** means any structure built in, under or over any Highway including (without limitation):

- bridges, footbridges, pipe gantries, culverts, pipes, tunnels, chambers, cellars, shafts, soakaways, manholes and storm water balancing tanks;

- retaining walls, headwalls, basements, cellars and reinforced earth where the face is at an angle of 70° or more;

- projecting or spanning buildings environmental barriers high mast lighting CCTV masts and portal and cantilever sign / signal gantries; and

- any such structure(s) built in or within 3.66 metres of any Highway or highway to be constructed as part of the Works which support(s) any highway or highway to be constructed as part of the Works;

**"Stage 3 Safety Audit"** See *[Form 1.2] - Definitions*;

**"Stage 4 Safety Audit"** See *[Form 1.2] - Definitions*;

**"Street"** See *[Form 1.2] - Definitions*;

**"Street Authority"** See *[Form 1.2] - Definitions*;

**"Street Works"** See *[Form 1.2] - Definitions*;

**"Traffic"** See *[Form 1.2] - Definitions*;

**"Traffic Regulation Order"** See *[Form 1.2] - Definitions*;

**"Traffic Signal Equipment"** means that part of the Works relating to traffic signal and data transmission equipment as shown on the Drawings;

**"Working Day"** See *[Form 1.2] - Definitions*;

**"Works"** means those works to be carried out on Main Road and the Adoption Areas and specified in the First Schedule and more particularly described in and shown in the Specification and the Drawings and all other things ancillary thereto including all road water drainage systems together with any Remedial Works and shall (where the context so admits) mean any part or parts of them.

## 2    STATUTORY PROVISIONS

2.1    This Agreement is made pursuant to Section 111 of the Local Government Act 1972, Section 1 of the Localism Act 2011 and Sections *[24] [72]* of the 1980 Act and all other powers enabling the Council in that behalf.

2.2    The Council hereby authorises the Developer to carry out the Works as the agent of the Council.

2.3    Save as expressly provided by it, this Agreement does not authorise any interference with the convenience of persons using any Street or affect the rights of the owners of premises adjoining any Highway or Street or the rights of Statutory Undertakers.

2.4    This Agreement is made without prejudice to and shall not be construed to be a licence under any of Sections 171, 176, 177, 178 or 179 of the 1980 Act.

2.5    Nothing in this Agreement shall operate to take away or prejudice the right of the Council to exercise the powers conferred upon it by the 1980 Act in respect of the Highways or other powers available to the Council if the Developer, Owner or the Surety shall fail to perform all or any of their obligations under this Agreement.

## 3    SECURITY FOR COSTS

3.1    No part of the Development or the Works shall commence unless and until the Bond has been executed by a Surety in the Bond Figure for the due performance of the Developer's obligations under this Agreement in the form of the draft bond annexed hereto[161] or such other form as the Council may agree.

3.2    The Developer may deposit an agreed sum by way of security for any such claims instead of the provision of a Bond.

## 4.    THE DESIGN

4.1    No part of the Works shall be commenced unless and until the Specification, the Drawings and the Programme have been submitted to and approved by the Engineer.

4.2    The Engineer shall approve or submit to the Developer his written comments in full upon the submitted Specification, Drawings and the Programme not later than *[****]* Working Days from receipt and the Developer shall not commence the Works until the Engineer's written approval has been provided.

4.3    If the Developer shall wish to revise any of the Specification and/or the Drawings and/or the Programme it shall notify the Engineer in writing of any proposed revisions

---

[161]    See Form 7 below.

and the Engineer shall approve or submit to the Developer his written comments in full upon those matters within *[****]* Working Days of receipt of them PROVIDED that if the Engineer does not propose to give his approval in relation to any of those matters then he shall inform the Developer in writing as soon as is reasonably practicable.

# 5      CONSTRUCTION OF WORKS

5.1      The Developer hereby covenants with the Council to diligently to carry out the Works at no cost to the Council in accordance with the provisions of this Agreement and to complete the Works (which date of completion shall for the purposes of this Sub-Clause be evidenced by the issue of the Certificate of Practical Completion) as the agent of the Council and in accordance with the Specification, the Drawings and the Programme to the satisfaction of the Engineer and within *[****]* Months of commencement of the Works and the Developer shall (without prejudice to the foregoing):

(a)    give to the Council at least *[****]* Working Days' written notice of the Developer's intention to commence the Development and at least *[****]* Working Days' written notice of its intention to commence the Works;

(b)    keep to a minimum the period of occupation of the Highways so as to ensure the safety of Traffic and the minimum disruption to users of and traffic flow on the Highway;

(c)    comply with all instructions given by the Council regarding the method of working within the Highway; and

(d)    undertake or procure all stages of the Safety Audits to the satisfaction of the Engineer.

5.2      No part of the Development or the Works shall commence unless and until the Adoption Areas have been transferred to the Council as local highway authority at no cost to the Council and free from encumbrances other than such as shall already have been created prior to the date of this Agreement (with the exception of any purely financial charges) *[such transfer to be in the form of the draft Transfer annexed hereto (or such other form of transfer as may be prescribed from time to time by H M Land Registry)]* and has paid the Council's legal costs and disbursements in connection with such transfer.

5.3      Before commencement of the Works and at no expense to the Council to obtain such consents licences or permissions as may be required for the purposes of carrying out the Works and the installation of the traffic signal equipment and to comply with the same and indemnify and keep the Council indemnified from and against all liabilities, costs, claims, actions, demands or expenses which may arise from the Developer's failure to obtain or to comply with such consents licences or permissions.

5.4     To execute and complete or to procure the execution and completion by all necessary parties without cost to the Council of such deeds of grant as are necessary to secure to the Council full and exclusive drainage rights in respect of such parts of the Drainage System as are situate outside the limits of the Highways and such other easements as may be required by the Council for the future maintenance of any Structure forming part of the Works as constructed.

5.5     If the Developer intends to suspend construction of the Works for a period of more than *[****]* Working Days, the Developer shall notify the Engineer in writing of:

(a)     the intended suspension not less than *[****]* Working Days before the start of the suspension; and

(b)     the Developer's intention to re-commence construction of the Works not less than *[****]* Working Days before such re-commencement;

and if the Developer fails to notify the Engineer as provided by this clause, the inspection fee referred to in Clause *[****]* shall be increased by such amount as the Engineer, exercising absolute discretion, sees fit to reimburse the Council any additional cost incurred by the Council in inspecting the Works because of such failure.

5.6     If, by any impediment, prevention or default, whether by act or omission by the Council (except to the extent caused or contributed to by any default, whether by act or omission of the Developer), the Council delays the carrying out and completion of the Works *[or the Developer's obligations under Clause [****]]*, the Engineer shall grant an extension of time to complete the Works *[or the Developer's obligations under Clause [****]]* for a further period or periods, by giving written notice to the Developer and such extension shall be commensurate with the delay suffered by the Developer that was caused by such impediment, prevention or default.

## 6     TEMPORARY WORKS

6.1     During the period when the Works are being executed the Developer shall institute at its own expense temporary measures to be approved by the Engineer prior to the commencement of the Works  to maintain the flow of traffic on the Highways.

## 7     SAFETY OF ROADWORKS

7.1     During the period over which the Works are being executed the Developer shall comply with the provisions of the Traffic Signs Manual 2009 chapter 8  (published by the Department of Transport) and any amendment thereto or any provisions replacing the same for lighting and signing the Works or such other measures as may be reasonably required by the Engineer.

7.2    If the Council considers that the Developer's actions are putting the users of the Highways at risk then the Council can, without notice, take such actions (at the cost of the Developer) as the Council considers appropriate to protect the users of the Highways.

## 8    SUPERVISION

8.1    The Developer shall nominate a suitably qualified supervisor to oversee and manage the construction of the Works and to act as liaison between the Developer and the Council.

## 9    PAYMENTS

9.1    The Developer shall pay to the Council upon the execution hereof -

(a)    the Council's legal and administrative costs in connection with the preparation and completion of this Agreement; and,

(b)    a fixed sum consultancy fee of £[****] ([****] Pounds) in respect of the highway management and transportation advice and assistance given to the Developer prior to the date hereof.[162]

9.2    The Developer shall pay to the Council within [****] Working Days of demand[163] the costs expenses incurred by the Council in project management checking the design of and carrying out periodic site inspections of the Works as certified by the Council's finance officer for the time including (without limitation):

(a)    personnel costs based on the following hourly rates (exclusive of VAT):

(i)    £[****] for a junior technician

(ii)    £[****] for a project manager

in all cases adjusted in accordance with any changes in the Council's standard hourly rates which may occur after [****] to be calculated on a time basis at [****] monthly intervals the first payment period being the period of [****] Month[s] from the date of commencement of the Works;

(b)    such payments from time to time during the course of the Works the costs and expenses incurred by the Council in the testing of any materials carried out by the Council;

---

[162]    Query whether these costs should be secured in advance by way of an abortive costs agreement.
[163]    Query whether the Developer should put the Council in funds before the commencement of the works. Note the cash-flow disadvantages of payments in arrears.

(c)     the costs incurred by the Council in connection with the design, ordering, supply, supervising the controller, programming and testing installation and commissioning and inspection and maintenance of the Traffic Signal Equipment;

(d)     any costs incurred by the Council in connection with the diversion and/or protection of the apparatus of Statutory Undertakers as evidenced by copies of their invoices (as certified by the Engineer); and

(e)     any costs incurred by the Council in making and implementing any Traffic Regulation Order[s] which the Engineer deems *[is] [are]* necessary because of the Works and whether made or implemented prior to during or following the completion of the Works.

9.3     For the purposes of this Agreement, the expression "costs" shall include all costs, expenses, disbursements and all relevant in-house administrative costs.

9.4     The Developer shall pay the Commuted Sum to the Council in accordance with Clause *[****]*.

## 10      INTEREST ON OVERDUE PAYMENTS

See *[Form 1.12]* - *Payments*

## 11      THE COUNCIL'S COVENANTS

11.1     The Council hereby covenants with the Developer that it will at the request and cost of the Developer subject to its statutory duties from time to time and then as expeditiously as possible use such powers as are reasonably available to the Council to assist the carrying out of the Works (including highway drainage).

## 12      ACCESS TO HIGHWAY

12.1     The Council without prejudice to its statutory powers and duties hereby gives to the Developer licence to enter, and to remain upon, with or without workmen, plant and machinery, so much of the highway under the Council's control as the Engineer shall agree is reasonably necessary for the Developer to carry out its obligations under this Agreement and it is hereby agreed and declared that such licence extends to breaking open (subject where appropriate to making good its surface) and without limitation to the foregoing carrying out works in, on or under the said highway.

## 13      ACCESS TO WORKS

13.1     The Developer shall during the progress of the Works and the Maintenance Period give or procure for the Engineer and any person or persons duly authorised by him unfettered access to every part of the Works and permit him or them to inspect the same as they proceed and all materials used or intended to be used therein and shall give effect to any reasonable and proper requirements made or reasonable and proper direction given by the Engineer to conform to the Drawings and/or the Programme and the Specification.

13.2    The Developer shall not cover up or put out of view any part of the Works without the approval of the Engineer and shall afford full opportunity for him to examine and measure any work which is about to be covered up or put out of view and to examine foundations before permanent work is placed thereon and shall give at least Two (2) Working Days' notice to the Engineer whenever any such work or foundations is or are ready or about to be ready for examination and the Engineer shall without unreasonable delay unless he considers it unnecessary and advises the Developer accordingly attend when required by the Developer upon at least Two (2) Working Days' notice for the purpose of examining and measuring such works or of examining such foundations.

13.3    The costs of all inspections, sampling, and other actions pursuant to these clauses shall be at the expense of the Developer and, if borne by the Council in the first instance, shall be refunded to the Council in accordance with the provisions of Clause *[****]*.

## 14    TESTING OF MATERIALS

14.1    Before commencement and during the construction of the Works the Developer shall submit for approval to the Engineer a list of suppliers from whom it wishes to obtain materials for incorporation in the Works together with test certificates for such materials and shall at its own cost provide the Engineer with any samples of materials he may reasonably request for testing purposes.

14.2    The Engineer may in his reasonable discretion test or require the testing of materials, plant, workmanship used or proposed to be used in the Works and to reject any materials, plant or workmanship so tested which he may reasonably and properly find to be not in accordance with the Specification and/or the Drawings or otherwise not fit for purpose.

14.3    The Developer shall as soon as is reasonably practicable replace or repair any materials, plant or workmanship which have been found not in accordance with the Specification and/or the Drawings with such as are so in accordance.

14.4    The Engineer shall be allowed reasonable access and admission to the Works or the places where materials or plant for the Works may be stored or in the course of preparation, manufacture or use.

14.5    The Developer shall as soon as is reasonably practicable remove such materials, plant and workmanship as are rejected by the Engineer which are not capable of repair or remedy from the site of the Works and if the Developer shall wish to continue to store such rejected materials, plant and workmanship on the site of the Works they shall be stored separately from those materials, plant and workmanship which have not been so rejected or which the Developer shall wish in future to use in execution of the Works.

14.6     The costs of all inspections, sampling, and other actions pursuant to these clauses shall be at the expense of the Developer and, if borne by the Council in the first instance, shall be refunded to the Council in accordance with the provisions of Clause *[****]*.

14.7     Such sampling and testing shall be in accordance with the current editions of the '*Design Manual for Roads and Bridges*' and the '*Manual of Contract Documents for Highway Works*' or such other standard or guidance as may be agreed and at the Developer's expense.

## 15     OPENING OF THE WORKS

15.1     During the construction of the Works and prior to the issue of the Final Certificate the Engineer may issue instructions to the Developer to open up or expose any of the Works which has been covered up without previously being inspected by the Engineer.

15.2     Should the Developer fail to comply with any such instructions the Council may so open up or expose the Works causing as little damage or inconvenience as is possible to or in respect of any other part or parts of the Works and (without prejudice to Clause *[****]*) the reasonable and proper cost of such taking up or exposure and reinstatement shall be met by the Developer.

15.3     If the Works are covered up by the Developer after giving at least Two (2) Working Days' notice of its intention so to do and the Engineer shall have failed to inspect within that period and shall subsequently require the Works or any part of them to be uncovered for the purposes of inspection:

(a)     if inspection reveals that the relevant part or parts of the Works has or have been completed in accordance with the Drawings and/or the Specification all reasonable and proper costs in respect of such uncovering and inspection and of reinstating the part or parts of the Works uncovered shall be borne by the Council and the Council shall be liable for any consequential costs, expenses or damages which shall be directly or indirectly attributable to delay or interference occasioned by such uncovering testing and reinstatement;

(b)     if inspection reveals that the relevant part or parts of the Works has or have not been completed in accordance with the Drawings and the Specification all reasonable and proper costs in respect of such uncovering and inspections and of reinstating the part or parts of the Works uncovered shall be borne by the Developer.

15.4     Save for those mentioned in Clause 15.3(a), the costs of all inspections, sampling, and other actions pursuant to these clauses shall be at the expense of the Developer and, if borne by the Council in the first instance, shall be refunded to the Council in accordance with the provisions of Clause *[****]*.

## 16  STATUTORY UNDERTAKERS

16.1    Prior to the commencement of the Works the Developer shall give notice to all relevant Statutory Undertakers of the proposals to carry out the Works and the installation of the traffic signal equipment as if they were works for road purposes or major highway works as defined in Section 86 of the 1991 Act and at the same time deliver a copy of such notice to the Engineer.

16.2    The Developer shall at no cost to the Council carry out or procure the carrying out of any works or measures as are required by Statutory Undertakers in consequence of the proposal to carry out the Works and the installation of the traffic signal equipment to the plant and equipment of Statutory Undertakers on the site of the Works and the traffic signal equipment including payment of the costs of any diversions or new installations necessary for their completion and the Works shall be deemed not to have been completed until the cost of any such diversions or new installations has been paid by the Developer PROVIDED THAT in the event that any requirement made by any Statutory Undertaker shall be unreasonable the Council shall at the reasonable request of the Developer join with the Developer in resisting such requirement.

16.3    The Developer shall cause all highway or other drains or sewers, gas and water mains, pipes, electric cables (if any) or telephone cables (if any) which are to be laid by the Developer under the Works together with all necessary connections from them to the boundary of the Works to be laid in so far as is practicable under the Works before the foundations of the Works are laid and shall also in so far as is practicable cause the connections from electric cables to any street lamps to be laid before the paving of any footways comprised in the Works is carried out.

## 17  PREVENTION OF MUD BEING CARRIED ON THE HIGHWAY

17.1    The Developer shall make provisions (at no cost to the Council) at the Site and on the Highways to prevent the deposit of mud dust and other materials on the Highways by vehicles and/or plant leaving the site of the Works.[164]

## 18  TRAFFIC CONTROL

18.1    At all times when the Works are being executed the Developer shall from time to time institute at its own expense reasonable measures approved by the Engineer (before their implementation) to maintain the flow and safety of Traffic on the Highways and shall use reasonable endeavours to procure that contractors' site traffic in respect of the Works

---

[164]   This will not be necessary if already covered by a condition of the relevant planning permission.

and the Development shall adhere to such route or routes when approaching or departing from the site of the Works as may from time to time be agreed with the Council.

## 19    TRAFFIC REGULATION ORDERS

19.1    The Council shall use reasonable endeavours to make and confirm any Traffic Regulation Order required to carry out the Works PROVIDED that the Council shall not be obliged to initiate or pursue any Traffic Regulation Order unless and until the Developer has paid to or secured to the satisfaction of the Council a sum equivalent to the estimated costs of making and confirming any such order and also provided the Council with an indemnity in respect of any costs which might arise from or be incurred in respect of any such proceedings, whether the Order is completed or confirmed or not.

## 20    CDM REGULATIONS

20.1    For the purposes of the CDM Regulations, the Parties confirm that:

*[****]* is the Client;

*[****]* is the Principle Contractor; and

*[****]* is the Principle Designer.

## 21    CERTIFICATE OF PRACTICAL COMPLETION

21.1    On the completion of the Works in accordance with this Agreement to the satisfaction of the Engineer in all respects including (without limitation) that:

(a)    the lighting has been installed, tested, energised and is operational and any corrective works to the lighting which have been required by the Engineer have been completed by the Developer to the satisfaction of the Engineer;

(b)    the Works have been inspected and any corrective works to the Works which have been required by the Engineer have been completed by the Developer to the satisfaction of the Engineer;

(c)    the provision of the proposed Drainage System has been secured by way of an agreement or agreements with *[****]* Water Company (or such organisation which may discharge the functions of *[****]* Water Company);

(d)    the Developer has provided a Costed Risk Analysis;[165] and

---

[165]    The Council will then have to consider how it wishes to secure its position in respect of any such contingent liabilities. One option might be to consider an extended bond to cover such contingent liabilities.

(e)    the Developer has provided the Health and Safety File to the Council

the Engineer shall issue the Certificate of Practical Completion to the Developer and from the date thereof:

(a)    the Adoption Areas shall become highways maintainable at the public expense; and

(b)    the liability of the Surety pursuant to this Agreement shall be reduced to £*[****]* (*[****]* Pounds).

## 22    SITE CLEARANCE

22.1    On completion of the Works the Developer shall clear away and remove from the site of the Works and all Highways constructional plant, surplus material, rubbish and temporary works of every kind and leave the site of the Works and the Highway in good and tidy conditions and if the Developer shall fail to do so, then the Council may carry out all actions it deems necessary to leave the site of the Works and the Highway in good and tidy conditions and the Developer shall reimburse the Council's costs of doing so.

## 23    OBLIGATIONS DURING MAINTENANCE PERIOD

23.1    During the Maintenance Period:

(a)    the Developer (at its own expense) shall maintain the Works and carry out such repairs and maintenance as may be necessary to facilitate the safe and convenient use by the public of the Works;

(b)    the Developer shall at its own expense undertake the routine maintenance of and be responsible for the payment of energy charges in respect of all street lights and illuminated traffic signs erected in respect of the Works and energised in accordance with this Agreement;

(c)    the Developer shall forthwith at its own expense reinstate and make good to the satisfaction of the Engineer any defect in or damage to the Works which may have arisen from any cause whatsoever or have been discovered during the Maintenance Period (including any defect in or damage to the street lighting system and the Drainage System) of which the Developer has been notified in writing by the Engineer; and

(d)    neither the Owner nor the Developer shall place or erect on any part of the Works or Main Road (or the highway verges thereof) any structure, advertisement or notice or plant any tree or vegetation thereon without the consent of the Council.

## 24    FINAL CERTIFICATE

24.1    On the completion of not less than Twelve (12) Months' of the Maintenance Period in accordance with this Agreement to the satisfaction of the Engineer in all respects including (without limitation) that:

(a)    associated landscaping works have been completed to the satisfaction of the Engineer;

(b)    the Works have been inspected and all Remedial Works and other corrective works or reinstatement have been completed by the Developer to the satisfaction of the Engineer;

(c)    the provision of the Drainage System been secured;

(d)    all relevant Safety Audits have been completed and any actions arising from them and which the Engineer has required to be carried out have been completed to the satisfaction of the Engineer; and

(e)    the Commuted Sum and all monies and Interest due to the Council pursuant to this Agreement have been paid in full

the Engineer shall issue the Final Certificate to the Developer and from the date thereof the liability of the Surety pursuant to the Bond shall (save as to any liabilities which accrued before that date) be released in full.

## 25    INDEMNITIES

25.1    The Owner and the Developer hereby indemnify the Council in respect of all actions, claims, demands, expenses and proceedings arising out of or in connection with or incidental to the carrying out of, or use of, the Works or Highways including any claims under the Land Compensation Act 1973.

25.2    The Owner and the Developer hereby undertake and agree with the Council that in the event of any claim or claims arising in connection with or incidental to or in consequence of the carrying out of the Works or use of the Highways and being made against the Council for any one or more of the following payments:

(a)    compensation, including (without limitation) any Land Compensation Costs;

(b)    damages;

(c)    costs;

(d)    charges;

349

(e)    the cost of any works or measures considered necessary by any Statutory Undertaker in consequence of the making of any connection to its system or apparatus; and

(f)    any other payment arising in connection with or incidental to or in consequence of the carrying out of the Works

and the Owner and the Developer will hold the Council fully indemnified from and against each and every said claim and shall indemnify the Council in respect of the same.

## 26    *PUBLIC LIABILITY INSURANCE*

26.1    The Developer shall at all times during the period of this Agreement maintain full comprehensive public liability insurance in the sum of not less than £[****] ([****] Pounds) for any one occurrence or series of occurrences arising out of one event against liability to any person arising from the construction, operation or maintenance of the Works or the exercise of any rights granted by the Council and shall allow the Council to inspect the certificate of insurance at all reasonable times.

## 27    *DELEGATION OF DEVELOPER'S OBLIGATIONS*

27.1    The performance of the obligations on the part of the Developer to carry out the Works on behalf of the Council may (subject to the approval of the Council) be delegated to a contractor or sub contractor or sub contractors on the Council's list of approved contractors PROVIDED THAT:

(a)    the Developer shall remain liable to the Council for the due performance and observance of this Agreement;

(b)    the contract by which the obligations contained in this Agreement are delegated (the "Contract") shall in any event contain terms and conditions no less stringent than the terms and conditions contained in this Agreement and shall incorporate the Specification, the Programme and the Drawings; and

(c)    the Contract shall secure the amount of insurance cover against losses and claims for injuries or damage to persons or property arising out of or in consequence of the Works shall be not less than £[****] ([****] Pounds) in respect of any one incident or such other sum as may be specified the Council in writing.

## 28    *DETERMINATION*

28.1    If at any time:

(a)    the Developer fails to perform or observe any of the conditions, stipulations or obligations on its part contained in this Agreement; or

(b)    if a receiving order in bankruptcy is made against the Developer or the Developer's business is being wound up or dissolved or if the Developer is insolvent or enters into a composition or scheme of arrangement (otherwise than for the purpose of amalgamation or reconstruction),

THEN the Council may (without prejudice to any of its rights claims or remedies against the Developer and the Surety in respect of any non-performance or non-observance of this Agreement) determine this Agreement (except for Clauses *[****]* of this Agreement) by notice in writing delivered to the Developer and send a copy of any such notice to the Surety.

## 29    POWER TO EXECUTE THE WORKS IN DEFAULT

29.1    If at any time:

(a)    the Developer fails to perform or observe any of the conditions, stipulations or obligations on its part contained in this Agreement; or

(b)    a receiving order in bankruptcy is made in respect of the Developer's legal estate or if the Developer's business is being wound up or dissolved or if the Developer is insolvent or enters into a composition or scheme of arrangement (otherwise than for the purpose of reconstruction or amalgamation),

the Council may without prejudice to any of its statutory rights or powers or any other right claim or remedy under this Agreement send to the Developer notice in writing (hereinafter referred to as the "Default Notice").

29.2    The Default Notice shall:

(a)    specify the works ("the Default Works") to be carried out in order that the Works may be executed or completed (as the case may be) in accordance with this Agreement;

(b)    specify a timetable for the carrying out of the Default Works; and

(c)    contain an estimate by the Engineer of the cost of carrying out the Default Works (whether by the Council or by a contractor appointed by the Council) including (without limitation) the cost of preparation (including any necessary survey) of the Final Drawings; the costs of maintaining the Highways and any Remedial Works or Default Works prior to the Highways becoming maintainable at the public expense; and, the usual establishment charges of the Council (together hereinafter referred to as the "Default Sum") AND the amount of any such expenditure shall be that certified by the Engineer, whose certificate shall be final and binding upon all Parties.

29.3    The Default Sum shall not exceed:

(a)    the sum of £[****] ([****] Pounds) where the relevant Default Notice is issued before the issue of the Certificate of Practical Completion;

(b)    the sum of [£[****] ([****] Pounds) where the relevant Default Notice is issued on and after the issue of the Final Certificate.

29.4    If the Default Works are not completed within the period required by the Council in the Default Notice (or within such further period as may be agreed by the Council) the Council may carry out the Default Works mentioned in the Default Notice and apply the Default Sum together with interest accrued thereon to the cost of carrying out any Default Works not carried out by the Developer or to the cost of maintaining the Highways and the Default Works prior to the Highways becoming highways maintainable at the public expense as may be the case (or as being the cost of both) and also retain the amount determined by the Engineer as being the amount of the appropriate usual establishment charges of the Council.

ALSO SEE:

**[Form 1.10] - Council's statutory duties**

**[Form 1.11] - No partnership or agency**

**[Form 1.15] - Assignment**

**[Form 1.16] - Dispute provisions**

**[Form 1.17] - Waiver**

**[Form 1.18] - Third parties**

**[Form 1.19] - Service of notices**

**[Form 1.20] - Chargee's consent**

**[Form 1.21] - Jurisdiction**

**[Form 1.22] - Force majeure**

IN WITNESS whereof .........

## FIRST SCHEDULE

### The Works

The Works shall be carried out in accordance with the Specification, the Drawings and the Programme and shall include the following elements of construction work -

(a) excavation to reduce levels including breaking out existing carriageways and footways where necessary;

(b) all necessary alterations to the existing road drainage systems including the provision and installation of new road gullies and pipeworks;

(c) all necessary alterations to Statutory Undertakers' plant and equipment;

(d) the provision and installation of all necessary ducts;

(e) the provision of a dedicated electricity supply direct from the electricity supplier's network;

(f) any reconstruction or overlay of the existing carriageways necessary to ensure the structural integrity of the highways affected by the Works;

(g) the construction of new footways including all necessary edgings and textured footway at controlled pedestrian crossing places;

(h) the breaking out of all redundant areas of carriageway and their reinstatement with top soil and seeding;

(i) the provision and installation of new columns, lamps, lanterns and cabling where necessary including the lighting of any new traffic islands and roundabouts and including any necessary modification to existing columns, lamps, lanterns and cabling;

(j) the provision and installation of all necessary road signs, safety barriers and markings including any necessary modification to existing signs, barriers and markings;

(k) the regrading of verges, topsoiling and the provision and laying of new grass or landscaping within the proposed highway boundaries;

(l) any other minor items of accommodation work including (without prejudice to generality) noise attenuation measures necessary to complete the Works;

(m) all site clearance including removal of trees, shrubs, bushes and fences; and

(n)    all placing, compaction and grading of suitable fill materials.

## *SECOND SCHEDULE*

### Attachments

- The draft Bond

- The Specification

- The Drawing

# Form 7: Simple Bond

BY THIS BOND

*[****]* of *[****]* (the *"Developer"*) and *[****]* of *[****]* (the *"Surety"*) are jointly and severally bound to *[****]* of *[****]* (the *"Council"*) this day of *[20**]* in the sum of £*[****]* (*[****]* Pounds) to the payment of which sum the Developer and the Surety hereby jointly and severally bind themselves, their successors and assigns.

WHEREAS by an Agreement made between the Council (1) *[and]* the Developer (2) *[and [****] (3)]* dated the *[****]* day of *[****]*/*[20**]* (the *"Agreement"*) the Developer covenanted with the Council to commence, execute, perform, complete and maintain the highway works mentioned therein in such manner and within such time and subject to such conditions and stipulations as are particularly specified and set forth in the Agreement and also to pay to the Council such sums as therein provided.

NOW THE CONDITIONS of this Bond are such that if the Developer shall duly observe and perform all the terms, provisions, covenants, conditions and stipulations of the Agreement including (without limitation) the payment of all costs and fees on the Developer's part to be observed and performed according to the true purport, intent and meaning thereof or if on default by the Developer the Surety shall satisfy and discharge the costs, expenses and damages sustained by the Council thereby up to the amount of this Bond then this obligation shall be null and void but otherwise shall be and remain in full force and effect but no alteration in the terms of the Agreement made by agreement between the Council and the Developer and no allowance of time by the Council under the Agreement nor any forbearance or forgiveness in or in respect of any matter or thing concerning the Agreement on the part of the Council shall in any way release the Surety from any liability under this Bond.

IN WITNESS whereof ............

# Form 8: Improvement Works Agreement

BETWEEN:

(1) *[****]* COUNTY COUNCIL (the "Council") of County Hall, *[****]*

(2) *[****]* TOWN COUNCIL (the "Town Council") of *[****]*

### RECITALS:

A. The Council is the local highway authority for highways in the County of *[****]* pursuant to the 1980 Act.

B. The Land is part of a highway maintainable at the public expense and is vested in the Council.

C. The Town Council is desirous of carrying out the Improvement Works as the agent of the Council.

IT IS HEREBY AGREED AND DECLARED by and between the Parties hereto as follows:

### 1    INTERPRETATION

1.1     In this Agreement where the context so admits:

**"1980 Act"** means the Highways Act 1980;

**"Engineer"** means the Director of Planning and Economy of the Council for the time being or his deputy;

**"Improvement Works"** means the installation of a *[****]*, the planting of shrubs and trees, the construction of a footpath and the installation of lighting as more particularly shown on the drawing marked "Site Plan and Detail Plan" which is attached to this Agreement together with all associated works;

**"Land"** means the highway verge at *[****]* shown edged red on the plan marked "Location Plan" attached to this agreement;

**"Maintain"** includes inspect, repair, adjust, alter, remove or reconstruct and any derivative of *"maintain"* is to be construed accordingly;

**"Parties"** means (collectively) the Council and the Town Council;

**2      ENABLING LEGISLATION**

2.1      This Agreement is made in pursuance of powers contained in Sections 96 and 282 of the 1980 Act and Section 111 of the Local Government Act 1972 and the Localism Act 2011 and all other enabling provisions.

2.2      This Agreement does not authorise any interference with the convenience of persons using any street or affect the rights of the owners of land adjoining any highway or street or the rights of statutory undertakers or the operator of a telecommunications core system or a driver information system.

**3      THE IMPROVEMENT WORKS**

3.1      The Town Council shall carry out and complete the Improvement Works (at the Town Council's expense) in a good and workmanlike manner and with proper materials in accordance in all respects with "the Site Plan and Detail Plan" attached to this Agreement to the satisfaction of the Engineer and within a maximum period of *[****]* Months from the date of this Agreement.

3.2      The Improvement Works must be carried out in accordance with planning permission reference *[****]* and the approved plans referred to in that permission.

3.3      The Town Council may connect the lights which form part of the Improvement Works to the electricity supply for street lighting.

**4      INDEMNITIES**

4.1      The Town Council hereby indemnifies the Council in respect of all actions, claims, demands, expenses and proceedings arising out of or in connection with or incidental to the carrying out operation or use of the Improvement Works including any claims under the Land Compensation Act 1973 and any regulations made thereunder and any statutory re-enactment or modification thereof other than those arising out of or in consequence of any act, neglect, default or liability of the Council.

**5      HIGHWAY AUTHORITY CONSENTS**

5.1      Pursuant to Section 96(5) of the 1980 Act, the Council hereby consents to the Town Council exercising the powers conferred on the Council under sections 96(1) and (2) of the 1980 Act so far as required to enable the Town Council to carry out and complete the Improvement Works and to carry out its other obligations in this Agreement.

5.2      The Parties agree that the Town Council shall act as the Council's agent so far as the Improvement Works (or any part thereof) are carried out pursuant to Section 282 of the 1980 Act.

## 6 TOWN COUNCIL'S ONGOING OBLIGATIONS

6.1 Save as provided by this Agreement, the Town Council shall not make any alterations or additions to the Land and not without the previous consent in writing of the Council, such consent not to be unreasonably withheld by the Council.

6.2 The Town Council shall maintain the whole of the Land including keeping the lighting, footpath, grass and planting in good repair and condition.

6.3 The Town Council shall not use the Land for any other purpose than the installation and maintenance of the Improvement Works.

6.4 The Town Council shall:

6.4.1. keep the Improvement Works in good condition;

6.4.2. be responsible for complying with all requirements of the Health and Safety legislation and to bear the cost of such compliance;

6.4.3. keep the Land in a clean condition and free from litter;

6.4.4. make arrangements for the disposal of all refuse from the Land; and

6.4.5. pay to the Council the costs incurred to the energy company in supplying electricity to the lights forming part of the Improvement Works.

6.5 The Town Council shall not:

6.5.1. display any advertisements on the Land;

6.5.2. deposit or leave outside the Land any goods whatsoever; or

6.5.3. park any vehicles on the Land.

## 7 PUBLIC LIABILITY INSURANCE

7.1 The Town Council shall at all times during the period of this Agreement maintain full comprehensive public liability insurance in the sum of not less than £[****] ([****] Pounds) for any one occurrence or series of occurrences arising out of one event against liability to any person arising from the construction operation or maintenance of the Improvement Works or the exercise of the rights hereby granted by the Council and shall allow the Council to inspect the certificate of insurance at all reasonable times.

## 8      COSTS AND CHARGES

8.1      Before starting the Improvement Works, the Town Council shall (unless it has already done so) pay to the Engineer on demand the inspection fee of £*[****]* (*[****]* Pounds), which fee shall be applied towards the expenses of the Council in respect of the inspection of the Improvement Works as they proceed and the testing of materials used or intended for use therein.

## 9      INSPECTIONS

9.1      The Town Council shall during the progress of setting out and constructing the Improvement Works give to the Engineer (and any person authorised by him) free access to every site of such operations and permission to inspect them and all materials used or intended for use in them and shall if required by the Engineer to do so uncover or open up any work to enable it to be inspected and if so required shall remove any structure or materials which in the opinion of the Engineer are defective and shall at the expense of the Town Council re-execute any such work and substitute proper and suitable materials to the satisfaction of the Engineer.

## 10      DETERMINATION

10.1      Subject to Clauses 11.2 and 11.3 of this Agreement, this Agreement shall cease and determine on *[****]* or such later date as may be agreed in writing by the Parties.

10.2      If at any time the Town Council fails to perform or observe any of the conditions, stipulations or obligations on its part contained in this Agreement THEN the Council may (without prejudice to any of its rights claims or remedies against the Town Council in respect of any non-performance or non-observance of this Agreement) determine this Agreement by notice in writing delivered to the Town Council.

10.3      If it determines that the Land shall be used for purposes other than the retention and use of the Improvement Works, then the Council shall be entitled to terminate this Agreement, such termination to be subject to the service of not less than *[****]* weeks' written notice upon the Town Council.

10.4      The Town Council shall upon termination of this Agreement remove all of the Improvement Works and restore the Land to its original condition or such other condition as may be agreed in writing by the Council.

## 11      COSTS OF AGREEMENT

11.1      The Town Council shall pay the costs of preparation of this Agreement in the sum of £*[****]* (*[****]* Pounds).

ALSO SEE:

*[Form 1.10] - Council's statutory duties*

*[Form 1.11] - No partnership or agency*

*[Form 1.15] - Assignment*

*[Form 1.16] - Dispute provisions*

*[Form 1.17] - Waiver*

*[Form 1.18] - Third parties*

*[Form 1.19] - Service of notices*

*[Form 1.21] - Jurisdiction*

*[Form 1.22] - Force majeure*

IN WITNESS whereof .................

# Form 9: Cranage Licence

THIS LICENCE is made BY DEED on the *[****]* day of *[****]* 20*[**]*

BETWEEN:

(1) *[****]* ( the "Licensee"); and

(2) *[****]* ( the "Council").

WHEREAS:

A. The Council is the local highway authority for the highways known as *[****]* (the "Highways").

B. The Licensee is the owner of land at *[****]* (the "Site").

C. The boundaries of the Site are shown on the attached drawing marked *[****]* (the "Site Plan").

D. The Licensee is desirous of erecting and operating a tower crane (as more particularly described in the Schedule to this Licence (the "Crane") with a jib radius of *[****]* metres on land at the junction of the Highways (the "Site").

E. The jib of the Crane will from time to time oversail the Highways as shown on the Site Plan.

F. The Council is minded to grant a licence to the Licensee to oversail the Highways.

## *LICENCE*

1.        THE COUNCIL hereby grants to the Licensee this licence under Section 177 of the Highways Act 1980, Section 1 of the Localism Act 2011 and Section 111 of the Local Government Act 1972 to use the Crane so as to oversail the Highways upon the terms and subject to the conditions hereinafter specified and stipulated in the Schedule to this Licence and subject also to the relevant conditions contained in the said Section 177 and the Licensee hereby undertakes with the Council to observe the said terms and conditions and provisions and warrants that it is the owner of the Site.

2.        This Licence allows the Licensee to traverse the airspace above the Highways by way of the jib of the Crane.

3.        This Licence shall be for the period commencing on *[****]* and terminating on *[****]* (the "Licence Period").

4.      This Licence shall not be assigned.

5.      The Licensee shall pay to the Council on the granting of this Licence the sum of *[****]* pounds in respect of the legal and other expenses incurred by the Council in connection with the grant of the Licence and shall also pay to the Council on demand the sum or sums specified by the Council in accordance with the conditions hereinafter mentioned.

6.      The Council may give to the Licensee fourteen (14) days' notice in writing terminating this Licence if any of the following events occur:

   (a)    the Licensee fails to comply with the terms and conditions of this Licence;

   (b)    the Crane becomes the subject of legal proceedings or threatened legal proceedings against the Council; or

   (c)    the Licensee parts with control or possession of the Crane or of the Site without obtaining the Council's consent

in any case notwithstanding that the Licence period in Clause 3 above has not expired.

7.      The Licensee shall indemnify and keep indemnified the Council, its servants and agents against all liability for any loss of or damage to property or injury to persons and any other loss, damage, costs and expenses caused or incurred by the erection, operation, maintenance, dismantling, transportation and removal of the Crane or the lifting or conveyance of any load carried by the Crane or the exercise of the rights granted by this Licence.

8.      This Licence does not authorise any interference with the convenience of persons using the Highways or affect the rights of the owners of premises adjoining the Highways or the rights of statutory undertakers or the operator of a telecommunications core system or a driver information system.

9.      Nothing in this Licence will vest in the Licensee any easement or right whatsoever other than the limited and conditional privilege expressly conferred upon the Licensee by the issuing of this licence.

10.     This Licence shall not create the relationship of landlord and tenant.

11.     The Contracts (Rights of Third Parties) Act 1999 is hereby excluded and shall not apply.

IN WITNESS whereof .................

## SCHEDULE - THE CONDITIONS

1.      The Crane shall be a *[****]* tower crane (being a "*conventional tower crane*" as defined in the Notification of Conventional Tower Cranes Regulations 2010).

2.      THE Licensee shall provide adequate drainage from the Crane so as to prevent water falling onto the Highways.

3.      THE Licensee shall ensure that any maintenance, repair or other works carried out to or in connection with the Crane shall be done with no disturbance to the Highways or the user of the Highways.

4.      The Licensee shall at all times during the Licence Period maintain full comprehensive public liability insurance in the sum of not less than £*[****]* (*[****]* Pounds) for any one occurrence or series of occurrences arising out of one event against liability to any person arising from the erection, operation, maintenance, dismantling, transportation and removal of the Crane or exercise of the rights granted by this License and the Licensee shall allow the Council to inspect the certificate of insurance at all reasonable times.

5.      The Licensee shall permit the Council to inspect the Crane or any part thereof after reasonable previous notice (except in the case of emergency) has been given to the Licensee.

6.      The Crane shall not be used to lift, carry or otherwise convey any load whatsoever outside the boundaries of the Site unless previously approved in writing by the Council.

7.      The Crane shall, at all times, be operated by a properly qualified, skilled and competent operator and shall not be used for any load that is unsuitable or larger or heavier than it is designed to carry.

8.      The crane supervisor shall be competent and suitably trained and shall have sufficient experience to carry out all relevant duties and authority to stop the lifting operation if he judges it dangerous to proceed.

9.      Records of thorough examinations and tests of the Crane must be readily available to the Council on reasonable notice, secure, and capable of being reproduced in written form.

10.     For the purposes of this Licence, the phrase "*thorough examination*" has the same meaning as in regulation 2(1) of the Lifting Operations and Lifting Equipment Regulations 1998.

# Index